The rough guide.

written and researched by

Jules Brown and J.D. Dickey

ROUGH
GUIDES

www.roughguides.com

Contents

African American DC colour section following p.112

Colour maps following p.304

◄◄ The US Capitol at night ◄ Steps to the Supreme Court

Introduction to

Washington, DC

The dominion of American politicians of all stripes, rich with the lore and legend of presidents and power brokers past, Washington more than lives up to its reputation as the most powerful place on earth. And it looks the part too, with lovely Neoclassical buildings arrayed along grand boulevards, some of the finest museums in North America and an affecting set of war memorials honouring centuries of fallen soldiers. With the gleaming symbols of America's three branches of government – the White House, Capitol and Supreme Court – dominating the landscape, it's easy to be stunned by the spectacle of so much power in such a small space, but Washington has much more to offer than this. Beyond its political core is a flesh-and-blood city, whose vibrant neighbourhoods hold their own compelling set of attractions.

With only 600,000 residents (it's smaller than just about every foreign capital you could think of), Washington is compact and manageable – from the ease of riding its Metro system to the pleasures of walking and biking around – distinguishing it from the huge, sprawling American cities to its north. Even better, most of the city's attractions are free. All of this makes Washington hugely popular with short-term visitors – some twenty million flock here each year, making it one of the most visited destinations in the country.

There's evidence of Washington's prestigious history everywhere you look, thanks to a legacy as the national capital dating back more than

200 years. Planned in the 1790s by Pierre Charles L'Enfant and sited as part of a political compromise between Northern and Southern states, the District suffered from poor planning and shambling infrastructure throughout the nineteenth century, but in the twentieth really came into its own, when the urban development of its grand corridors finally began to fulfil L'Enfant's vision of a proud imperial city. And while it's had its problems – riots in the 1960s, severe poverty and crime in the decades after, and political disenfranchisement throughout (its citizens can't elect representatives for any federal office except the presidency) – in recent years Washington has been experiencing a cultural and economic renaissance.

▲ Rotunda, US Capitol

Fact file

• The city of Washington has the same boundaries as the federal District of Columbia and holds 600,000 people – though thirteen times as many people reside in the metropolitan region, making it one of the country's top five urban centres.

• DC is 54 percent black, 35 percent non-Latino white, 8 percent Latino, and 3 percent Asian.

• Originally, the District held several other cities: Georgetown and Anacostia, since annexed by Washington, and Arlington and Alexandria, now part of Virginia.

• The city has four quadrants, from largest to smallest: NW, NE, SE, SW. They all meet at the US Capitol, the only place in town without a quadrant or a street address.

• Washington, in more than two hundred years, has been ruled by mayors, district governors and commission boards, but only from 1820 to 1869 and 1975 to the present has the leader been elected by city voters. The current mayor is Vincent Gray.

• The District's biggest employer is the federal and city government, providing one in three jobs.

• From 1788 to 2010, 43 different men became president (with Grover Cleveland as the 22nd and 24th president for his non-consecutive terms), representing five political parties and serving tenures from one month (William Henry Harrison) to twelve years and one month (FDR).

The capital sound

To those not in the know, Washington, DC may not seem like one of the country's essential locations on the musical heritage map. However, through the decades the District has created a special niche for itself in several key musical styles. The oldest are, of course, **blues** and **gospel**, which really became established when Southern blacks moved here en masse after the Civil War, bringing traditions of spirituals, work songs and ballads with them. You can hear such music today in churches and in clubs like *Blues Alley* (p.226) and *Madam's Organ* (p.227). But much more prevalent is the sound of **jazz**. This quintessential DC style was championed by **Duke Ellington**, perhaps America's greatest composer, and lives on in a bevy of great clubs including *Bohemian Caverns* (p.226) and *HR-57* (p.227). The other prime draw in town is **indie rock**, which was fuelled by late 1970s and early 1980s hardcore punk acts like Bad Brains, Minor Threat and Henry Rollins, all locals. You can still hear that kind of thrash, along with more relaxed alternative rock, at great clubs like *9:30* and *Black Cat* (both p.227). **Country and folk music** both have city fans but are mainly played in the Virginia suburbs and at places like *Wolf Trap* (p.177). For true local energy and creativity, though, funk and hip-hop make regular appearances in the city's rock and blues clubs, and the best offshoot of these two styles is the city's own **go-go** music, basically funk with a staggered beat, perfected by hometown master **Chuck Brown**, whose own frenetic concerts are still the best place to hear this spirited, upbeat music in all its glory (check out ⓦwww .windmeupchuck.com for information).

The museums, monuments and memorials are still must-sees: icons on the National Mall honouring past presidents, world-class museums like the National Gallery of Art, and affecting war memorials such as the black wall for the country's Vietnam vets. But Washington is much more than these showpiece emblems of national pride. Its Downtown, for one, is now one of the most engaging on the East Coast, with fun museums like the International Spy

▲ Barack Obama mural, 14th St

Museum, acclaimed restaurants such as *Ten Penh* and *The Source*, and scores of great bars and hotels taking residence in classy historic structures, adding a real verve to the town's formerly quiet nightlife. You could also venture into some of DC's livelier precincts – the gay nexus of Dupont Circle or hipster hangout Adams Morgan – or to the genteel hills of Upper Northwest. Indeed, once you've taken in the crowd-pleasers around the National Mall, you should spend as much time as possible in the District's neighbourhoods, where you'll get a better sense than anywhere of DC as a real, functioning city.

Another facet of Washington that's key to the city's culture is its ethnic and cultural diversity. The election of President Barack Obama in 2008 is only the most visible sign of this (and Obama received a greater percentage of the vote in DC than in any American state), but long before the Chicagoan arrived in town, the District had a lengthy history of

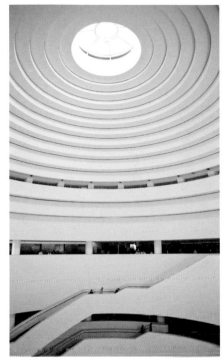
▲ National Museum of the American Indian

African-American culture and endeavour. All-star jazz and blues clubs like *Bohemian Gardens* and *Blues Alley*, classic soul-food joints such as *Ben's Chili Bowl* and *Rocklands*, and famed institutions like Howard University are just some of the more eye-catching emblems of this heritage, which is as fundamental a part of the District's identity as the National Mall itself.

What to see

There's no better way to come to grips with the city than by taking a two-mile stroll along the grassy centrepiece of the **National Mall**, the city's visual axis. You'll come back here time and again to view the powerful tributes to Washington, Lincoln, Jefferson, FDR and war veterans, or to browse the collections of the outstanding Smithsonian museums and the National Gallery of Art. At the Mall's eastern end, the US Capitol marks the geographic centre of the city, as all neighbourhoods and quadrants radiate out from its familiar white, cast-iron dome. **Capitol Hill** is one of DC's oldest districts, rich in nineteenth-century row houses, and ripe for a stroll from the Capitol itself to other defining buildings like the Supreme Court and Library of Congress. South of the Mall are two of the most popular attractions in DC – the Bureau of Engraving and Printing and the US Holocaust Memorial Museum – while the city's **Southwest Waterfront** area boasts the thriving Fish Wharf and, just east, the new Nationals Park baseball stadium. North of the Mall, the heavily visited section around the **White House** and **Foggy Bottom** contains headquarters for numerous federal bureaucracies and international institutions, as well as heavyweight attractions like the Corcoran Gallery of Art, the Renwick Gallery, Kennedy Center and the infamous Watergate Complex.

Between the White House and Union Station, **Downtown** was where nineteenth-century Washington first set up its shops and services, along the spine of Pennsylvania Avenue. These days, the so-called Penn Quarter has been revitalized, boasting compelling galleries and upscale restaurants. The neighbouring **Federal Triangle** is notable for the National Archives and an array of splendid Neoclassical buildings, while in the business district along and around **K Street**, you'll find a slew of fancy hotels, top-notch restaurants and the odd church of historical note. More engagingly, the historic townhouses and mansions of chic **Dupont Circle** hold a gaggle of low-key museums and an enclave of art galleries, not to mention some of DC's best clubs and restaurants. To the north, fun and funky **Adams Morgan**, with its diners and live-music venues, gets trendier by the day, while to the east, historically black **Shaw** is undergoing rapid gentrification around the thriving nightlife corridor of U Street.

▶ National Portrait Gallery

DC itineraries

No matter where you go, the District rewards almost any kind of itinerary, its attractions being more than enough for a city twice its size. The following itineraries provide a few suggestions; if they're a little too packed for your taste, take it easy and save a few sights for your next visit.

Two days

Day one Washington Monument; Vietnam Veterans Memorial; Lincoln Memorial; National Museum of American History; *Old Ebbitt Grill* (lunch; p.206); tour of Congressional visitor centre and US Capitol; Library of Congress; *Zaytinya* (dinner; p.207); basketball game at Verizon Center (p.246).

Day two White House tour; National Portrait Gallery; *Acadiana* (lunch; p.206), International Spy Museum; stroll along Pennsylvania Boulevard; Ford's Theatre; *DC Coast* (dinner; p.208); nightlife at a Dupont Circle bar such as *Brickskeller* (p.221) or downtown club like *Josephine* (p.225).

Five days

(The above, plus...)

Day three Georgetown shopping along M Street and Wisconsin Avenue; boat ride on the C&O Canal; Old Stone House; *Moby Dick House of Kabob* (lunch; p.210); Embassy Row and Phillips Collection in Dupont Circle; stroll along 18th Street NW in Adams Morgan and U Street in Shaw; *Henry's Soul Café* (dinner; p.213); jazz show at *HR-57* (p.227).

Day four World War II Memorial; US Holocaust Memorial Museum; Smithsonian Castle; *Ella's Pizza* (lunch; p.200), US Supreme Court, National Museum of Natural History or National Air and Space Museum; *The Monocle* (dinner; p.204); show at Woolly Mammoth Theatre (p.235) or Arena Stage (p.234).

Day five Washington National Cathedral; National Zoo; *Vace* (lunch; p.213), Arlington National Cemetery; Old Town Alexandria; *The Majestic* (dinner; p.217); classical music concert or opera at the Kennedy Center (p.230).

West of Foggy Bottom, venerable **Georgetown** is the quintessential hangout of the chattering classes (as well as university students), who make the many good shops, galleries, bars and restaurants here their own. To the north, the first bona fide city suburbs were in **Upper Northwest**, where well-to-do areas like Woodley Park and Cleveland Park feature such enjoyable sights as the National Zoo, the landmark National Cathedral, and the glades, dales and riverbanks of Rock Creek Park.

Across the Potomac, **Northern Virginia** holds a number of appealing sights: **Arlington** hosts a world-famous national cemetery; fetching **Old Town Alexandria** is known for its well-preserved eighteenth- and nineteenth-century buildings; and further out are the key historical sites of **Mount Vernon**, George Washington's estate, battlefields such as **Manassas** and, in West Virginia, the Civil War flashpoint of **Harpers Ferry**.

When to go

Without question, the best times to visit Washington, DC are the spring and autumn, when the weather is at its most appealing – moderate temperatures and mild precipitation – plus, in April, DC's famous cherry trees are in bloom. By contrast, summer in the capital is thoroughly unpleasant, with hot and humid days made worse by throngs of visitors packed cheek by jowl at the major attractions. Winter weather is equally dreary, with ice-cold temperatures, plenty of snow and rain, and howling winds blowing in off the Potomac River. However, the one benefit of winter over summer is the relative lack of visitors – you're likely to have many of the sights to yourself, or, at the very least, you can expect some relief from the school groups and tour buses that are legion during the rest of the year.

Average monthly temperatures and rainfall

	Jan	Mar	May	Jul	Sep	Nov
Temperatures						
Max/min (°F)	42/27	53/35	75/54	87/68	78/59	55/38
Max/min (°C)	6/-3	12/2	24/12	31/20	26/15	13/3
Rainfall						
mm	86.4	91.4	94	111.8	94	66

16 things not to miss

It's not possible to see everything that Washington, DC has to offer in one trip – and we don't suggest you try. What follows is a selective taste of the city's highlights: stirring memorials and tasty meals, engaging events and tranquil urban retreats, arranged in five colour-coded categories to help you find the very best things to see, do and experience. All highlights have a page reference to take you straight into the Guide, where you can find out more.

01 National Cherry Blossom Festival Page **241** • When DC's beautiful cherry trees are blooming in late March and early April around the Tidal Basin, the city celebrates with a holiday parade, pageants, concerts, fireworks and lantern-lighting.

02 **Rock Creek Park** Page **159** • Six miles and 1800 acres set along a forest and gorge offer rugged trails for hiking, winding paths for cycling and rollerblading, and nineteenth-century remnants like a functional grist mill and parts of a Civil War fort.

04 **Washington National Cathedral** Page **157** • The sixth-biggest cathedral in the world is a Gothic Revival icon of American religion and politics, hosting regular services attended by Washington's elite.

03 **Ben's Chili Bowl** Page **212** • Sitting along the historic U Street corridor, this venerable diner doles out the city's best chili dogs and cheese fries.

05 **Digging into history** Pages **83** & **121** • Although the Declaration of Independence and Constitution attract the most attention, there are millions of other pieces of American history and culture ready for your viewing, whether at the National Archives or Library of Congress.

06 **The Whistler Collection** Page **72** • The works of James McNeill Whistler dominate the Freer Gallery of Art: some 1200 pieces, in addition to his gloriously decorated Peacock Room, are on display.

07 **Arlington National Cemetery** Page **172** • Deservedly the nation's most famous military cemetery, where myriad white crosses mark the graves of nearly a quarter of a million US soldiers.

09 **International Spy Museum** Page **130** • The golden age of spycraft in the Cold War is alive and well at the exceptionally popular downtown attraction, which features hundreds of tales of intrigue and elaborate devices – including James Bond's Aston Martin.

08 **Seafood** Pages **23, 93, 201** & **205** • Dig into a mess of steamers at the Fish Wharf or enjoy a fabulous meal at places such as Kinkead's or Johnny's Half Shell.

10 **Lincoln Memorial** Page **50** • This Greek temple on a knoll is the best-loved and most dramatic of the city's presidential memorials.

12 Vietnam Veterans Memorial

Page **51** • Arguably the most affecting war memorial to be found anywhere, this dramatic, black-granite chevron carved into the earth is engraved with the names of the 58,000 men who died in the jungles of Southeast Asia.

11 National Gallery of Art

Page **63** • The jewel of Washington, DC or even American, art museums, this grand institution hosts a wide collection of international sculpture and Old Masters, highlighted by a handful of evocative Vermeers.

13 Rare pandas

Page **158** • The National Zoological Park boasts wetlands, nature trails and botanic gardens, but celebrity pandas Mei Xiang and Tian Tian always take centre stage.

14 Taking in a concert at Wolf Trap

Page **177** • A great place to see American music in all its glory, this rustic Virginia site is a showcase for bluegrass, blues, country and folk music, with a pair of concert "barns" adding to the atmosphere.

15 Mount Vernon Page **183** • The most rewarding day-trip from the city is to George Washington's Virginia estate, his home for forty years and his burial place.

16 Old Ebbitt Grill Page **206** •

One of the city's finest dining establishments, more than a century-and a-half old, still appeals for its clubby tavern atmosphere and fine oysters, chops and burgers.

Basics

Basics

Getting there

Unless you live along America's Eastern seaboard, the easiest way to get to Washington, DC is to fly. Three airports serve the Washington metropolitan area: Reagan National (DCA), the city's domestic airport, located just south of town along the Potomac; Dulles International (IAD), the main international airport, about 45 minutes west, in Virginia; and Baltimore-Washington International (BWI), a good alternative about an hour north of central DC, in Maryland.

Amtrak provides **train service** to DC within the US and Canada, though this is typically a leisurely and expensive journey; Greyhound and Peter Pan **buses** are cheaper, albeit less enjoyable, options. DC is easily accessible **by car**, but you might not want to drive once you've reached the city, as it has an outstanding – and safe – public transport system.

Flights from the UK and Ireland

There are daily **nonstop flights** to Washington, DC from **London Heathrow** with British Airways, United Airlines and Virgin Atlantic; BMI British Midland flies from **Manchester**, with connections through London, most days of the week. These flights take about eight hours, though return flights are always an hour or so shorter due to tailwinds. Outbound flights usually leave Britain midmorning, and inbound flights from the US usually arrive in the early morning. Other airlines serving DC fly from Heathrow or London **Gatwick** via their respective American or European hubs. These flights can add an extra two to five hours to your trip each way, depending on how long you have to wait for your connection.

Fares to Washington, DC can cost more than £450 return between June and August and at Christmas, though £375–400 is the more typical range. Prices in winter often fall to £300. The nonstop flights from Heathrow tend to be among the cheapest. With BMI, you can usually add on a connecting domestic flight to Manchester from one of the other UK regional airports for little or no extra cost; with other airlines, add-on fares from UK regional airports to London cost around £100 return. More flexible tickets to

Shopping for flights

Within the US and Canada, **prices** for flights to DC are usually relative to the date of departure, length of stay and seat availability. If you're booking from abroad, tickets will be the most expensive during Europe's high season – June to August, despite this being DC's hottest and most humid period – less pricey in spring and autumn, and cheapest during winter, excluding the Christmas and New Year holiday period. If you're planning to arrive in DC during any major American holiday, be sure to make reservations well in advance.

To guarantee the cheapest economy fares, tickets usually have to be purchased at least 21 days in advance, and you must have at least one Saturday-night stopover. These tickets are nonrefundable and subject to "change fees", meaning that if you alter your return date or destination, you must pay the difference in the two prices along with a fee of $30–100 (though Southwest Airlines is notable for not charging this fee). It's usually cheaper to fly during the week than on the weekend, and seasonal specials or student discount fares can bring the price down even more. Remember to allow for the extra cost of duty fees and airport taxes of 8 to 15 percent; most airlines have also instituted an onerous new policy of charging for checked bags, usually starting at $25 per item.

DC, requiring less advance-booking time or allowing changes or refunds, often cost an additional £100 or more.

Aer Lingus and United offer flights from **Dublin** to Washington, DC, usually with a stop in New York or Boston. Air France and Delta fly between the same cities via Paris, New York and Atlanta (10–15hr). Other airlines, such as British Airways, will route you through London, which takes about the same amount of time. Alternatively, you could arrange your own Dublin-to-London flight with low-cost airlines like easyJet or Ryanair and pick up a connecting flight to DC. Return fares from Dublin to DC start at around €600 in the low season, rising to €700–820 in high season. Although Dulles is often the first choice for international travellers, you may be able to save up to €100 by landing in Baltimore's BWI airport, though you'll probably have to connect in London.

Flights from the US and Canada

Washington, DC is well connected to the rest of the US, as well as to Canada, by air, and air travel is the first transport choice for most North American travellers. The most convenient airport for domestic arrivals into DC is **Reagan National Airport** (DCA), just south of the Pentagon and linked to central DC by the Metro. Most major carriers offer daily service here, but direct service is usually limited to the major cities on the Eastern seaboard.

Most of the major airlines have direct service to **Dulles International** (IAD), out in suburban northern Virginia, 25 miles from downtown Washington. Southwest Airlines and US Airways have good deals for people willing to fly into **Baltimore** (BWI) and reserve in advance.

Fares are lowest in the Northeast corridor. From **New York** and **Boston**, you can pay as little as $120 round-trip, though $150–200 is more typical; fares are around $200–250 from **Chicago** and $220–260 from **Miami**. The price of flights from the **West Coast** is more likely to fluctuate – round-trip tickets from **LA** can cost as little as $250 (but will more likely start at $300), with prices from San Francisco and Seattle starting at $400.

Air Canada has direct flights to DC from **Toronto** and **Montréal**; from **Vancouver**, you'll have to change planes, most likely in Chicago. American carriers such as Delta, Northwest and United also operate flights from these cities, often in combination with Canadian airlines. Special deals bring round-trip fares as low as Can$380 from Toronto, though you're more likely to pay Can$400–500, Can$50 more from Montréal. From Vancouver, winter getaways start at Can$600 round-trip (usually with one stop) and go up to Can$700–750 the rest of the year.

Flights from Australia, New Zealand and South Africa

As there are no direct flights to Washington, DC from Australia or New Zealand, the cheapest way to get there is to fly via **Los Angeles** with Qantas, American or United, and add a connector via any domestic US airline for Aus$260–320/NZ$330–400 more. Flights from Sydney or Melbourne to LA cost Aus$1200–1800, depending on the season, with airline specials and student fares sometimes reducing that by Aus$100–300.

From **New Zealand**, most flights are out of Auckland; add about NZ$200 for Christchurch and Wellington departures. Seasonal fares are NZ$1400–1900, with special deals and student fares reducing prices significantly. Specialist agents can advise about US air passes, which are the cheapest way to fly to DC from whichever American hub you've arrived at. Seat availability is limited, so it's best to book at least several weeks ahead.

Travel to America is not particularly cheap from **South Africa**; prices are about the same out of Cape Town or Johannesburg but are several hundred rand more from Durban and other smaller cities. To get to Washington, DC, you'll need to transfer at Dakar, London, Atlanta, New York, or other cities, sometimes a combination of several; one-stop itineraries are quite possible, though nonstops are fairly uncommon and usually offered for the steepest prices. Basic fares start at around ZAR12,000, including taxes, and rise as high as ZAR25,000 or more at peak times.

Four steps to a better kind of travel

At Rough Guides we are passionately committed to travel. We feel strongly that only through travelling do we truly come to understand the world we live in and the people we share it with – plus tourism has brought a great deal of **benefit** to developing economies around the world over the last few decades. But the extraordinary growth in tourism has also damaged some places irreparably, and of course **climate change** is exacerbated by most forms of transport, especially flying. This means that now more than ever it's important to **travel thoughtfully** and **responsibly**, with respect for the cultures you're visiting – not only to derive the most benefit from your trip but also to preserve the best bits of the planet for everyone to enjoy. At Rough Guides we feel there are four main areas in which you can make a difference:

- Travel with a purpose, not just to tick off experiences. Consider **spending longer** in a place, and getting to know it and its people.
- Give thought to how often you **fly**. Try to avoid short hops by air and more harmful night flights.
- Consider **alternatives to flying**, travelling instead by bus, train, boat and even by bike or on foot where possible.
- Make your trips **"climate neutral"** via a reputable carbon offset scheme. All Rough Guide flights are offset, and every year we donate money to a variety of charities devoted to combating the effects of climate change.

Trains

The sprawling metropolitan area between Boston and Washington has the most dependable **Amtrak** service in the country (book through ☎1-800/872-7245, ⓦwww .amtrak.com). The high-speed, 150mph **Acela** Express has cut the travel time from New York City to Washington, DC to two hours and forty-five minutes, down from three and a half hours, and to six and a half hours from Boston, down from nine hours. If you're travelling from New York City or points south, the Acela is probably the most convenient way to reach Washington, DC, not least because it drops you right in the middle of town, at Union Station.

One-way **fares** for the regular service begin around $100 from **New York** and $175 from **Boston**. Depending on the season, fares for the reserved-seating Acela Express trains can be a third more or up to twice as high. If you're travelling from cities outside the Northeast, ticket prices are comparable to or higher than the equivalent airfare, and if you want any extras, like a sleeping compartment, it will cost you a lot more: the one-way, three-day rail journey from **Los Angeles**, for example, costs around $400–700 with an economy bedroom, but only $270 without it. In general, Amtrak isn't a budget option, although some of the journeys are pleasant enough – for example, the *Crescent*, which travels from New York to New Orleans via DC, makes for a rewarding 24hr trip between Washington and the Big Easy, and there is regular Amtrak service to DC from **Toronto** (16hr; Can$350 return) and **Montréal** (14hr; Can$200–250 return), both via New York City. Amtrak often has **seasonal specials**; check its website or call its toll-free number to check.

Rail passes

Only one **rail pass** covers Washington, DC. It's mainly useful if you're on an extended tour of the region and have plenty of time to explore. The **USA Rail Pass** covers varying time periods, and the longer the period, the more "segments" (individual train rides) you're allowed for travel within the US. For 15 days, eight segments are offered ($389); 30 days gets you 12 segments ($579); and 45 days allows 18 segments ($749). Many trains fill quickly, so it's worth making reservations well ahead.

Buses

Buses are cheaper and run more frequently than trains, but they take forever and, in a worst-case scenario, you may need to use one of those toilets. **Greyhound** is the chief bus operator to DC (☎1-800/229-9424, ⓦwww.greyhound.com); in addition, **Peter Pan** Bus Lines (☎1-800/343-9999, ⓦwww.peterpanbus.com) offers service to Washington, DC from major East Coast cities, sometimes in combination with Greyhound. Return fares for the six-hour trip from **New York City** start at $100, though they can be as little as $75 with one week's advance purchase. Paying in advance, tickets are around $110 from **Boston** (11hr), $60 from Philadelphia (5hr), $200 from **Chicago** (22hr) and $270 from **Los Angeles** (2 days; 12–18hr). Return fares from **Montréal** are Can$160 (17hr), and around Can$250 from **Toronto** (26hr). On all routes, you'll pay a bit more if you travel between Friday and Sunday, though discounted seven-day advance-purchase tickets and student, senior and "companion" (two-for-one) fares are often available. Greyhound's nationwide toll-free information service (☎1-800/231-2222) can give you routes and times, plus phone numbers and addresses of local terminals. You can also make reservations at the same number.

Bus passes

The Greyhound Discovery Pass offers unlimited travel within a set time limit; you can order online at ⓦwww.discoverypass.com. A seven-day pass costs $239, fifteen days for $339, thirty days for $439, and the longest, a sixty-day pass, is $539. The website has a list of international vendors. The first time you use your pass, the ticket clerk will date it (which becomes the start date of the pass), and you will receive a ticket that allows you to board the bus. Repeat this procedure for every subsequent journey.

Driving

Driving to DC gives you a certain amount of freedom and flexibility, but you'll probably never use your car once you reach the city, since the public transport system is so good. The box below gives an idea of the distances and times involved in driving to DC. Routes into the city are explained on p.24, where you'll also find some useful tips on the intricacies of driving in DC itself.

Car-rental deals vary wildly, though in general you'll find better prices over the weekend than during the week, given the business orientation of the town. You can often make **significant savings** by booking in advance with a major firm that has representation in DC; most agencies in the city have offices at the airports, and at Union Station. When booking, be sure to get free unlimited mileage and be aware that rates can go up by as much as $200 if you want to pick up the car in one location and leave it at another. Collision Damage Waiver (sometimes called Liability Damage Waiver) costs around $15 a day, but without it you are liable for every scratch to the car, even those that aren't your fault. Then again, don't be suckered into insurance you already have; call your credit card company to see if it offers free insurance if you use your card to pay. **If you are under 25**, be prepared for hefty surcharges on top of the usual rates.

Car-rental companies

Advantage ⓦwww.advantage.com.
Alamo ⓦwww.alamo.com.
Avis ⓦwww.avis.com.
Budget ⓦwww.budget.com.
Dollar ⓦwww.dollar.com.
Enterprise ⓦwww.enterprise.com.
Fox Rent-a-Car ⓦfoxrentacar.com.
Hertz ⓦwww.hertz.com.
National ⓦwww.nationalcar.com.
Payless ⓦwww.paylesscar.com.
Rent-a-Wreck ⓦwww.rentawreck.com.
Thrifty ⓦwww.thrifty.com.

Driving to DC

Distances from each city:
Boston: 350 miles (8hr).
Chicago: 710 miles (16hr).
Los Angeles: 2690 miles (3 days).
Miami: 1057 miles (24hr).
Montréal: 610 miles (14hr).
New York: 240 miles (5hr 30min).
San Francisco: 2845 miles (3 days).
Seattle: 2868 miles (3 days).
Toronto: 570 miles (12hr).

Airlines, agents and operators

Airlines

Aer Lingus www.aerlingus.com.
Air Canada www.aircanada.com.
Air France www.airfrance.com.
Air New Zealand www.airnewzealand.com.
Air Pacific www.airpacific.com.
Air Tran www.airtran.com.
Alaska Airlines www.alaskaair.com.
American Airlines www.aa.com.
bmi www.flybmi.com.
British Airways www.ba.com.
Cathay Pacific www.cathaypacific.com.
China Airlines www.china-airlines.com.
Continental Airlines www.continental.com.
Delta www.delta.com.
easyJet www.easyjet.com.
Frontier Airlines www.frontierairlines.com.
Icelandair www.icelandair.com.
JAL (Japan Airlines) www.jal.com.
jetBlue www.jetblue.com.
Korean Air www.koreanair.com.
Lufthansa www.lufthansa.com.
Qantas Airways www.qantas.com.au.
Ryanair www.ryanair.com.
Singapore Airlines www.singaporeair.com.
South African Airways www.flysaa.com.

Southwest www.southwest.com.
United Airlines www.united.com.
US Airways www.usairways.com.
Virgin Atlantic www.virgin-atlantic.com.

Agents and operators

North South Travel UK ☎01245/608 291,
www.northsouthtravel.co.uk. Friendly, competitive
travel agency, offering discounted fares worldwide.
Profits are used to support projects in the developing
world, especially the promotion of sustainable tourism.
STA Travel UK ☎0871/2300 040,
US ☎1-800/781-4040, Australia ☎134 782,
New Zealand ☎0800/474 400, South Africa
☎0861/781 781; www.statravel.co.uk.
Worldwide specialists in independent travel; also
student IDs, travel insurance, car rental, rail passes
and more. Good discounts for students and
under-26s.
Trailfinders UK ☎0845/058 5858, Ireland
☎01/677 7888, Australia ☎1300/780 212;
www.trailfinders.com. One of the best-informed
and most efficient agents for independent travellers.
Travel CUTS Canada ☎1-866/246-9762, US
☎1-800/592-2887; www.travelcuts.com.
Canadian youth and student travel firm.
USIT Ireland ☎01/602 1906, Northern Ireland
☎028/9032 7111; www.usit.ie.
Ireland's main student and youth travel specialists.

Arrival

National Airport has good access to downtown Washington, DC; from the other airports, you can't count on being downtown in much less than an hour, though the various bus, train and subway transfers are smooth enough. Taking a taxi from Dulles or Baltimore-Washington International Airport won't save much time, especially if you arrive during rush hour, though filling a taxi with three or four people may save you a few dollars. Those travelling by train or bus arrive at the most central locations: Union Station and the downtown Greyhound terminal, respectively. Union Station is easily linked by Metro to the city centre.

By air

Dulles International

The area's major airport, and one of the top five busiest in the country, **Dulles International** (IAD; ☎703/572-2700,

www.metwashairports.com), 26 miles west of DC in northern Virginia, handles most international and some domestic flights. The drive to or from central DC can take up to an hour or more in heavy traffic, and rarely less than forty minutes. **Taxis** going downtown cost $60. There's also a

SuperShuttle bus from Dulles (see above; one-way $29). It's cheaper, if a little more time-consuming, to take the **Washington Flyer Express** bus (T1-888/927-4359, Wwww.washfly.com; one-way $10, return $18) to the **West Falls Church Metro station**, a thirty-minute trip; from there it's a twenty-minute train ride into central DC. However, the most inexpensive option is to take public transport all the way into town: catch **Metrobus #5A** (daily 6.30am–11.40pm every hour, weekdays from 5.30am; 1hr–1hr 30min; $6) from the airport, which connects with the Metrorail at the Rosslyn and L'Enfant Plaza Metro stations.

National Airport

The most convenient destination for domestic arrivals is **National Airport** (DCA; T703/417-8000, Wwww.metwashairports .com) – officially Ronald Reagan Washington National Airport – four miles south of central DC and across the Potomac in Virginia. By car or by bus it takes 30 minutes to an hour to reach the centre of town from the airport, depending on traffic, though the National Airport **Metro station** is linked directly to Metro Centre, L'Enfant Plaza and Gallery Place–Chinatown on the Blue and Yellow lines, making the subway the clear choice for transport if you don't have too much luggage. A **taxi** to central DC costs around $15–20 (including airport surcharge). Another option is the **SuperShuttle** bus (one-way $12; T1-800/258-3826, Wwww .supershuttle.com), which drops you at your hotel, though you'll have to ride with up to six strangers.

Baltimore-Washington International Airport

Other international and domestic arrivals land at **Baltimore-Washington International Airport** (BWI; T410/859-7111, Wwww .bwiairport.com), 25 miles northeast of DC and 10 miles south of Baltimore. This, too, is up to an hour's drive from central DC, with **taxis** costing around $60. It's cheaper to take the commuter rail (a free shuttle service connects the airport with the BWI rail terminal, a 10–15min ride). The most economical choice is the southbound Penn Line of the **Maryland Rail Commuter Service** (MARC; Mon–Fri 5am–11.10pm; every 20min–1hr; one-way $6; T410/539-5000, Wmta.maryland.gov) to Washington's Union Station, a forty-minute trip. You can also take the quicker **Amtrak** trains from BWI to Union Station (daily 6.20am–11pm; every 30min; one-way $10): a half-hour journey with regular service, twenty minutes with the speedier Acela Express trains, which are $34 one-way. It's also possible to take a combination of **Metro and bus**: take Metrobus #B30 nonstop to Greenbelt station (every 40min; Mon–Fri 6am–10pm, Sat & Sun 8.45am–10pm; one-way $6), where you can switch to the Metro Green Line.

When **leaving DC**, give yourself plenty of time to get to the airport, especially if you're driving: it can take up to 30 minutes to reach National, and an hour to get to Dulles or BWI with minimal traffic. Once there, security checks can keep you waiting in line for 15 to 45 minutes, so try to leave two hours or more before your flight.

By train and bus

The grand edifice of **Union Station**, 50 Massachusetts Ave NE, three blocks north of the Capitol, welcomes arrivals from all over the country, including major East Coast routes from Philadelphia, New York and Boston. Train operators include the nationwide **Amtrak** (T1-800/872-7245, Wwww.amtrak.com) and the local **MARC** system (T410/539-5000, Wmta.maryland.gov), which connects DC to Baltimore, BWI Airport and suburban Maryland. From the station you can connect to the Metro, rent a car or catch a taxi.

Greyhound (T1-800/229-9424, Wwww .greyhound.com) and **Peter Pan** (T1-800/343-9999, Wwww.peterpanbus .com) buses from Baltimore, Philadelphia, New York, Boston and other cities stop at the terminal at 1005 1st Street NE at L Street, five long blocks (a half-mile) north of Union Station. The Union Station Metro stop is about a $6 taxi ride away.

By car

Driving into DC is a sure way to experience some of the East Coast's most hellish traffic. The eight-to twelve-lane freeway known as the **Capital Beltway** encircles the city at a ten-mile radius from the centre and is busy nearly around the clock. It's made up of two separate highways: I-495 on the western half and I-95/I-495 in the east. If you're visiting only Washington, DC and some of its neighbouring points of interest (including nearly every sight in this book), a car is superfluous due to the capital's excellent transport system. Only if you're wandering farther afield in the region will you need your own vehicle, and even then only to visit smaller towns without transport links to the capital.

Approaching the city **from the northeast** (New York/Philadelphia), you need I-95 (south), before turning west on Route 50; that will take you to New York Avenue, which heads directly into the White House but goes first through a rather bleak industrial wasteland on the northeast edge of town. **From Baltimore** there's the direct Baltimore–Washington Parkway, which also joins Route 50. Indeed, Route 50 is the main

route into DC from the east (Annapolis, Maryland and Chesapeake Bay). **From the south**, take I-95 to I-395, which crosses the river via the George Mason Memorial Bridge – part of the colossal "14th Street Bridge Complex" – and deposits you south of the Mall near the waterfront. **From the northwest** (Frederick, MD, and beyond), take I-270 until you hit the Beltway, then follow I-495 (east) to Connecticut Avenue south; this is one of the more attractive approaches to the city, and also one of the slowest. **From the west** (Virginia) use I-66, which runs across the Theodore Roosevelt Bridge to Constitution Avenue, where DC first appears in the image of the Lincoln Memorial. At peak periods in the Beltway, high-occupancy-vehicle restrictions apply on I-66 eastbound (6.30–9am) and westbound (4–6.30pm). See the "Washington, DC Metropolitan Area" colour map at the back of this book for highways into the city

Getting around

Most places in and around downtown – including the major museums and monuments, and the White House – are within walking distance of one another, while an excellent public transport system connects central DC to outlying sights and neighbourhoods. The Washington Metropolitan Area Transport Authority (WMATA) operates a subway system (Metrorail) and a bus network (Metrobus), plus you can get around by taxi or bike. Driving a car can be very frustrating, with the District's thick congestion and maddening squares and traffic circles resulting in gridlock amid a horn-blaring cacophony.

The Metro

Washington's subway – the **Metrorail**, or **Metro** – is quick, cheap and easy to use. It runs on five lines that cover most of the downtown areas and suburbs (with the notable exception of Georgetown), branching out from the centre of the District in all directions to just beyond the Capital Beltway, where the outlying stations have parking lots for commuters' cars. Each line is colour-coded and studded with various interchange stations: Metro Centre, L'Enfant

Plaza and Gallery Place–Chinatown are the most central downtown. Stations are identified outside by the letter *M* on top of a brown pylon; inside, the well-lit, vaulted halls make the Washington Metro one of the safest subway systems in the world – though security precautions have, as with everything else in town, been tightened since 9/11. Keep in mind that while the system itself may be generally safe, a few of its stations, like those in Anacostia, are in unsafe neighbourhoods.

New extensions are regularly proposed, most recently an extension to Dulles Airport, which will link with the rest of the system at East Falls Church and be dubbed the **Silver Line**. Completion is due by 2016, with closer stations to Washington, DC opening a few years before that.

The Metro's **operating hours** are Monday to Thursday 5am to midnight, Friday 5am to 3am, Saturday 7am to 3am, and Sunday 7am to midnight. Trains run every five to seven minutes on most lines during rush hours, and every ten to twelve minutes at other times. Pick up a copy of the useful **Metro guide** (available in most stations; free), which gives the train and bus routes to the city's various attractions. The **Metro System route map** is available at Metro offices (see below) and at ⓦwww.wmata.com.

Tickets and passes

Each passenger needs a **farecard**, which must be bought from a machine before you pass through the turnstiles. Fares are based on when and how far you travel and usually cost $1.60 (one-way, peak or off-peak) if you're travelling around central DC, the Mall and the Capitol (maps and station-to-station ticket prices are posted by the machines, as well as online). **One-way fares** range from $1.60 (base rate) to $2.75; the minimum **peak-rate fare** is $1.95 and the maximum is $5, charged Mon–Fri 5–9.30am, 3–7pm and weekends from midnight until closing. Children under five ride free, and seniors are admitted for half of the standard price.

Farecards work like debit cards – you "put in" an amount of money when you purchase the card, and the fare is subtracted after each train ride. If you're going to use the Metro several times, it's worth putting in more money

– most stations have machines that accept debit and credit cards. Feed the card through any turnstile marked with a green arrow, and then retrieve it. When you do the same thing at the end of your journey, the machine prints out on the card how much money remains. If you've paid the exact amount, the turnstile keeps the card; if you don't have enough money remaining on the card for the journey, insert it into one of the special exit-fare machines, deposit more money, and try the turnstile again. If you are going to catch a bus after your Metro ride, get a **rail-to-bus transfer pass** at the station where you enter the rail system. The self-service transfer machines are on the mezzanine next to the escalator leading to the train platform.

If you plan on making at least five trips a day around central DC, the **Metrorail One-Day Pass** ($9) is a good choice, buying unlimited travel after 9.30am on weekdays and all day at weekends. There's also a **7-Day Fast Pass** ($47), for seven consecutive days of unlimited travel, but a better deal for visitors is the **7-Day Short Trip Pass** ($32.35), which saves you money and will take you to every sight you'll probably want to see, from the waterfront up to the zoo, as well as National Airport; the only thing outside the covered area is Alexandria, Virginia, for which you'll have to pay a few cents extra. All passes are available at Metro Centre station (12th and F sts NW; Mon–Fri 8am–6pm), Metro Headquarters (600 5th St NW; Mon–Fri 9am–3pm), Metro Pentagon (upper level bus bay; Mon–Fri 7am–4pm) and many supermarkets, or via ⓦwww.wmata.com.

Buses

WMATA runs DC's subway and **bus** systems, which operate during largely the same hours (though some buses run until

---

Washington Metropolitan Area Transport Authority

For route information and bus and Metro timetables call ☏202/637-7000 or visit ⓦwww.wmata.com.

Other helpful numbers
General information ☏202/962-1234.
Transport Police ☏202/962-2121 (emergencies only).
Service Disruption Notices ☏202/962-1212.
Lost and Found ☏202/962-1195 (also online).

Washington city tours

There are a number of **tour operators** eager to show you the many sights of Washington, DC. Some of the more popular **tour bus** services are useful, since they allow you to get on and off the bus at will and shuttle you out to the area's far-flung sights. **River cruises** are worth considering, especially in summer when the offshore breezes come as a welcome relief. **Specialist tours** show you a side of Washington you may not otherwise see, like historic buildings, sites and famous people's homes. For more information, contact Cultural Tourism DC (☎202/661-7581, ⓦwww .culturaltourismdc.org), whose website lists various tours (most $10–20).

Buses and trolleys

Gray Line ☎202/289-1995, ⓦwww.graylinedc.com. A variety of tours in and around DC, including a day tour of downtown sights ($55), combo tours of Alexandria and Mount Vernon ($55), and a trip to Monticello ($92).

Old Town Trolley Tours ☎1-888/912-8687, ⓦwww.historictours.com/washington. Trolleys take you around Downtown, the National Mall, Georgetown and Washington National Cathedral ($35), and a "Monuments by Moonlight" tour shows you the Mall's presidential and war memorials after dark ($35). Tickets available at trolley stops and downtown hotels.

Tourmobile ☎202/554-5100, ⓦwww.tourmobile.com. Narrated bus (daily 9.30am–4.30pm) covering Downtown and Arlington Cemetery ($27), Mount Vernon ($32) and the Mall by night ($30). Tickets available at the office on the Ellipse, at kiosks on the Mall (there's one at the Washington Monument), at the cemetery visitor centre and on the bus.

Cruises and river trips

Atlantic Kayak Tours ☎301/292-6455 or 1-800/297-0066, ⓦwww.atlantickayak .com. Kayak tours of DC monuments near the water and sights along the Potomac, including tours of Piscataway Creek, a Potomac tributary, and the Dyke Marsh Wildlife Area (April–Oct; $45–50). Also moonlight tours, day trips and overnight wildlife excursions. No experience necessary; all equipment included.

Capitol River Cruises ☎1-800/405-5511 or 301/460-7447, ⓦwww.capitolriver cruises.com. Sightseeing cruises leaving hourly (April–Oct noon–9pm; 45min) from Georgetown's Washington Harbour, at the end of 31st St NW; $14 per person, reservations not required.

DC Ducks ☎1-800/844-7601, ⓦwww.dcducks.com. Converted amphibious carriers cruise the Mall and then splash into the Potomac (1hr 30min; $33). Hourly departures from Union Station (mid-March to Oct daily 10am–4pm).

Walking and specialist tours

African American Heritage Tour ☎202/636-9203, ⓦwww.washington-dc-tours.com. Half-day trips to sights important to black history, including the Frederick Douglass National Historic Site and Martin Luther King Jr Memorial. $25; by reservation only.

Bike the Sites ☎202/842-2453, ⓦwww.bikethesites.com. Two- to four-hour guided bike tours of the city's major sights ($30–48, including bike and helmet), plus tours of Mount Vernon and customized tours of the District. Also rents bikes for $5–10 an hour or $35–65 a day. Tour reservations required.

Lantern Lights ☎703/548-0100, ⓦwww.alexcolonialtours.com. The "Ghosts and Graveyard Tour" in Old Town Alexandria takes you through haunted nineteenth-century homes and eerie cemeteries, as costumed guides tell bone-chilling tales of historical horror. Tours (Oct & Nov only; $10) depart from the Ramsay House visitor centre at 221 King St.

Washington Walks ☎202/484-1565, ⓦwww.washingtonwalks.com. Two-hour guided walks with themes like "Before Harlem, There Was U Street", "Memorials by Moonlight", "Most Haunted Houses" and so on (all tours $15).

3am on weekdays). The **base fare** for most bus journeys is $1.70, payable to the driver, though surcharges and zone crossings can raise the price, and express routes will cost $3.85 a ride. The same peak-hour rates on the Metro apply to the buses. The **Weekly Pass** ($15) applies to all regular routes and reduces express trips by $1.50, and buys seven days' worth of unlimited base-fare trips. Other systems are in Alexandria (the **DASH**) and en route to Mount Vernon, which you can reach on a **Fairfax Connector** bus. Both systems link with the Metro; for timetable information contact DASH (tickets $1.50; ☎703/746-3274, ⊛www.dashbus .com) or Fairfax Connector (non-express routes $1.70, express $7; ☎703/339-7200, ⊛www.fairfaxconnector.com).

WMATA also offers the special "**DC Circulator**" service (☎202/962-1423, ⊛www .dccirculator.com), geared toward tourists and conference travellers, which will take you from Union Station to Georgetown via K Street, or from the Convention Centre to the Southwest waterfront by way of 7th Street and the National Mall. Other shuttle routes loop around the museums of the Mall itself; connect Adams Morgan, Shaw and Logan Circle with Downtown's Franklin Square; link the Nationals baseball stadium with the Mall; and connect Dupont Circle with Georgetown and the Rosslyn Metro stop in Arlington. Buses run daily from 7am to 9pm, with some routes having extended hours until midnight on weekdays and 2am at weekends; check the website for timetables. Tickets are $1 on all routes, and the usual passes and transfers are allowed.

Taxis

Taxis complement DC's public transport system and are especially valuable in outposts like Georgetown and Adams Morgan, which aren't on the Metro. If you know you're going to be out late in these neighbourhoods, it's a good idea to book a return taxi in advance.

Fares are $8–10 from Georgetown to Dupont Circle, $15–20 between Reagan National Airport and central DC, and $5–10 for quick jaunts from the National Mall to Downtown. Groups may be asked to pay $1.50 for each passenger in addition to the first one. Once you get out of DC, into Maryland or Virginia, fares can be much more expensive ($60 to the airports, for example). Taxis from those states are legally allowed to deposit you at your Washington destination but may not shuttle you from one DC spot to another.

You can either flag taxis down on the street or use the ranks at hotels and transport terminals; there are always taxis at Union Station. If you call a taxi in advance, there's a $2 surcharge. For more information, call the **DC Taxicab Commission** at ☎202/645-6018 or visit ⊛dctaxi.dc.gov.

Driving

You shouldn't drive in the capital unless you absolutely have to. **Traffic jams** can be nightmarish, the DC street layout is a grid overlaid with unnerving diagonal boulevards, and without a map it's easy to get lost and find yourself in the middle of an urban wasteland. If you must head out of the city by car, either rent one at the end of your stay (at Union Station), or leave your car at your hotel for the duration – though this will cost $20–30 per night at any decent downtown hotel. For lists of car rental agencies, see p.22.

One-way streets can play havoc with the best-planned driving routes, while the traffic-control system in place during the city's **rush hours** (Mon–Fri 6.30–9.30am & 3–7pm, plus lunchtime) means that many lanes, or even whole streets, **change direction** at particular times of the day and left turns are periodically forbidden. Read the signs carefully.

Car parks and garages charge from $6 per hour to $25 a day. Searching for free, **on-street parking** is likely to cost you a lot of time and energy; there are limited-wait (two- to three-hour) parking spots around the Mall (Jefferson and Madison Drives, Independence Ave SW) and in West Potomac Park, but they're extremely popular. **Parking meters** cost between 75 cents and $2 per hour and tend to operate between 7am and 6.30pm, but in popular neighbourhoods (U Street, Adams Morgan, Georgetown, Downtown, around the Mall) they may run until 10pm. At other times, just when you think you've found the perfect spot, it will almost certainly be reserved for workers, or on a street that becomes one-way during rush hour, or temporarily illegal to park on because it is rush hour.

If you're stopped by the police when driving, you'll be required to produce a driver's licence, the car's registration papers and verification of insurance (though the latter two will be waived if you are driving a rental, as long as you can provide proof of rental). Should your car get towed away, call the local **Department of Motor Vehicles** at ☏202/727-5000 and expect to pay $100 or more to get it back. Vehicles towed after 7pm on a Friday won't be returned until after 9am the following Monday.

Bikes

If you want to use your bike more for sport than for transport while in the city, see the "Sports and outdoor activities" chapter, as well as the entries for bike-friendly locales such as Rock Creek Park (p.159) and the C&O Canal (p.166). Given the traffic, few visitors will actually want to brave the DC streets on a bicycle, though several outfits can provide maps and advice on traffic conditions, and Bike the Sites offers tours (see box, p.27). **Bike rental** costs $5–10 an hour, $15–50 a day, or $100–130 a week; you'll need to leave a deposit and/or a credit card or passport number. Bikes are permitted on the Metro except on weekdays during rush hour (7–10am and 4–7pm) and on major holidays such as the Fourth of July. See p.244 for a list of bike-rental companies.

The media

DC is unquestionably the savviest city for political media in the United States; much of what makes headlines around the world is born in the capital's press briefings. Though closed to the general public, White House briefings are broadcast live on C-SPAN and covered in detail in the next day's Washington Post. Nevertheless, overseas visitors will probably find American news coverage too parochial; to keep in touch with day-to-day events back home, you'll have to buy a foreign newspaper.

Newspapers and magazines

DC's major newspaper, the liberal *Washington Post*, is one of America's most respected dailies, landing every morning on the doorsteps of the most powerful people in the world. It routinely wins Pulitzer prizes, the nation's highest award for journalism, though its most famous one was in the 1970s for its investigation of the Watergate scandal that brought down the Nixon administration. You can read the paper free at ⓦwww.washingtonpost.com, but registration is required. The only local competitor to the *Post* is the deeply conservative, Moonie-published *Washington Times*. The country's one truly national daily, *USA Today* – aka "McPaper" – is headquartered across the Potomac in Virginia and known for being thick on splashy graphics and thin on investigative journalism (though you wouldn't know it from visiting the newspaper owner's triumphalist Newseum downtown; see p.118). Any upscale hotel will offer you a choice of this paper or the *Post* in the morning.

Free weeklies include the alternative *CityPaper* (ⓦwww.washingtoncitypaper.com), a tabloid-size paper appearing on Thursdays that's known for its progressive slant on current affairs and its arts and entertainment listings. Glossy **monthly magazines** include the arts-and-leisure publication *Washingtonian* (ⓦwww.washingtonian.com) and PR-focused *Where: Washington* (ⓦwww.wheremagazine.com).

Newspapers from other US cities, as well as **foreign newspapers and magazines**, can be bought at Union Station and major bookshops such as Kramerbooks (see p.252).

TV and radio

The four **television networks** – NBC, ABC, CBS and Fox – broadcast news and talk shows from 6am or 7am to 10am Monday to Friday and air their evening local news programmes from 5pm to 6.30pm and again at 11pm, also on weekdays. National news is on at 6pm and 6.30pm. The city's public-TV channel, WETA (@www.weta.org/tv), broadcasts a compelling mix of documentaries, political investigations and history programmes. Most hotel rooms have some form of cable TV, though the number of channels available varies. Check the daily papers for schedules. Cable news stations include MSNBC, CNN, CNN Headline News and Fox News. ESPN is your best bet for sports, MTV for youth-oriented music videos and programmes, and VH-1 for people outside the MTV demographic. HBO, Showtime and AMC present Hollywood

flicks and award-winning TV shows, while Turner Classic Movies takes its programming from the Golden Age of Hollywood.

The state of commercial **radio** in Washington, DC, as elsewhere in America, is dismal: a slew of radio stations is owned by the goliath Clear Channel and Infinity networks, and a few other national heavyweights. For quality news and programming, tune in to WAMU at 88.5 FM (@wamu.org), which airs National Public Radio broadcasts (Mon–Fri 5–9am & 4–7pm) and independently produced journalism and cultural-affairs shows. NPR also makes its appearance, along with classical-music favourites, on the other public radio station in town, WETA (90.9 FM; @www.weta.org/fm). Other worthwhile stations are usually broadcast online only from universities such as George Washington (@www.gwradio.com), Georgetown (@www.georgetownradio.com) and Howard (WHUR, also on 96.3 FM; @www.whur.com), which together play a mix of jazz, folk, blues, hip-hop and alternative rock, along with talk shows and intermittent cultural programmes.

Travel essentials

Costs

The nation's capital is a lot more affordable than most big American cities. What's particularly appealing about DC is how much you can do here **free**: entry to most museums, the US Capitol and the White House; outdoor concerts, festivals, parades and children's events – none of them costs a cent. And although not free, the **inexpensive** Metro and buses get you to DC's main attractions for $1.70 per ride for buses, and $1.60 for rail. Where admission is charged, **children** and (usually) **senior citizens** get in for half-price, and full-time **students** (holding an International Student ID Card, or ISIC), anyone under 26 (with International Youth Travel Card), and **teachers** (with International

Teacher Card) often receive discounts. Contact discount and/or student travel agencies for applicable ID cards.

The presence of so many students, interns and public servants means that many **bars and restaurants** have great deals, too. That's not to say that you can't spend money here; the city has some of the country's finest and most expensive hotels and restaurants, and the odd attraction can be on the pricey side. Still, sticking to a budget in DC shouldn't be too hard.

Average costs

Accommodation will be your biggest single expense: expect the lowest rate for a double hotel room to be around $100–150 a night, though spartan hostels, motels and a few B&Bs will cost less. This price range can also apply to weekend deals and rooms booked in the less popular winter months. Excluding accommodation, count on spending a **minimum** of $50 a day, which should cover breakfast, a cheap lunch, a budget dinner and a beer. Taking taxis, eating fancier meals and going out for drinks will cost more like $100 or more a day. If you want to go to the theatre, rent a car or take tours, then double that figure.

Taxes and tipping

Sales tax in Washington, DC is among the lowest in the country at 6 percent; this tax is in addition to the marked price on goods. **Restaurant** meals incur a 10 percent tax, while the **hotel tax** is 14.5 percent, on top of the room rate.

One point of eternal discussion is **tipping**. Many workers in service industries get paid very little and rely on tips to bolster their income. Unless you've had abominable service (in which case you should tell the management), you really shouldn't leave a bar or restaurant without leaving a tip of at least **fifteen percent**, and about the same should be added to taxi fares. For superior service, pay twenty percent. A hotel porter deserves roughly $1 for each bag carried to your room; a coat-check clerk should receive the same per coat. When paying by credit card you're expected to add the tip to the total bill before filling in the amount and signing.

Crime and personal safety

Washington, DC has had an unfortunate reputation for **crime**. You'll be told that it's the "murder capital" of the United States, and stories of drug dealers doing business just blocks from the White House are in routine circulation among visitors and locals alike.

It's true – DC ain't Kansas. However, almost all the crime that makes the headlines takes place in neighbourhoods that tourists won't be venturing into (the parts of Northeast and Southeast DC away from tourist-friendly zones, for example). When neighbourhoods are borderline, this guide will tell you where you should and

shouldn't go; if a sight or museum you really want to see is in a risky part of town, take a taxi there and back. But this shouldn't be necessary in the places where you will be spending most of your time: Downtown, the Mall, Dupont Circle, Georgetown, all the major tourist sights, the Metro system and the main nightlife areas are invariably well guarded, well lit and well policed.

Security issues

While travelling around the capital, you'll soon get used to the city's security procedures. At the biggest-name attractions on the Mall or Capitol Hill, you can expect airport-like security: your bags, coats and belongings will be passed through an X-ray machine and you'll have to walk through a metal detector. At less-trafficked museums and attractions, a guard will inspect your bags at the door.

Be sure to **carry some form of ID** at all times. Two pieces should suffice, one of which should have a photo; a passport or driver's licence and credit card(s) are best. University photo ID might be sufficient but is not always recognized as official ID. An International Student Identity Card (ISIC) is often not accepted as valid proof of age in bars or liquor stores. Overseas visitors (often surprised to learn that the legal drinking age in the US is 21) might want to carry their passport to prevent unnecessary hassles.

Mugging and theft

Because DC attracts so many tourists, it certainly has its share of **petty crime**. Keep your wits about you in crowds, and make sure your wallet or purse is secured. After the Metro has closed down, take taxis home from bars, restaurants and clubs; never go wandering in an unfamiliar or deserted area, especially at night. Always be careful when using **ATMs**, especially in untouristed areas. Try to use machines near downtown hotels, shops or offices, and during the daytime. If the worst does happen, it's advisable to hand over your money and afterward to find a phone and dial ☎911, or hail a taxi and ask the driver to take you to the nearest **police station**. Here, report the theft and get a reference number on the report so you can claim insurance and/or travellers' cheque refunds.

Having bags that contain travel documents stolen can be a big headache, so make photocopies of everything important before you travel and keep them separate from the originals. **If your passport is stolen** (or if you lose it), call your country's embassy (see opposite) and pick up an application form for a temporary passport, or have one sent to you. Complete the application and submit it with a notarized photocopy of your ID and a reissuing fee, often around $30. The process of issuing a new passport can take up to six weeks, so plan accordingly.

Keep a record of the numbers of your **travellers' cheques** separate from the actual cheques; if you lose them, call the issuing company on the toll-free number below. The missing cheques should be reissued within a couple of days, and you can request an emergency advance to tide you over in the meantime.

Numbers for lost cards and cheques

American Express Cards ☎1-800/528-4800, cheques ☎1-800/221-7282.
Citibank/Visa Cheques ☎1-800/645-6556.
Diners Club ☎1-800/234-6377.
Discover ☎1-800/347-2683.
Mastercard ☎1-800/826-2181.
Thomas Cook/Travelex Cheques ☎1-800/223-9920.
Visa Cards ☎1-800/847-2911, cheques ☎1-800/227-6811.

Electricity

The US operates on 110V 60Hz and uses two-pronged plugs with the flat prongs parallel. Foreign devices will need both a plug adapter and a transformer, though laptops and phone chargers usually automatically detect and cope with the different voltage and frequency.

Entry requirements

Basic requirements for entry to the US are detailed (and should be frequently checked for updates) on the US State Department website ⓦtravel.state.gov.

Under the Visa Waiver Program (VWP), if you're a citizen of the UK or most other European states, Australia, New Zealand, Japan, or other selected countries (36 in all), and visiting the US for less than ninety days, at a minimum you'll need an onward or return ticket, a visa waiver form and a Machine Readable Passport (MRP). The **I-94W Nonimmigrant Visa Waiver Arrival/ Departure Form** can be provided by your travel agency or embassy, or you can get the form online at the US Customs website, ⓦwww.cbp.gov. The same form covers entry across the US borders with Canada and Mexico (for non-Canadian and non-Mexican citizens). Under no circumstances are visitors who have been admitted under the Visa Waiver Program allowed to extend their stays beyond ninety days. If you're in the Visa Waiver Program and intend to work, study or stay in the country for more than ninety days, you must apply for a **regular visa** through your local US embassy or consulate.

Canadian citizens should have their passports on them when entering the country. If you're planning to stay for more than ninety days you'll need a **visa**. Without the proper paperwork, Canadians are barred from working in the US.

Citizens of **all other countries** should contact their local US embassy or consulate for details of current entry requirements, as they are often required to have both a valid passport and a nonimmigrant visitor's visa. To obtain such a visa, complete the application form available through your local American embassy or consulate and send it with the appropriate fee, two photographs and a passport. Visas are not issued to convicted criminals, those with ties to radical political groups, and visitors from countries identified by the State Department as being "state sponsors of terrorism" (North Korea and Iran, for example). Complications also arise if you have a communicable disease or have previously been denied entry to the US for any reason. Furthermore, the US government now electronically fingerprints most visitors and applies spot background checks looking for evidence of past criminal or terrorist ties.

For further information or to get a **visa extension** before your time is up, contact the nearest US Citizenship and Immigration

Service office, whose address will be online or at the front of the phone book under the Federal Government Offices listings. You can also contact the National Customer Service Centre at ☎1-800/375-5283 or ⓦwww .uscis.gov/contact_us.

Customs

Upon your entry to the US, Customs officers will relieve you of your Customs declaration form, which you receive with your waiver form when it is handed out on incoming planes, on ferries and at border crossing points. It asks if you're carrying any fresh foods and if you've visited a farm in the last month.

As well as food and anything agricultural, it's prohibited to carry into the country any articles from such places as North Korea, Iran, Syria or Cuba, as well as obvious no-no's like protected wildlife species and ancient artefacts. Anyone caught sneaking **drugs** into the country will not only face prosecution but be entered in the records as an undesirable and probably denied entry for life. For duty-free allowances and other information regarding Customs, call ☎202/354-1000 or visit ⓦwww.customs.gov.

Embassies in Washington, DC

Australia 2005 Massachusetts Ave NW ☎202/558-2216, ⓦwww.austemb.org.
Canada 501 Pennsylvania Ave NW ☎202/682-1740, ⓦwww.canadianembassy.org.
Ireland 2234 Massachusetts Ave NW ☎202/462-3939, ⓦwww.embassyofireland.org.
New Zealand 37 Observatory Circle NW ☎202/328-4800, ⓦwww.nzembassy.com/usa.
South Africa 3051 Massachusetts Ave NW ☎202/232-4400, ⓦwww.saembassy.org.
UK 3100 Massachusetts Ave NW ☎202/588-6500, ⓦwww.fco.gov.uk.

Health

The US has no national healthcare system, and, while new legislation was passed in 2010, the implementation dates are far spread out and the law itself is a bit of a patchwork, especially for foreign travellers. You're still well advised to protect yourself from exorbitant medical costs with a good insurance policy (see below). If you have a serious accident while you're in Washington, emergency

services will get to you sooner and charge you later. For **emergencies**, dial toll-free ☎911 from any phone. For medical or dental problems that don't require an ambulance, most hospitals have a walk-in emergency room: for your nearest hospital or dental office, check with your hotel or dial ☎411.

Should you need to see a **doctor**, lists can be found online or in the *Yellow Pages* under "Clinics" or "Physicians and Surgeons". Be aware that even consultations are costly, usually around $95–145 each visit, payable in advance. Keep receipts for any part of your medical treatment, including prescriptions, so that you can claim against your insurance once you're home.

For minor ailments, stop by a local **pharmacy**; a few in DC are open 24hr. Foreign visitors should note that many medicines available over the counter at home – codeine-based painkillers, for one – are **prescription-only** in the US. Bring additional supplies if you're particularly brand-loyal.

Travellers from Europe, Canada and Australia do not require **inoculations** to enter the US.

Insurance

UK residents would do well to take out an **insurance policy** before travelling to cover against theft, loss and illness or injury. Before paying for a new policy, however, it's worth checking whether you are already covered – some all-risks home insurance policies may cover your possessions when overseas, and many private medical schemes include coverage when abroad.

After exhausting the possibilities, you might want to contact a **specialist travel insurance** company. A typical policy usually provides cover for the loss of baggage, tickets, and – up to a certain limit – cash or cheques, as well as cancellation or curtailment of your journey. Most of them exclude so-called dangerous sports unless an extra premium is paid: in America, this can mean scuba diving, whitewater rafting and windsurfing. Many policies can be changed to exclude coverage you don't need – for example, sickness and accident benefits can often be excluded or included at will. If you do take medical coverage, ascertain whether benefits will be paid as treatment

Rough Guides travel insurance

Rough Guides has teamed up with WorldNomads.com to offer great **travel insurance** deals. Policies are available to residents of over 150 countries, with cover for a wide range of **adventure sports**, 24hr emergency assistance, high levels of medical and evacuation cover and a stream of **travel safety information**. Roughguides.com users can take advantage of their policies online 24/7, from anywhere in the world – even if you're already travelling. And since plans often change when you're on the road, you can extend your policy and even claim online. Roughguides.com users who buy travel insurance with WorldNomads.com can also leave a positive footprint and donate to a community development project. For more information go to ⓦ **www.roughguides.com/shop**.

proceeds or only after you return home, and if there is a 24-hour medical emergency number. When securing **baggage coverage**, make sure that the per-article limit – typically under £500 – will cover your most valuable possession. If you need to make a claim, you should keep receipts for medicines and medical treatment, and in the event you have anything stolen, you must obtain an official theft report from the police.

For information on **rental-car insurance**, see p.22.

Internet

Given that the military-industrial complex itself had much to do with the creation of the **internet** (which it called Arpanet), it's not surprising that Washington, DC is one of the most connected cities on the planet. The spread of wireless hot spots all over the region means anyone travelling with a laptop or PDA enabled for wi-fi should have no trouble getting connected, often at fast speeds at no cost. At some **cafés** you'll need to use your credit card to sign up for a service, though many other cafés have unsecured access or will give you the password when you buy a coffee or muffin. You'll also come across a few dedicated **internet cafés**, with a dozen or more machines usually charged at around $5–10 an hour.

Public libraries almost invariably have **free internet access** – just ask at the front desk. You may have to wait for an opening, or sign up for a later slot. Many motels, hotels and hostels also offer internet access with a machine or two in the lobby, but again, wi-fi is taking over.

If you're not staying somewhere that offers internet access, you may be forced to hunt down a FedEx Kinko's or similar spot (look under "Copying" in the *Yellow Pages*). You can log on at a major hotel's business centre, but that can get pricey. And if you're so inclined before catching a flight at Dulles or National, you can use one of the credit card-activated internet kiosks.

Useful websites

The Hill ⓦ hillnews.com. Aimed at those who can't get enough of inside-the-Beltway news, gossip and intrigue. Covers current events, committee hearings, lobbying, campaign activity and spirited punditry.
Metromix ⓦ dc.metromix.com. Good spot for the latest on hip restaurants, happening clubs and events, plus movie reviews, blog entries and other opinionated, youth-oriented angles on the city.
Station Masters ⓦ www.stationmasters.com. Very effective site highlighting major attractions, buildings and roads around Metrorail stations. Gives the location of parking facilities, station escalators and elevators, and train routes.
Thomas ⓦ thomas.loc.gov. Online resource for legislative information. The only site with biographies of every member of Congress since 1774, the full text of the Constitution and other such documents, committee reports, roll calls of votes, and more.
Washington Art ⓦ www.washingtonart.com. Website where DC-area visual artists display their work online. Includes exhibition information, art discussions and links to other local art sites.
White House Historical Association ⓦ www .whitehousehistory.org. Online tours of the president's house, plus special features on the various presidents, resources for children and teachers, and a chance to buy a White House Christmas ornament for your tree.

Laundry

The larger hotels provide **laundry** service at a price. Cheaper motels and hostels may have self-service laundry facilities, but in general you'll be doing your laundry at a laundromat. Found all over the place, they're usually open fairly long hours and have a powder-dispensing machine and another to provide change. A typical wash and dry might cost $4–6.

Mail

Post offices are usually open Monday to Friday, from 9am to 5pm, although some are also open on Saturday from 9am to noon or 1pm. Ordinary **mail** within the US costs 44¢ for letters weighing up to an ounce. Postcards cost 28¢ or 44¢, depending on size. The return address should be written in the upper left corner of the envelope. Domestic letters that don't carry a **zip code** are liable to get lost or at least seriously delayed; you can find these codes at ⑩www .usps.com, and post offices – even abroad – should have zip-code directories for major US cities. You can drop mail off at any post office or in the blue **mailboxes** found on street corners throughout the city. **Airmail** from DC to Europe takes less than a week.

You can have mail sent to you c/o General Delivery (known elsewhere as poste restante), at the central **Benjamin Franklin Post Office**, 1200 Pennsylvania Ave NW, Washington, DC 20004 (Mon–Fri 9am–5pm), which will hold mail for thirty days before returning it to the sender – so make sure the envelope has a return address. Alternatively, any decent hotel will hold mail for you, even in advance of your arrival.

Rules on sending **parcels** are very rigid: packages must be sealed according to the instructions given at ⑩www.usps.com. To send anything out of the country, you'll need a green **Customs declaration form**, available from the post office. Rates for airmailing a parcel weighing up to 1lb to Europe, Australia and New Zealand are $15–18.

Maps

The maps in this guide, along with the free city plans you'll pick up from tourist offices, hotels and museums, will be sufficient to help you find your way around DC. If you want something a bit more comprehensive, best is the small, shiny, foldout *Streetwise Washington DC* map ($6.95, ⑩www.street wisemaps.com), available from book, travel and map stores in major cities. If you are travelling to the more unfamiliar outlying parts of the city, you can pick up the comprehensive *Thomas Guide: Washington DC Metro* ($25; ⑩www.thomasguidebooks.com).

If you'll be travelling beyond DC, the **free road maps** issued by each state are usually fine for general driving and route planning. To get hold of one, either write to the state tourist office directly or stop by any state welcome centre or visitor centre. Camping shops have a strong selection as well.

The **American Automobile Association** (☎1-800/222-4357, ⑩www.aaa.com) provides free maps and assistance to its members, and to British members of the AA and RAC. You can visit the local branch at 1405 G St NW, Washington, DC 20005 (Mon–Fri 9.30am–5.30pm; ☎202/481-6811, ⑩www.aaamidatlantic.com).

Money

US currency comes in **notes** of $1, $5, $10, $20, $50 and $100. All are the same size, though denominations of $5 and higher have in the last few years been changing shades from their familiar drab green – with the $100 bill particularly loaded with high-tech, anti-counterfeiting elements. The dollar comprises one hundred cents, made up of one-cent pennies, five-cent nickels, ten-cent dimes, and 25-cent quarters. Quarters are most useful for buses, vending machines, parking meters and telephones, so always carry plenty. For the latest exchange rates, see ⑩www.xe.com.

Most **banks** are open Monday to Friday 9am to 5pm; some stay open until 6pm on Friday, and a few open on Saturday from 9am to noon. For banking services – particularly currency exchange – outside normal business hours and on weekends, try major hotels or branches of Thomas Cook or Travelex.

Travellers' cheques

US **travellers' cheques** are the safest way for overseas visitors to carry money, and the better-known cheques, such as those issued by American Express and Visa, are treated as cash in most shops. The usual fee for travellers' cheque sales is one or two percent, though this fee may be waived if you buy the cheques through your home bank. It pays to get a selection of denominations, particularly tens and twenties. Keep the purchase agreement and a record of serial numbers separate from the cheques themselves. In the event that cheques are lost or stolen, report the loss immediately (see p.32 for emergency numbers). Most companies claim to replace lost or stolen cheques within 24 hours.

Credit and debit cards

Credit cards are the most widely accepted form of payment for major hotels, restaurants and retailers, even though a few smaller merchants still do not accept them. You'll be asked to show a credit card when renting a car, bike or other such item, or to start a tab at hotels for incidental charges; in any case, you can always pay the bill in cash when you return the item or check out of your room. Most major credit cards issued by foreign banks are honoured in the US. Visa, MasterCard, American Express and Discover are the most widely used.

Credit cards can also come in handy as a backup source of funds, and they can save on exchange-rate commissions. Most debit cards connected to international financial networks will work on the road as they do at home, but be wary of steep **ATM** charges for using cards outside your own bank's system – these start at $3–4 and can rise with each transaction.

If your card is **stolen**, you'll need to call the dedicated emergency number (see p.32) and provide information on where and when you made your last transactions.

Opening hours and public holidays

As a general rule, **museums** are open daily 10am to 5.30pm, though some have extended summer hours; a few art galleries stay open until 8 or 9pm one night a week, often Thursday. Smaller, private museums close for one day a week, usually Monday or

Tuesday, and may be open 9am to 4pm or have more limited hours. **Federal office buildings**, some of which incorporate museums, are open Monday to Friday 9am to 5.30pm. Most **national monuments** are open 24hr daily, though they tend to be staffed only between 8am and 11.30pm, and their gift shops will have more limited hours (typically daily 9am–5.30pm). **Shops** are generally open Monday to Saturday 10am to 6pm or 7pm; some have extended weekend hours. In neighbourhoods like Georgetown, Adams Morgan and Dupont Circle, many stores open on Sunday, too, usually noon to 5pm. **Malls** tend to be open Monday to Saturday 10am to 7pm or later, and Sunday noon to 6pm. For **bank** opening hours, see under "Money"; for **post office** hours, see under "Mail".

While some diners stay open 24hr, most **restaurants** open daily around 11am for lunch and close at 9 or 10pm. Places that serve breakfast usually open early, between 6 and 8am, serve lunch later, and close around 2pm to 3pm. Dance and live-music **clubs** often won't open until 9 or 10pm; many serve alcohol until 2am and then either close for the night or stay open until dawn without serving booze.

Public holidays and festivals

On the **national public holidays** listed below, stores, banks, and public and federal offices are likely to be closed all day, as are many clubs and restaurants. Shopping malls, supermarkets, and department and

National public holidays

Jan 1 New Year's Day
Jan 3rd Monday Dr Martin Luther King Jr's Birthday
Feb 3rd Monday Presidents' Day
May Last Monday Memorial Day
July 4 Independence Day
Sept 1st Monday Labor Day
Oct 2nd Monday Columbus Day
Nov 11 Veterans' Day
Nov 4th Thursday Thanksgiving
Dec 25 Christmas Day

Dialling codes

Calling home

Note that the initial zero is omitted from the area or city code when dialling the UK, Ireland, Australia and New Zealand from abroad.

Canada 1 + area code.
Australia 00 + 61 + city code.
New Zealand 00 + 64 + city code.
UK 00 + 44 + city code.

Republic of Ireland 00 + 353 + city code.
South Africa 00 + 27 + city code.

Capital region area codes

202 District of Columbia (all)
240 Western Maryland
301 Western Maryland (overlay with above)
304 West Virginia

540 Northern Virginia, not incl. most DC suburbs
571 Virginia suburbs of DC, incl. Alexandria and Arlington
703 Virginia suburbs of DC, incl. Alexandria and Arlington (overlay)

---

chain stores, however, tend to remain open. The Smithsonian museums and galleries are open every day except Christmas. The traditional **summer season**, when many attractions have extended hours, runs from Memorial Day to Labor Day.

DC's full **festival calendar** is detailed in Chapter 15. During certain times, like the National Cherry Blossom Festival in spring, Memorial Day weekend, the Fourth of July, and Labor Day weekend, it can be very difficult to find accommodation, so it's important to book well in advance.

Telephones

With excellent reception in all but the remotest areas, taking your **mobile phone** to DC makes a lot of sense. Ask your provider to confirm that your phone will work on US frequencies (most do these days) and get it set up for international use. **Roaming** rates can be pretty high, so if you're planning to make a lot of calls, it may work out cheaper to **buy a phone** in the city, though the lower cost is counterbalanced by the need to tell all your friends your new phone number. Basic, new phones can be picked up for as little as $30.

Cheap, prepaid phone cards allow calls to virtually anywhere in the world. Most convenience stores sell them; look for signs posted in shop windows advertising rates, which can vary dramatically, and check the fine print to make sure you're getting a good deal – many companies tack on exorbitant fees if you try to use their cards from a pay phone.

Calling from your **hotel room** will cost considerably more than calling from a public phone. Major hotels often charge a connection fee of at least $1 for most calls (waived if they're toll-free), and international calls will cost a small fortune. While an increasing number of public phones accept credit cards, these can incur astronomical charges for long-distance service, including a high "connection fee" that can bump charges up to as much as $7 a minute.

Most **telephone numbers** in this guide have a **202 area code**, for Washington, DC. Calls within the greater DC metropolitan area are counted as local even if they require a different code. Detailed information about calls, codes and rates are listed online and at the front of the *White Pages* **telephone directory**. A local call on a public phone, where you can find them, usually costs 50¢.

Useful numbers

Emergencies ☎911
Directory information ☎411
Directory enquiries for toll-free numbers ☎1-800/555-1212
Long-distance directory information ☎1-(area code)/555-1212
International operator ☎00

Any number with ☎800, ☎866, ☎877 or ☎888 in place of the area code is **toll-free**. Most major hotels, government agencies and car rental firms have toll-free numbers, though some can be used only within the area – dialling is the only way to find out. Numbers with a ☎1-900 prefix are toll calls, and will charge you a high fee for just a few minutes of use.

Photography

With fabulous scenery abounding, many parts of the DC area can be a delight to **photograph**. Bring plenty of digital memory or be prepared to visit photo shops periodically and burn your images onto CD. As ever, try to shoot in the early morning and late afternoon when the warmer, lower-angled light casts deeper shadows and gives greater depth to your shots.

As with everything in the capital region, care must be taken when taking snapshots around any kind of government installation. Most parks and monuments welcome photography, and museum policies depend on the institution and the exhibit. It is never a good idea to take photos of military bases, security infrastructure or anything else that suggests you're looking for a weak spot for some sort of attack – at best, you'll be questioned by a guard; at worst, you'll have your digital memory taken from you and be escorted from the premises.

Senior travellers

Establishments vary in their definition of **seniors**: in some places it's over-55s, in others over-65s. Seniors can regularly find discounts of anywhere from 10 to 50 percent at movie theatres, museums, hotels, restaurants, performing arts venues and the occasional shop. On Amtrak, they can get a 15 percent discount on most regular fares. On Greyhound the discount is smaller, in the range of 5 to 10 percent. If heading to a national park, the **Senior Pass** ($10) provides a lifetime of free entry to federally operated recreation sites, as well as half-price discounts on concessions such as boat launches and camping. At other sites like museums and galleries, a discount in the range of five to twenty percent may be offered.

Time

Washington, DC runs on **Eastern Standard Time** (EST), which is five hours behind Greenwich Mean Time (GMT). Thus, when it's noon Monday in DC it is 9am in California, 5pm in London, 2am Tuesday in Sydney and 4am Tuesday in Auckland.

Tourist information

The main sources of **tourist information** for the District are the DC Chamber of Commerce and the Washington DC Convention and Tourism Corporation. Both of these offices can send you brochures, visitor guides, events calendars and maps in advance of your trip, and answer any questions once you've arrived.

On arrival, you'll find maps and other guides available in the airports, Union Station and hotels. The most useful item to pick up is the free *Washington DC Visitors Guide*, with listings, reviews and contact numbers. Once in the city, your first stop should be the **DC Visitor Information Centre**, Ronald Reagan Building, 1300 Pennsylvania Ave NW (spring and summer Mon–Fri 8.30am–5.30pm, Sat 9am–4pm; autumn and winter Mon–Fri 9am–4.30pm; ☎1-866/324-7386, ⓦwww.itcdc.com), which can help with maps, tours and region-wide information.

Other resources include the **White House Visitor Information Centre** (see below), which has details on the Executive Mansion along with National Park sights all over the District, and the **Smithsonian Institution** building on the Mall (see box, p.53), which is the best stop for Smithsonian Museum information. You'll also come across National Park Service rangers – in kiosks on the Mall, and at the major memorials – who should also be able to answer general queries. Additionally, neighbourhoods like Georgetown and cities like Alexandria have their own visitor centres covering their respective sights.

Tourist offices

Alexandria, VA in the Ramsay House, 221 King St ☎703/746-3301, ⓦvisitalexandriava.com. Daily 10am–8pm, Jan–March closes 5pm.
Arlington, VA 1905 E Randol Mill Rd ☎817/461-3888 or 1-800/342-4305, ⓦwww.arlington.org /arlington-cvb. Mon–Sat 9am–5pm, Sun noon–4pm.

DC Chamber of Commerce 506 9th St NW, Downtown ☎ 202/638-7330 or 1-866/324-7386, ⓦ www.dcchamber.org. Mon–Fri 9am–4.30pm.
Georgetown 1057 Thomas Jefferson St ☎ 202/653-5190, ⓦ www.georgetowndc.com. Wed–Fri 9am–4.30pm. Doubles as a visitor centre for the nearby C&O Canal.
National Park Service National Capital Region 1849 C St NW, Foggy Bottom ☎ 202/208-4747, ⓦ www.nps.gov. Mon–Fri 9am–5pm.
Washington, DC Convention and Tourism Corporation (WCTC) 901 7th St NW, 4th Floor, Downtown ☎ 202/789-7000 or 1-800/422-8644, ⓦ www.washington.org. Telephone and mail enquiries only.
White House Visitor Centre Downtown ☎ 202/208-1631, ⓦ www.nps.gov/whho. Daily 7.30am–4pm. Maps, brochures and information about major city sights.

Special events lines

Dial-A-Museum ☎ 202/357-2020. Mon–Sat 9am–4pm. Smithsonian Institution exhibits and special events.
Dial-A-Park ☎ 202/619-7275. Events at National Park Service facilities.
Post-Haste ☎ 202/334-9000. *Washington Post* information line for news, weather, sports, restaurants, events and festivals.

Travellers with disabilities

The Americans with Disabilities Act requires all public buildings to be **wheelchair accessible** and provide suitable toilet facilities, and almost all street corners have dropped kerbs, public telephones are equipped for hearing-aid users, and most public transport has accessibility aids such as subways with elevators and buses that "kneel" to let riders board. Even movie theatres are required to allow people in wheelchairs a reasonable, unimpeded view of the screen. Most hotel and motel chains offer accessible **accommodation**, though the situation may be more problematic at B&Bs built a century ago, where a narrow stairway may be the only option.

Getting around

Major **car rental** firms can provide vehicles with hand controls for drivers with leg or spinal disabilities, though these are typically available only on the pricier models. Regarding parking regulations, licence plates for the disabled must carry a three-inch-square international access symbol, and a placard bearing this symbol must be hung from the car's rearview mirror.

American **air carriers** must by law accommodate customers with disabilities, and some even allow attendants of those with serious conditions to accompany them for a reduced fare. Almost every Amtrak train includes one or more cars with accommodation for disabled passengers, along with wheelchair assistance at train platforms, adapted on-board seating, free travel for guide dogs, and discounts on fares, all with 24 hours' advance notice. Passengers with hearing impairment can get information by calling ☎ 1-800/523-6590 (TTY) or checking out ⓦ www.amtrak.com.

By contrast, travelling by **Greyhound** and **Amtrak Thruway** bus connections is often trouble. Buses are not equipped with platforms for wheelchairs, though intercity carriers are required by law to provide assistance with boarding, and disabled passengers may be able to get priority seating. Call Greyhound's ADA customer assistance line for more information (☎ 1-800/752-4841, ⓦ www.greyhound.com).

The **Washington Convention and Tourism Corporation** (see above) produces a free handout on the city's accessibility for people with disabilities; call ☎ 202/789-7000 or visit ⓦ www.washington.org. Each **Metro** station has an elevator (with Braille controls) to the platforms, and the trains' wide aisles can accommodate wheelchairs. Most Metro buses have lowering platforms, and reduced fares and priority seating are available. ⓦ www.wmata.com outlines the system's features in some detail under "Accessibility". There is also a free guide offering information on Metro access for the disabled at Metro stations, or you can call ☎ 202/637-7000 or 202 638 3780 (TDD). Travellers who are visually impaired or who use a wheelchair can call **Mobility Link** at ☎ 202/962-6464 for information.

Site access

Blind or disabled citizens or permanent residents of the US can obtain the America the Beautiful Access Pass, a free lifetime entrance pass to those federally operated parks, monuments, historic sites, recreation areas and wildlife refuges that charge entrance fees. It also provides a fifty percent discount on fees charged for facilities such as camping, boat launching and parking. The pass is available from the National Park Service (⊛www.nps.gov/fees_passes.htm) and must be picked up in person from the areas described.

Most **monuments and memorials** in DC have elevators to viewing platforms and special parking facilities, and at some sites large-print brochures and sign-language interpreters are available. (Call ☎202/619-7222 for more information on any site operated by the National Park Service.) All **Smithsonian museums** are wheelchair-accessible, and with notice staff can serve as sign-language interpreters or provide large-print, Braille or recorded material. The free *Smithsonian Access* is available in large print or Braille, or on audiocassette; call

☎202/357-2700 or 202-357-1729 (TTY). It's also available, as is an accessibility map, at ⊛www.si.edu.

Information

National **organizations** facilitating travel for people with disabilities include SATH, the Society for the Advancement of Travellers with Handicaps (☎212/447-7284, ⊛www.sath.org), a nonprofit travel-industry grouping made up of travel agents, tour operators and hotel and airline management; contact them in advance so they can notify the appropriate members. Mobility International USA (☎541/343-1284, ⊛www.miusa.org) answers transport queries and operates an exchange programme for people with disabilities. Access-Able (☎303/232-2979, ⊛www.access-able.com) is an information service that assists travellers with disabilities by putting them in contact with other people with similar conditions.

The City

The City

The National Mall

Occupying a majestic spread of two miles between the US Capitol and the Potomac River is the cultural and political axis of the United States, the **National Mall** (24hr; staffed with rangers daily 9.30am–11.30pm; ⓦ www.nps.gov/nama). The prime target for nearly every visitor to DC, this enormous swath of green in the middle of the city is a showpiece filled with many of the city's biggest-ticket attractions, including nine famous Smithsonian Institution **museums** and the National Gallery of Art, itself spread over two huge buildings. The Mall also contains several of the city's (and the country's) most iconic **monuments and memorials**, dedicated to presidents and war veterans. The 2000ft-long, 160ft-wide **Reflecting Pool**, supposedly inspired by the Taj Mahal's landscaping and the Palace of Versailles' pools and canals, runs through the middle of the western half of the Mall, between the Washington Monument and the Lincoln Memorial. Though only two and a half feet deep at its centre, it nonetheless holds almost seven million gallons of water.

The Mall's central spot in a planned capital city has made it an eyewitness to some of the most historically significant **social and political events of the twentieth century**: the 1963 March on Washington brought Dr Martin Luther King Jr to the steps of the Lincoln Memorial to deliver his "I Have a Dream" speech; in 1967, at the height of the anti–Vietnam War protests, the March on the Pentagon began at those same steps. In the current era, various protests and events have been held by figures from across the political spectrum, from Louis Farrakhan to Glenn Beck. For all its grandeur and tumult, however, the Mall is also a place to relax and party, notably at the annual Festival of American Folklife and on the Fourth of July (see p.241).

As a visitor to Washington, you'll find the Mall almost inescapable on any tourist-oriented route. You'll need three days or so to visit all its major sights, but it's better not to spend whole days at the Mall, if only to avoid complete cultural overload. Many of the attractions lend themselves to being seen with a combination of other city sights: the western monuments with the White House and Foggy Bottom (see Chapter 4); the Jefferson and Roosevelt memorials with the sights along the Water-front (see Chapter 3); and the museums on the Mall's east side interspersed with a stroll around Capitol Hill (see Chapter 2) or Downtown (see Chapter 5).

Some history

Despite the size and prominence the Mall enjoys today, from the early to mid-nineteenth century it was something of an embarrassment – a wild, stagnant piece of marshy land that some saw as a metaphor for the country's then-unrealized potential.

A 400ft-wide avenue leading west from the Capitol was at the heart of French military engineer **Pierre Charles L'Enfant**'s original 1791 plan for the city; along it, he envisioned gardens and mansions for the political elite. However, by the

1

THE NATIONAL MALL

▲ Capitol Hill

US Court House

National Archives

PENNSYLVANIA AVE NW

National Gallery of Art East Building

National Museum of the American Indian

3RD ST SW

3RD ST SW

FEDERAL CENTER SW Ⓜ

VIRGINIA AVE

4TH ST SW

4TH ST SW

CONSTITUTION AVE NW

National Gallery of Art West Building

National Air & Space Museum

INDEPENDENCE AVE SW

4TH ST SW

C ST SW

SCHOOL ST

E ST SW

6TH ST SW

G ST SW

I ST SW

Ice rink & Sculpture Garden

MARYLAND AVE SW

6TH ST SW

6TH ST SW

▲ Federal Triangle

7TH ST SW

Smithsonian Institution

National Museum of Natural History

Sculpture Garden

Hirshhorn Museum

D ST SW Ⓜ

L'ENFANT PLAZA

7TH ST SW

MAINE AVE SW

WATER ST SW

9TH ST SW

Arts & Industries Bldg

Enid A Haupt Garden

National Museum of African Art

L'ENFANT PROMENADE (10TH ST)

Washington Channel

National Museum of Asian Art

WATER ST SW

National Museum of American History

MADISON DR NW

SMITHSONIAN Ⓜ

SMITHSONIAN DR

JEFFERSON DR

12TH ST SW

Francis Case Memorial Bridge

OHIO DRIVE

Dept of Commerce

14TH ST NW

C ST SW

Department of Agriculture

D ST SW

15TH ST NW

Holocaust Museum

RAOUL WALLENBERG PL

14TH ST SW

Bureau of Engraving & Printing

East Potomac Park

▲ Foggy Bottom

CONSTITUTION AVE

Ticket kiosk

Washington Monument

John Paul Jones Memorial

National World War II Memorial

Tidal Basin Paddle Boats

EAST BASIN DR SW

Jefferson Memorial

EAST BASIN DR

OHIO DRIVE SW

▲ Pentagon

Vietnam Veterans Memorial

Vietnam Women's Memorial

Constitution Gardens

Reflecting Pool

West Potomac Park

Korean War Veterans Memorial

DC War Memorial

Tidal Basin

INDEPENDENCE AVE SW

WEST BASIN DR SW

Martin Luther King Jr National Memorial

West Potomac Park

OHIO DRIVE

FDR Memorial

George Mason (14th St) Bridge

Potomac River

Lincoln Memorial

▲ Arlington National Cemetery

N

0   500 yds

middle of the nineteenth century, the Mall was little more than a muddy, bug-infested swamp where cows, pigs and goats grazed on the open land, while the malodorous city canal (linking the C&O Canal in Georgetown with the Anacostia River) ran along the north side, stinking with rotting refuse, spoiled fish, entrails and dead animals from Washington's Centre Market on 7th Street.

Following the construction of the **Smithsonian Institution Building** between 1849 and 1855, eminent landscape gardener **Andrew Jackson Downing** was hired to design an elegant green space in keeping with L'Enfant's plan. However, the money only stretched to one tree-planted park near the Smithsonian, and nobody dared venture there at night, since it quickly became the haunt of ruffians and criminals. The Mall continued to deteriorate, and as the city grew, its south side became home to sweltering meat markets and warehouses, while the grand avenue L'Enfant imagined was crisscrossed by the ungainly tracks of the Baltimore and Potomac Railroad.

In the post-Civil War era, the city canal was filled in (it's now Constitution Avenue); Centre Market was closed; a Board of Public Works was established to build sewers, pavements and streets; and mature trees were planted. Several of Downing's plans were resurrected, extending beyond the Mall to incorporate the grassy Ellipse and the gardens on either side of the White House, finally placing the Mall at the ornamental heart of the city – though the true shape of its grandeur would take another fifty years to be realized.

Led by Senator James McMillan, members of the 1901 **McMillan Commission**, charged with improving the Mall and the city's park system, returned from Europe fired up with plans to link the Mall with a series of gardens and memorials, and to demolish an unsightly train station. McMillan's proposals eventually prevailed and, following the completion of the Lincoln Memorial in 1922, the Mall was extended west of the Washington Monument for the first time, reaching to the banks of the Potomac River and incorporating the grounds known today as West Potomac Park (though much of the watery turf of the western Mall still had to be filled in and made to resemble something other than a swamp). More improvements were made in the 1930s under the auspices of President Roosevelt's Works Progress Administration (WPA), including the planting of the city's now-famous elm trees, and the **National Park Service** was granted stewardship of the Mall and its monuments.

The Jefferson Memorial was erected in 1943 by John Russell Pope, who also designed the contemporaneous National Gallery of Art in a similarly proper Classical style. The 1960s and 1970s ushered in **museums** of a more modern ilk, and **monuments** to fallen warriors (most notably the Vietnam Veterans Memorial) followed from the 1980s up to the present. The most recent proposal, the National Museum of African American History and Culture, on the northeast side of the Washington Monument, is due for completion in 2015.

Monuments and memorials

The Mall is laid out for easy navigation: **monuments and memorials** lie to the west, surrounding the Reflecting Pool, while **museums** sit to the east, and the Washington Monument stands between the two sides.

Other than the Washington Monument, which sits about a quarter of a mile west of the Smithsonian stop, the various memorials and monuments on the western Mall are **not easily accessible by Metrorail**; the closest stops are Foggy Bottom–GWU and Farragut West to the north, but they are more than two-thirds of a mile from the Lincoln Memorial and further from the rest. You can also tackle the memorials from the west: take the Metrorail to the Arlington Cemetery stop, arriving at the Lincoln Memorial on foot by way of the striking Arlington Memorial Bridge. The closest approach, however, may be to take Metrobus #13 (routes A, B, F or G), which loops around the north side of the entire Mall along Constitution Avenue to the cemetery and Pentagon and back, or the Tourmobile, which also runs along Constitution Avenue (see box, p.27).

The Washington Monument

Along with the US Capitol, if there's one structure that symbolizes DC, it's the **Washington Monument**, 15th St NW at Constitution Ave (daily 9am–5pm, summer until 10pm; Smithsonian Metro) – an unadorned marble obelisk built in memory of America's successful revolutionary general and first president. Simple, elegant, majestic and, above all, huge, it's the centrepiece of the National Mall and immediately recognizable from all over the city.

L'Enfant's original city plan proposed erecting an equestrian statue of George Washington in the centre of the Mall, but nothing was built for several decades. Impatient at Congress's apparent lack of enthusiasm for the work, in 1833 Chief Justice John Marshall and a very aged James Madison established the National Monument Society to foster a design competition and subscription drive. Fantastic plans were announced to honour the general, but considering the meagre subscriptions gathered, the Society settled for a giant **obelisk**.

Early excavations revealed that L'Enfant's chosen spot was too marshy to build on, and when the cornerstone was finally laid on July 4, 1848, it was on a bare knoll 360ft east and 120ft south of the true intersection (which explains why the monument is off-centre on the map), near an abattoir and the fetid Washington Canal. Added to this were construction and political woes that gave the monument an air of failure for two decades, leaving it an incomplete stump just 152ft high – likened by Mark Twain to a "factory chimney with the top broken off".

After the Civil War, Congress finally authorized government funds to complete the monument and appointed **Lieutenant Colonel Thomas Casey** of the Army Corps of Engineers to the work. Casey suffered his own tribulations, not least of which was the discovery that the original marble source in Maryland had been exhausted; you can still see the transition line at the 150ft level, where work resumed with marble of a slightly different tone. At long last, by December 1884, the monument was finally complete. The tallest all-masonry structure on the planet, it stands just over 555ft tall, measures 55ft wide at the base, tapers to 34ft at the top, and is capped by a small aluminium pyramid.

Visiting the monument

Once you gain access, a seventy-second **elevator ride** whisks you past the honorary stones in the stairwell and deposits you at the 500ft level, from where the **views** – glimpsed through surprisingly narrow windows on all four sides – are, of course, tremendous. There's not much else at the top, other than a few displays, and you'll doubtless be ready to descend within fifteen minutes.

Due to security concerns, concentric stone rings have been built into the sloping knoll around the monument to prevent vehicles from getting too close to the structure. Surprisingly, the new design is not unappealing, unlike the process you must endure to gain access to the monument in the first place.

To visit, pick up a free **ticket** from the 15th Street kiosk (on the Mall, south of Constitution Ave; daily 8am–4.30pm), which will allow you to turn up at a fixed time later in the day. You'll need to get to the kiosk early, as tickets often run out quickly. You can also book a ticket in advance with the National Park Service (☎1-877/444-6777; $1.50), which you then pick up at the ticket office.

National World War II Memorial

The stirring **National World War II Memorial**, 17th St SW at Independence Ave (daily 24hr, staffed 9.30am–11.30pm; Smithsonian or Farragut West Metro), opened in 2004 in the centre of the Mall just west of the Washington Monument, to honour America's veterans from that conflict. Two arcs on each side of a **central fountain** have a combined total of 56 stone pillars (representing the number of US states and territories at the time of the war), 17ft high and decorated with bronze wreaths. In the middle of each arc stands a 43ft tower, one called "Atlantic" and the other "Pacific" for the two major theatres of battle, and within each tower are four interlinked bronze eagles and a sculpted wreath that, despite its bulk, seems to float above you in midair.

Beyond the carefully considered architecture and the FDR and Eisenhower **quotations** that are chiselled on the walls, a curving wall of four thousand golden stars reminds you of the 400,000 fallen US soldiers – a number matched only by the colossal carnage of the Civil War. Less conspicuous on the wall is a small, honorary piece of officially inscribed "graffiti" from the war era, "Kilroy Was Here", showing the titular scamp with his long nose poking out.

The DC War Memorial and John Paul Jones statue

Just south of the World War II Memorial, you go from the Mall's newest war memorial to its oldest, the **District of Columbia War Memorial** (24hr), built in 1931 to commemorate soldiers who fought in World War I. A small Doric temple hidden in a grove of trees just north of Independence Avenue, it was built in commemoration of the district's own soldiers who sacrificed their lives in a foreign war. Usually free of tourists or any visitors whatsoever, it offers a quiet and relaxing respite from the hubbub of the Mall.

Due south of the World War II Memorial and east of the DC War Memorial stands the proud **statue of John Paul Jones** – stranded on a traffic island at 17th Street and Independence Avenue. If the sculpted figure of America's first naval hero looks a bit wary, it's only appropriate: ironically, the World War II Memorial, which is in his line of sight, honours the alliance of the US with Britain – the European power Jones spent years trying to intimidate with his coastal raids and nautical tactics.

The Jefferson Memorial

Although **Thomas Jefferson** was America's first Secretary of State, its third president, author of the Declaration of Independence, and the closest thing to a Renaissance Man ever produced in America, it took until 1943 for his **memorial** to be built, in West Potomac Park, southeast bank of the Tidal Basin near 14th St SW and Ohio Drive (daily 24hr, staffed 9.30am–11.30pm; Smithsonian Metro). By the twentieth century, however, the memorial site proved contentious: the obvious site lay on the southern axis, south of the Washington Monument, and many bemoaned the destruction of some of the city's famous cherry trees when the ground around the Tidal Basin was cleared, while others argued that the memorial would block the view of the river from the White House. More practically, the site proved difficult to reach, since the basin blocked direct access from the north. This, in fact, provides much of its charm today, as the sinuous walk around the tree-lined basin makes for a fine approach.

John Russell Pope's design was in keeping with Jefferson's own tastes: not only was it influenced by the Greek and Renaissance Revival styles that Jefferson had helped popularize in the United States after his stint as ambassador to France in the 1780s (eventually displacing the British-favoured Georgian style), but it also echoed closely the style of Jefferson's own country home at Monticello, in Charlottesville, Virginia.

Today the Jefferson Memorial is one of the most recognizable and harmonious structures in the city: a white marble temple, reminiscent of Rome's Pantheon, with steps down to the water's edge and framed by the cherry trees of the Tidal Basin. The huge bronze statue of Jefferson, by **Rudulph Evans**, gazes determinedly out of the memorial, while the inscription around the frieze sets the high moral tone, trumpeting: "I have sworn upon the altar of God eternal hostility against every form of tyranny over the mind of man". Inside, on the walls, four more texts flank the statue, including words from the 1776 Declaration of Independence. On the lower level, a small **museum** devoted to Jefferson reminds visitors of why the man is still worth admiring, even as it alludes to his discomforting, hand-wringing defence of slavery, and has a bevy of historical displays and mementos from his era.

The Tidal Basin

The fetching **Tidal Basin** fills most of the space between the Lincoln and Jefferson memorials. This large inlet, formerly part of the Potomac River, was created in 1882 to prevent flooding, while the famous **cherry trees** – a gift from Japan – were planted around the edge in 1912. The annual Cherry Blossom Festival in early April celebrates their blooming with concerts, parades, and displays of Japanese lanterns, making this perhaps the best time of the year to visit DC, despite the considerable crowds. To take it all in from the water, rent a pedal boat from the **Tidal Basin Boat House**, on the basin's northeast side at 1501 Maine Ave SW (mid-March to Aug daily 10am–6pm; Sept & Oct Wed–Sun same hours; two-seaters $12/hr, four-seaters $19/hr; ☎202/479-2426, ⓦwww.tidalbasin paddleboats.com) – it's a real treat for children and a great way to experience waterside views of several famous monuments and memorials.

The Franklin Delano Roosevelt Memorial

Designed by Lawrence Halprin and dedicated in 1997, the **Franklin Delano Roosevelt Memorial** (daily 24hr, staffed 9.30am–11.30pm; Smithsonian Metro or #13 bus from Constitution or Independence avenues), honouring the man who was president from 1933 to 1945, sprawls across a seven-acre site on the southwestern banks of the Tidal Basin and is made up of a series of interlinking granite outdoor galleries – called "rooms" – punctuated by waterfalls, statuary, sculpted reliefs, groves of trees, and shaded alcoves and plazas. It's among the most successful – and popular – of DC's memorials, and there's an almost Athenian quality to its open spaces, resting places, benches and inspiring texts. On a bright spring or autumn day, with the glistening basin waters and emerging views of the Washington Monument and Jefferson Memorial, it's one of the finest places in the city for a stroll.

A wartime leader and architect of the New Deal, Roosevelt's political spirit is captured in a series of carved **quotations**, appearing on the walls, that defined his presidency – perhaps most famously in the words "The only thing we have to fear is fear itself". The four galleries of rustic stone (one for each of his terms in office) turn upon seminal periods: the first has a torrent of water symbolizing the miseries of the Great Depression; in the second gallery stand George Segal's sculpted figures of a city breadline, a dust-bowl couple in a rural doorway, and an elderly man listening to one of Roosevelt's famous radio fireside chats; in the third gallery, alongside a **seated statue of FDR** and the heartfelt message "I have seen war...I hate war", a tangle of broken granite blocks with water tumbling over them represents the World War II years. The memorial ends in the fourth gallery, where a timeline of dates and events is inscribed in the steps; a statue of perhaps Roosevelt's greatest ally, his wife, Eleanor, stands; and a still pool represents his death in Warm Springs, Arkansas, just before the end of World War II.

There's great significance, too, in something most visitors don't notice about the memorial, namely that it is fully accessible to people in wheelchairs. The main sculpture of FDR portrays him simply as being seated – his legs largely covered by the flowing cape he wore at the 1945 Yalta conference with Winston Churchill and Joseph Stalin – while a later addition near the entrance shows the president clearly in his wheelchair, an image he took such careful pains not to reveal during his presidency, as he had been paralyzed by polio at age 39.

By the end of 2011, the **Martin Luther King Jr National Memorial** (details at ⓦ www.mlkmemorial.org) will be unveiled on the northern flank of the FDR Memorial, between it and the Lincoln Memorial, honouring the late civil rights leader and his legacy on a walkway that will also commemorate the various heroes and victims of the civil rights struggle in the 1950s and 60s and up to the present day.

The Korean War Veterans Memorial

The **Korean War Veterans Memorial** (daily 24hr, staffed 8am–11.45pm; Smithsonian or Foggy Bottom–GWU Metro) lies south of the Reflecting Pool, just a few minutes' walk from the Lincoln Memorial. Dedicated in 1995, it is distinguished by a Field of Remembrance with nineteen life-size, heavily armed combat troops sculpted from stainless steel. The troops advance across a triangular plot with alternating rows of stones and plant life and head toward the Stars and Stripes positioned at the vertex. A reflecting black granite wall, with the inscription "Freedom is not free", and an etched mural depicting military support crew and medical staff flank the ensemble. It's not an entirely successful piece of

Lincoln and the Gettysburg Address

Abraham Lincoln's **Gettysburg Address**, beginning with the words "Four score and seven years ago", is the most famous piece of American political oratory of the nineteenth century, its themes of human freedom, democracy, and a developing idea of equality springing from the carnage and sacrifice displayed at an epic Civil War battle in the eponymous Pennsylvania town several months earlier. The address was meant to dedicate the grounds of a cemetery to hold the many thousands of war dead, and Lincoln's classical rhetoric was more than equal to the solemn task at hand – all in around two and a half minutes. Indeed, the official photographer at the dedication hadn't even got his equipment ready before the president sat down again. Edward Everett, former senator and one-time Secretary of State, spoke first at the ceremony – for two and a half hours; he later admitted his long-winded oratory hadn't accomplished a fraction of what Lincoln's had. If you'd like a glimpse at one of the few remaining copies of the address, the Library of Congress (see p.83) sometimes puts one on public display, hermetically sealed with argon gas to keep the document from decaying.

sculpture, due mainly to the statues' faces being cruder and less expressive than those of the presidents and other war heroes sculpted along the Mall.

Almost 55,000 Americans were killed in the conflict on the Korean peninsula. The memorial lists the fifteen other countries that volunteered forces, with Britain, France, Greece and Turkey in particular suffering significant losses. While the memorial commemorates soldiers from allied countries, it doesn't give the number of Korean casualties: by some estimates, about three million (North and South) Korean civilians died – in addition to half a million North Korean, 50,000 South Korean, and possibly one million Chinese soldiers.

The Lincoln Memorial

As one of the country's most recognizable symbols, the **Lincoln Memorial,** West Potomac Park at 23rd St NW (daily 24hr, staffed 9.30am–11.30pm; Foggy Bottom–GWU Metro), represents both the United States' political ideology and its culture of social activism. The memorial is perpetually host to speeches, protests, events and marches; less tempestuously, it effortlessly provides a backdrop for some of the most stirring photographs in town. The Reflecting Pool, the Washington Monument and the US Capitol lie to the monument's east on the Mall's axis, and the Potomac River and Arlington National Cemetery are to its west – a bit less visually symmetrical, though no less stirring a view.

Proposals to erect a monument to the "Railsplitter" were raised as early as 1865, the year of Lincoln's assassination. In 1901 the McMillan Commission approved the construction of a Greek temple in the marshlands of the newly created West Potomac Park, and work began on the memorial in February 1914 under the aegis of New York architect **Henry Bacon**.

Loosely modelled on the ancient Greek Temple of Zeus, the memorial has 36 Doric columns that symbolize the number of states in the Union at the time of

History at the Lincoln Memorial

Although Lincoln is inextricably linked to the nation's abolition of slavery and long struggle with **civil rights**, ironically, at the memorial's dedication in May 1922, President Warren G. Harding and Lincoln's surviving son, Robert, watched the proceedings from the speakers' platform while Dr Robert Moton, the president of the Tuskegee Institute, who was scheduled to make the principal address, was forced to watch from a roped-off, racially segregated area. The memorial thereafter became a centrepiece in **demonstrations** urging the recognition of civil and human rights: Spanish Civil War veterans from the Abraham Lincoln Brigade marched here in 1938; a year later, on Easter Sunday, black opera singer **Marian Anderson** performed from the steps to a crowd of 75,000, having been refused permission by the Daughters of the American Revolution to appear at their nearby Constitution Hall. Anderson pointedly dedicated her performance to "the ideals of freedom for which President Lincoln died". Perhaps the memorial's brightest day was August 28, 1963, when, during the March on Washington for Jobs and Freedom, **Dr Martin Luther King Jr** delivered his "I Have a Dream" speech to 200,000 people who had gathered here. Five years later, in May and June 1968, after King's assassination, his successors brought the ill-fated Poor People's March to the memorial. During the height of the Vietnam War two years later, **Richard Nixon** made a strange and unexpected late-night visit to the site, where he discussed the war with sleepy protesters – a legendary event not covered by the media. Since then, the memorial has hosted everything from Louis Farrakhan's Million Man March in 1995 to George W. Bush's 2001 inaugural party, to Glenn Beck and Sarah Palin's massive right-wing pep rally in 2010.

Lincoln's death, while bas-relief plaques on the attic parapet commemorate the country's 48 states at the time of the memorial's completion in 1922 (Alaska and Hawaii get a mere inscription on the terrace). But for all its beauty, the temple is upstaged by what is inside – the seated statue of Lincoln by **Daniel Chester French** (1850–1931), which faces out through the colonnade. Full of resolve, a steely Lincoln clasps the armrests of a throne-like chair with determined hands, his unbuttoned coat falling to either side. The American flag is draped over the back of the chair. It's a phenomenal work, one that took French thirteen years to complete, fashioning the 19ft-tall statue from 28 blocks of white Georgia marble.

Climbing the steps to the memorial and meeting the seated Lincoln's gaze is one of DC's most profound experiences. After your introductions, look out over the Reflecting Pool and down the length of the Mall, then turn back and gaze at the **murals** on the north and south walls. Jules Guerin painted these images, which represent (on the north wall) Fraternity, Unity of North and South, and Charity, and (on the south wall) Emancipation and Immortality. Underneath the murals are carved inscriptions of Lincoln's two most celebrated **speeches** – the Gettysburg Address of November 19, 1863 (see box, p.49), and Lincoln's Second Inaugural Address of March 4, 1865, in which he strove "to bind up the nation's wounds" caused by the Civil War.

The Reflecting Pool and Constitution Gardens

The view from the Lincoln Memorial would lose a significant part of its appeal were it not for the lengthy **Reflecting Pool** that reaches out from the cenotaph's steps toward the Washington Monument. The reflections in the water are stunning, particularly at night when everything is lit. Especially striking is the fact that all the memorials around the pool, save for that of Lincoln, commemorate twentieth-century wars.

Like the Lincoln Memorial, the pool was built in 1922. It was supposedly inspired by the Taj Mahal's landscaping and Versailles' pools and canals – in particular, how those designs demonstrated control over nature. Classical order was key to the pool's simple geometric layout, standing in contrast to the swamp that occupied much of the turf before the twentieth century. Though the surrounding area of West Potomac Park was originally to be landscaped as a grand garden park, financial concerns and aesthetic considerations produced, in 1976, the less flamboyant **Constitution Gardens**, a fifty-acre area of trees and dells surrounding a kidney-shaped lake on the north side of the Reflecting Pool south of Constitution Avenue. A plaque on the island in the centre commemorates the 56 signatories of the Declaration of Independence; every September 17, Constitution Day, the signing of the Constitution is celebrated in the gardens by, among other things, an outdoor naturalization service for foreign-born DC residents.

The Vietnam Veterans Memorial

On the western side of Constitution Gardens, and due northeast of the Lincoln Memorial, the **Vietnam Veterans Memorial**, Henry Bacon Drive and Constitution Ave at 21st St NW (daily 24hr, staffed 9.30am–11.30pm; Foggy Bottom–GWU Metro), is one of the most poignant tributes to be found anywhere. The Vietnam veterans who conceived of having a memorial in Washington intended to record the sacrifice of every person killed or missing in action without making a political statement. Once the grounds had been earmarked, a national competition was held in 1980 to determine the memorial's design, and a 21-year-old Yale student from

Ohio named **Maya Lin** won, her entry provided in pursuit of a class project. (The original design is held and sometimes displayed in the Library of Congress's Jefferson Building.) Lin decided that the **names** of the fallen would be the defining feature of the memorial, and she chose to record them on walls of reflective black granite that point to the city's lodestars – the Lincoln Memorial and Washington Monument – and gradually draw you into a rift in the earth.

The **names** of the 58,256 American casualties of the Vietnam War are etched into east and west walls that each run for 250ft, slicing deeper into the ground until meeting at a vertex 10ft high; they appear in chronological order (1959–75), and to each is appended either a diamond (a confirmed death) or cross (missing in action, made into a diamond if the death is confirmed). It's a sobering experience to walk past the ranks of names and the untold experiences they represent, not least for the friends and relatives who come here to leave tokens at the foot of the walls and make rubbings of the names. Brass-bound directories on each side of the memorial list the names and their locations. The annual Veterans' Day ceremony held at the memorial on November 11 is one of the most emotional in the city, with the memorial walls decked in wreaths and overseen by military colour guards.

Elsewhere at the site, the **Three Servicemen Statue** depicts young soldiers who, despite their weaponry, have an air of vulnerability and confusion, while the **Vietnam Women's Memorial** honours the 11,000 American women who were stationed in Vietnam (eight were killed), with a bronze sculpture vaguely reminiscent of a pietà.

Scheduled for construction in 2012 closer to the Lincoln Memorial, the **Vietnam Veterans Memorial Centre** will be a $100 million, two-level underground museum providing displays, photographs and a timeline of the conflict.

Museums and galleries

There are nine **museums and galleries** along the eastern side of the Mall, most of them national in name and scope, and all but one (the National Gallery of Art) coming under the aegis of the **Smithsonian Institution**. Since they're all **free**, expect them to be packed with families and school groups. At the top of many people's list are the kid-friendly national museums for Air and Space, Natural History, and American History, and the more adult-oriented National Gallery of Art. Less-visited institutions include the Hirshhorn Museum for modern art and sculpture, the National Museum of Asian Art (with its separate Sackler and Freer galleries), and the National Museum of the American Indian. The route below continues the one left off in the "Monuments and memorials" section, heading east from the Washington Monument on a clockwise path from the Reflecting Pool. Note that by 2015, the proposed **National Museum of African American History and Culture** (Ⓦnmaahc.si.edu) will occupy a prominent position at the start of this route, immediately west of the American History museum and at the northeast foot of the Washington Monument.

National Museum of American History

The major museums east of the Washington Monument begin with a procession of big-name Smithsonian institutions. The first of these, on the north side of the Mall, is the **National Museum of American History**, 14th St NW and Constitution Ave (daily 10am–5.30pm; ☎202/633-1000, Ⓦwww.americanhistory.si.edu;

Federal Triangle or Smithsonian Metro), deservedly one of the country's most popular museums, with objects taken from nearly four hundred years of American and pre-American history.

The museum's roots lie in prodigious bequests made to the original Smithsonian Institution, beginning with pieces left over from Philadelphia's 1876 **Centennial Exhibition**. Each item collected was destined for the "National Museum" (now the Arts and Industries Building), but since this meant displaying stuffed animals alongside portraits, postage stamps and patent models, the Smithsonian was soon forced to specialize. Although an ungainly 1950s modernist box was built to house the collection, it proved ugly and far from user-friendly. Later, the museum was closed for several years and reopened in 2008, as a still modern but brighter and airier design with a skylight cutting through the building, an open layout, and better access between floors.

The museum has gift shops on each of the three main floors (with the one on the top storey reserved for military and political paraphernalia), and the junk-food-oriented **Stars and Stripes Café** on the lower level and the more well-rounded lunches of the **Constitution Café** on the first floor (both have wi-fi). Ask at the information desks for details about free **tours**, **lectures** and **events**, including demonstrations of antique musical instruments, printing presses and machine tools. The desks, at Mall (second-floor) and Constitution Avenue (first-floor) entrances, are staffed from 10am to 4pm.

First floor

Upon entering from Constitution Avenue, the first thing visitors to the museum will notice is the spacious layout of the **first floor**. A wide common area off the lobby is lined with **"artefact walls"** that show off some of the items that the museum previously had to keep in storage. These glassed-in walls provide eclectic artefacts for you to muse over, anything from 200-year-old tavern signs and toy chests to the **John Bull**, the nation's oldest functioning steam locomotive, dating from 1831.

Traditionally, the regular gallery displays on the first floor have showcased the technological advancements and the economic, industrial and agricultural prowess that brought the US to its position of global power. Also on view, **"Science in American Life"** covers every scientific development you can think of from recent decades – including mobile phones, birth control, microwave ovens, nylon, nuclear power and plastics. There are also displays devoted to currency, power machinery and electrical power – as well as a charming re-creation of Julia Child's kitchen – but the real showpiece of the first floor is **"America on the Move"**, an unapologetic celebration of urban, rural and long-distance transport from the nineteenth century to the present. The exhibition starts with the locomotive in the post–Civil War era and in rough chronological order covers the cultural, economic and social impact of transport up to the modern age. To most visitors, the main story here will be familiar: how the US began with covered wagons and trains (shown with a huge locomotive from the Southern Railway), was revolutionized by early automobiles (from the first car to make a transcontinental trip, in 1903, to later Model Ts, Studebakers and Chryslers), and ended up having to deal with urban gridlock and finding alternative means of transport (a walk-in Chicago elevated train is a highlight). Beyond this are equally interesting side stories of the new age in transport – from the old East Coast docks giving way to transpacific container shipping in the 1960s, to the roadside cultures that developed around highways like Route 66.

Second floor

The **second floor** is connected to the first floor by a wide stairway and illuminated by a towering five-storey skylight – a dramatic setting for what's a more scattershot series of exhibits. Upon entering from the National Mall, one of the first things you'll see will be silvery abstract flag art that leads to the Star-Spangled Banner Gallery (see below), the museum's focus and one of the reasons why it draws as many visitors as it does. Other galleries include "**Communities in a Changing Nation**", in which nineteenth-century America is showcased through various social environments – a slave cabin from South Carolina, an indigent peddler's cart, a wealthy Gothic Revival bedroom interior; "**Within These Walls**", two hundred years of history brought into focus through the stories of five families and their Massachusetts home; and "**Ain't Nothin' Like the Real Thing**", an ode in photos and artefacts to Harlem's Apollo Theatre and the historic role it played in the African-American community and on America's musical landscape.

"**First Ladies**" begins with portraits of each presidential wife, from Martha Washington onwards. Though there's an attempt to provide biographical padding, and exhibits exhort viewers to appreciate First Ladies as political partners or preservers of White House culture and history, the real fun here is in the frocks. Helen Herron Taft was the first to present her inaugural ball gown to the Smithsonian for preservation, starting a tradition that allows the museum to display a backlit collection of considerable interest, if not always taste. Other outfits provide revealing historical snapshots: Jackie Kennedy's brocaded dress and jacket raised hemlines in America almost overnight.

Star-Spangled Banner Gallery

The museum's highlight is undoubtedly its recently created gallery devoted to the faded and battered red, white and blue flag that inspired the writing of the US national anthem: the **Star-Spangled Banner**, which survived the British bombing of Baltimore harbour during the War of 1812.

With dimensions of about 30ft by 34ft, and weighing 150 pounds, it has fifteen stars and fifteen stripes, representing the fifteen states in the Union at the time of the war. The flag is famously tattered from the battle and the intercession of two centuries, but it is still something of a marvel, preserved through years of painstaking labour by historians and technicians and enclosed in a new viewing chamber in a darkened fire- and waterproof room controlled for temperature, humidity and excess oxygen. Before you get to it, you'll head through an immersive multimedia corridor that will get you into the spirit of 1812, giving military and political details on the American defence of Baltimore harbour at Fort

McHenry that began after the British successfully sacked Washington in 1814. **Francis Scott Key**, a 35-year-old Georgetown lawyer and part-time poet, witnessed the battle. Attempting to negotiate the release of American prisoner Dr William Beanes, Key had been held on board a British ship that night and, come "dawn's early light", was amazed to see not only that the flag was still "so gallantly streaming", but that the cannons of the outnumbered Americans had forced the British to withdraw. Taking the bombardment as his inspiration, Key dashed off a poem titled **"The Defense of Fort McHenry"**, which he set to the tune of a contemporary English drinking song called "To Anacreon in Heaven".

The rest of the gallery provides artefacts, photos and assorted media about the flag and the song throughout the centuries. These range from the varying musical interpretations – everything from the most gung-ho patriotic anthems to counter-cultural incarnations such as Jimi Hendrix's electrified Woodstock version – to the myriad uses of the American flag as a national icon, whether as a totem of near-religious devotion or a handy symbol of protest.

Third floor

If the two-hundred-year-old flag is the centrepiece of the second floor, the third floor's undeniable highlight is the gallery devoted to **Abraham Lincoln**, which details the life and lore of this most formidable of US presidents (the sixteenth), who kept the Union from fracturing during the Civil War and ensured the end of slavery in 1865. That same year he was famously assassinated, an event which forms no small part of the exhibit, with artefacts such as the top hat and coat he was wearing on the night of his death, to the eerie image of his death mask, to the hoods worn by the conspirators in the murder when they were executed. The rest of the gallery doesn't quite have the same dramatic import, but it's still fascinating to check out the tools the "railsplitter" used in his youth, the political mementos and writings that followed his rise to national power, and the haunting portraits taken throughout his life, which follow his progress from a rangy young lawyer to a beleaguered, wizened figure, burdened by the crushing demands of his office and of the era.

A bit lighter in content, **"The American Presidency: A Glorious Burden"** focuses on various aspects of presidential life, and displays a wide array of objects, including George Washington's general's uniform and Revolutionary War sword, the "fireside chat" microphone through which Franklin Roosevelt soothed an America mired in the Great Depression, and a pair of Mao and Nixon table-tennis paddles, souvenirs from the days of "Ping Pong Diplomacy". Those with a taste for nostalgia will enjoy **"American Popular Culture"**, which includes such oddments as Dorothy's slippers from *The Wizard of Oz*, Muhammad Ali's boxing gloves, Michael Jordan's NBA jersey, a baseball autographed by Babe Ruth, Archie Bunker's chair, Dizzy Gillespie's trumpet, and a *Star Trek* phaser.

Finally, as if the surfeit of war memorials around town weren't reminder enough, **"The Price of Freedom"** covers America's long-standing support of, and occasional ambivalence about, its armed forces. One indisputable highlight is the oak gunboat *Philadelphia*, the oldest US man-of-war in existence, along with a Vietnam-era Huey helicopter, General Washington's linen tent (his campaign headquarters during the Revolutionary War) alongside his camp chest complete with tin plate and coffeepot, and weapons from Colonial muskets to modern machine guns.

National Museum of Natural History

Founded in 1911, the **National Museum of Natural History**, 10th St NW and Constitution Ave (daily 10am–5.30pm; ☎202/633-1000, ⓦwww.mnh.si.edu;

Federal Triangle or Smithsonian Metro), is one of DC's oldest museums and one of the best places in the capital to take children – a fact that sometimes makes it a daunting experience for adults without them. The museum's imposing three-storey entrance rotunda feels like the busiest and most boisterous crossroads in all DC, with troops of screeching school kids chasing each other nonstop around a colossal African elephant. The museum owns more than 125 million specimens and artefacts and is regularly working to show off more of its holdings to the public. Stop by the **information desk** at the elephant's hooves to pick up floor plans, check on any temporary exhibitions, and ask about the **free guided tours** (Tues–Fri 10.30am & 1.30pm), which show you the highlights in around an hour. These tours are particularly helpful, since this is one of the Smithsonian's most confusingly laid-out museums. The ground-floor, glass-domed **Atrium Café** serves a variety of foods, while the first-floor **Fossil Café** is more for sandwiches and salads; there are also **IMAX screenings** ($9) of short nature- and science-oriented documentaries and Hollywood family flicks.

First floor

Although the café and gift shops are on the ground floor off Constitution Avenue, the **first floor** is regarded as the main entrance. You'll have to squeeze past countless other visitors if you hope to get a peek at the big-ticket items. The showpiece is the **Dinosaurs** section, with hulking skeletons reassembled in imaginative poses and accompanied by informative text. The massive diplodocus, the most imposing specimen, was discovered in Utah in 1923, at what is now Dinosaur National Monument. The museum's pride and joy, however, is the 65-million-year-old triceratops (dubbed "Hatcher"), which, these days, is more paleontologically accurate following a high-tech face-lift. Stay in this section long enough to tour the related displays on the **Ice Age**, **Ancient Seas**, **Fossil Mammals** and **Fossil Plants** – each covering molluscs, lizards, giant turtles and early fish in exhaustive, engaging detail with the aid of diagrams, text and fossils. Near the end of the circuit, you'll unexpectedly get a look at what is claimed to be an early-human form of **burial**, though the display – a nearly naked caveman tied up with ropes in a dank hole – looks more like something out of *Pulp Fiction* than *Nova*.

Taking up a good chunk of the west side of the first floor is the **Hall of Mammals**, where some three hundred replicas focus on mostly fur-wearing, milk-producing creatures in a variety of simulated environments. If you can, check out the African savanna animals, which strive to drink at a watering hole in the same desperate manner in which viewers vie for a look at them, and the various big cats, chimps, shrews, moles, dogs, and other creatures that are biologically related to *Homo sapiens*.

North of the Hall of Mammals is the 25,000-square-foot **Sant Ocean Hall**, which has hundreds of displays and specimens – among them, a 50ft-long whale model – to describe the biological and ecological world of the sea in different places around the world. It also uses historical and present-day models to show the remarkable diversity of the oceans, increasingly under peril from such threats as global warming, overfishing and pollution.

The recently installed **Hall of Human Origins** gives the lowdown on evolution, describing how its processes work and giving insight into the development of human and human-like creatures from the last six million or so years. Also imaginative is the **"African Voices"** exhibit between the Ocean Hall and the Ice Age displays, which does as well as can be expected for a section that covers people from an entire continent. Bursting with colourful displays, films and tunes – plus tools, garments, icons and trinkets – the exhibit has Africans tell their stories in testimonials and on video monitors. Best are items like a huge "antelope mask" for tribal rituals, an "airplane coffin" from Ghana in the shape of a KLM jet, and a section on the global reach of African mudcloth (handwoven cotton cloth painted with intricate designs), detailing the intersection of native symbolism and Western consumerism.

Second floor

On the second floor is "**Western Cultures**", where displays veer between ancient Egypt, Greece and Rome, and showcase a number of ancient artefacts such as death masks, iconic statues, votive offerings, tools, ritual beads and coffins – as well as the odd Ice Age mummy.

The IMAX theatre and various temporary galleries also occupy this level, so there's less space for the permanent collection. The natural history sections tend toward the creepy-crawly, including an array of **reptiles** – snakes, Gila monsters and lizards among them – but don't miss the splendid **Insect Zoo**, where behind screens you can watch tarantulas, roaches, crickets, bird-eating spiders, worms, termites and a thriving bee colony. Less-creepy insects are on display in the new **Butterfly and Plant gallery**, which features the strategies of each to propagate their kind through coevolution but more importantly offers a great living butterfly house, with thousands of the brightly coloured creatures flittering about.

On the other side of the floor, the **Hall of Geology, Gems and Minerals** is centred on the astounding National Gem Collection, notably the legendary 45-carat **Hope Diamond** once owned by Marie Antoinette, and the bearer of a legendary curse. Crowds stare as if hypnotized at the well-guarded rock as it rotates in its display case, and at a pair of the French queen's diamond earrings and a genuine crystal ball that is the world's largest flawless quartz sphere. Also prominent is the museum's **rock and mineral** selection. Scientists have identified around 4000 minerals so far and it seems as though each one is represented here in its glorious shape, texture and colour. Almost as fascinating is the **Mine Gallery**, where, in a small, curving tunnel, are assembled actual walls from mines across the country – from a Missouri lead mine's rocky panels to those bearing zinc, copper and microcline.

National Gallery of Art – West Building

Despite having a prime spot on the Mall and sitting cheek-by-jowl amid the big-ticket Smithsonian museums, the estimable **National Gallery of Art**, Constitution Ave, between 4th and 7th sts NW (Mon–Sat 10am–5pm, Sun 11am–6pm; ⊤202/737-4215, ⓦwww.nga.gov; Archives-Navy Memorial Metro), is not part of that institution, contrary to what some assume. This museum is easily one of the nation's greatest, probably only second to New York's Met in the quality, depth and breadth of its collections, and not surprisingly, you can't hope to see the whole of it in one visit. Many concentrate on seeing what they can in the sizable **West Building**, the original gallery structure (see p.63 for the newer **East Building**), whose entire first floor (where most of the art can be found) has almost one hundred display rooms, full of works ranging from thirteenth-century Italian to nineteenth-century European and American art. To make best use of limited time, latch on to one of the daily **free tours** and programmes; pick up a schedule at the gallery's information desks, located on the main floor (Mall entrance) and the ground floor (Constitution Ave at 6th St).

The West Building's collection starts in Room 1 of the West Wing and proceeds chronologically, beginning with thirteenth- to fifteenth-century Italian art and wrapping up with nineteenth-century French art. To track down the specific

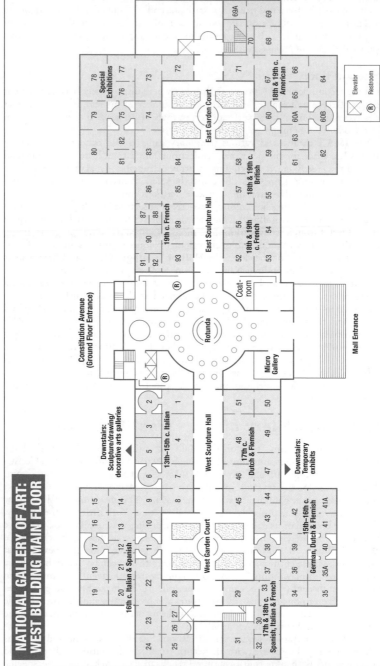

NATIONAL GALLERY OF ART: WEST BUILDING MAIN FLOOR

National Gallery, East Building ▲

East Garden Court

East Sculpture Hall

18th & 19th c. American

18th & 19th c. British

18th & 19th c. French

19th c. French

Special Exhibitions

Constitution Avenue (Ground Floor Entrance)

Rotunda

Coat-room

Micro Gallery

Mall Entrance

West Sculpture Hall

West Garden Court

13th–15th c. Italian

Downstairs: Sculpture/drawing/ decorative arts galleries ▲

Downstairs: Temporary exhibits ▶

17th c. Dutch & Flemish

16th c. Italian & Spanish

15th–16th c. German, Dutch & Flemish

17th & 18th c. Spanish, Italian & French

☒ Elevator

Ⓡ Restroom

Sculpture Garden & ice-skating rink ▲

location of a particular work, the museum offers an interactive computer system that allows you to locate and view some of the two thousand works in the gallery. (Alternatively, you can search the collection via the museum's excellent website.) Special exhibitions and installations are detailed in a monthly calendar, which also lists the free classical music **concerts** held in the West Building's serene West Garden Court.

Thirteenth- to fifteenth-century Italian art (Rooms 1–15)

The gallery's oldest works are the stylized thirteenth-century Byzantine **icons** (holy images) in which an enthroned Mary holds the small figure of an adult Christ. The Sienese artist **Duccio di Buoninsegna** was one of the first to move beyond strict Byzantine forms; the faces of the subjects in his *Nativity*, a panel taken from the base of his *Maestà* altarpiece in Siena Cathedral, display genuine emotion. The artist **Sassetta**, also from Siena, was popular with some twentieth-century avant-gardists for his strange sense of space and fantastic imagery, as seen in his eye-opening *St Anthony Triptych*. Much more influential, however, was the Florentine artist **Giotto**, whose humanism and use of perspective would eventually lead to the Renaissance. Giotto's *Madonna and Child* marks an extraordinary departure in its attempt to create believable human figures.

The action then moves to fifteenth-century Florence, the home of the Renaissance. The prominent *tondo* (circular painting) depicting the *Adoration of the Magi* was started by the monk **Fra Angelico** but completed by **Fra Filippo Lippi**, who invested the biblical scene with his full range of emotive powers. But for dynamic realism there's nothing to compare with **Andrea del Castagno**'s decorative shield showing *The Youthful David* preparing to fling his sling; Florentines would have understood that Goliath's decapitated head at David's feet was a warning to any of their city's squabbling neighbouring states.

In other rooms relating to Florentine artists, all eyes are drawn to **Leonardo da Vinci**'s *Ginevra de' Benci*, an engagement portrait done when Leonardo was only 22, and the only work by the artist in the US. The painting's subject is a 16-year-old Florentine beauty with alabaster skin sitting before a spiky juniper bush – an image meant to symbolize chastity and to be a pun on her name, Ginevra (the Italian word for juniper is *ginepro*). Works by **Sandro Botticelli** include his rendering of the *Adoration of the Magi*, set in the ruins of a Classical temple from which the frame of a new structure, representing Christianity, rises.

Sixteenth-century Italian and Spanish art (Rooms 16–28)

By the beginning of the sixteenth century, new artistic ideas were emerging in other Italian cities, and the accomplished Bellini family was at the forefront of the scene. Nowhere is this more evident than in **Giovanni Bellini**'s *The Feast of the Gods*, which depicts deities feasting to bawdy excess in a bucolic setting. Bellini created this painting between 1511 and 1514, just a few years before his death in 1516. In 1529, **Titian**, his former pupil and the forerunner of Mannerism, restyled it by removing a grove of trees and adding a striking mountain in the background. The gallery's diverse Titian collection includes an image of *Saint John the Evangelist on Patmos* and *Venus with a Mirror*.

The High Renaissance artist **Raphael** has only one major piece here: the *Alba Madonna*, in which the Virgin and Child are seated on the ground, leaning against a tree stump – a pose intended to emphasize their humility. As the High and Late Renaissance yield to the Mannerist era, **Bronzino**'s striking *A Young Woman and Her Little Boy* is a highlight of this period. Here the favoured court portraitist creates almost doll-like figures, with fair skin and precocious features.

Seventeenth-century Spanish, Italian and French art, and later Spanish and Italian art (Rooms 29–37)

In the draconian grip of the Counter-Reformation, Spanish art remained deeply spiritual in character. The paramount artist of this time was **El Greco**, and the gallery is distinguished for having the most important El Greco collection outside of Spain. Its *Christ Cleansing the Temple* portrays Jesus, leather whip in hand, laying into assorted traders and money-lenders. More typical of the artist's style, though, is the dour *Laocoön*, in which the Trojan priest and his two sons are attacked by serpents sent by the Greek gods.

The *Saint Lucy* of **Francisco de Zurbarán** is a spiritual study that carries an accompanying shock as your eyes are drawn to those of the saint: hers have been plucked out and laid on a dish that she holds. Much more skilful, Zurbarán's contemporary **Diego Velázquez** was the finest Spanish painter of the seventeenth century, and his unfinished *Needlewoman* is a reserved study of a woman that offers a nice play of subtle light and shadow.

Spain's greatest eighteenth-century artist was the flamboyant **Francisco de Goya**, who, beginning in 1789, was court painter to Charles IV. The gallery owns several of his works, primarily portraits, including the famous *Señora Sebasa Garcia*, in which the artist abandons background entirely to focus on the elegant *señora*.

Also in these rooms are works by France's leading seventeenth-century painters – like **Georges de la Tour** and popular landscapist **Claude Lorrain** – who often set off for Rome, the capital of the Baroque scene. Lorrain's ideas of natural beauty, as represented in *Landscape with Merchants*, were firmly shaped by his years in and around Rome, with the sweeping topography enveloping the tiny humans near the bottom of the canvas; and the careful balance of light and dark in la Tour's *The Repentant Magdalene* recalls the artist's debt to the pre-eminent painter of the chiaroscuro style, Caravaggio.

Fifteenth- and sixteenth-century German, Dutch and Flemish works (Rooms 38–41)

Albrecht Dürer is a principal figure among early German Northern Renaissance masters, and his *Lot and His Daughters* is a moralistic piece that grafts realistic Italian Renaissance figures onto a landscape typical of Northern European religious paintings of the time. Also worth a look are **Matthias Grünewald**'s agonized *The Small Crucifixion* – one of only twenty Grünewald paintings in existence, and the only one in the US – and portraits by **Hans Holbein the Younger**, whose proud and pudgy *Edward VI as a Child* is an image of Henry VIII's heir and son with Henry's third wife, Jane Seymour, while his *Portrait of a Young Man* is a much humbler rendering of a fellow with silken shirt and somewhat goofy hat.

Elsewhere, fifteenth-century artist **Jan van Eyck**'s *Annunciation* shows a remarkable depth of colour and texture. Even more striking is the tiny panel by **Rogier van der Weyden** of *Saint George and the Dragon*, in which the artist probably used a magnifying glass to paint individual tree branches and pinprick windows. Also worth a close look are **Hieronymus Bosch**'s *Death and the Miser*, a ghoulish tour de force, and **Quentin Massys**'s grotesque *Ill-Matched Lovers*.

Seventeenth-century Dutch and Flemish art (Rooms 42–51)

Anthony van Dyck was an immensely popular portraitist of Italian, English and Flemish nobility. His earliest image here of the seventeen owned by the gallery, *Portrait of a Flemish Lady*, a skilled rendering of a rigid sitter wearing a thick collar like a giant headcuff, was painted when Van Dyck was just nineteen. His teacher,

Peter Paul Rubens, offers the striking *Daniel in the Lions' Den*, in which virtually life-size lions bay and snap around an off-centre Daniel.

Rembrandt's *The Mill* – a brooding study of a cliff-top mill, backlit under black thunderclouds – is a famous image, with its dark and light connotations of good and evil. There are a dozen other priceless Rembrandts on view, among them the distant, imperious *Man in Oriental Costume*; the famed *Lucretia*, in which the legendary poisoner poses artfully with a knife; and a late-middle-aged *Self-Portrait*, with the artist gazing deeply and poignantly at the viewer.

Pieter de Hooch offers genre depictions of quiet domestic households in *A Dutch Courtyard* and *The Bedroom*, while **Jan Steen**'s festive *The Dancing Couple*, despite its cheerful imagery, is a subtle warning against excess. Portraits of bourgeois gentlemen in lacy or ruffled collars and tall hats were bread-and-butter work for **Frans Hals**, and eight of these pieces are on display here.

This gallery and the Met are almost the only places in the US where you can see a selection of the work of **Johannes Vermeer**. In *Girl with the Red Hat*, the sitter is seemingly interrupted by the viewer from her reverie; *A Lady Writing* depicts the eponymous figure again gazing back at the viewer, in soft lighting and perfect detail; and *Woman Holding a Balance* is a beautiful allegory of a woman holding a scale before an array of jewellery, while in the dark background, an ominous painting of the Last Judgment shows Jesus rendering a different sort of verdict.

Eighteenth- and early nineteenth-century French art (Rooms 53–56)

Marble busts of Voltaire by **Jean-Antoine Houdon** – who also did sculptures of George Washington – usher in the gallery's eighteenth-century French painting and sculpture collection. The main attraction, however, is arch-Neoclassicist **Jacques-Louis David**'s portrait of *Napoleon in His Study at the Tuileries*, in which the artist employs the sword, crisp uniform, military papers and imperial emblems to bolster the little corporal's image.

By way of contrast, **Jean-Siméon Chardin**'s still lifes and everyday scenes impress with their subtlety and elegance of detail; indeed, Chardin's influence continues to be as great as ever, especially with delicate works like that of a young boy blowing *Soap Bubbles*. Elsewhere, works by **Antoine Watteau** include the delightfully absurd *Italian Comedians* – a group portrait of clowns and players – and the decorative Rococo-style oval panel depicting *Ceres*, the Roman goddess of the harvest, surrounded by the signs of the summer zodiac, Gemini, Cancer and Leo.

There's also a major showing of **Jean-Honoré Fragonard**, who knocked out his Rococo "fantasy portraits" in as little as an hour, but the greatest academic painter of the era was **Jean-Auguste-Dominique Ingres**, whose wondrous *Madame Moitessier* is a figure of a darkly clad matron, with stern expression, pearls and rosy garland, that's been described by one critic as "the most imperial and commanding of Ingres's female portraits".

Eighteenth- and nineteenth-century British art (Rooms 57–59 & 61)

The gallery's limited number of **British works** include pieces by **William Hogarth**, whose subtly satirical painting *A Scene from The Beggar's Opera* illustrates characters that would later turn up in the musical standard "Mack the Knife"; **Joshua Reynolds**'s more regal portrait of *John Musters*; and **Thomas Gainsborough**'s cliffside cove of a *Seashore with Fishermen*, a rugged nature scene.

Other works are firmly within the British tradition, particularly the harmonious landscapes by **John Constable** – with *The White Horse* as a particularly lovely example – and the influential works of **J.M.W. Turner**, which run the gamut from the hazy, atmospheric luminance of the *Approach to Venice* to *Keelmen Heaving in Coals by Moonlight*, a light-drenched harbour scene set in the industrial north of England, to the early *Junction of the Thames and the Medway*, all stormy waves, bracing winds and nautical desperation. Finally, take care to see **Henry Fuseli**'s striking *Oedipus Cursing His Son, Polynices*, in which the tragic figure points dramatically to his son with the stern visage of an angry patriarch.

Eighteenth- and nineteenth-century American art (Rooms 60 & 62–71)

The gallery has an eclectic collection of eighteenth- and nineteenth-century American art, from **Gilbert Stuart**'s many images of the leading American men of his age, including George Washington of the early *Vaughan Portrait* and the more familiar *Athenaeum Portrait*, to **John Singleton Copley**'s *Watson and the Shark*, whose depiction of a shark attack off the coast of Cuba caused a stir in London at the time, to **Benjamin West**'s splendid historical scenes, including the political propaganda of *The Battle of La Hogue*, which pits seventeenth-century English and French naval forces against each other. Portraiture here includes works by two of West's pupils, **Thomas Sully** and **John Trumbull**, the latter of whom depicted a half-smiling *Alexander Hamilton* and later painted the murals in the Capitol.

Some of the better nineteenth-century American art on view includes **Thomas Cole**'s four *Voyage of Life* paintings, haunting images that follow a figure from childhood to old age; German-born **Albert Bierstadt**'s shimmering, turquoise *Lake Lucerne*; and **Frederic Edwin Church**'s *El Rio de Luz*, depicting a glorious vista of hazy sunshine beaming across primordial, almost jungle-like riparian terrain.

Philadelphia-based **Thomas Eakins**'s work introduces the gallery's late nineteenth-century collection, with his precisely rendered *Biglin Brothers Racing* a good example of his penchant for sporting images, in this case rowing. **James Abbott McNeill Whistler** is dominant, too; his standout work here is *The White Girl*, subtitled *Symphony in White, No. 1*, a full-length study of the artist's mistress.

Nineteenth-century French art (Rooms 80–93)

The gallery has an exceptional collection of nineteenth-century French paintings, with most Impressionist, post-Impressionist, Realist and Romantic artists of note represented. **Claude Monet**'s signature works include two facades of Rouen Cathedral. Significant, too, are *The Japanese Footbridge*, whose water-lily theme he was to return to again and again until his death in 1926, and *Woman with a Parasol*, whose true subject is the vibrant summer light rather than the human figures (Monet's wife and child).

There are also female portraits by the American-in-Paris **Mary Cassatt**, such as *Mother and Child*, with its flat blocks of colour and naturalistic models, and the earlier *Woman with a Red Zinnia* and *The Boating Party*. The gallery has a number of **Edouard Manet** works on view, from the black-and-white austerity of *The Dead Toreador* to the swirling still life of *Oysters*. Also well represented is **Edgar Degas**, whose paintings *Before the Ballet* and especially *The Dance Lesson* are iconic works of near-perfect form and composition.

Works by **Vincent van Gogh** include *The Olive Orchard*, a subject he found to be spiritual and complex; the *Farmhouse in Provence*, filled with strikingly rich colours; and the eerie *Self-Portrait*, understandably one of the National Gallery's most viewed works. Even more impressive, the museum's **Cézanne** collection encompasses still lifes, portraits and landscapes from most periods of the artist's long life, including *The Artist's Father*, in which he perched his father uncomfortably in a high-backed chair in front of an image of one of his paintings. More kinetic are the works by **Henri de Toulouse-Lautrec**, whose dancers, madams and café patrons reflect his affection for Montmartre fleshpots, in particular *Marcelle Lender Dancing the Bolero in "Chilperic"*, a sprightly vision of colour, movement and energy.

Sculpture, decorative arts, prints and drawings

The ground floor hosts changing exhibitions of sculpture, decorative arts, prints and drawings. The gallery owns more than two thousand pieces of **sculpture**, including many Italian and French pieces from the fourteenth to eighteenth centuries, and nineteenth-century French pieces by Rodin, Degas and Maillol, among others. Also worth seeking out are Honoré Daumier's 36 small portrait busts, intended for use in his printed caricatures; Houdon's contemplative head of George Washington; Gianlorenzo Bernini's marvellous bust of Baroque titan Francesco Barberini; and an anonymous early Baroque sculpture of the fabled she-wolf suckling *Romulus and Remus*, recounting the legendary birth of Rome.

Among the works of **decorative art** are Flemish tapestries; eighteenth-century French furniture; Renaissance majolica, chalices and religious paraphernalia; Chinese porcelain; engraved medals; and stained-glass windows by Renaissance artist Giovanni di Domenico. Equally impressive is the gallery's collection of **prints and drawings** – 65,000 works, from the eleventh to the twentieth centuries.

The Sculpture Garden and ice-skating rink

Adjacent to the West Building, the **Sculpture Garden** (Mon–Sat 10am–5pm, Sun 11am–6pm) exhibits a small but impressive selection of contemporary sculpture, with floating cubes and eight-tonne slabs of elegantly twisted steel scattered across a six-acre enclosure. Roy Lichtenstein's *House I* is a skewed comic-book image made into a pancake-flat sculpture of a house, and Barry Flanagan's pensive rabbit posing as the *Thinker on a Rock* is an irreverent homage to Rodin's nineteenth-century tour de force. There are also representative works by Joan Miró, David Smith, Louise Bourgeois, Sol LeWitt, Isamu Noguchi, and Claes Oldenburg, whose gargantuan *Typewriter Eraser* guards the western gate along Constitution Avenue. Don't miss the installation of one of Hector Guimard's famed Art Nouveau designs, which formerly graced an entrance to the Paris Metro, all sweeping, sinewy lines and curvaceous letters.

At the centre of the garden, an **ice-skating rink** ($7 admission) doubles as a **fountain** in the summer. Two-hour skating sessions begin on the hour from mid-November to March, weather permitting ($20–30). Skates are available for rent ($3) and lockers are on hand to stow your valuables.

National Gallery of Art – East Building

Although the National Gallery's **East Building**, on Constitution Ave, between 3rd and 4th sts NW (Mon–Sat 10am–5pm, Sun 11am–6pm; ☏202/737-4215, ⓦwww.nga.gov; Archives-Navy Memorial Metro), was opened in 1978 to accommodate the museum's ever-expanding collection of twentieth-century European and American art, there still isn't enough exhibition space to display the entire collection. This is partly due to **I.M. Pei**'s audacious modern design, which is dominated by public areas and a huge atrium, and partly due to the packed roster of special shows, which often displace the museum's own holdings. So if there's something you specifically want to see, call ahead to make sure it's there.

Inside, dominating the atrium, a huge steel-and-aluminum mobile by **Alexander Calder**, *Black, White and Ten Red*, hangs from the ceiling, its red and black (and one blue) paddle-like wings moving slowly with the air currents. Also in the atrium, **Max Ernst**'s eerie sculpture *Capricorn* shows a surreal horned potentate on his metal throne.

Twentieth-century exhibitions begin chronologically on the upper level and include pre-1945, mostly European works. Selections rotate, but it's all but certain that some works by **Pablo Picasso** will be on view. Among the National Gallery's substantial collection are the Blue Period pieces *The Tragedy* and *Family of Saltimbanques*, plus *Nude Woman*, which Picasso completed after fully turning to Cubism. Also in this area, and usually displayed near the Picasso pieces, **Henri Matisse**'s restrained early works give way to his exuberant *Pianist and Checker Players*, depicted in his own apartment in Nice.

Modern American art

On the ground level are rooms devoted to American art up to World War I. Works in the collection include **Childe Hassam**'s *Allies Day, May 1917*, a packed New York streetscape of flags and crowds; **John Marin**'s *Grey Sea*, a moody study of form and colour; **Marsden Hartley**'s pointed and stylized *Landscape No. 5*; **Grant Wood**'s bucolic ode to *Haying*; **John Sloan**'s evocative *The City from Greenwich Village*; and **Edward Hopper**'s poignant *Cape Cod Evening*. **George Bellows**'s assured portrait of *Florence Davey* in no way prepares you for his other paintings, notably the brutal prizefight pictures *Club Night* and *Both Members of This Club*, in which you can almost feel the heat as the crowd bays for blood. There's a similar energy in Bellows's brilliantly realized *Blue Morning*, set on a New York construction site.

Post-1945 art (mostly American) is usually shown downstairs in the lower levels. **Andy Warhol**'s Pop Art works are as familiar as they come, with classic serial examples of *Mao Tse-Tung*, *Let Us Now Praise Famous Men* and *Green Marilyn*. Separate rooms are often set aside for the works of artists using huge canvases: the gallery owns large, hovering slabs of blurry colour by **Mark Rothko**, which have been known to transfix acolytes for long periods at a time, as well as the thirteen stations of the cross by **Barnett Newman**, a series of big canvases built around the visual rhythm of black-and-white stripes. Other highlights include **Jasper Johns**'s *Targets*, which are among his more influential works; **Chuck Close**'s *Fanny/Fingerpainting*, a mighty portrait of an elderly black woman realized from a brilliantly marshalled canvas of finger splotches; **Jackson Pollock**'s *Number 1, 1950 (Lavender Mist)*, a spray of finely drizzled, multicoloured drippings; **Clyfford Still**'s big, jagged shards of colour, often without titles; and delightfully odd works by **Claes Oldenburg**, such as *Clarinet Bridge*, *USA Flag* and, best of all, *Soft Drainpipe – Red (Hot) Version*, a huge, soft-red sculpture that looks as much like a drooping phallus as anything under the sink.

National Museum of the American Indian

As you continue clockwise around the mall, skirting the Capitol Reflecting Pool and heading back west along Jefferson Drive, you'll hit the **National Museum of the American Indian** (daily 10am–5.30pm; Federal Centre SW Metro), instantly recognizable by its curvaceous modern form with undulating walls the colour of yellow earth – designed to represent the natural landscape. This stone-and-glass building with muted hues, terraced facade, and small-scale forest and wetland landscapes sits on an awkward plot, but it is nonetheless in a position of prominence near the Capitol.

The museum is designed to recognize and honour the many tribes of the Americas, including such groups and nations as the **Iroquois**, **Sioux**, **Navajo**, **Cherokee** and countless others. The collections reach back thousands of years and incorporate nearly a million objects, including ceramics, jade and goldwork, textiles and other artefacts from civilizations such as the **Olmec, Maya** and **Inca** – in many ways a world away from the culture of the Iroquois and the North American peoples.

The museum is staggering in its scope, attempting to provide a straightforward narrative to hundreds of different peoples and cultures that, in many cases, had little to do with one another except for being located in the Western Hemisphere. The temporary exhibits take in everything from different styles of native dresses to contemporary native rock stars. The permanent collection lies in several huge galleries with themes that are overarching, to say the least: **"Our Universes"** touches on religious and cosmological conceptions of eight selected peoples, from Chile to Alaska, and tries to provide some defining thread; **"Our Peoples"** does much the same for eight tribes from Brazil to Montana, with the much more consistent narrative element of the depredations of white missionaries, conquistadors, traders and government agents; and **"Our Lives"** again uses the device of eight representative peoples to show the characteristics and challenges of modern Indian life, mostly in North America.

National Air and Space Museum

If there's one DC museum tourists have heard about, and just one they want to visit with their kids, it's almost always the **National Air and Space Museum**, Independence Ave and 6th St SW (daily 10am 5.30pm; ☎202/633-1000, ⓦwww .nasm.si.edu; L'Enfant Plaza Metro) – which, since its opening in 1976, has captured the imagination of ten million people a year. The excitement begins in the entrance gallery, which throws together some of the most celebrated flying machines in history, while more than twenty monstrous galleries on two floors accommodate objects the size of, well, spaceships as well as the huge crowds, so even on busy days it's not too much of a struggle to get close to the exhibits. You may have to wait a while to get into the **IMAX theatre**, but otherwise the worst queues are in the café.

The **information desk** is at the Independence Avenue entrance; here you can catch a free tour (daily 10.30am & 1pm) and enquire about shuttle pickup to the **Udvar-Hazy Center** satellite museum (see p.186). If you want to visit the **Einstein Planetarium** or see an IMAX movie in the Lockheed Martin Theater (each is $9 per show), buy tickets when you arrive or book in advance (☎202/633-4629).

First floor: Milestones of Flight

The entry hall, known as **"Milestones of Flight"**, is a huge atrium filled with all kinds of flying machines, rockets, satellites and assorted aeronautic gizmos that are bolted to the floor, hung from the rafters and couched in cylindrical holes. For many the highlight is peeking up at the *Spirit of St Louis*, which flew into history on May 20, 1927, when 25-year-old Charles Lindbergh piloted it during the first solo transatlantic crossing. Elsewhere you can see spy planes, the 1957 Sputnik satellite, sound-barrier-breaking fighters, mail planes and Cold War-era missiles. Less portentously, there's *SpaceShipOne*, a three-man, privately built spacecraft that on three separate occasions in 2004 was hoisted into the heavens by plane, briefly reached the thermosphere of outer space, and returned to earth safely – all within 25 minutes.

First floor: other galleries

For many visitors, most of the interesting sights are on the east side of the first floor and relate to space travel. **"Space Race"** traces the development of space

THE NATIONAL MALL

NATIONAL AIR AND SPACE MUSEUM: FLOOR PLAN

FIRST FLOOR

Museum Shop

America by Air

Flight Simulators

Milestones of Flight

Lockheed Martin IMAX Theater

Space Race

Moving Beyond Earth

Lunar Exploration Vehicles

Food Court

Early Flight

Jet Aviation

Golden Age of Flight

How Things Fly

Looking at Earth

Explore the Universe

MALL ENTRANCE

INDEPENDENCE AVENUE

SECOND FLOOR

Einstein Planetarium

Lockheed Martin IMAX Theater

Beyond the Limits

Sea-Air Operations

Exploring the Planets

Pioneers of Flight

Wright Brothers Gallery

Apollo to the Moon

Temporary Exhibits

Great War in the Air

World War II Aviation

flight. Highlights include Wiley Post's early version of a "pressure suit", which resembles something out of a 1950s sci-fi flick with its tin-can helmet, leather gloves, metal collar, and rubber tubes poking out, and a Mark V deep-sea diver's suit from 1900, a distant cousin of the outfits worn by 1960s astronauts on their moonwalks. A display of lunar exploration vehicles starts with unmanned probes – the *Ranger*, *Lunar Orbiter* and *Surveyor* – and gives way to the ludicrously flimsy lunar module *Eagle*, in which Neil Armstrong and Edwin "Buzz" Aldrin made their historic descent to the moon. In the adjoining gallery, one of the newer exhibits, **"Moving Beyond Earth"**, focuses on the contemporary uses of space through multimedia presentations and various kiosks and interactive displays. Some of the topics include the outfits and gear used by visitors to the International Space Station and astronauts on board the space shuttle, as well as the mechanics behind the Hubble Space Telescope.

In a similar vein, **"Explore the Universe"** offers a broad view of astronomy, astrophysics and cosmology with an arsenal of high-tech items including spectroscopes and spectrographs, X-ray telescopes, early observation tools like reflecting telescopes, chunky lenses and curious "Armillary Spheres", and a replica of the huge, forbidding metal cage used for telescopes at California's Mount Wilson Observatory.

The other galleries on the first floor are less eventful. **"Jet Aviation"** will appeal to engineers and military buffs for its selection of groundbreaking fighters from the World War II era, while the **"Golden Age of Flight"** encompasses early exploration and air-racing craft. In **"Early Flight"** you can see Otto Lilienthal's glider (1894), which first inspired the Wright brothers, while **"How Things Fly"** is an interactive room aimed at those who need a refresher course to understand the museum's exhibits. It's worth glancing at **"Looking at Earth"**, where aerial photographs include pictures of San Francisco after the 1906 earthquake (snapped from a kite), 1860 photos of Boston taken from a balloon, and German castles recorded by camera-carrying pigeons.

Second floor

Those who want to recount the heroism demonstrated during the world wars will be drawn to the west side of the second-floor galleries: the **"Great War in the Air"** bursts with dog-fighting biplanes, and **"World War II Aviation"** has a classic set of American and foreign fighters. In the middle of the gallery, **"Pioneers of Flight"** has a hodgepodge of record-breaking aircraft, from the first helicopter to complete a journey around the globe, to the *Fokker T-2*, the first aeroplane to make a nonstop flight across North America, to the bright-red *Lockheed Vega*, flown solo across the Atlantic in May 1932 by Amelia Earhart. Nearby, **"Exploring the Planets"** provides an introduction to the basic facts you need to know about our solar system and the means we've employed for charting it – prominently the Voyager space probe.

Even better is **"The Wright Brothers"** – where the focus is the handmade **Wright Flyer** in which the Wright brothers made the first powered flight in December 1903 at Kitty Hawk, North Carolina. Just 20ft above the ground, that flight lasted twelve seconds and covered 120ft; within two years the Wrights were flying more than twenty miles at a time, though it was forty years before the Smithsonian formally recognized the brothers' achievement; the original Wright Flyer wasn't accepted into the fold until 1985.

Although the remaining galleries are fairly interesting and feature deep-space photography and the role of computers in space exploration, most visitors make a beeline for **"Apollo to the Moon"**, the most popular and crowded exhibit. The gallery centres on the *Apollo 11* (1969) and *17* (1972) missions, the first and last flights to the moon. There are Neil Armstrong's and Buzz Aldrin's spacesuits, a Lunar Roving Vehicle (basically a Space Age golf cart), *Apollo 17*'s flight-control deck, tools, navigation aids, space food, clothes, charts, and an astronaut's survival kit (complete with shark repellent for splashdown). In a side room, each space mission is detailed, beginning in May 1961 when, on a fifteen-minute flight aboard *Freedom 7*, Alan B. Shepard Jr became the first American in space.

Hirshhorn Museum and Sculpture Garden

The **Hirshhorn Museum**, Independence Ave at 7th St SW (daily: museum 10am–5.30pm, Sculpture Garden 7.30am–dusk; ☎202/633-4674, ⓦwww .hirshhorn.si.edu; L'Enfant Plaza or Smithsonian Metro), is a huge, cylindrical drum of a building that, with its impenetrable concrete facade and colossal scale, is a perfect example of late modernist architecture at its most inhuman. Luckily, the art inside is much better. In addition to the voluminous permanent collection, there are changing exhibitions of contemporary art, thematic shows, and a **sculpture garden** with an outdoor **café**, plus free daily **guided tours** of the collection and art **films** a couple of evenings a week in the Ring Auditorium. Starting in 2011, the museum plans to erect a giant **blue bubble** twice a year to fill much of its circular courtyard; the plastic bubble is a temporary exhibit designed to hold shows, performances and lectures, and promises to enliven the drab old architecture quite a bit.

The Hirshhorn's two upper floors are split into concentric inner and outer loops, with its main galleries winding along the nearly windowless exterior wall. The first floor is mostly entry space, while the lower level and second floor are given over to new acquisitions and temporary exhibits. That leaves the bulk of the permanent collection on the third floor, and since it's rotated regularly, you may or may not see some of the items described below. Highlights include contemporary American and European sculpture, international modern art from the twentieth century, and European sculpture from 1850 to 1935.

The collection

If the museum has one recognized strength, it's **French sculpture**, one of the best selections outside France. **Jean-Baptiste Carpeaux**, principal French sculptor of the mid-nineteenth century, is represented with eleven works, among them a thoughtful bust of *Alexandre Dumas, the Younger*, along with **Auguste Rodin**, whom he directly influenced, evident in his *Portrait of Balzac* and other pieces. Of the dozens of bronzes by **Henri Matisse**, most notable is *The Serf*, a stumpy portrait of a downtrodden spirit, while alongside **Edgar Degas**'s usual muscular ballerinas are energetic studies of women washing, stretching and emerging from a bath. Masks and busts by **Pablo Picasso** trace his (and sculpture's) growing alliance with Cubism: contrast the almost jaunty bronze *Head of a Jester* with the severe *Head of a Woman, Fernande Olivier*, produced just four years later.

More contemporary sculpture includes an abundance of 1950s **Henry Moore**, from the rather gentle *Seated Figure Against a Curved Wall* to the more imposing *King and Queen*, a regal pair of seated five-foot-high bronze figures whose curved laps and straight backs look as inviting as chairs. Look, too, for **Nam June Paik**'s *Video Flag*, composed of seventy thirteen-inch monitors, with a flurry of images spanning the presidents from Truman to Clinton; **Sol LeWitt**'s *13/11*, a white-painted wooden lattice of cubes on the floor; **Joseph Cornell**'s assorted art boxes, among them *Medici Princess*, in which a replica of a fetching Mannerist-era portrait by Bronzino stares out from behind blue glass, while an open drawer below is filled with intriguing castoffs such as bracelets, pearls, a Tuscan map and a powder-blue feather. And outdoors in the **sculpture garden**, you'll find such worthies as

Rodin's *The Burghers of Calais*, his famous depiction of the six robed bourgeois of the French town surrendering to the English in 1347; **Matisse's** four voluptuous human *Backs* in relief; **Gaston Lachaise's** proud, bronze *Standing Woman (Heroic Woman)*; and various works of Joan Miró, Barbara Hepworth and David Smith.

The Hirshhorn's cache of **modern paintings** starts with figurative works from the late nineteenth and early twentieth centuries and wends its way toward Abstract Expressionism and Pop Art, along the way covering everything from the surrealism of Salvador Dalí and Max Ernst to the organic abstractions of Alexander Calder.

American art, too, makes a good showing: there are works by **John Singer Sargent**, including a gentle study in white of *Catherine Vlasto*; **Mary Cassatt**, mostly a series of pastel drawings of children; and **Thomas Eakins**, such as the curious images of George Reynolds taken with double exposure showing his nude figure leaping or walking across the frame in multiple positions. Other pieces include the monumental landscapes of **Albert Bierstadt**; busy painted collages of military medals, hats and ribbons by **Marsden Hartley**, namely *Painting no. 47, Berlin*; and some bleak paintings of isolated urbanites by **Edward Hopper**. In addition, the Hirshhorn's collection of work by Abstract Expressionist **Willem de Kooning** is one of the most impressive anywhere (though often travelling to other museums), and just about every noteworthy twentieth-century artist – Georgia O'Keeffe, Robert Rauschenberg, Louise Bourgeois, Clyfford Still, Piet Mondrian, Jasper Johns, Roy Lichtenstein and Andy Warhol – turns up for good measure as well.

The Smithsonian Building

The most striking edifice on the Mall, the **Smithsonian Building**, 1000 Jefferson Drive SW (daily 8.30am–5.30pm; ☎202/633-1000, ⓦwww.si.edu; Smithsonian Metro), is widely known as **"the Castle"** for its Gothic combination of ruddy brown sandstone, nave windows and slender steeples. It serves as headquarters for the Smithsonian Institution, an independent trust holding nearly 140 million artefacts in nineteen museums (and one zoo). Inside you can see a short video highlighting the role of the institution, interact with touch-screen Smithsonian information displays and electronic wall maps, and check out scale models of all the major city plans for DC, from L'Enfant's designs onward. You can also stop by the information desk for the latest details on events at all the galleries. Smithsonian founder **James Smithson** (see box, p.70), who never visited America in life, found a place here in death: his ornate, Neoclassical tomb stands in an alcove just off the Mall entrance. It was placed here in 1904, 75 years after his death in Italy.

Minor Smithsonian attractions

Sitting between the Smithsonian Castle and the Hirshhorn Museum, the **Arts and Industries Building** is another fitting holdover from the Victorian era, with its playful polychromatic brick-and-tile patterns and striking Gilded Age verve reminding you just what drew so many people to this first addition to the "National Museum" in 1881. However, despite its enticing design and historic value, the building is due to undergo a complete renovation and won't be open to the public anytime soon. Still on view, though, are the regular children's programmes at its **Discovery Theater** (tickets $6; ☎202/633-8700, ⓦdiscoverytheater.org), while right outside is the popular **carousel**. Even more appealing are the lovely **Enid A. Haupt Gardens** (free tours May–Sept Wed 1pm) nearby, where you'll find several topiary bison and well-tended plots of decorative flowers.

The Smithsonian story

James Smithson, a gentleman scientist and the illegitimate son of the first Duke of Northumberland, never visited the US, but bequeathed half a million dollars "to found at Washington, under the name of the Smithsonian Institution, an establishment for the increase and diffusion of Knowledge" – provided that his surviving nephew should die without an heir. His nephew did just that in 1835, six years after Smithson's death, and it took Congress until 1846 to decide what sort of institution to create. In the end, the vote was for a multi-use building that would hold a museum, art gallery and laboratory: the original Smithsonian Institution Building, known as "the Castle", was completed in 1855.

A new wrinkle occurred when America observed its centennial in 1876. The government invited its constituent states and forty foreign nations to display a panoply of inventions and exhibits that would celebrate contemporary human genius. The subsequent Centennial Exhibition in Philadelphia was a roaring success, though at its close most of the exhibits were abandoned by their owners, who couldn't afford to take or ship them home. Congress made the Smithsonian responsible for the items and approved funds for a new "National Museum" (now the Arts and Industries Building) to house them. Opened in 1881 in time to host President Garfield's inaugural ball, the building soon became rooted in people's consciousness as the "nation's attic", since quite apart from the Centennial exhibits – which included an entire American steam locomotive and Samuel Morse's original telegraph – the Smithsonian also made acquisitions that weren't of a strictly educational nature. Over the years, as the National Museum filled to bursting, most of the Smithsonian holdings were farmed out to new, specialized museums, with proposals for new museums coming every few years after.

National Museum of African Art

In the same area of the Mall as the Smithsonian Building, the **National Museum of African Art**, 950 Independence Ave SW (daily 10am–5.30pm; ☎202/633-4600, ⓦwww.nmafa.si.edu; Smithsonian Metro), is a granite-and-limestone cube that holds the nation's foremost collection of traditional art from sub-Saharan Africa, including some six thousand diverse sculptures and artefacts culled from a wide variety of tribal cultures, displayed in a series of permanent galleries and bolstered by special exhibitions. For an overview of the collection, the free guided **tours** (daily except Fri) are an excellent introduction (pick up a schedule at the ground-floor information desk). It's also worth noting that the **gift shop** on the first level is one of DC's most appealing, selling woven and dyed fabrics and clothes as well as the usual books and postcards.

The collection

Unlike most other Smithsonian museums on the Mall, the African art museum has few permanent installations, and instead centres on temporary shows that present themed groupings of the items from its broad **collection**. Therefore, you can't expect to encounter the same items from year to year. Nonetheless, for many shows you're likely to see a wide variety of **ceramic bowls** (perfectly round, despite being hand-formed), including one with a hippo head for a spout, and carved legs and delicate ivory animal figures from the ceremonial beds used to carry the dead to the cemetery for burial. Ivory inlays from these burial beds come in the form of ibex, hyenas, vultures and the hippo god Taweret – standing up and wearing a skirt.

Political, religious and ceremonial art – mostly from West and Central Africa – makes up some of the museum's most elaborate holdings, highlighted by rounded, stylized, terracotta **equestrian and archer figures** from Mali (thirteenth to fifteenth century). A number of works (fertility fetishes) represent a woman and child, including wooden carvings from Nigeria that would have sat at one end of a ceremonial drum. From Cameroon, wooden sculptures of a regal male figure show him holding his chin in his hand (a sign of respect), wearing decorative bead clothing covered with symbolic representations of spiders (a wily opponent) and frogs (fecundity). There's much to learn, too, about the African concepts of **divinity** and **beauty**: a carved figure from the Ghanaian Asante people shows a seated male and female with disk-shaped heads, a form considered to be the aesthetic ideal. One of the most engaging works, a headrest from the Luba people of the Congo, is supported by two caryatid figures who, if you look around the back, have their arms entwined.

National Museum of Asian Art

As you finish up the National Mall museum circuit, on Independence Ave SW between 10th and 12th sts, you come to the two institutions that make up the **National Museum of Asian Art** (daily 10am–5.30pm; ✆202/633-4880, Ⓦwww.asia.si.edu; Smithsonian Metro). The first, the pyramidal **Arthur M. Sackler Gallery**, displays artworks and devotional objects in well-lit, underground galleries; the other, connected by subterranean passage, is the **Freer Gallery of Art**, an airy Italian Renaissance palazzo of granite and marble with small, elegant galleries encircling a herringbone-brick courtyard. The permanent collections are described below; temporary exhibitions might cover themes such as painted Chinese literary adaptations, contemporary Southeast Asian ceramics, and early Islamic texts from Iran.

The **information desk** at ground level of either building should be your first stop. Ask about the highly informative, free guided **tours** (daily at noon; other hours vary). The gallery also has a **shop**, with a fine range of prints, fabrics, ceramics and arty gewgaws, and an Asian art research **library** (Mon–Fri 10am–5pm).

Arthur M. Sackler Gallery

The most prominent permanent exhibition is **"The Arts of China"**, which highlights the Sackler Gallery's collection of up to 3000-year-old Chinese art. It includes a variety of items, including ritual wine containers decorated with the faces and tails of dragons; ceramic, multicoloured temple guard figures designed to ward off evil spirits with their fearsome expressions; and imperial porcelain richly embellished with symbolic figures and motifs – as in a plate depicting a young boy holding a pomegranate full of seeds, and one of ladies holding fans with painted butterflies, representing fertility.

Elsewhere, **"Sculpture of South and Southeast Asia"** traces the spread of devotional sculpture across the continent. The earliest piece here is from ancient Gandhara (now part of Pakistan and Afghanistan), a third-century carved head of the Buddha whose features were directly influenced by images from Greece and Rome, with which Gandhara traded. Later Hindu temple sculpture from India includes bronze, brass and granite representations of Brahma, Vishnu and Shiva; there's also a superb thirteenth-century stone carving of the elephant-headed Ganesha, the remover of obstacles – his trunk burnished by years of illicit touching by museum visitors.

Other galleries aren't quite as eye-catching, intended more for specialists than the lay public in some cases. **Ancient Persian metalwork and ceramics** include vessels, weapons and ornaments made between 2300 and 100 BC, many of which are animal-shaped or painted with animal motifs, while a ceramic trio from northern Persia resembles metal, such was the craftsman's skill in firing. **Korean ceramics** include hundreds of pieces (wine bottles, tea bowls, ewers and more) across a broad scope of time (200–1900 AD) and were used for everything from simple household tasks to encasing human ashes.

Freer Gallery of Art

The **Freer Gallery**'s collection of **Japanese art** is one of its best, and includes painted folding screens called *byobu* ("protection from the wind") with seasons or themes from Japanese literature, ranging in length from two to ten panels. Other choice items include the nineteenth-century porcelain dish shaped like Mount Fuji and – one of the oldest pieces here – a twelfth-century standing Buddha of wood and gold leaf.

Other rooms are devoted to **Chinese art**, ranging from ancient jade burial goods to a series of ornate bronzes (1200–1000 BC), including ritual wine servers in the shape of tigers and elephants. There's also a stunning series of ink-on-paper hand scrolls, though the calligraphy (literally, "beautiful writing") isn't just confined to paper – jars and tea bowls, even ceramic pillows, are painstakingly adorned. In addition, **Egyptian art** comprises a remarkable collection of richly coloured glass vessels, bronze figurines and carved plaques, most around 4000 years old. Of the **Buddhist**, **South Asian** and **Islamic art**, a remarkably well-preserved Pakistani stone frieze from the second century AD details the life of the Buddha, while the eye will delight in the gold jewellery set with rubies and diamonds, the Turkish ceramics (many repeating garden motifs), and a fine inlaid Persian pen box emblazoned with animal heads and engraved with the name of the artist and the owner.

Whistler collection

Also in the Freer Gallery, thanks to the enthusiasms of its founder Charles Freer, are a great number of works by **James Abbott McNeill Whistler** (1834–1903). Among these are a *Self-Portrait* in which the artist looks very much the man at ease with Left Bank life; *The Golden Screen*, depicting a seated woman in Japanese dress in front of a fine painted screen; and three evocative *Nocturnes*, which use combinations of blue, silver, grey and gold to illuminate the hazy colours of landscapes at Chelsea, Bognor and Valparaiso Bay. Most famous is *Arrangement in White and Black*, which contrasts the ghostly white dress and parasol of Whistler's mother with the dark shades of the background; and *The Little Red Glove*, harmonizing glove and bonnet with the subject's auburn hair.

Whistler is also well represented by the magnificent **Peacock Room**, which has been taken from the dining room of a London client. Using a technique similar to Japanese lacquerware, Whistler covered the leather-clad walls, ceiling, shelving and furnishings with blue paint, gold-painted peacock feathers, gilt relief decor, and green glaze; above the sideboard he placed two golden painted peacocks trailing a stream of feathers – the aggressive birds supposedly emblematic of the relationship between painter and patron. The other American art on view in the Freer is more scattershot, enlivened by **John Singer Sargent**'s *Breakfast in the Loggia*, a scene in the arcaded courtyard of a Florentine villa, and **Winslow Homer**'s *Sailors Take Warning (Sunset)*, a moody grouping of two women and a weathered captain on a bleak hillside before a darkening sky.

2

Capitol Hill

Housing the American federal legislature, **Capitol Hill** is the seat of lawmaking for a nation of 300 million people, centred on the towering silhouette of the white-domed **US Capitol**, which tops the shallow knoll at the eastern end of the Mall. The building – whose Neoclassical design is meant to evoke the ideals of ancient Greece and Rome that inspired the founding fathers – is the political and geographical centre of the city, and many of DC's diagonal boulevards lead directly to it.

The Capitol isn't the only important structure on this hill. Around it sit more essential components of American government, including the **United States Supreme Court** and vast **Library of Congress**; scattered attractions like the historic **Sewall–Belmont House** and the lush **US Botanic Garden**; and buildings that hold the offices of senators and representatives. For many, that is the extent of the neighbourhood, but the Hill is actually home to diverse residential areas, where politicians, aides, lobbyists and even commoners live. The southeast stretches of **Pennsylvania Avenue** provide a few worthy distractions, while **Lincoln Park**, with its memorial to the Great Emancipator, marks the neighbourhood's eastern limit. The spruced-up area around grand old **Union Station** lies to the north.

As a neighbourhood, Capitol Hill has faced a lengthy climb to respectability. When Pierre L'Enfant and his surveyors began laying out the city, the cross drawn on what was then Jenkins Hill was the focus of a grand, Baroque-style city plan. The US Capitol was erected on the site of that cross, and in 1800 Congress moved in. But this marshy backwater outpost was slow to develop: it froze in the bitter winters and sweltered in the harsh summers; from their boarding houses around the Capitol, legislators had to trudge the muddy length of Pennsylvania Avenue for an audience with the president in the White House. After the **War of 1812** broke out, the British diverted a force away from Quebec and upstate New York and made a play for Washington and Baltimore – a plan designed more to shame the American government than to achieve any strategic goal. The Capitol was the first to burn, prompting many to suggest abandoning the city altogether and setting up political shop somewhere more hospitable.

However, with the conclusion of the war, the damaged structures were rebuilt, and as the capital and the federal government grew in stature in later years, so too did the Hill. During the nineteenth century, rows of elegant **townhouses**, which today form the keystone of Capitol Hill's status as a protected historic district, began to appear. Eventually, major federal institutions that had been housed since 1800 in the ever-expanding Capitol complex moved into new homes of their own: first the Library of Congress in 1897, then the Supreme Court in 1935. Later in the twentieth century, massive office buildings were erected to accommodate legislators and their staff, reflecting the government's growth in stature, size and bureaucracy.

The US Capitol

The towering, rib-vaulted dome of the **US Capitol** (Capitol South or Union Station Metro) soars between north and south wings, respectively occupied by the **Senate** and **House of Representatives**, the two legislative bodies of Congress. The building, with its grand halls and statues, committee rooms and ornate chambers, is one of the few places in DC where you get a tangible sense of the immense power wielded by the nation's elected officials. Unlike the White House – where you're kept away from any real action – when Congress is in session, you can watch from third-floor galleries as elected leaders get down to business (see p.79).

The Capitol is the only building in the city without an address, as it stands foursquare at the centre of the street plan: the city quadrants extend from the building, and the numbered and lettered streets count away from its central axis. For the same reason, the building doesn't have a front or a back, simply an "East Front" and a "West Front". The **public entrance** is at the East Front, where, from 1829 to 1977, all the presidents were inaugurated. In 1981 Ronald Reagan was sworn in on the west side, and the six inaugurations since then have followed this precedent. When Congress is in session (from January 3 until close of business, usually in the autumn) the lantern above the dome is lit, and flags fly above Senate and House wings.

Visiting the Capitol

The $600 million **Capitol Visitor Centre** (Mon–Sat 8.30am–4.30pm; ☎202/226-8000, ⓦwww.visitthecapitol.gov) is where most visitors get their first internal view of the Capitol – deep underground. It's quite a showpiece, indeed, with two great central galleries. The massive **Exhibition Hall** is where you can find out all about the building – including an 11ft. model of the dome – and the role it played in the nation's democracy, with biographies and information about some of the key figures in congressional history, and the various inaugurations that have taken place here. In the even larger **Emancipation Hall** there are, among other things, a plaster cast of the Statue of Freedom atop the Capitol, two skylights offering a fine view of the dome, and around two dozen statues that state governments have donated to National Statuary Hall but ended up here instead in the overflow space, among them the figures of Sacagawea, Helen Keller and Kamehameha I – the first king of Hawaii. There are also the requisite gift shops and restaurants, a pair of theatres devoted to each chamber of Congress, a tunnel to the Thomas Jefferson building of the Library of Congress, and acres of office space, media production facilities, and related infrastructure for politicians and their staffs. Not surprisingly for its cost, the entire below-ground site is huge, occupying up to three-quarters the size of the Capitol's footprint, which makes it one of the most sizeable visitor centres in the world.

To go anywhere beyond the visitor centre and check out the highlights noted below, such as National Statuary Hall and the Rotunda, you'll need an advance online **reservation** through ⓦwww.visitthecapitol.gov, or, if an American citizen, you can reserve through the office of your home-state US representative or senator. A small number of same-day **tour passes** are also provided through information desks on the lower level of the Visitor Centre, though you'll want to arrive early in the day for a chance of grabbing one. Entry into the chambers of the House of Representatives and the Senate requires much more frisking and scanning, although it may be worth it to see the legislative machinery of the American government at work. The only downside is that you can only get a visitor's pass (one for each chamber) through the local or Washington, DC office of your home-state representative or senator; foreign visitors can also try to request a pass through their home country's embassy in Washington.

CAPITOL HILL

I ST NW · NORTH CAPITOL ST · CAPITOL ST NW
H ST NW · H ST NE
G ST NW · G ST NE
MASSACHUSETTS · National Postal Museum · UNION STATION · G ST NE · MORRIS PL NE · PICKFORD PL
F ST NW · 5TH ST NE · 6TH ST NE · 7TH ST NE · 8TH ST NE · 9TH ST NE
F ST NE
E ST NW · Union Station · ACKER ST NE
E ST NE
Columbus Memorial Fountain
NW · LEXINGTON PL NE
NE · MARYLAND AVE NE
D ST NW · D ST NE
National Japanese American Memorial · UNION STATION PLAZA · Senate Office Buildings · Stanton Park
Taft Memorial · Russell · Dirksen · Hart · C ST NE · MASSACHUSETTS AVE NE
CONSTITUTION AVE NE · Sewell-Belmont House
Peace Monument · Frederick Douglass Museum · A ST NE
PENNSYLVANIA AVE NW · US Senate · US Capitol · Supreme Court · Visitor Center · Jefferson Building · Folger Shakespeare Library · EAST CAPITOL ST
Capitol Reflecting Pool · Grant Memorial · US House of Representatives · John Adams Building · A ST SE
Garfield Memorial · Library of Congress
US Botanic Garden · Rayburn · INDEPENDENCE AVE SE
Bartholdi Fountain · Longworth · Cannon · Madison Building · SEWARD SQUARE · Eastern Market
FEDERAL CENTER SW · SW · C ST SW · House Office Buildings · SE · PENNSYLVANIA AVE SE · EASTERN MARKET
D ST SE · CAPITOL SOUTH · Folger Park · Ebenezer Church · D ST SE
Marion Park
Southeast DC ▼

0   200 yds

ACCOMMODATION		CAFÉS & RESTAURANTS		BARS & CLUBS		GAY RESTAURANTS & BARS	
Capitol City Hostel	E	Au Bon Pain	5	18th Amendment	20	Banana Café &	
Capitol Hill Suites	G	Bistro Bis	8	Argonaut	1	Piano Bar	25
George	B	Café Berlin	11	Bullfeathers	23	Mr. Henry's	19
Hyatt Regency		Johnny's Half Shell	9	Capitol City Brewing Co.	4	Phase One	26
Washington	C	Las Placitas	24	Capitol Lounge	13	Remington's	22
Liaison Capitol Hill	D	Le Bon Café	12	The Dubliner	7		
Maison Orleans	H	Market Lunch	14	Kelly's Irish Times	6		
Phoenix Park	A	The Monocle	10	Pour House	15		
William Penn House	F	Montmartre	17	The Pug	2		
		Mr. Henry's	19	Rock and Roll Hotel	3		
		Peregrine Espresso	18	Tune Inn	16		
		Pizza Boli's	21				

Some history

A chaste plan, sufficiently capacious and convenient for a period not too remote, but one to which we may reasonably look forward, would meet my idea in the Capitol.

George Washington, 1792

Before the Revolution, relevant colonial matters were decided across the Atlantic in Parliament or locally by royal governors and their (frequently hand-picked) assemblies. Even with the tide of independence, the concept of **federalism** was still a nebulous one, and the colonies' aggregate assemblies met in all sorts of places, from New York City in 1765 (protesting the Stamp Act), to 1777 in

Baltimore, to a half-dozen spots in Pennsylvania for the first and second Continental Congresses from 1774 to 1781. After the Constitution was ratified in 1788, plans were formulated for a more permanent, site-specific location for the federal legislature, and the design of the seat of that government, the US Capitol, was thrown open to public competition in 1792. **Dr William Thornton**, an amateur whose grand Neoclassical offering brought a splendour deemed appropriate for Congress's meeting place, won the competition. On September 18, 1793, in a ceremony rich with Masonic symbolism, the square-and-compass-engraved cornerstone of the Capitol was laid by second-term president George Washington, himself a Mason. By the time the government moved to DC from Philadelphia seven years later, however, the Capitol was nowhere near completion.

When Congress assembled for the first time in the brick-and-sandstone building on November 22, 1800, only a small north wing housing the Senate Chamber, the House of Representatives, the Supreme Court and the Library of Congress was ready. The building's ceilings leaked, and the furnaces installed to heat the structure produced intolerable temperatures. Adams's successor, **Thomas Jefferson** (the first president inaugurated at the Capitol), appointed the respected **Benjamin Latrobe** as surveyor of public buildings in an attempt to speed up work, and by 1807 a south wing had been built for the House of Representatives. In addition, Latrobe added a second floor to the north wing, allowing separate chambers for the Supreme Court and the Senate.

British troops burned down the Capitol and the White House in 1814. With President Madison having fled the city, Washington, DC's future was uncertain. Nonetheless, Congress met for four years in a quickly built temporary capitol made of brick on the site of today's Supreme Court, and restoration work

Capitol conflicts

As an iconic symbol of democracy for more than two centuries, the US Capitol has been an obvious hub for **political demonstrations**. In 1894, Jacob S. Coxey led an "army" of unemployed people from Ohio and points west to demand a public works programme to create jobs; he was arrested for trespassing, and the few hundred men with him slunk off home. In the decades following, the Capitol would be the focus of demonstrations from groups as diverse as women's suffragists and members of the KKK. In 1932, 17,000 unemployed soldiers in the so-called **Bonus Army** – demanding an early payment of their World War I military pensions – camped outside the Capitol, then set up shanties in Anacostia, where they were driven off by a force of federal soldiers led by George Patton and Douglas MacArthur. Decades later, in May 1968, the weary citizens of the Poor People's March set up makeshift tents and shelters they called "Resurrection City", which came to a similarly unsuccessful conclusion. More recently, in 1995, Nation of Islam leader Louis Farrakhan harangued white America from the terrace steps while addressing attendees of the Million Man March.

On occasion, the building itself has come **under attack**. Shots were fired in the Capitol in 1835, and in 1915, 1971 and 1983 various miscreants detonated bombs in the building (no one was injured). The worst attack was in the summer of 1998, when a lone gunman stormed the building, killing two Capitol police officers and injuring several members of the public.

It was, of course, the 2001 terrorist attacks in DC and New York City that really led to clarion calls for further **restricting public access** to the building. This was duly achieved, and new barriers were erected and an underground visitor centre built to control access much more effectively, but despite all the newfangled security measures, the building is still remarkably open to the public – provided you don't mind getting patted down, scanned and searched several times before you get inside.

continued on what little was left of the original Capitol. By 1826 the Capitol finally appeared in a respectable form, complete with a central rotunda topped by a low wooden dome clad in copper.

By the 1850s Congress had again run out of space. Plans were laid to build magnificent, complementary wings on either side of the building and to replace the dome with something more substantial. In 1857 the new south wing accommodated the **House Chamber**, and two years later the **Senate Chamber** moved to the new north wing. In 1861, the **Civil War** threatened to halt work on the **dome**, but Abraham Lincoln, recognizing the Capitol as a potent symbol of the Union, was determined that the building should be completed. A cast-iron dome was painstakingly assembled, at three times the height of the previous dome, and in December 1863 the glorious project came to fruition. Hoisted on top of the white-painted dome was the 19ft-high **Statue of Freedom** by sculptor Thomas Crawford. Resplendent in a feathered helmet and clutching a sword and shield, the statue is also known as "Armed Liberty".

The surrounding terraces were added after the Civil War, and when extra office space was required in the 1870s, separate **House and Senate office buildings** were built in the streets on either side of the Capitol. However, with the Capitol dome being much larger than its predecessor, the visual effect of the portico and its columns was altered considerably, and subsequent reconstructions of the East Front have tried to make the architecture more harmonious: the porch was rebuilt in 1904, followed 55 years later with a more general construction programme that included the replacement of the old sandstone columns with marble – the originals are now poised on a grassy plot by themselves at the National Arboretum (see p.153). The East Front was extended in 1962 and faced in marble to prevent the original sandstone from deteriorating further; so far the West Front – now the oldest part of the building – has avoided modern accretions, though it was restored in the 1980s.

The Rotunda

Standing in the **Rotunda**, you're not only at the centre of the Capitol, but at point zero of the entire District of Columbia. William Thornton, the Capitol's first architect, took Rome's Pantheon as his model, so it's no wonder that this is a magnificent space: 180ft high and 96ft across, with the dome canopy decorated by Constantino Brumidi's mighty **fresco** depicting the *Apotheosis of Washington*, showing George Washington surrounded by symbols of democracy, arts, science and industry, as well as female figures representing the thirteen original states.

From the floor, it's hard to see much detail of either frieze or fresco, and eyes are drawn instead to the eight large **oil paintings** that hang below the frieze. Four of the paintings depict events associated with the "discovery" and settlement of the country (like, again, Columbus's arrival and the Pilgrims' disembarkation), though most notable are the four Revolutionary War pieces by **John Trumbull**, who trained under Benjamin West, the first American artist to study in Europe. One depicts the signing of the **Declaration of Independence**, showing the key figures who drafted the document – Jefferson, John Adams and Ben Franklin among them – presenting it to Continental Congress president John Hancock while other legislators stand or sit at rigid attention.

Busts and statues of prominent American leaders fill in the gaps in the rest of the Rotunda. Washington, Jefferson, Lincoln and Jackson are all here, along with a modern bust of Dr Martin Luther King Jr and a gold facsimile of the Magna Carta. In such august surroundings more than thirty people – including members of Congress, military leaders, eminent citizens and eleven presidents – have been **laid in state** before burial. The most recently honoured was the nation's 38th president, Gerald Ford, who died in December 2006 at age 93, making him the longest-lived former president.

National Statuary Hall

From the Rotunda you move south into one of the earliest extensions of the building – the 1807 section that once housed the chamber of the **House of Representatives** (rebuilt in 1819). It's designed in grand Roman style with Classical elements of sandstone pilasters and marble capitals, a D-shaped space with stylized coffered ceiling and oculus.

After the House moved into its new wing in 1857, the chamber was used for various temporary purposes until Congress decided to turn it into the **National Statuary Hall** and invited each state to contribute two statues of its most famous citizens. Around forty statues are still on display in the hall, with the others scattered around the corridors in the rest of the building, including such figures as Vermont patriot Ethan Allen and Texas revolutionary Sam Houston, missionaries like Marcus Whitman and Brigham Young, Congressional heavyweights like William Jennings Bryan and Daniel Webster, and, more questionably, Confederates like Robert E. Lee and Jefferson Davis.

Adelaide Johnson's 1921 *Suffrage Monument*, which was moved to the Rotunda after languishing in the Crypt (see opposite), shows women's rights pioneers Susan B. Anthony, Lucretia Mott and Elizabeth Cady Stanton poking their heads out of a large, mostly uncut, block of granite, as if entombed there. It is one of only six statues of women in the entire building.

Old Senate Chamber

North of the Rotunda is the **Old Senate Chamber**. This splendid semicircular gallery, with its embossed rose ceiling and eight Ionic columns made from Potomac marble, was built in 1810 and reconstructed from 1815 to 1819, after the British had done their worst to the city. The Senate met here until 1859, when it moved into its current quarters. The Supreme Court moved in and stayed until 1935, when it, too, was given a new home. After that the Old Senate Chamber sat largely unused until it was restored to its mid-nineteenth-century glory for the Bicentennial in 1976. Its furnishings are redolent of that period; the members' desks are reproductions, but the gilt eagle topping the vice president's chair is original, as is the portrait of George Washington by Rembrandt Peale. Contemporary engravings helped restorers reproduce other features of the original Senate chamber, like the rich red carpet emblazoned with gold stars. The original carpet received severe punishment from spit tobacco, despite the provision of a cuspidor by every desk.

Old Supreme Court and the Crypt

Before 1810, the Senate met on the floor below the **Old Senate Chamber**, in a room that architect Benjamin Latrobe later revamped to house the **Supreme Court**, which sorely needed a permanent home. By 1819 the Court had settled in the chamber, where it remained until 1860, when it moved again – this time upstairs, to the chamber just vacated by the Senate.

The **Old Supreme Court Chamber** is quite a visually appealing spot, occupying a semicircular space topped with ten ribs that converge at a central node, giving the ceiling the appearance of a sunburst or umbrella, with the busts of the nation's first five chief justices sitting in prominent niches. Sitting on chairs whose individual designs reflected the personal preference of each, the justices held court at mahogany desks behind a mahogany rail, with lovely natural light coming in through the windows; unfortunately, the room has been lit by artificial means since the extension of the East Front of the Capitol blocked the view in the 1950s. By that time, the Court had been gone for a century and the chamber served as a law library and congressional committee space, before being relegated to a mere storeroom until just before the Bicentennial, when it, too, was restored to its mid-nineteenth-century appearance on the basis of original etchings and plans for the building.

The **Crypt** lies underneath the Rotunda, on the same level as the Old Supreme Court Chamber. Lined with Doric sandstone columns, it was built in 1827 and designed to house George Washington's tomb, a plan that was never realized (Washington is buried with his wife, Martha, at Mount Vernon). The Crypt instead is an **exhibition centre**, displaying details of the plans submitted for the 1792 architectural competition and the Capitol's construction.

House and Senate chambers

With beefed-up security measures, public access to the **House and Senate chambers** has been cut back. If you're an American citizen, you can apply to your representative's or senator's office in advance for a pass valid for the entire (two-year) session of Congress, and enter the Senate from the north side of that wing and the House of Representatives from its south side. Foreign visitors wanting a look will need to get tickets from their embassy.

The chambers may be almost empty, or deep in torpor, when you show up, which is fine if all you want is a flavour of either place. If you're lucky, you may watch members introduce legislation or even vote on various bills or issues. The House chamber is the more striking of the two, with its decorative frieze and oil paintings; from here the president addresses joint sessions of Congress and delivers his annual **State of the Union** speech. You can enter the House even when it's not in session, but the Senate must be open for business for the public to be allowed admittance.

Legislative offices

Only political junkies will be interested in poking around the six legislative **office buildings** that contain the **committee rooms** where most of the day-to-day political activity of the Senate and House takes place. The first of these office buildings – all named after past politicians – were the imperious Cannon and Russell, built in 1907–09, and the last, the modern Hart, in 1982; they follow the pattern of the Capitol in that the Senate office buildings (Russell, Dirksen and Hart) are to the north and the House office buildings (Cannon, Longworth and Rayburn) are to the south. Especially worth a look are the magisterial, column-encircled rotundas of the Beaux-Arts-style Cannon and Russell buildings. In the Senate buildings, each politician's office is marked by an American flag and his or her state flag in the corridor outside the door. Office hours can be erratic, depending on the relative activity of the politicians hived inside; **committee hearings**, usually held in the morning, are listed in the *Washington Post*'s "Today in Congress" section.

Capitol Reflecting Pool

Facing the National Mall, the West Front of the Capitol provides a striking image of imperial power that is heightened by the mirror image shown in the **Capitol Reflecting Pool** at its base. The pool itself, with its surrounding benches and sloping wall, is an excellent spot to rest before tackling the museums on the Mall, and offers a bit of aesthetic pleasure and a picturesque backdrop for souvenir photos of the Capitol.

West Front memorials

The **memorials** on the **West Front** memorialize notable post-Civil War-era figures. At the junction of the Capitol grounds with Pennsylvania Avenue NW and Maryland Avenue SW, the 1887 **James Garfield Memorial** – honouring the assassinated twentieth president – shows a noble, steadfast Garfield posing atop a granite pillar, while below sit three allegorical sculptures relating to his days as a student, soldier and statesman. However, the most significant structure is just north, the 250ft-long **Ulysses S. Grant Memorial**, lauding the general-in-chief of the Union forces under President Lincoln during the Civil War. Dedicated in 1922, the monument depicts a sombre Grant on horseback, guarded by lions, flanked by a charging cavalry unit on one side and an artillery unit moving through thick mud on the other.

Further north, at the corner of Pennsylvania Avenue and 1st St NW, stands the 44ft-high marble pillar of the **Peace Monument**, so-called for the partially nude figure of the Roman goddess of Peace that faces the Capitol; it is matched on the opposite side of the building by the goddess Victory and childlike forms of Mars and Neptune, in training for war and seacraft, respectively. The Peace Monument was built in 1878 and commemorates Civil War soldiers lost at sea, and with its evocative, austere form, is a moving if little-noticed sculpture.

North of the Reflecting Pool towards Union Station, a small park bordered by Constitution and Louisiana avenues contains the **Robert A. Taft Memorial and Carillon**, a bronze statue and 100ft-high concrete bell tower, which sounds on the hour, erected in 1958. The memorial honours the veteran senator (and son of President William Howard Taft), who during the mid-twentieth century was known simply as "Mr. Republican". Unlike Taft himself, the carillon's 27 bells are all fairly huge and loud, the largest of them weighing seven tonnes.

A reminder of a darker chapter in the nation's history can be found just north, at the triangular intersection of New Jersey, Louisiana and D streets, where the **National Japanese American Memorial** commemorates the Japanese American units and soldiers who fought in World War II, including twenty Medal of Honor winners. It's highlighted by a central 14ft-tall marble and bronze sculpture of two intertwined cranes held to their pillar by barbed wire, which they attempt to break through with their beaks. The symbolic reference is, of course, to the 120,000 Japanese American citizens who were rounded up in the xenophobic climate after Pearl Harbor and sent to internment camps in the American West.

US Botanic Garden

The closest museum or institution to the Capitol, the **US Botanic Garden**, 245 1st St SW (daily 10am–5pm; free; Federal Center SW), sits near a corner of the National Mall. Its centrepiece is a grand conservatory crowned by an 80ft-tall **Palm House**, the results of a renovation that transformed the Victorian-style structure, built in 1933, into a state-of-the-art greenhouse, where it's now possible to grow plants from almost everywhere in the world. More than four thousand plants are currently on view, of a collection of around 10,000. Especially intriguing are the climate-controlled rooms devoted to colourful ranks of tropical, subtropical and desert plants; the orchid section, two hundred varieties of which are visible at any one time; and the **Jungle Room**, stuffed with equatorial trees and other plants and humid almost to the point of discomfort.

On the west side of the facility is a newer addition to the site, the **National Garden**, whose themed plots include a lovely **Rose Garden**; a pleasant **Regional Garden** thick with blooms from plants of the mid-Atlantic area; a **Butterfly Garden** that employs trees, shrubs and flowers such as primrose, milkweed and coneflower to attract the colourful winged insects, as well as hummingbirds; and a **First Ladies Water Garden** built around a fountain meant to symbolize the various accomplishments of the wives of the presidents.

Bartholdi Fountain

South of the Botanic Garden, across Independence Avenue at 1st Street SW, stands the 30ft-high **Bartholdi Fountain**, submitted by French sculptor Frédéric-Auguste Bartholdi to the 1876 Centennial Exhibition in Philadelphia. (A decade later Bartholdi would create the Statue of Liberty.) Congress bought the fountain in 1877 for display on the Mall, where its original gas lamps – illuminated at night – made it a popular evening hangout. Moved to this site in 1932, it's often deserted today, but it's as good a spot as any to catch your breath before taking the long walk down the Mall.

East Capitol neighbourhood

All the other notable buildings and institutions of Capitol Hill – like the Supreme Court and Library of Congress – lie on the east side of the Capitol, within half a dozen blocks of one another. Here, in the charming and historic **East Capitol neighbourhood**, amid the grand old Georgian and Federal townhouses, a few historic old homes, such as the Sewall-Belmont House, add to the picturesque setting, making it a good spot for a daytime walk – at night, the further you drift from the Capitol, the dicier the neighbourhoods get.

US Supreme Court

The third branch of American government, the judiciary, has its apex at the **Supreme Court of the United States**, 1st St and Maryland Ave NE (Mon–Fri 9am–4.30pm; ☎202/479-3211, ⓦwww.supremecourtus.gov; Union Station or Capitol South Metro). Not only is the court the final word on what is and isn't constitutional, it's also the nation's arbiter for disputes between states, between the federal government and states, between federal and state judges, and between individuals appealing all kinds of legal decisions – from boundary disputes to death sentences. Since it was established at the Constitutional Convention of 1787, the Court has functioned as both the guardian and interpreter of the **Constitution**, but it only really began flexing its muscles in the early 1800s under the sway of Chief Justice John Marshall (see box, p.82). Its familiar motto is "Equal Justice For All" – the legend inscribed upon the architrave above the double row of eight columns facing 1st Street.

Inside, the main corridor – known as the **Great Hall** – has a superb carved and painted ceiling, white walls lined with marble columns, and busts of all the former chief justices. At the end of the corridor is the surprisingly compact **Court Chamber**, with damask drapes and a moulded plaster ceiling done up in gold leaf, flanked by more marble columns. A frieze runs around all four sides, its relief panels depicting various legal themes, allegorical figures, and ancient and modern lawgivers. When in session, the chief justice, currently John Roberts, sits in the centre of the **bench** (below the clock), with the most senior justice on his right (left as you face the bench) and the next in precedence on his left; the rest sit in similar alternating fashion so that the most junior justice sits on the far left. The chairs for each justice are made in the Court's own carpentry shop, and the Court even has its own police force.

You used to be allowed to reach the ground floor via the building's wondrous **spiral staircases**, but in today's more security-obsessed era, you'll have to content yourself with an elevator ride. The lower floor has its own Great Hall (overseen by a mighty statue of Chief Justice Marshall lounging in his chair) and a permanent exhibition about the Court. A free, short movie fills you in on the Court's legal

The supremacy of the Supreme Court

The **Supreme Court** was established by the Constitution to oversee the balance between the federal government and the states, and between the legislative and executive branches of government. By tradition, it comprises nine justices, who are by law appointed by the president and approved by the Senate. Once approved, the justices are in for life and can be removed only by impeachment and (successful) trial by Congress – which has never happened.

The Court (and the associated system of district courts) convened for the first time in February 1790. At the end of the following year, the ratification of the **Bill of Rights** in effect gave the Supreme Court an additional role: to defend the liberties enshrined in the Bill, directing the country as to what was and wasn't constitutional. However, it wasn't until 1803 and the case of *Marbury v Madison* that the Court's power of **judicial review** – the ability to declare a law or action of Congress or the president unconstitutional – was established, and the court with **John Marshall** at the helm became an institution unto itself. Since then, the Supreme Court has repeatedly shaped the country's social and political legacies by ruling on and, in the following cases, upholding the constitutionality of slavery (in the 1857 *Dred Scott* case), segregation (1896's *Plessy v Ferguson*), desegregation (1954's *Brown v Board of Education*), abortion rights (1973's *Roe v Wade*) and freedom of the press (1971's *New York Times Co. v the United States*, over whether the *Times* had the right to publish the leaked Pentagon Papers, which revealed expanded US involvement in Vietnam).

Whichever way the Court rules, and despite its firm roots in the Constitution, it depends ultimately on the mood of the people for its authority. If it produces opinions that are overwhelmingly opposed by inferior courts, or by the president or Congress, there's not much it can do to enforce them. Indeed, Congress has the constitutional right (Article 3, Section 2) to **restrict the Court's jurisdiction** – a prerogative rarely taken, since in the battle for public opinion, Congress rarely wins when opposed to the perceived supremacy of the court.

and political background, while architectural notes, sketches and photos trace the history of the building itself.

Visiting the Court

The Court is **in session** from October to June. From the beginning of October to the end of April, arguments are heard every Monday, Tuesday and Wednesday from 10am to noon and 1pm to 3pm on occasion. (In May and June, the Court works out its rulings and presents them to the public.) The sessions, which almost always last one hour per case, are **open to the public** on a first-come, first-served basis. Arrive by 8.30am if you really want one of the 150 seats, and keep in mind that for some high-profile cases, such as those involving abortion rights, civil liberties or freedom of speech, people sometimes wait in line overnight. More casual visitors simply join a separate line, happy to settle for a three-minute stroll through the standing gallery. When Court is not in session, guides give free **lectures** in the Court Chamber (Mon–Fri 9.30am–3.30pm; hourly on the half-hour).

Sewall-Belmont House

North of the Supreme Court, across Constitution Avenue at 2nd Street, is the red-brick townhouse known as the **Sewall–Belmont House**, 144 Constitution Ave NE (☎202/546-1210, ⓦwww.sewallbelmont.org; Union Station Metro), one of the oldest residences in the city. The dainty building was built in 1800 by Robert Sewall and rented in 1801 to Albert Gallatin, Treasury secretary to presidents

Jefferson and Madison. Gallatin participated in negotiations for the Louisiana Purchase (1803), which was signed in one of the front rooms, and the Treaty of Ghent, which ended the War of 1812.

In 1929, the house was sold to the **National Woman's Party** and was home for many years to Alice Paul, the party's founder and author of the 1923 Equal Rights Amendment. The house still serves as party headquarters and maintains a museum and gallery dedicated to the women's and suffrage movements. A short tour makes much of the period furnishings, and the carriage house contains the country's earliest feminist library. Portraits, busts and photographs of all the best-known activists adorn the halls and walls, starting in the lobby with sculptor Adelaide Johnson's busts of Susan B. Anthony, Elizabeth Cady Stanton and Lucretia Mott, the trio whom Johnson would memorialize with her collective sculpture *Suffrage Monument* in the Capitol (see p.78).

The building was closed for restoration at the time of research; contact the phone number and website above for information on its reopening.

Folger Shakespeare Library

The renowned **Folger Shakespeare Library**, 201 E Capitol St, on the south side of the Supreme Court (Mon–Sat 10am–5pm; ☎202/544-4600, ⓦwww.folger .edu; Union Station or Capitol South Metro), has a split architectural personality. The white-marble facade is decorated in Art Deco with geometric window grilles, and panel reliefs depict scenes from the Bard's plays. The look inside, however, is quite different: a dark oak-panelled Elizabethan **Great Hall** features carved lintels, stained glass, Tudor roses and a sculpted ceiling.

Founded in 1932, the Folger holds more than 600,000 books, manuscripts, paintings and engravings – making it the world's third-largest repository of books in English printed prior to the mid-seventeenth century   only a fraction of which focuses strictly on Shakespeare. The **Great Hall** displays changing exhibitions about the playwright and various historical and literary themes. The reproduction-Elizabethan **Folger Theatre** annually hosts a trio of performances, usually two by the Bard and another by a contemporary such as Marlowe, and in the same theatre are regular lectures and readings as well as medieval and Renaissance music concerts. Finally, an Elizabethan **garden** on the east lawn grows herbs and flowers common in the sixteenth century, while the **gift shop** sells everything from assorted editions of the Stratford lad's plays to jokey T-shirts based on Shakespearean quotations.

Try to visit when a free ninety-minute **guided tour** is offered (Mon–Fri 11am & 3pm, Sat 11am & 1pm). The **library** itself – another sixteenth-century repro-duction – is designed for registered scholars and open to the public only during the Folger's annual celebration of Shakespeare's birthday (usually the Saturday nearest April 23).

Library of Congress

The **Library of Congress**, 1st St SE at Independence Ave (hours vary; see each building below for individual hours; ☎202/707-8000, ⓦwww.loc.gov; Capitol South Metro), is the nation's official copyright office and the world's largest library (it's said that, on average, ten items per minute are added to its holdings). Books are just part of its unimaginably vast collection: 142 million items, from books, maps and manuscripts to movies, musical instruments and photographs, are kept on 745 miles of shelving in closed stacks spread out over three buildings – where they stay, as the Library of Congress does not circulate its materials beyond the complex, except to members of Congress and other public officials.

After the British burned the Capitol and its nascent national library in 1814, **Thomas Jefferson** offered his considerable **personal library** as a replacement; this collection comprised more than six thousand volumes, which Jefferson had accumulated during fifty years of service at home and abroad, picking up, he said, "everything which related to America". A year later, Congress voted to buy this stupendous private collection for almost $24,000 – about $300,000 today.

In 1866 the library acquired the thousands of books hitherto held by the **Smithsonian Institution**, and in 1870 it was declared the national copyright library. Not surprisingly, the library soon outgrew its original home, and in 1897 the exuberantly eclectic **Thomas Jefferson Building** (Mon–Sat 8.30am–4.30pm) opened across from the Capitol, complete with domed octagonal Reading Room and adorned with hundreds of mosaics, murals and sculptures. The building was projected to have enough space to house the library until 1975, but by the 1930s it was already too full. In the surrounding blocks, the **John Adams Building** (Mon, Wed & Thurs 8.30am–9.30pm, Tues, Fri & Sat 8.30am–5pm) was erected in 1939, followed by the **James Madison Memorial Building** (Mon–Fri 8.30am–9.30pm, Sat 8.30am–5pm) in 1980.

Visiting the Library

The **Adams** and **Madison** buildings both have their charms, but the latter really appeals for its **Mary Pickford Theater**, where you're likely to see lectures, exhibits, films, seminars and other cultural fare (also offered on other floors). Yet with its full range of activities, including musical concerts in its **Coolidge Auditorium**, the magnificent **Jefferson Building** is the library's unquestioned centrepiece. At its **visitor centre** (ground-level entrance on 1st St SE) you can learn about the building's highlights and pick up a calendar of upcoming events. You're allowed to wander around inside, but you'd do well to catch one of the free library **tours** (Mon–Sat 10.30am, 11.30am, 1.30pm, 2.30pm & 3.30pm, Sat last tour at 2.30pm).

This Renaissance Revival structure is based around a **Great Hall** that is duly awe-inspiring, rich with marble walls and numerous medallions, inscriptions, murals and inlaid mosaics. A treasured copy of the Gutenberg Bible is on display, while upstairs the visitors' gallery overlooks the octagonal marble-and-stained-glass **Main Reading Room**, a beautiful galleried space whose columns support a dome 125ft high. The mural in the dome canopy, *The Progress of Civilization*, represents the twelve nations supposed to have contributed most to world knowledge.

The library's huge collection is showcased on the second floor in the **main gallery**, where periodic exhibitions are based around broad subjects, with library materials showcased in themed cabinets. It's hard to predict exactly what you'll see, but previous displays have included items such as Walt Whitman's Civil War notebooks, the original typescript of Martin Luther King Jr's "I Have a Dream" speech, a copy of Francis Scott Key's *Star-Spangled Banner*, first editions of Dante and Machiavelli, and a multitude of music scores, historic photographs, early recordings, magazines and baseball cards, as well as colonial money bearing the inscription "To counterfeit is death".

Using the Library

Anyone over 18 carrying photo ID can use the library, and some one million readers and visitors do so each year. To find what you're looking for, head for the information desks or touch-screen computers in the Jefferson or Madison buildings. The **Main Reading Room** in the Jefferson Building is just one of 22 reading rooms, and the rules are the same in each. This is a research library, which means you can't take books out; in some reading rooms you have to order what you want from the stacks. You can also access papers, maps and musical scores, and the advent of the **National Digital Library** means that many now come in machine-readable format (the desks in the Main Reading Room are wired for laptops and there are CD-ROM indexes). Major exhibitions, as well as prints, photographs, films and speeches, are also available online. For research advice, call ℡ 202/707-6500; for reading room hours and locations, call ℡ 202/707-6400.

Pennsylvania Avenue SE and around

To most visitors, the section of **Pennsylvania Avenue** running southeast from the Capitol will be much less familiar than the stretch running northwest from it, where the presidential inaugural parade is held. Still, over the course of six blocks or so, you can find some of DC's more appealing ethnic restaurants and noteworthy bars, mainly devoted to sports and politics. Although you shouldn't wander around the district south of E Street on your own after dark, two churches in this area stand out and can be safely visited in daylight. The utilitarian red-brick **Ebenezer United Methodist Church**, 420 D St SE (Mon–Fri 10am–3pm, Sun service 9am), has the neighbourhood's oldest black congregation. Founded in 1827, the church was the site of DC's first public school for black people; it was a short-lived affair (1864–65), but a pioneering one, since the teachers were paid out of federal funds. Further south, **Christ Church**, at 620 G St SE (Mon–Fri 9am–4pm, Sun service 11am), is an early work (1806) by Capitol architect Benjamin Latrobe, notable mainly to architecture buffs for its charming Gothic Revival facade, but also the site of regular Episcopal worship by early American presidents. Ten blocks east, many notable politicians and others can be found at the Christ Church-run **Congressional Cemetery**, 1801 E St SE (Mon–Fri 9am–5pm; tours April–Oct Sat 11am; ℡ 202/543-0539, ⓦ www.congressionalcemetery .org), among them great Washington architect Robert Mills, marching-band composer John Philip Sousa, jovial House speaker Tip O'Neill and notorious FBI director J. Edgar Hoover.

Eastern Market

The classic **Eastern Market**, 306 7th St SE (Tues–Fri 7am–7pm, Sat 7am–6pm, Sun 9am–5pm), was built in 1873 and has been in operation since the nineteenth century. Designed by Adolph Cluss, the building had operated continuously since its opening, until April 2007, when a **fire** caused considerable damage and closed the place down. It reopened in 2009 to glorious effect, with a better layout, more light and generally a more welcoming atmosphere. A welter of vendors does roaring business in the market, selling seafood, deli meats, sides of beef and other foodstuffs. On the weekend, on the streets outside the market proper, a **farmers' market** and **arts and crafts market** (Sat & Sun 9am–5pm) takes place, where you can buy produce and flowers, or antiques and junk. Back along 7th Street, delis, coffee shops, antiques stores and clothes shops make this area one of the Hill's most appealing hangouts.

East Capitol Street and Stanton Park

East Capitol Street, one of the city's four axes and one of the first streets on the Hill to be settled, starts between the Supreme Court and the Library of Congress's Jefferson Building. For its first ten or so blocks, its wide, tree-lined reach is peppered with wooden and brick townhouses, some dating from before the Civil War, others sporting the trademark late Victorian turrets and "rusticated" (roughened) stonework.

The typical row house at 316 A St NE was home to black orator and writer **Frederick Douglass** when he first moved to the capital in 1870 to take up the editorship of the *New National Era*, a newspaper championing the rights of African Americans. His family owned the adjacent property, too, where Douglass lived with his first wife, Anna, until 1877, when they moved to the grander Cedar Hill in Anacostia. The complex is now home to a nonprofit institution that shares space with the **Frederick Douglass Museum** (tours by appointment only at ☎202/547-4273, ⓦwww.nahc.org/fd/index.html), and has done a marvellous job of restoring the home to its nineteenth-century splendour, with rich cabinetry and other woodwork, elegant Victorian chairs and chandeliers, a courtyard, art galleries and a grand piano. From here, it's just a few blocks north to **Stanton Park**, named after Lincoln's secretary of war during the Civil War but highlighted by an equestrian statue of Revolutionary War general **Nathanael Greene**, who had a significant role in the 1781 battle of Yorktown, which basically guaranteed America's independence from Britain.

Lincoln Park

In 1876, on the eleventh anniversary of Abraham Lincoln's assassination, the slain sixteenth president was honoured in **Lincoln Park**, further along East Capitol Street between 11th and 13th streets. To contemporary eyes the **Emancipation Memorial** may seem a bit paternalistic – the bronze statue portrays Lincoln, proclamation in one hand, standing over a kneeling slave, exhorting him to rise – but it was actually daring for its day, funded mainly by the contributions of black soldiers who had fought for the Union. Working from a photograph, sculptor Thomas Ball re-created in the slave the features of **Archer Alexander**, the last man to be seized under the Fugitive Slave Act, which empowered slave-owners to capture escaped slaves even if they fled to free states. Under Lincoln's gaze, Alexander is breaking his own shackles.

Facing Lincoln, across the park, is a memorial to **Mary McLeod Bethune**, educator, women's rights leader and special adviser to Franklin Delano Roosevelt. Robert Berks, also responsible for the 8ft head of JFK in the Kennedy Centre (see p.112), depicts Bethune leaning on her cane, reaching out to two children. (Across town near Logan Circle stands another memorial to Bethune, the Bethune Council House; see p.137.)

Union Station

On the border of the north side of Capitol Hill and the eastern fringe of Downtown is DC's magnificent **Union Station**, 50 Massachusetts Ave NE, a huge Beaux-Arts building that glimmers with skylights, marble detail and statuary, culminating in a 96ft-high coffered ceiling whose model was no less than ancient Rome's Baths of Diocletian. On the east side of the building are connections to most of DC's train and transport systems (see p.137); and inside there are stores, restaurants, car rental agencies and ticket counters.

For five decades, Union Station sat at the head of an expansive railway network that linked the country to its capital: hundreds of thousands of people arrived in the city by train, catching their first glimpse of the Capitol dome through the station's great arched doors. Incoming presidents arrived at Union Station by train for their inaugurations – Truman was the last – and were met in the specially installed Presidential Waiting Room (now a diner); some, like FDR and Eisenhower, left by train in a coffin after lying in state at the Capitol. By 1958, though, with the gradual depletion of train services, Union Station was left unkempt and underfunded, and left under threat of demolition. That didn't happen, but the structure wasn't restored until 1988. The station stands at the centre of a grand redevelopment plan that was designed to resurrect a formerly neglected part of the city, and it has done so to some degree.

It's also worth taking a stroll outside in Union Station Plaza, the landscaped approach to the station that stretches all the way down to the Capitol grounds. The **Columbus Memorial Fountain** in front of the station was dedicated in 1912 and features a statue of the Genovese explorer standing on the prow of a ship, between two lions and male and female figures representing the old and new worlds. A replica of Philadelphia's **Liberty Bell** stands nearby.

National Postal Museum

Built between 1911 and 1914, the **City Post Office**, Massachusetts Ave NE at N Capitol Ave (daily 10am–5.30pm; free; Union Station Metro), was a working post office until 1986, when it was renovated at a cost of $200 million, in part to house the **National Postal Museum**, along with restaurants and retailers. Before you descend to the lower-level galleries, take a quick look at the building itself, whose white Italian marble reaches are some of the most impressive in the city. Also, look up and read how the postal service is not only "Carrier of News and Knowledge", but also "Messenger of Sympathy and Love", "Consoler of the Lonely" and "Enlarger of the Common Life", among other questionable claims.

The collection

The **collection** includes sixteen million artefacts, but since many of these are stamps, only a few of which are on display, it's not that daunting a show. Indeed, the museum's strength is in its selectivity, judiciously placing the history of the mail service within the context of the history of the United States itself.

Escalators down to the galleries dump you in "**Moving the Mail**", which features soaring models of early mail planes – from a 1911 Wiseman-Cooke craft that vaguely resembles the Wright Flyer to a 1939 Stinson Reliant monoplane – as well as an 1851 mail coach with bourgeois riders inside and a walk-through Southern Pacific railcar with artefacts on display and a video. Beyond here is "**Binding the Nation**", which begins with the **first postal route**, the seventeenth-century King's Best Highway between New York and Boston – a dark and spooky tour through a primeval wood. The story continues with small models of steamships and clipper ships, a crude "mud wagon" that did the literal dirty work of nineteenth-century mail delivery, and the saddles and spittoons, among other artefacts, of the relay-rider system of the famed **Pony Express**.

Elsewhere in the museum are other oddments related to postal-service history. Only in the "**Philatelic Gallery**" do you get a look at the museum's philatelic collection (up until this point, there's barely a stamp in sight). Here you'll find some splendid curiosities as well as frequently rotated exhibitions; you might see anything from ultra-rare vintage stamps to detailed coverage of famous series, like Ducks of America.

Before leaving, you can print out your own free, personalized **postcard** from the machines in the lobby, then buy a stamp in the shop and mail it home.

Southwest Waterfront and Southeast DC

S outh of the Mall begins a series of neighbourhoods that lie along or around the shoreline of the Potomac and Anacostia rivers, united by little else than the accident of geography. The **Waterfront** district, or **Southwest Waterfront**, is among the most prominent, with a range of Washington's most historic buildings as well as many modern complexes. In the vicinity are the United States Holocaust Memorial Museum and the Bureau of Printing and Engraving, immediately south of the Mall, and the Potomac waterfront's marinas and fish market. If you venture further east, into the dicier sections of **Southeast Washington**, you'll find the US Navy Museum and its cache of nautical artefacts, the baseball stadium Nationals Park; and, across the Anacostia River in Anacostia, the Anacostia Community Museum and the Frederick Douglass National Historic Site. Much of Southwest Waterfront around the Potomac's Washington Channel is accessible by public transport, but a bigger effort will be required to reach the limited attractions of Southeast DC. Visitors are advised to head directly to the individual sights listed there – and then come straight back again – as this part of town is not tourist-friendly, and to be avoided at night.

Some history

For a century after the city was founded, DC's nearest accessible riverbanks (in today's West Potomac Park) were too marshy and malarial to develop. The only practicable wharves and piers were those built along the Channel, but they, too, stagnated and began to flourish only after the Tidal Basin was created in 1882.

Despite the undeveloped character of the nearby river, Southwest thrived as a fashionable neighbourhood in the early nineteenth century because it was close to the Capitol. But in the 1870s, the railway arrived and sliced its way through the area, diminishing its social cachet and causing the wealthy to flee north. The people left behind were mostly white European immigrants and poor blacks who worked at the goods yards, storage depots and wharves. The work eventually dried up, the swamp-ridden housing became increasingly dilapidated, and by the 1920s the area had degenerated into a slum.

In the 1950s Congress decided to end the squalor once and for all, not with any sort of social investment, but simply by demolishing huge swaths of the neighbourhood – up to 5000 buildings in all – displacing thousands of families to make room for behemoth federal agencies like the Department of Agriculture. More buildings were added in the 1960s and 70s, and the rather haphazardly

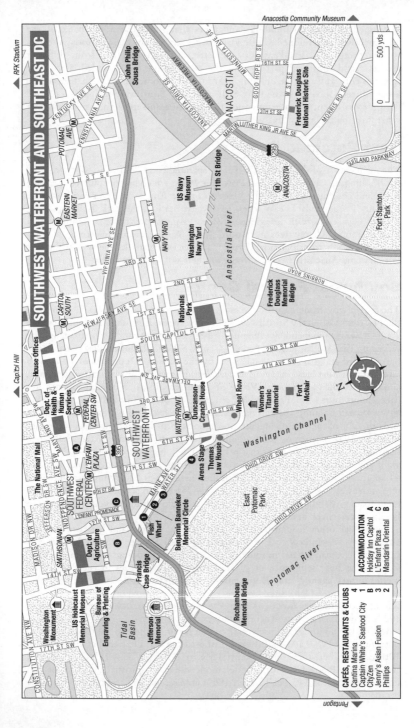

Anacostia Community Museum

RFK Stadium

Capitol Hill

Pentagon

SOUTHWEST WATERFRONT AND SOUTHEAST DC

John Philip Sousa Bridge

KENTUCKY AVE SE

PENNSYLVANIA AVE SE

POTOMAC AVE

ANACOSTIA

MINNESOTA AVE SE

GOOD HOPE RD SE

16TH ST SE

W ST SE

13TH ST SE

Frederick Douglass National Historic Site

MORRIS RD SE

ANACOSTIA DRIVE SE

ANACOSTIA FREEWAY

MARTIN LUTHER KING JR AVE SE

SUITLAND PARKWAY

EASTERN MARKET

11TH ST SE

11th St Bridge

395

ANACOSTIA

Fort Stanton Park

VIRGINIA AVE SE

3RD ST SE

M ST SE

US Navy Museum

NAVY YARD

Washington Navy Yard

Anacostia River

ROBBINS ROAD

Frederick Douglass Memorial Bridge

CAPITOL SOUTH

NEW JERSEY AVE SE

2ND ST SE

1ST ST SE

SOUTH CAPITOL CT

Nationals Park

O ST SW

2ND ST SW

4TH AVE SW

House Offices

The National Mall

Dept. of Health & Human Services

FEDERAL CENTER SW

SOUTHWEST WATERFRONT

3RD ST SW

I ST SW

K ST SW

M ST SW

N ST SW

DELAWARE AVE SW

Duncanson-Cranch House

4TH ST SW

Wheat Row

Fort McNair

Women's Titanic Memorial

'Z

L'ENFANT PLAZA

FEDERAL CENTER SW

L'ENFANT PROMENADE

G ST SW

WATER ST

MAINE AVE

6TH ST SW

7TH ST SW

Arena Stage

Thomas Law House

Washington Channel

OHIO DRIVE SW

INDEPENDENCE AVE SW

MARYLAND AVE SW

395

SOUTHWEST FEDERAL CENTER

Dept. of Agriculture

SMITHSONIAN

12TH ST SW

D ST SW

Fish Wharf

Benjamin Banneker Memorial Circle

East Potomac Park

OHIO DRIVE SW

JEFFERSON DR NW

MADISON DR NW

14TH ST SW

Francis Case Bridge

Rochambeau Memorial Bridge

Potomac River

CONSTITUTION AVE NW

17TH ST SW

Washington Monument

US Holocaust Memorial Museum

Bureau of Engraving & Printing

Tidal Basin

Jefferson Memorial

3

SOUTHWEST WATERFRONT AND SOUTHEAST DC

0   500 yds

ACCOMMODATION
Holiday Inn Capitol	A
L'Enfant Plaza	C
Mandarin Oriental	B

CAFÉS, RESTAURANTS & CLUBS
Cantina Marina	4
Captain White's Seafood City	1
CityZen	B
Jenny's Asian Fusion	3
Phillips	2

developed commercial buildings and piers that lined the north bank of the Channel were redeveloped to lure visitors. As any visitor can tell, today the area is something of a Frankenstein's monster, stitched together from different aesthetic and historical parts – and the experiment hasn't ended, with new schemes constantly on the drawing board to make something of what should be a magnificent section of the city. Still, much of Southwest seems like a failed design experiment, with grim concrete hardscape and modernist malls dotting what must be DC's least lively quarter.

East Potomac Park

The main course of the Potomac River is separated from Southwest Waterfront by the Washington Channel and **East Potomac Park**, which begins south of the Tidal Basin and continues down to the junction of the Anacostia River south of Fort McNair. Though it lacks easy access to a Metro station, the park itself is pleasant enough – walkable, with nice views across to Virginia, plus there are tennis courts, fishing grounds, cherry trees and a public pool. At the park's southern tip and just across the water from National Airport, **Hains Point** marks the spot where the Potomac and Anacostia rivers converge on their way to the Atlantic.

Southwest Federal Center

The federal government's grunt work is done in concrete fortresses just south of the National Mall in the **Southwest Federal Center**. Almost all the agencies here are bounded by Independence Avenue, 3rd Street, E Street and 14th Street, and are served by two Metro stations: Federal Centre SW and L'Enfant Plaza. The block between 3rd and 4th streets is taken up by the hulking **Department of Health and Human Services** – the only federal building in the area open to the public, and home to the government's **Voice of America** offices, 330 Independence Ave (free 45min tours Mon–Fri noon & 3pm, reservations required; ℗202/303-4990, ⓦwww.voatour.com); the entrance is around the back, on C Street between 3rd and 4th. One of the world's biggest international broadcasters, the VOA was established in 1942 as part of the war effort and given its own charter in 1960 to transmit programmes overseas that promote US values and culture. Guided tours walk you through the radio and TV studios from where broadcasts are made in 44 languages and transmitted to 115 million listeners in 120 countries. One place you won't hear the VOA, however, is in the US: a 1948 act prohibits the government from proselytizing to its own citizens by radio (though if you really want to hear, you can check out a broadcast online).

Southwest's other federal buildings occupy a no-man's-land between 4th and 14th streets. Architects such as **Edward Durrell Stone**, **Marcel Breuer** and **I.M. Pei** have had a hand in some of the imperious buildings, plazas and streetscapes. The only semblance of old-fashioned style emerges in the oldest (and westernmost) agency, the **Department of Agriculture** (Independence Ave between 12th and 14th); sited here since 1905, the original building on the north side of Independence Avenue is connected by slender arches to the much larger 1930s Neoclassical structure across the avenue.

Beyond the buildings themselves, the main focus of the Federal Center's development in the 1960s and 1970s was **L'Enfant Plaza**, at D Street between 9th and 10th streets, where there's now a central Metro station. It's easy to feel a twinge of sympathy for Pierre L'Enfant – alone among the city's spiritual founders, he gets not a monument in DC but a barren 1960s concrete square and subway station as his memorial.

United States Holocaust Memorial Museum

One of the city's most disturbing and unforgettable sites is the **United States Holocaust Memorial Museum**, 14th St between C St and Independence Ave SW (daily 10am–5.30pm; ℡ 202/488-0400, ⓦ www.ushmm.org; Smithsonian Metro), which presents an intimate look at the persecution and murder of six million Jews by the Nazis. The solemn mood is reflected by the museum's stark architecture and evocative design: half-lit chambers, a floor of ghetto cobblestones, an obscenely cramped barracks building, and an external roofline that resembles the guard towers of a concentration camp. You don't need tickets to see the special exhibitions or to enter the museum and the interactive Wexner Learning Centre, but between March and August you do need tickets with fixed entry times (between 10am and 3.45pm) to get into the permanent exhibit, "The Holocaust". **Tickets** are free but limited to four per person. You can pick them up from 10am daily at the 14th Street entrance; they're usually sold out by mid-morning. Advance tickets can be purchased for a dollar fee through the website.

The Holocaust exhibition spans the museum's second, third and fourth floors; you start at the top and work your way down. The main galleries are not considered suitable for children under the age of 11, but the feature "**Remember the Children: Daniel's Story**" is designed for those over the age of 8, following the story of a young boy's witness to the events of Nazi Germany. The 14th Street entrance is at first-floor level, where you'll find the **information desk**, children's exhibit and shop. On the lower level, the moving **Children's Tile Wall** is composed of three thousand panels made by US schoolchildren to honour the 1.5 million European children slaughtered by the Nazis.

Fourth floor

The first rooms on the fourth floor use storyboards, newspaper articles and film clips to chronicle the "**Nazi Assault**" and rise to power from 1933 to 1939. The presentation begins with a direct shock: horrifying images of concentration camps and victims gathered from US Army archives in 1945, the year the camps were finally liberated. From there the exhibition jumps back a dozen years to the beginning of the terror. Assuming state power in 1933, the Nazi party quickly goes to work marginalizing and oppressing the Jews of Germany, and what begins as a boycott of Jewish businesses and book-burning quickly leads to the organized looting of Jewish shops and the parading of German women who had "defiled" their race by associating with Jews. Anyone who didn't fit the Nazi ideal, like gays (who were forced to wear an identifying pink triangle), black people, gypsies, Jehovah's Witnesses and Freemasons, was persecuted and imprisoned as an "enemy of the state". Beyond a glass wall etched with the names of the hundreds of Eastern European Jewish communities wiped off the map forever, a towering stack of photographs from 1890 to 1941 records the breadth of life in just one of them – the *shtetl* (community) of Eishishok, in what's now Lithuania.

Third floor

The third floor covers the World War II era of Hitler's "**Final Solution**", with prominence given to the gassing of Jews at a death camp in Poland in December 1941, one of the earliest massacres. A few months before, some 33,000 Jews had been slaughtered at Babi Yar in Kiev following the German invasion of the Ukraine capital. In the Warsaw uprising of 1943, Jews fought the Nazis for a month despite having no real weapons or supplies. Eventually all the surviving Jews were brought to the camps in packed freight cars; you can walk through one here that stands on railway tracks taken from the camp at Treblinka.

The most harrowing part of the exhibition deals with life and death in the concentration camps. A pile of blankets, umbrellas, scissors, cutlery and other personal effects taken from the hundreds of thousands of prisoners underscores the fact that the prisoners had expected to be put to work, but instead most were gassed within hours. A re-created barracks building from Auschwitz provides the backdrop for the spoken memories of some survivors, as well as a shocking film of gruesome medical experiments carried out on selected prisoners. The third floor ends with photographic coverage of the Eishishok *shtetl* and its experience with the Final Solution, when a town and community that had existed for more than nine hundred years were summarily destroyed in just two days.

Second floor

As the Nazi front collapsed across Europe during 1945, many groups became involved in efforts to aid the Jews. The **"Last Chapter"** on the second floor recounts the heroism of individuals such as Raoul Wallenberg (whose name now graces the street where the museum sits) and the response of certain governments (the Danish in particular). Much of the floor offers multimedia testimony of camp survivors and details the Allied forces' liberation of the camps; film reels show German guards being forced to bury mountains of bodies in mass graves, while locals were made to tour the camps to witness the extent of the horror. Although Nazis were later prosecuted during the Nuremberg trials, most of those responsible for the planning, maintenance and administration of the camps were never tried; some were treated leniently or acquitted altogether.

Bureau of Engraving and Printing

The bland bureaucratic buildings found east of 14th Street and south of Independence Avenue are virtually indistinguishable from one another, with one exception – the **Bureau of Engraving and Printing** at 14th and C sts SW (☎202/874-2330 or 1-866-874-2330, ⓦwww.moneyfactory.com; Smithsonian Metro), where US currency, government securities and postage stamps are created (though coins are produced by the US Mint – not in DC). The Bureau offers one of DC's most popular tours; each year nearly half a million people take the free twenty-minute tour of what is, effectively, a large printing plant, cranking out millions of dollars in currency every day, and $120 billion a year. Indeed, the making of US currency is a surprisingly low-tech operation; engravers work in teams on each bill with dyes to create intaglio steel plates, from which the bills are printed in sheets of 32, checked for defects, and loaded into large barrows. On a separate press, they're then overprinted with serial numbers and seals, sliced up into single bills, and stacked into "bricks" of four thousand notes before being sent out to the twelve Federal Reserve districts, which issue the notes to local banks.

Between May and August you must pick up tickets for **tours** in advance, but you can, and should, start waiting in line at 8am, as tickets are often gone by 11.30am. The rest of the year you can show up later, just before 10am, without tickets, though you'll still have to wait in line. Tours run every 15 minutes from 9 to 10.45am and from 12.30 to 2pm, with additional summer hours from 2 to 3.45pm and from 5 to 7pm. A forty-minute Congressional/VIP tour providing an in-depth, behind-the-scenes look at the plant is available for US citizens who make arrangements through their representative's office (Mon–Fri every 15min 4–4.45pm; also May–Aug Mon–Fri 8.15am & 8.45am). You can also skip the tour and just drop by the **visitor centre** (daily: March 8.30am–3.30pm, April–Aug 8.30am–7.30pm), perhaps to purchase an overpriced bag of shredded currency that you can send to the folks back home.

Benjamin Banneker Memorial Circle

From the printing plant, following D Street east to 10th Street and south over the freeway, you'll reach **Benjamin Banneker Memorial Circle**, where there's a viewpoint over the Washington Channel and the rest of the Waterfront. A memorial and fountain here honour Banneker, an African American born in Maryland in 1731 to a former slave. Almost entirely self-taught, Banneker distinguished himself as a mathematician, clockmaker, astronomer and inventor before being invited, at the age of 60, to assist Andrew Ellicott in surveying the land for the new capital. He also published several editions of a successful almanac and spent the last years before his death in 1806 corresponding with Thomas Jefferson, who he hoped would abandon his prejudices against African Americans. The Memorial Circle occupies freeway-caged land on the so-called **L'Enfant Promenade**, which connects L'Enfant Plaza with the Waterfront.

The Washington Channel and around

The developed shoreline of the Potomac's **Washington Channel** is accessible by Metro (Waterfront station, at 4th and M sts SW). If they're not coming to dock their boat in one of the upscale marinas in the area, most people come here to eat seafood at one of the scattered **restaurants** along Maine Avenue or Water Street SW, west of 7th; all have terraces and patios with views across to East Potomac Park. Otherwise, the main attraction is the **Fish Wharf** (daily 8am–9pm), also known as the Maine Avenue Fish Market. Floating on permanently moored steel barges, this is the oldest continuously operating fish market in the country, and haggling is encouraged. Impressive displays include huge trays of Chesapeake Bay fish, shrimp, clams, oysters and, especially, Maryland blue crabs, which are available live or steamed.

Further down Maine Avenue, east of 7th Street, the recently renovated **Arena Stage** (see p.234) is one of the most prestigious playhouses in the city. Continuing south, you'll come to the **Thomas Law House**, 1252 6th St SW (c.1794–96), one of DC's oldest surviving townhouses, and the **Duncanson–Cranch House**, around the corner at 468 N St SW; both date from the same era and offer a humble reminder of the tasteful Federal style that used to permeate this neighbourhood before 1960s urban renewal was allowed to run amok. If you cut past here to 4th Street, you can see **Wheat Row** (1315–1321 4th St SW), a strip of Federal houses built in 1794 and striking for their elegant early American design. They were all built on speculation, in the city's first real-estate bubble.

Channel and river collide south of here with the spit of land occupied by the off-limits **Fort McNair**. Fortified in 1791, the fort became home to the **Washington Arsenal** in 1804, and inside, at the **US Penitentiary**, the conspirators in the Lincoln assassination were imprisoned, tried and executed. Just outside the fort at Washington Channel Park, at 4th and P sts SW, the **Women's Titanic Memorial** commemorates the men who gave up their lifeboat spaces (and, thus, their lives) to women and children on the fateful 1912 voyage of the *Titanic*.

Along the Anacostia River

Unlike those along the Potomac, the neighbourhoods along the **Anacostia River** in Southeast DC have been mostly starved of redevelopment money, with a few exceptions. The new **Nationals Park** has been smartly built thanks to DC's enthusiasm for sport, and the **Washington Navy Yard** has always been well funded, as an early bulwark of America's defence infrastructure. The other major attractions of the area – such as the **Frederick Douglass National Historic Site** across the river in Anacostia, and the **Anacostia Community Museum** – exist in blighted neighbourhoods that most tourists steer well clear of, but are deserving of a visit if you take care to come by day in a taxi.

Nationals Park

The glitzy **Nationals Park** (Navy Yard Metro), sitting at a bend in the Anacostia River and a bend along Capitol Street SE, is a $600 million showpiece for baseball (see p.246) that seats more than 41,000 rabid souls. From the upper decks you can spot some of the landmarks along the Mall, and the sightlines are generally good. Otherwise, beyond sports and a smattering of development around the park, there's not much to see here.

Washington Navy Yard and the US Navy Museum

The **Washington Navy Yard**, at 805 Kidder Breese St SE (Mon–Fri 9am–5pm, Sat & Sun 10am–5pm; ☎ 202/433-6826; free; Navy Yard Metro), was one of the first naval yards in the country. Established in 1799, it has been in continuous operation ever since, excluding an interruption that began in 1812, when the commander burned the base to prevent the invading British Army from capturing it. Shipbuilding ceased in 1874, but ordnance production continued until 1962; since then, the base has served as a naval supply and administrative centre. Before entering the yard to visit the US Navy Museum, you'll need to show photo ID to the guard at the gate (designed by Benjamin Latrobe in 1804) at 9th and M streets. As with all federal sites, call ahead to make sure it hasn't been closed for security reasons.

The **US Navy Museum** is housed in the Navy Yard's former gun factory in Building 76 and adorned on the outside with cannon and deck guns from the Civil and 1898 wars. The museum traces the history of the US Navy since it was created in 1794 in response to attacks on American ships by Barbary pirates. Displays include uniforms, ship figureheads, vicious cat-o'-nine-tail whips, and a walk-through frigate gundeck. Separate galleries detail every US naval conflict from the War of 1812 to the present day, while other exhibits highlight every-thing from US polar explorations begun in the 1840s to the necessity of submarines in combat and intelligence operations. The World War II displays are particularly affecting; you can sit in anti-aircraft guns, watch crackly archive film footage, and view an account of the sinking of a PT-109 patrol boat by a Japanese destroyer on August 2, 1943. The boat's commander, John Fitzgerald Kennedy, towed the boat's badly burned engineer ashore, despite an injured back. There's also the upended casing for the prototype of *Little Boy*, the atomic bomb that killed 140,000 people in Hiroshima.

Anacostia

On the south side of the Anacostia River, across from the Navy Yard, is Washington's most notorious neighbourhood, though it wasn't always so. **Anacostia** thrived during post-Civil War reconstruction, when African Americans slowly started to move in and create a vibrant community. But the "white flight" to the suburbs gathered speed in the 1950s, assisted by the damaging social effects of the "wall" of the I-295 freeway built here and the 1968 riots that damaged much of the area's infrastructure. The neighbourhood still suffers from dilapidated housing, unemployment and crime. Still, the two attractions below are worth a visit, though you should go by taxi – either from Anacostia Metro station or from across the river.

Frederick Douglass National Historic Site

Frederick Douglass – former slave, abolitionist leader and blistering orator – was 60 years old when, in 1877, he moved to the white brick house known as **Cedar Hill**, 1411 W St SE (daily: May–Sept 9am–5pm, Oct–April 9am–4.30pm). Its mixed Gothic Revival–Italianate architecture, twenty-one rooms and fifteen acres were typical of the homes built twenty years earlier in what was then called Uniontown, though at that time they were sold only to whites. Douglass, DC's newly appointed US marshal, was the first to break the racial barrier, paying $6700 for the property and living out the last eighteen years of his life here.

You can view the home only on a free thirty-minute **tour** (usually daily 9am, 12.15pm, 3pm, 3.30pm & 4pm), for which you must reserve a place when you arrive or by calling ☎1-888/444-6777 (for a $1.50 fee). The tours begin in the **visitor centre** below the house, where a short docudrama and a few exhibits provide details about Douglass's life. Mementos on display include President Lincoln's cane, given to Douglass by Mary Lincoln, and a desk and chair from Harriet Beecher Stowe. Most of the fixtures are original and illustrate middle-class life in late nineteenth-century Washington. Douglass kept chickens and goats outside in the gardens, and the only water source was a rainwater pump, but inside the kitchen the domestic staff had access to all the latest technology. Douglass chose to work either in his study, surrounded by hundreds of books, or in the outdoor "Growlery" – a stone cabin he used for solitary contemplation.

Anacostia Community Museum

The official mission of the Smithsonian's **Anacostia Community Museum**, 1901 Fort Place SE (daily 10am–5pm; ☎202/633-4820, ⓦanacostia.si.edu), is to document black life in Anacostia and throughout America through the collection and preservation of artefacts such as household objects, family photos, folk artworks and writings. A favourite item is the fur coat opera singer Marian Anderson wore to her famed 1939 concert on the steps of the Lincoln Memorial. Also on display (though the collection rotates its exhibits regularly) are contemporary quilts and a small art collection of works by local artists like Samella Lewis, John Robinson and Elena Bland. The museum is perhaps best known for its temporary exhibitions, some of which have highlighted black artists and writers, the Great Migration that brought blacks north after the Civil War, and slavery throughout America from the seventeenth to nineteenth centuries.

The White House and Foggy Bottom

Since 1800, when John Adams moved into the unfinished building, the **White House** has been home to every US president and has survived the ravages of fire, war and potential acts of terror to stand as an enduring symbol of American power.

Along with the US Capitol, the White House was one of two original cornerstones of L'Enfant's master plan for the city. It is still very much in the centre of things: to the south lies the National Mall; to the southeast and east, the Federal Triangle and the colossus of the Treasury Building; to the north, historic Lafayette Square and the modern towers of Downtown; and to the west, **Foggy Bottom** – the bureaucratic district north of Constitution Avenue that runs to the Potomac River.

Foggy Bottom is best known for federal buildings such as the **State Department** and cultural and educational institutions like the **Kennedy Centre** and **George Washington University**. The city's first art museum was opened here in the 1860s, in what is now the **Renwick Gallery**, though its collection was eventually moved to the nearby **Corcoran Gallery of Art**, one of the city's best museums. Less reputable, however, is one of Foggy Bottom's biggest draws: the **Watergate Complex** that was the site of the 1972 break-in that led to President Nixon's unprecedented resignation.

The White House

The **White House**, 1600 Pennsylvania Ave NW (tours Tues–Thurs 7.30–11am, Fri 7.30am–noon, Sat 7.30am–1pm; events ☎202/456-2200, tours ☎202/456-7041, Ⓦwww.whitehouse.gov; McPherson Square or Farragut West Metro), residence and office of the president of the United States, is the most famous house at the most famous address in America. For millions, the chance to tour the president's home and possibly be in the same building as the most powerful person in the world is irresistible.

In the nineteenth century, though there were armed sentries at every door and plainclothes policemen mingled with visitors, virtually anyone could turn up at the president's house without an introduction. As late as the 1920s, the general public was allowed to saunter across the lawns and picnic on the grounds, and President Warren G. Harding would answer the front door himself.

THE WHITE HOUSE AND FOGGY BOTTOM

CAFÉS & RESTAURANTS

Blue Duck Tavern	1
The Breadline	14
Capitol Grounds	5 & 8
Cosi	15
DISH	7
Kinkead's	12
Lawson's Deli	10
Notti Bianchi	13
Primi Piatti	9
Thai Coast	4

BARS & CLUBS

51st State Tavern	3
Froggy Bottom Pub	6
Lindy's Red Lion	11
Marshall's	2

ACCOMMODATION

Fairmont	A
Hay-Adams	E
Lombardy	C
Ritz-Carlton	B
River Inn	D
State Plaza	F

THE WHITE HOUSE AND FOGGY BOTTOM

Federal Triangle
Downtown
Dupont Circle
Georgetown

MCPHERSON SQUARE
McPHERSON SQUARE (M)
St John's Church
Lafayette Statue
Andrew Jackson
Kosciusko Statue
Treasury
Hamilton Statue
National Place
White House Visitor Center
Department of Commerce

15TH ST NW
16TH ST NW
17TH ST NW
FARRAGUT SQUARE
FARRAGUT WEST (M)
Decatur House
Blair and Lee Houses
LAFAYETTE SQUARE
EAST EXECUTIVE AVE NW
The White House
THE SOUTH LAWN
WEST EXECUTIVE AVE NW
1st Division Monument
Sherman Statue
Zero Milestone
Haupt Fountains
The Ellipse
2nd Division Memorial
Boy Scout Memorial
Original Patentees Monument
Bulfinch Gatehouse
CONSTITUTION AVE NW

Renwick Gallery
Winder Building
Eisenhower Executive Office Building
Octagon
Corcoran Gallery of Art
American Red Cross
DAR Museum/Constitution Hall
Organization of American States
Art Museum of the Americas
Bolivar Statue
Lockkeeper's House

17TH ST NW
18TH ST NW
19TH ST NW
20TH ST NW
21ST ST NW
22ND ST NW
23RD ST NW
24TH ST NW
25TH ST NW
29TH ST NW

World Bank
IMF
Rawlins Park
Department of the Interior
United Church
Federal Reserve
Vietnam Veterans Memorial
Arts Club of Washington
Lisner Auditorium
George Washington University
GWU Hospital
FOGGY BOTTOM-GWU METRO (M)
Academic Center
St Mary's Church
National Academy of Sciences
Einstein Statue
Department of State
John F. Kennedy Center for the Performing Arts
Watergate Complex
SNOW COURT
WEST END
WASHINGTON CIRCLE

L ST NW
K ST NW
I ST NW
H ST NW
G ST NW
F ST NW
E ST NW
D ST NW
C ST NW

PENNSYLVANIA AVE NW
NEW HAMPSHIRE AVE
VIRGINIA AVE NW
ROCK CREEK AND POTOMAC PKWY

Theodore Roosevelt Memorial Bridge
Lincoln Memorial
National Mall
National World War II Memorial
Rosslyn

0   100   200 yds

These days, self-guided **tours** of the White House are open to all (a reversal of the Bush administration's crimped policy), but you must reserve in advance. US citizens can book through their home-state representative or senator; the Capitol switchboard number to access their Washington offices is ☎202/224-3121. Foreign visitors should contact their embassies in Washington for information on getting access. Reservations are available up to six months in advance. Once you arrive, keep in mind you will be thoroughly searched and scanned, and that items such as backpacks, large bags, hand lotions, cameras and strollers may keep you from being allowed inside; call for more details.

A few blocks southeast, the **White House Visitor Centre**, in the Department of Commerce at 1450 Pennsylvania Ave NW (daily 7.30am–4pm; ☎202/208-1631, Ⓦwww.nps.gov/whho), is worth a visit in its own right. Permanent exhibits highlight topics like the First Families and White House architecture, plus there are concerts, lectures, free maps and brochures, and a gift shop. It can also provide information on other federally operated sites, museums and parks, and give you the lowdown on current entry requirements and security restrictions for each.

Some history

In 1792 the design of what was known as the **President's Mansion** was thrown open to competition; President Washington's only request was that it command respect without being too extravagant or monarchical. **James Hoban**, an Irish immigrant and professional builder, won the $500 prize for his Neoclassical design, influenced by the Georgian manor houses of Dublin. Advertisements were placed in European newspapers for skilled craftspeople, but logistics ultimately dictated that local slaves and Scottish masons from the Potomac region be used for the work. Progress was slow: the house of grey Virginia sandstone wasn't completed in time to house Washington, whose second term ended in 1797.

America's second president, **John Adams**, moved into the unfinished building on November 1, 1800, a few days before he lost his bid for re-election. East and west terraces were built during the administration of **Thomas Jefferson**, who also installed the first indoor toilets and hired a French chef. Under **James Madison**, the interior was redecorated by Capitol architect Benjamin Latrobe, but during the **War of 1812**, British soldiers burned it down in August 1814, forcing Madison and his wife to flee. Hoban was charged with reconstructing the building after the war, and it was ready to reopen in 1817 – but with one significant change: to conceal fire damage to the exterior, the house was painted white.

Throughout the nineteenth century, the White House was decorated, added to and improved upon by each new occupant, though occasionally there were setbacks. To celebrate his inauguration in 1829, **Andrew Jackson** invited some of his followers back to the White House, who then proceeded to wreck the place before being lured onto the exterior lawn with tubs of orange juice mixed with whiskey; Jackson was forced to spend the first night of his presidency in a hotel. He did, however, install the building's first indoor bathroom in 1833. Gaslights were added in 1848, central heating and a steam laundry in 1853, the telephone in 1877, and electric lighting in 1891– though air conditioning didn't follow until 1909.

During the Civil War, troops were briefly stationed in the White House's East Room, and the South Lawn was used as a field hospital. The East Room is also where seven US presidents have lain in state – the first being **Abraham Lincoln** just after the close of the Civil War in 1865.

It wasn't until **Theodore Roosevelt**'s administration (1901–09) that fundamental structural changes were made to the building, as well as expansions to accommodate the president's family and staff. Elevators were added, and an executive West Wing – incorporating the president's personal **Oval Office** – was built. The famous Rose

Garden was planted outside the Oval Office in 1913 at the behest of President Wilson's wife, Ellen, and was used for ceremonial purposes. An entire residential third floor was added in 1927, an East Wing followed in the 1940s, and during World War II came an air-raid shelter, swimming pool and movie theatre.

Because presidential families lived in the White House during these renovations, the projects were often done too quickly, so that by 1948 the entire building was on the verge of collapse. **Harry Truman** – who had already added a poorly received balcony ("Truman's folly") to the familiar south-side portico – had to move into nearby Blair House for four years while the structure was stabilized. New foundations were laid, all the rooms were dismantled, and a modern steel frame was inserted. The Trumans moved back in 1952, and since then there have been no significant alterations – unless you count Nixon's bowling alley, Ford's outdoor pool and Clinton's jogging track.

The interior

White House **tours** allow you to view rooms on the ground and State (principal) floors. The Oval Office, family apartments and private offices on the second and third floors are off limits. Once inside, you can wander one-way through or past a half-dozen rooms, but in many rooms you can't get close enough to appreciate the paintings or the furniture. Caught up in the flow of the crowd, most people are outside again within thirty minutes.

Until Jackie Kennedy and her Fine Arts Committee put a stop to the practice, each incoming presidential family changed, sold or scrapped the furniture according to their taste, while outgoing presidents took favourite pieces with them. Presidents can no longer redecorate the historic, nonliving quarters any way they see fit and must submit changes to the State Rooms to the Committee for the Preservation of the White House. While doubtless well intentioned, such practice also has the effect of turning the building into one of the world's largest live-in museums, with the residents safely out of view.

The East Wing to the East Room

Visitors enter the **East Wing** from the ground floor and traipse first past the Federal-style **Library**, panelled in timbers rescued from a mid-nineteenth-century refit and housing thousands of books by American authors. Opposite is the **Vermeil Room**, once a billiard room but now named for its extensive collection of silver gilt; the portraits are of recent First Ladies, whose individual tastes have had significant bearing on what the place looks like. Across from the stairs, the **China Room**, true to its name, displays the services of the various presidents from George Washington on; it's been used as such only for the last century, though – before that it was little more than a storage cupboard. Since the adjoining **Diplomatic Reception Room** is often closed off for foreign heads of state and ambassadors, you're next likely to move upstairs to the **State Floor**, where the **East Room** – the largest room in the White House – is the first stop. It has been used in the past for weddings, for lyings in state, and other major ceremonies, and has a grand appearance with long, yellow drapes, a brown marble fireplace, and glass chandeliers from c.1900. Between the fireplaces hangs the one major artwork on general display: Gilbert Stuart's celebrated 1797 portrait of a steely George Washington, rescued from the flames by Dolley Madison when the British torched the White House.

The Green, Blue and Red rooms, and the State Dining Room

The last rooms on the tour are more intimate in scale. The **Green Room**, its walls lined in silk, was Jefferson's dining room and JFK's favourite in the entire house.

Portraits line the walls, Dolley Madison's French candlesticks are on the mantel-piece, and a fine, matching green dinner service occupies the cabinet. The room is often used for receptions, as is the adjacent, oval **Blue Room**, whose ornate French furniture was bought by President Monroe after the 1814 fire. In 1886, Grover Cleveland was married in here, the only time a president has been married in the White House. The **Red Room** is the smallest of the lot, decorated in early nineteenth-century Empire style and sporting attractive inlaid oak doors, with the antiques herein meant to reflect the room's design scheme, despite being acquired mostly after the 1950s. Finally, the oak-panelled **State Dining Room** harks back to the East Room in scale and style and hosts banquets for important guests. From here you loop back through the cross halls and exit on the north side of the White House, opposite Lafayette Square.

The South Lawn

The White House is surrounded by greenery, but its most famous patch is the **South Lawn**, the grassy stretch that was first designed by Thomas Jefferson, only to be reconstructed by Frederick Law Olmsted Jr during the FDR era. The White House helicopter **Marine One** lands on the lawn, and the president can often be seen on TV brushing past news reporters here. However, you can't wander around the grounds unless you're here for a garden tour or for the White House's most famous outdoor event: the **Easter Egg Roll**, which usually involves children painting eggs and rolling them across the grass, a White House staffer dressed as the Easter Bunny, and various department heads and B-level celebrities reading stories and trying to act mirthful. Free tickets for this event, on the Monday after Easter, are distributed by a nationwide lottery; to try your luck, contact ⓦwww .whitehouse.gov/eastereggroll.

The Ellipse

The **Ellipse**, also known as President's Park South, is the large green expanse south of the White House that is open to the public, and a popular spot for softball, Frisbee and flag football, among other diversions. Before 1900 the Ellipse variously hosted military camps, tent revival meetings, tennis courts, baseball fields, horse and mule corrals and a dump. Landscaped considerably in the last century, since 1978 it's been home to the rather stumpy **National Christmas Tree**, a Colorado blue spruce that the president lights every year to mark the start of the holiday season.

On the Ellipse's northern edge, at E Street opposite the South Lawn, is the **Zero Milestone**, which was intended to mark the point from where all distances on US highways would be measured, but now it only applies to those in the District. On the Ellipse's eastern side (along 15th St) is the bronze **Boy Scout Memorial**, commemorating the site of the first Boy Scout Jamboree location, in 1937. Nearby, the simple granite **Monument to the Original Patentees** honours the eighteenth-century landowners who ceded land so that the city could be built. At the Ellipse's southeastern corner, the stone **Bulfinch Gatehouse** at Constitution Avenue and 15th Street was one of a pair that stood at the Capitol grounds' western entrance. Today its partner stands across the Ellipse at Constitution and 17th. On the south end of the Ellipse are the pair of **Enid Haupt Fountains**, which flow up from 55-tonne slabs of rough Minnesota rainbow granite, and beyond them is the **Second Division Memorial**, paying tribute to the fallen soldiers of that Army group in World War II and the Korean War with a granite doorway symbolically blocked by a flaming sword. Another sculptural tribute, to the **First Division**, the oldest such grouping in the US Army, lies just north of the

Ellipse on the southwest side of the South Lawn, offering a gilded statue of Victory atop a pink granite column.

Around the White House

Appearing as a gleaming monolith at the edge of a lush green lawn on its south side, the White House is obscured on the east and west by two giant office buildings (the Treasury and Eisenhower Executive Office buildings, respectively) and sneaks up on you from the north. The security gates are not so imposing as you approach from **Lafayette Square**, so the northern side is your best bet for an unobscured snapshot of the president's house, and perhaps a chance to see a shadowy figure or two darting around inside.

Lafayette Square and around

The land due north of 1600 Pennsylvania Avenue was originally intended as part of the White House grounds, but in 1804 President Thomas Jefferson divided it in half and created a public park. Until 1824 the currently named **Lafayette Square** was known as **President's Square**. Over the years, redevelopment threatened the surrounding historic houses on several occasions, but in the 1960s Jacqueline Kennedy intervened, and modern monoliths were erected behind them – resulting in one of the stranger visual juxtapositions in DC, with warm old facades fronting drab office blocks.

In the park's centre is its only statue of an American, **Andrew Jackson**, shown astride a horse, surrounded by Spanish cannons (captured in Florida) and doffing his hat. Statues of foreign-born Revolutionary leaders are set at the corners of the square. In the southeast corner stands a likeness of the park's namesake, the **Marquis de Lafayette**, flanked by French admirals and being handed a sword by a female nude, symbolizing America – he raised an army on behalf of the American colonists and was a Revolutionary War general by the age of 19. Following the war Lafayette was imprisoned in France as a traitor, later to be released and become active once again in French politics, and during a return to the US in 1824 he was feted on the Mall and awarded various honours, including this eponymous park.

In the northeast corner of the park, a bronze memorial for **Tadeusz Kosciusko**, the Polish freedom fighter and a prominent engineer in Washington's army, features an angry imperial eagle killing a snake atop a globe while the general towers overhead. The inscription at the base is taken from Scottish poet Thomas Campbell: "And freedom shrieked as Kosciusko fell!" The other two statues, honouring American allies Comte de Rochambeau and Baron von Steuben, are a bit more traditional and less eventful.

Blair House complex

Built by the first US surgeon general in 1824, **Blair House**, at the southwestern corner of Lafayette Square, was named after a prominent Washington real-estate speculator, Francis Preston Blair, and has served as the guesthouse of choice for foreign dignitaries since the 1940s, and the house of two presidents while the White House was undergoing renovation: Harry Truman in the 1940s and Bill Clinton briefly in the 1990s. Next door, but considered part of the complex, the 1860 **Lee House** was where Robert E. Lee was offered – and refused – command of the Union Army. Off limits to the public, the Blair House complex in total spreads across four buildings and has two dozen bedrooms (and three dozen bathrooms) for associated officials, staff and hangers-on, with allegedly more space available than the White House itself.

Decatur House

US Capitol designer Benjamin Latrobe's red-brick 1819 **Decatur House**, 1610 H St NW (guided tours hourly: Fri & Sat 10.15am–4.15pm, Sun 12.15–3.15pm; $5; T202/842-0920, W www.decaturhouse.org), is the oldest home on the square. Latrobe built this house for Stephen Decatur, a precocious American hero who performed with distinction in the War of 1812 and as a navy captain fighting Barbary pirates. Decatur lived here only about a year, as he was killed in a duel by Commodore James Barron in 1820 as payback for Decatur's role in the court martial that convicted Barron of wartime incompetence. The Federal-style first floor, studded with naval memorabilia, is decorated in the fashion of the day. Most of the other rooms have Victorian-style inlaid floors, furnishings, mirrors, mouldings and the like; the slave quarters in the Gadsby Wing were unusual for being on an upper level instead of in the basement as was customary. Along with the guided **tour**, enquire about taking an audio tour of Lafayette Square, with content provided to visitors' mobile phones.

Hay-Adams Hotel

Across the street from the Decatur House is the **Hay-Adams Hotel**, H and 16th streets (see p.193), an impressive Renaissance Revival building with elegant arches and columns. The hotel sits on the former site of the townhouses of statesman **John Hay** (President Lincoln's private secretary) and his friend, historian and author **Henry Adams**. Their adjacent, grandly Romanesque Revival homes were the site of glittering soirées attended by Theodore Roosevelt and his circle and one of the city's better intellectual salons – an association that appealed to hotshot hotel developer Harry Wardman, who jumped at the chance to buy the properties in 1927. Although the townhouses were torn down, the hotel itself is quite magnificent, and has been at the heart of Washington politicking: Henry Kissinger lunched here regularly, Oliver North did much of his clandestine Iran-Contra fund-raising here, and the Clintons slept here before Bill's first inauguration.

St John's Episcopal Church

The tiny, yellow St John's Episcopal Church, across H Street from Lafayette Park (Mon–Sat 10.30am–2.30pm), was built by **Benjamin Latrobe** in 1815. The handsome, domed church was intended to serve the president and his family and is therefore known as the "**Church of the Presidents**"; all since Madison have attended at least periodically – sitting in the special pew (no. 54) reserved for them – and when an incumbent dies in office, **St John's** bells ring out across the city. The handsome 1836 building just east of the church, with a grand French Second Empire facade, is today a parish building, but in the nineteenth century it was home to the British Embassy.

Franklin, McPherson and Farragut squares

A block east of the church, **McPherson Square** is named after James B. McPherson, the Civil War general who saw action with Grant at Vicksburg and later became the highest-ranking Union officer to die in battle, when, commanding the Army of Tennessee, he was killed near Atlanta as his troops marched with Sherman into Georgia. His statue is presented on horseback in the square's centre. The more inviting **Franklin Square**, a block east on I Street between 13th and 14th streets, is a large, tree-covered expanse broken up by paths, benches and a central fountain, and overlooked by the Victorian-era, red-brick Franklin School, the place where Alexander Graham Bell sent his first message. Two blocks west of McPherson Square (at 17th), **Farragut Square** stands beneath the gaze of Admiral David Farragut, whose statue celebrates his reckless heroism during the Civil War battle of Mobile Bay ("Damn the torpedoes. Full speed ahead!") and was cast from the melted-down propeller of his ship.

Treasury Building

The **Treasury Building**, with its imposing Neoclassical bulk and grand colonnade, flanks the White House to the east and faces 15th Street. Built – or at least begun – in 1836 by Robert Mills, who created the Old Patent Office and Old Post Office, this is commonly judged to be the finest Greek Revival building in DC. During the Civil War, the basement was strengthened and food and arms were stored in the building, as Lincoln and his aides planned to hole up here if the city was attacked. The jaunty statue at the southern entrance, facing Hamilton Place, is of **Alexander Hamilton**, first secretary of the Treasury (and the man on the $10 bill; the Treasury Building itself is on the back). Washington's closest adviser during the president's first administration and co-writer of the famed *Federalist Papers*, he died young in an 1804 duel with Aaron Burr, Jefferson's vice president and scheming Tammany Hall founder. US citizens only may arrange to take free, one-hour guided **tours**, which take place on Saturday mornings (9am, 9.45am, 10.30am & 11.15am), by contacting their senators or representatives well ahead of time and providing sufficient background information, including a photo ID upon arrival. You can expect to see the luxurious suites of Salmon P. Chase, Treasury secretary during the Civil War and later Supreme Court justice, and Andrew Johnson, made president after Lincoln's assassination, along with conference and reception rooms, and the cast-iron face of the 1864 Vault, lined with three sheets of steel. The last room on the tour, the Cash Room, sounds promising – and is an eye-opener for its bronze chandeliers and marble floors – but it hasn't held currency since the 1970s. Don't come expecting to see money being printed, either; for that, you'll need to visit the Bureau of Engraving and Printing (see p.92).

Eisenhower Executive Office Building

The ornate, grey-granite **Eisenhower Executive Office Building**, 17th St and Pennsylvania Ave NW, was built in 1888 to house the State, War and Navy departments. Its architect, Alfred B. Mullet, claiming to be inspired by the Louvre, produced an ill-conceived monster of a French Empire-style building with hundreds of freestanding columns, extraordinarily tall and thin chimneys, a copper mansard roof, pediments, porticos and various pedantic stone flourishes. The design has never been terribly popular – Henry Adams called it an "architectural infant asylum" – but schemes to rebuild it have come to nothing, mainly because of the expense involved in tackling such a behemoth. Ironically, its namesake, the 34th president, proposed to demolish the building in 1957, but public outcry saved it from the wrecking ball.

These days its roomy interior provides office space for government and White House staff, and in that capacity has been at the centre of some of the country's most infamous political scandals, from Watergate to Iran-Contra. The building has long housed the offices of the vice president and the secretive National Security Council, so security here is almost as tight as it is at the White House and US

Capitol. To view the ornate public rooms, filled with marble and gilt, stained glass, tiled floors and wrought-iron balconies, you can arrange a **tour** (Saturday mornings only) by calling the Preservation Office at ☎202/395-5895 between 9am and noon on Tuesday and Wednesday, and providing plenty of information about yourself.

Renwick Gallery

The Second Empire flourishes of the Eisenhower Executive Office Building were directly influenced by the earlier, smaller and much more harmonious **Renwick Gallery** of American arts and crafts, which lies directly opposite across Pennsylvania Avenue (daily 10am–5.30pm; ☎202/633-7970, ⓦamericanart .si.edu/renwick; Farragut West Metro). Started by **James Renwick** (architect of the Smithsonian Castle) in 1859, the handsome red-brick building originally housed the private art collection of financier **William Wilson Corcoran**. Within twenty years his burgeoning collection had outgrown the site, and the new **Corcoran Gallery** was built just a couple of blocks south. In 1899 the US Court of Claims took up residence in the Renwick and, after it vacated, the by-then-decrepit building was saved and restored in the 1960s by the Smithsonian, which uses it to display selections from its **American Art Museum** and hosts excellent temporary exhibitions on decorative arts, modern jewellery and furniture, as well as sculpture, ceramics, abstracts, and applied art in all its manifestations.

The building's ornate design reaches its apogee in the deep-red **Grand Salon** on the upper floor, a soaring parlour preserved in the style of the 1860s and 1870s, featuring windows draped in striped damask, period portraits and landscapes stacked four and five high, velvet-covered benches, marble-topped cabinets, and splendid wood-and-glass display cases taken from the Smithsonian Castle. This was the main picture gallery in Corcoran's time, but today's artworks are minor compared to those in the Smithsonian's expansive National Portrait Gallery and American Art Museum.

South along 17th Street

From the Eisenhower Executive Office Building and the Renwick Gallery, you can stroll south down 17th Street toward Constitution Avenue and take in a number of attractions along the way, including the **Daughters of the American Revolution Museum** and the **Corcoran Gallery of Art**, the latter home to the city's earliest art collection (originally in the Renwick Gallery). Smaller, less heralded collections nearby are also worth a visit. Keep an eye out for the five-storey, iron-framed **Winder Building**, 604 17th St NW, which, in 1848, was the tallest building in Washington and the first to incorporate central heating; it now houses the office of the US trade representative. Between D and E streets is the white marble headquarters of the **American Red Cross**, at 430 17th St NW. Inside, in its second-floor assembly room, are gorgeous, three-panelled Tiffany stained-glass windows – supposedly the largest of their kind. You can take a peek on one of the tours offered by the organization (Wed & Fri 10am & 2pm; free; by reservation at ⓔtours@redcross.org or ☎202/303-7066).

Corcoran Gallery of Art

The **Corcoran Gallery of Art**, 500 17th St NW (Wed–Sun 10am–5pm, Thurs closes 9pm; ☎202/639-1700, ⓦwww.corcoran.org; Farragut West Metro; $10), is one of DC's best art museums in a town overflowing with them. Moving from what is now the Renwick Gallery at the end of the nineteenth century, the gallery occupies a beautiful Beaux-Arts building of curving white marble with a green copper roof, the light and airy interior enhanced by a double atrium. Its mighty American collection includes more than three thousand paintings, from colonial to contemporary; Neoclassical sculpture; and modern photographs, prints and drawings. Over the years, the permanent collection has expanded to include European works, Greek antiquities and medieval tapestries. Benefactors continue to bestow impressive gifts, like the large collection of Daumier lithographs donated by Dr Armand Hammer and the seven hundred works by two hundred nineteenth- and twentieth-century artists and sculptors, from Picasso to Calder, left by Olga Hirshhorn (wife of Joseph of the eponymous gallery). Works from the permanent collection are rotated throughout the year, and other pieces are sent out on tour; not everything mentioned below will be on display at any one time. Details of changing exhibitions are available at the **information desk**, inside the main entrance, which is also where you can sign up for the guided **tours** of the permanent collection (daily at noon, Sat & Sun also 3pm, Thurs also 7pm; free). The *Corcoran Café* (☎202/639-1786) has standard salads and sandwiches, with a good Sunday **brunch** (10am–2pm). There are also periodic **jazz and classical concerts**, films, lectures and other events.

European art

The gallery's collection of European art is a mixed bag, mainly comprising the 1925 bequest of **Senator William A. Clark**, an industrialist with more money than discretion. Among the more familiar names are **Degas**, whose vivid, nocturnal *Cabaret* resembles the work of Toulouse-Lautrec more than his own; **Renoir** and **Monet**, with pleasant landscapes; **Chardin**, whose *Scullery Maid* shows the title figure hunched over a barrel; **Picasso**, with a mid-level Cubist still life; and **Corot**, whose *Repose* features a notably sour-faced nude with Pan and his nymphs cavorting in the background. The only other European exhibits of real interest are the ones devoted to sixteenth-century French and Italian works, including some outstanding Italian majolica plates depicting mythological scenes, a thirteenth-century stained-glass window lifted from Soissons Cathedral, and two large, allegorical wool-and-silk French **tapestries** representing contemporaneous political and historical events.

In fact, the most striking piece of the gallery's European collection is not a painting but the corner room on the first floor known as the **Salon Doré** (Gilded Room), which originally formed part of an eighteenth-century Parisian home, the Hôtel de Clermont. Senator Clark bought the entire room and housed it here, then bequeathed it to the Corcoran. Framed mirrors (flanked by medallion-holding cherubs) make it seem larger than it actually is, and the rest of the luxurious details in the room include opulent floor-to-ceiling hand-carved wood panelling, gold-leaf decor, and ceiling murals.

American art

The Corcoran's American art collection is the real reason to visit. You'll find paintings by early American artists such as **Gilbert Stuart**'s presidential portraits, **George Inness**'s murky, dramatically lit *Sunset in the Woods*, and **Rembrandt Peale**'s equestrian *Washington Before Yorktown*, an illuminated image of a strong, deliberate general hours before the decisive battle for independence.

The gallery possesses a fine collection of landscapes, starting with the expansive *Niagara* by **Frederic Edwin Church** and the splendid *Last of the Buffalo* by **Albert Bierstadt**, portraying the Native American braves pursuing buffalo so numerous they darken the plain. In marked contrast, **Thomas Cole**'s *The Return* is a mythical medieval scene of an injured knight returning to a priory glowing in the evening light.

Nineteenth-century portraiture includes formal studies by artists like **John Trumbull** (who painted the Capitol murals) and **Charles Bird King**, who depicts statesman Henry Clay supporting an 1821 resolution for South American independence. Striking also is **Thomas Sully**'s rendering of Andrew Jackson on horseback, fresh from triumph at the Battle of New Orleans in 1814, though the general looks well aged even by that time. More lurid and eye-catching, **Hiram Powers**'s *The Greek Slave*, with her manacled hands and full-length nudity, so outraged contemporary critics that women visitors were prevented from viewing it while men were in the room.

The gallery also holds late nineteenth-century works by **John Singer Sargent**, **Thomas Eakins** and **Mary Cassatt**, among others. Sargent is responsible for one of the gallery's most loved pieces – the startling *Simplon Pass*, with its landscape of crags and boulders – as well as more familiar society portraits such as a regal *Mrs Henry White* and a scowling *Madame Edouard Pailleron*. **Winslow Homer**'s *A Light on the Sea* and **Richard Norris Brooke**'s *A Pastoral Visit* take on rare subjects for the time – working women and African Americans – Homer depicting a fiercely strong woman swathed in fishing nets and Brooke providing a beautifully lit scene out of black life in the rural South.

The gallery's pre-World War II collection includes works by **Childe Hassam**, **Rockwell Kent**, **Thomas Hart Benton** and **Edward Hopper**, whose sailing picture, *Ground Swell*, features a long, smooth sea and horizon, and just a hint of menace. Even better is **George Bellows**'s *Forty-Two Kids*, in which the urchins in question are playing half-naked on the rotting docks of New York's East River.

DAR Museum

The National Society of the **Daughters of the American Revolution (DAR)**, 1776 D St NW (Mon–Fri 8.30am–4pm; museum, shop and library also Sat 9am–5pm; period room tours Mon–Fri 10am–2.30pm, Sat 9am–4.30pm; ☎202/879-3241, ⓦwww.dar.org/museum; Farragut West Metro), has had its headquarters in Washington for more than a century. Founded in 1890, this thoroughly patriotic (if rigidly conservative) organization is open to women who can prove descent from an ancestor who served the American cause during the Revolution. Fuelled by the proud motto "God, Home, and Country", it busies itself with good-citizen and educational programmes, including one designed to promote "correct flag usage" throughout America: the Stars and Stripes adorning the rostrums in the Senate and the House in the US Capitol are gifts from the DAR, and just two of the more than 100,000 given away in the last century.

The DAR's annual congress (the week of April 19, anniversary of the Battle of Lexington) takes place in the massive adjoining **Constitution Hall** on 18th Street, designed with typical exuberance by John Russell Pope in 1929, and one of the finest buildings in the city. A blight on the organization's history, however, occurred in 1939, when the DAR refused to let peerless black contralto Marian Anderson perform there. Eleanor Roosevelt resigned from the organization in outrage, and Anderson gave her concert instead on Easter Sunday at the Lincoln Memorial to a rapt crowd of 75,000.

The collection

Although you won't find that shameful episode on display, the **DAR Museum** (entrance on D St) is happy to direct you to its **gallery**, where a hodgepodge of embroidered quilts, silverware, toys, kitchenware, glass, crockery, earthenware and just about anything else the Daughters have managed to lay their hands on over the years is on view. Although exhibits change, there's usually a fine selection of ceramics, popular in the Revolutionary and Federal periods (from which most of the collection dates). On request, one of the docents will lead you through the rest of the building, beginning in the spacious, 150,000-volume **genealogical library** that was once the main meeting hall.

What the Daughters are most proud of, however, are the **Period Rooms**, comprising no fewer than 31 period salons, mainly decorated with pre-1850 furnishings, each representing a different state, almost all of them east of the Mississippi. The New England room has an original lacquered wooden tea chest retrieved from Boston Harbor after the Tea Party in 1773; the California room replicates the interior of an early adobe house; and the New Jersey room displays furniture and panelling fashioned from the wreck of a British frigate sunk off the coast during the Revolutionary War – the elaborate chandelier was made from the melted-down anchor.

Foggy Bottom

For the most part, **Foggy Bottom**, lying between Pennsylvania and Constitution avenues from 17th to 25th streets, is a staunchly bureaucratic quarter with the buildings given over to various governmental, nonprofit and international organizations. The cultural activities at the **Kennedy Centre** provide one respite from the blandly white-collar, institutional tone, as does the historic **Octagon** house, and a smattering of attractions at some remove from each other. The nearest Metro stop is Foggy Bottom–GWU, which is convenient for **George Washington University**, Washington Circle and the Kennedy Centre, but is half a dozen blocks and a fifteen-minute walk from Constitution Avenue.

The murky story of Foggy Bottom

Settled in the mid-eighteenth century, **Foggy Bottom** began as a very small town on the shores of the Potomac (which reached further north in those days) and was known as Hamburg or Funkstown, after its German landlord **Jacob Funk**. Fashionable houses were built on the higher ground above today's E Street, though down by the river, in what's now **West Potomac Park**, it was a different story: industries making glass, beer and gas emptied effluents into the Potomac and the city canal, while workers' housing was erected on the low-lying malarial marshlands, blighted by rats, poison ivy, winter mud and murky fog.

The poor black and immigrant neighbourhood changed radically once the marshlands were drained in the late 1800s. Families and industries were displaced by the new West Potomac Park, and the southern limit was redefined by grand **Constitution Avenue**, which replaced the filled-in city canal. The smarter streets to the north formed the backdrop for the federal and international organizations that moved in before and after World War II, as the federal workforce rapidly expanded. Nowadays, given the predominance of government institutions here and the absence of any real street life outside of **George Washington University**, Foggy Bottom has seamlessly blended with the fabric of official Washington, becoming a wide swath of bureaucracy beginning at Capitol Hill and continuing on to the east bank of the Potomac River.

Organization of American States

Founded in 1890 "to strengthen the peace and security of the continent", the **Organization of American States** (OAS; Mon–Fri 9am–5.30pm; free; Farragut West Metro), 201 18th St NW, is the world's oldest regional organization, with 35 member states from Antigua to Venezuela. As one of its five buildings in the city, its headquarters occupy one of DC's more charming buildings, a squat white Spanish Colonial mansion built in 1910 that faces onto the Ellipse. From the main entrance on 17th Street – fronted by a gaunt statue of Columbus's patron, Queen Isabella of Spain – you pass through fanciful iron gates to a cloistered lobby, where a fountain and tropical trees reach to the wooden eaves and stone frieze above. You can then climb upstairs and walk through the gallery of national flags and busts of OAS founders, and take a peek in the grand Hall of the Americas.

A path leads from the Constitution Avenue side of the building through the so-called Aztec Garden to the smaller building behind. The **Art Museum of the Americas**, 201 18th St NW (Tues–Sun 10am–5pm; free; ℡202/458-6016, ⓦwww.museum.oas.org), shows rotating exhibits of Central and South American art, as well as temporary shows focusing on painting, photography, architecture and more. Some of it is quite good, more in line with what you'd find in a top-notch gallery than in the airless institutions of Foggy Bottom. In the main brick-floored gallery, the walls are lined with lively Latin American ceramics reaching to a wood-beamed roof, while just outside the museum, an equestrian statue of **Simón Bolívar** rides triumphantly on a curious horse with an almost circular neck.

Department of the Interior

The nation's principal landowner and conservation agency, the **Department of the Interior**, 1849 C St NW (hours vary; ℡202/208-4743, ⓦwww.doi.gov /interiormuseum; Farragut West Metro), was one of the earliest federal departments to take up residence in Foggy Bottom. The Department moved into architect Waddy Butler Wood's granite, square-columned building in 1937. Inside, grand WPA-era **murals** – like one commemorating Marian Anderson's 1939 concert at the Lincoln Memorial – decorate the walls.

After presenting ID at the reception desk, you'll be directed to the department's little-visited **museum**, which sheds light on agencies like the Bureau of Land Management, the National Park Service and the Bureau of Indian Affairs. The wood-panelled museum opened in 1938 with a mission to spend one percent of its budget on art, as part of a New Deal programme to hire unemployed artists. It's filled with stuffed bison heads, old saddles, fossils and minerals, paintings by nineteenth-century surveyors of the West, and eight elaborate dioramas featuring an Oklahoma land office, coal mine explosion, Alaska gold rush town and frontier fort. There are also regularly changing exhibitions of photography, paintings and sculpture, and Native American artefacts, much of it drawn from the museum's stock of 150 million items. At the time of writing, the museum was undergoing a long-overdue renovation and was expected to reopen in 2011; call for details. Around the corner from the museum, the **Indian Craft Shop** sells tribal art and crafts, the authentic jewellery, pottery and baskets making for unexpected souvenirs. Elsewhere in the building, the **National Park Service**'s information office (Mon–Fri 9am–5pm) has leaflets on almost every NPS park, museum and monument in the country; in DC, that includes all the sites on the Mall.

The Octagon

As with the Department of the Interior museum, the Octagon, 1799 New York Ave NW (hours vary; ☎202/626-7312; Farragut West Metro), is another Foggy Bottom stalwart that's undergoing a lengthy renovation – though this building's far more important; call for details on when the works will conclude and on opening hours and prices.

As one of the city's oldest homes, the Octagon doesn't have eight sides (debate continues as to what the name actually means), but nonetheless provides a glimpse of how elite Washington lived two centuries ago. Loosely adapted from the Georgian style, its rather simple brick exterior gives way to curving interior walls, arcing closet doors, and several period rooms open for touring. The circular entry hall sports its original marble floor, while beyond, a swirling oval staircase climbs up three storeys. The house had two master bedrooms and five regular ones to accommodate the owner, his wife and their fifteen children. In the dining and drawing rooms, period furnishings reveal how the house would have looked in its day – light, with high ceilings, delicate plaster cornicing and Chippendale accessories. The two portraits in the dining room are of the architect and the owner, and the beautifully carved stone mantel in the drawing room is an original, signed and dated 1799. Downstairs, the accessible basement gives you an idea of the kind of drudgery servants and slaves underwent while the owners lived in splendour above.

Constitution Avenue

From the Organization of American States building at the corner of 17th Street, **Constitution Avenue** – known as B Street until the 1930s – parades an attractive line of buildings framed by the greenery of Constitution Gardens across the way. The street isn't necessarily a destination in itself, but it's dotted with interesting sights along the way, from a few highlights on the north side to the Vietnam Veterans Memorial on the south side of the avenue. One architectural curiosity is the **Lockkeeper's House**, on the southwest corner of 17th Street and Constitution Avenue, a sturdy stone cabin that today is a simple park maintenance facility. However, it used to be the residence of the toll-taker for the terminus of the **C&O**

The many sides of the Octagon

Although no longer set amid fields and flanked by a line of fir trees, the Octagon, now dwarfed by the office buildings behind it, gives a good example of the private homes that once characterized the neighbourhood. It was built by wealthy Virginian plantation owner **John Tayloe** on a prime corner plot just two blocks from the new President's Mansion. Tayloe, a friend of George Washington, was so rich and well connected that he could afford to spend the substantial sum of $35,000 on the house and hire **William Thornton**, US Capitol designer, to build it.

The **War of 1812** guaranteed the house its place in history. Though the English torched the nearby President's Mansion, they spared the Octagon, possibly because the French ambassador was in residence at the time. President and Dolley Madison moved in after they returned to the city after the blaze. For six months in 1814–15, the president ran the government from its rooms, and on February 17, 1815, the **Treaty of Ghent**, making peace with Britain, was signed in the study (on a table still kept in the house). For much of the latter part of the nineteenth century, the Octagon was left to deteriorate, but at the turn of the twentieth century, the American Institute of Architects (AIA) bought it and used it as its headquarters until 1973; though it later found newer premises nearby, it still maintains the Octagon as a house museum.

Canal, which connected to Georgetown to the west. To the east flowed the dreaded **Washington City Canal**, which for half a century occupied what's now the avenue and, even more than a transport artery, was notorious as an open sewer and breeding ground for mosquitoes and disease. It was filled in during the 1870s.

Federal Reserve

The first building of any distinction along Constitution Avenue is the enormous, eagle-fronted **Federal Reserve**, 20th St NW between C St and Constitution Ave (Mon–Fri 10am–3.30pm by advance reservation only; ⓣ202/452-3324 for tours, ⓣ202/452-3778 for gallery, ⓦwww.federalreserve.gov; Foggy Bottom–GWU Metro). Designed by Paul Cret, who was also responsible for the OAS and the Folger Shakespeare Library (see p.83), it holds the department which controls the country's money supply and gold reserves and issues government securities; it's most familiar to the public as the body that decides the direction of US interest rates, and as such it played a serious role in the economic collapse and corporate bailouts of 2008. **Group tours** of the 1937 building are available for visitors of 18 years and over (ten-person minimum; call two weeks in advance) and include a film giving an overview of the organization's function, as well as a look at the boardroom, where key decisions are made. With two days' notice you can make a separate reservation to visit the Reserve's decent **art gallery**, which hosts temporary exhibits on Romantic-era French sculpture and American Abstract Expressionism, as well as collections borrowed from galleries owned by other central banks around the world. Its small permanent collection comprises a hodge-podge of donated pieces, from the bucolic works of antebellum landscape artist **Thomas Hotchkiss** to the modern colour-field paintings of **Ellsworth Kelly** to the abstractions of **Lee Krasner** and **Robert Motherwell**.

National Academy of Sciences

Congress created the **National Academy of Sciences**, 2100 C St NW (hours vary; ⓣ202/334-2000, ⓦwww.nas.edu; Foggy Bottom–GWU Metro), in 1863 to provide the country with independent, objective scientific advice. The building's facade is adorned with Greek inscriptions, and its cold Neoclassical lines are softened by a grove of elm and holly trees at the southwest (22nd St) corner, where Robert Berks's large bronze statue of **Albert Einstein** sits. Einstein is depicted lounging on a granite bench with the universe (in the shape of a galaxy map) at his feet; a piece of paper inscribed with the famous formula from his Theory of Relativity is in his hand.

The Academy also has a pair of **art galleries**, in its central rotunda and upstairs, that showcase pieces relating to its mission. Paintings, sculptures and multimedia projects by mostly unknown artists provide fascinating takes on astronomy, anatomy, cosmology, cartography and other scientific fields. Its auditorium also hosts occasional **music concerts** featuring the occasional big-name artist, in genres from Baroque to modern. As with a number of other Foggy Bottom buildings, however, the NAS is closed for a lengthy renovation, scheduled for completion in 2012.

Department of State

In 1960 the **Department of State**, C St between 21st and 23rd sts (Foggy Bottom–GWU Metro), moved out of the Executive Office Building and into its own headquarters – a long white building occupying two entire blocks in the southwest corner of Foggy Bottom. Established in 1789 and originally helmed by Thomas Jefferson, the nation's oldest and most senior Cabinet agency is effectively the federal foreign office. The 45-minute **tours** (Mon–Fri 9.30am, 10.30am & 2.45pm; free) need to be reserved via ⓦhttps://receptiontours.state .gov as much as three months in advance to guarantee a spot. The tours allow you to peek at the eight elegant **Diplomatic Reception Rooms**. During the 1960s, many of these rooms were redecorated and refurnished to provide more suitable chambers for receiving diplomats and heads of state, and are kitted out in styles ranging from Federal and Georgian to more spartan Neoclassical. Among the wealth of eighteenth- and nineteenth-century paintings, decorative arts and furniture is the desk on which the American Revolution's conclusive Treaty of Paris was signed.

Northern Foggy Bottom

The **northern side** of Foggy Bottom is pretty dull terrain, split between sites for institutional behemoths like the IMF and World Bank (adjacent on G St between 18th and 20th) and the uneventful campus for **George Washington University**. The main campus spreads over several city blocks between F, 20th and 24th streets and Pennsylvania Avenue; the nicest part is **University Yard**, between G and H, and 20th and 21st streets – a green, rose-filled park surrounded by Colonial Revival buildings. On the north side, the park's statue of Washington is yet another copy of the famous Houdon image. For more information on the university, visit the Marvin Centre at 801 21st St NW (☎202/994-6602, ⓦwww.gwu .edu), where you can pick up a map and get a self-guided walking tour of campus.

There are a few scattered points of architectural interest in northern Foggy Bottom. To the east, at 20th and G, the red Italianate **United Church** was built in 1891 for the descendants of the neighbourhood's Germanic immigrants, and offers an eye-catching bell tower. On the western side of the GWU campus, **St Mary's Episcopal Church**, at 730 23rd St, was established in 1887 as the first black Episcopal church in DC. A wealthy band of local citizens coughed up $15,000 to hire architect **James Renwick**, of Smithsonian Castle and Renwick Gallery fame, to construct it, and the stately red-brick Gothic structure is very much in keeping with the latter's high Victorian style.

Two blocks west on 25th Street (north of H), there's a run of carefully preserved nineteenth-century brick houses painted with vivid pastel colours; the most interesting ones are in **Snow Court** (between 24th and 25th streets, and I and K), DC's

Washington's university

Pierre L'Enfant's city plan allowed for the building of a university in the Foggy Bottom district, and it was certainly a development that George Washington himself was keen on; he even left money in his will to endow an educational institution. Like L'Enfant and Washington, many of the university's founders were Freemasons and liberally applied the society's emblem throughout the school (the Bible that inaugurates new university presidents once belonged to Washington himself). The nondenominational Columbian College, founded by an Act of Congress in 1821, was the precursor to today's **George Washington University** (GWU), which was renamed in 1873 and soon moved into its current site. Since then it has played a crucial role in the city's development, buying up townhouses and erecting new buildings on such a scale as to make it the second-biggest landholder in DC after the federal government. Famous alumni include Jacqueline Kennedy Onassis (who gets a building named after her), J. Edgar Hoover, Colin Powell, Allen and John Foster Dulles, crime author (and Harry's daughter) Margaret Truman, and Senate majority leader Harry Reid, as well as less expected figures like Courteney Cox and L. Ron Hubbard.

only surviving interior alley, where the homes are only 12ft wide. In the 1880s each one probably housed ten people; nowadays they change hands for up to half a million dollars. Lastly, north of **Washington Circle**, where four major roads converge, the **West End** neighbourhood – named after its presence at the edge of L'Enfant's city plan – is another of DC's newly gentrifying districts, though unless you've come to drop in at a hotel or restaurant, there's little to detain you.

Watergate Complex

If there's a single word synonymous with American political scandal, it's certainly "Watergate", which takes its name from the **Watergate Complex** on 25th Street NW at Virginia Avenue. This huge, curving, mid-1960s residential and commercial monster – named after the flight of steps behind the Lincoln Memorial that leads down to the Potomac – has always been a sought-after address, both for foreign ambassadors and the city's top brass. People like Bob and Elizabeth Dole and Caspar Weinberger have maintained apartments here for years, and White House intern Monica Lewinsky lived here before the Clinton impeachment scandal forced her from DC. In 1972, the Democratic National Committee was headquartered in the hotel's sixth floor. On June 17, five men connected to President Nixon's re-election campaign were arrested for breaking into the offices, and two years later, Nixon resigned from the presidency in disgrace. The hotel here has gone through a number of owners and closures, but there's no need to stay – it's something to pass by and gawk at, rather than visit.

Kennedy Centre

Washington didn't have a national cultural centre until 1971, when a $78 million white marble behemoth designed by Edward Durrell Stone was opened. The **John F. Kennedy Centre for the Performing Arts**, 2700 F St NW (☎202/467-4600, ⓦwww.kennedy-centre.org; Foggy Bottom–GWU Metro), continues to be the city's foremost cultural outlet: it has four main auditoriums, a variety of exhibition halls, and a clutch of restaurants and bars; is home to the **National Symphony Orchestra** and the **Washington National Opera**; and hosts touring theatre, musical and ballet groups. There's an information desk on your way in, and you're free to wander around. Provided there's no performance or rehearsal taking place, you can look inside the theatres and concert halls (most are open to visitors 10am–1pm). Free 45-minute **tours** depart every ten minutes from Level A (beneath the Opera House).

The **Grand Foyer** itself is a real sight: 630ft long and 60ft high, it's lit by gargantuan crystal chandeliers and contains an 8ft-high **bronze bust** of JFK in the moon-rock style favoured by sculptor Robert Berks. You can also drop by the **Hall of States**, where states' flags are hung in the order they entered the Union, and the **Hall of Nations**, which honours the nations recognized by the US. In addition, each of the theatres and concert halls has its own catalogue of artwork, from the **Matisse** tapestries outside the Opera House and the **Barbara Hepworth** sculpture in the Concert Hall to the **Felix de Welden** bronze bust of Eisenhower above the lobby of the Eisenhower Theater. The **Roof Terrace** level has several theatres and places to eat. While you're up here, step out onto the terrace for great **views** across the Potomac to Theodore Roosevelt Island, and north to Georgetown and Washington National Cathedral.

African American DC

Making up more than half of Washington, DC's population, African Americans have a long history in the region, one that stretches back to the colonial era. But only recently have historians begun to understand how inextricably black history is tied to America's growth from New World backwater to globe-trotting superpower. From its outset, the capital has been fundamentally shaped by black Americans, from the early days of slavery through the tumultuous Civil War period to the modern era: the current US president, Barack Obama, was himself the son of a Kenyan immigrant.

Oppression in the New World

As early as the 1600s, the English colonies around the Chesapeake Bay were developing sizable plantations and agrarian economies using **slave labour** imported from West Africa. Indeed, stylish residences such as Mount Vernon and the Carlyle House were built with and functioned through the aid of slave labour, their elegant facades contrasting with the back-breaking drudgery and oppression experienced in their kitchens and fields. Even the US Capitol was built from the toil of African American slaves, indicating just how fundamental they were in the creation and expansion of the capital region.

Mount Vernon ▲

Slave quarters at Mount Vernon ▲

Reproduction of the uniform worn by black Union troops ▼

The Antebellum and Civil War eras

While some early **free blacks** such as Benjamin Banneker achieved a place in the history books (by helping plan the capital, in his case), with the turn of the nineteenth century the majority of African Americans still were not free, and were consigned to performing the duties laid out by their masters, including many members of Congress. Lasting from 1861 to 1865, the **Civil War** was fought vigorously by **black troops wearing the Union blue**, who risked death or re-enslavement if taken by Confederate soldiers. Inspired by the sacrifice of these men, national figures such as Frederick Douglass emerged to champion the causes of slavery abolition, racial equality and economic justice, and were followed by leaders such as educator Mary McLeod Bethune, activist Mary Church Terrell and journalist William Calvin Chase.

Strivers' sections

After the Civil War, a flood of new migrants escaping the South sought refuge in Washington, DC many in working-class areas such as **Anacostia**. Although segregation was practised in many sections of DC, other neighbourhoods opened to the black middle class, including **Adams Morgan** and, especially, **Shaw**, where the so-called **Strivers' Section** of Edwardian residences filled up with well-heeled African Americans, and **U Street** became known as the "Black Broadway". Here would emerge the next group of black leaders, including jurist Thurgood Marshall, UN diplomat Ralph Bunche and civil-rights activist A. Philip Randolph, along with trailblazing figures in music and the arts like Langston Hughes, Marian Anderson and Duke Ellington.

▲ Martin Luthor King

▼ Crowds at Barack Obama's inauguration

The modern era

Although African Americans in the District have experienced setbacks in recent decades – everything from the devastation of the **1968 riots** to the **gentrification** of historically black neighbourhoods – rising incomes and new opportunities have led many residents to integrate once-forbidden white enclaves such as Georgetown and seek opportunity in city and national politics, business, science and arts. Today, along with obvious signs of political progress such as the election of president **Barack Obama**, the depth of the African American contribution to the District can be heard in the **fiery jazz** performances at Bohemian Caverns, seen in the **vivid exhibits** of the Anacostia Museum, and experienced at the many memorials and **historic sites** that honour those who made modern DC the city it is, and what it promises to become.

▼ Duke Ellington mural, Shaw

African American Civil War Memorial ▲

Mural, Bohemian Caverns ▼

Black heritage sites

Although the number of important black heritage sites in Washington, DC is too numerous to mention here, the following list is a good start. Washington's new National Museum of African American History and Culture, under construction on the National Mall, is due for completion in 2015.

▶▶ **Frederick Douglass National Historic Site** One of the District's most famous residents, Douglass is revered for his fight against slavery and his championing of equal rights for all citizens; his house in Cedar Hill provides a look at his life and career. p.95

▶▶ **Metropolitan AME Church** Dating to 1886, when it was constructed and financed by former slaves, this church is among the country's most prominent houses of worship, with a record of social activism and a few famous funerals, including that of Frederick Douglass. p.136

▶▶ **Howard University** This historically black college, founded after the Civil War, has produced legions of important Americans, from Toni Morrison to Andrew Young to Stokely Carmichael. p.150

▶▶ **Alexandria Black History Museum** Antique photos of early pioneers, as well as neighbourhoods and artefacts from the eras of slavery and segregation, at this Virginia institution. p.180

▶▶ **African American Civil War Memorial** Along with its adjacent museum, this is a great place to learn about the groundbreaking impact that the 150 regiments of "US Colored Troops" had on that historic conflict. p.150

▶▶ **Bohemian Caverns** Scores of legendary performers have appeared at this jazz supper club, including Duke Ellington, Cab Calloway, Billie Holiday and Sarah Vaughan. p.226

▶▶ **Lincoln Memorial** The Greek temple honouring the sixteenth president is just as identified with Martin Luther King Jr, who gave his famous 1963 "I Have a Dream" speech here, as it is with Abe Lincoln himself. p.50

5

Downtown to Dupont Circle

Washington, DC has a rather amorphous **Downtown**, in varying states of decay and revival, but it is for the most part a lively section of town that has, in the last few decades, recovered from much of the blight of the 1960s. During that time, riots, white flight and urban disinvestment did much to cripple the economic foundation of the area, but with urban-renewal dollars now steadily flowing, you'll find plenty of chic restaurants, niche museums, fancy hotels and more to explore and enjoy.

Technically, Downtown begins north of Constitution Avenue and northwest of Capitol Hill. Although the eight superstructures of the **Federal Triangle** have a few sights of interest (namely the National Archives), and **Pennsylvania Avenue** is the famed presidential inauguration route that holds a number of important historical sites, for the most part the most energetic part of Downtown is the **Penn Quarter**, centred on 7th and F streets NW – where you can dine at a fancy restaurant, have a few drinks in a sports bar, enjoy a basketball game or take in a play or a movie. In the vicinity are notable institutions such as the **National Portrait Gallery** and **American Museum of Art**, the **Museum of Women in the Arts**, and the infamous **Ford's Theatre** where President Lincoln was shot. From there it's only a short stroll to **Chinatown**, the place for a cheap but tasty lunch of noodles and dim sum.

Further north, **K Street** is DC lobbying central, where well-connected power-brokers get their way in Congress through various means. This part of Downtown is newer than that further south, and not quite as interesting – its appeal is limited to some historic buildings and institutions, the up-and-coming neighbourhood of **Logan Circle**, and the decent bars, clubs and restaurants of **Connecticut Avenue**.

The avenue leads out of Downtown northwest to **Dupont Circle**, with its hip restaurants and clubs, shops, charming old buildings and contemporary-art galleries. Northwest from the Circle, turn-of-the-twentieth-century mansions house the denizens of **Embassy Row**, private galleries cluster near the **Phillips Collection**, America's first modern art museum, and townhouse museums are peppered around the elite district of **Kalorama**.

Some history

The land between the Capitol and the White House, north of the Mall, was the only part of nineteenth-century Washington that remotely resembled a city.

DOWNTOWN : PENN QUARTER AND FEDERAL TRIANGLE

CAFÉS & RESTAURANTS	
Acadiana	1
Café Atlantico	29
Café Mozart	3
Corner Bakery	22
Courtyard Café	18
District Chophouse & Brewery	25
Eat First	8
Ebbitt Express	16
Ella's Pizza	17
Full Kee	10
Haad Thai	2
J&G Steakhouse	23
Jaleo	27
Kanlaya Thai	11
Matchbox	6
Old Ebbitt Grill	15
Proof	9
The Source	31
Teaism	28
Ten Penh	30
Tosca	19
Zaytinya	13
Zengo	14
Zola	21

ACCOMMODATION	
Courtyard Washington	G
Grand Hyatt	E
Hampton Inn	D
Harrington	J
Henley Park	C
HI-Washington DC	A
JW Marriott	I
Monaco	F
Morrison-Clark Inn	B
Willard InterContinental	H

BARS & CLUBS	
Capitol City Brewing Co.	4
Fado	7
Gordon Biersch Brewery	20
Iron Horse Tap Room	26
RFD Washington	5
Rocket Bar	12
Round Robin	24

Union Station

▲ G, I, Washington Historical Society & Convention Center

3RD ST NW
4TH ST NW
5TH ST NW
6TH ST NW
7TH ST NW
8TH ST NW
9TH ST NW
10TH ST NW
11TH ST NW
12TH ST NW
13TH ST NW
14TH ST NW
15TH ST NW

MASSACHUSETTS AVE NW

H ST NW

JUDICIARY SQUARE

CHINATOWN

Pension Building (National Building Museum)

National Law Enforcement Officers Memorial

Old City Hall

Lincoln Statue

Marshall Statue

John Marshall Park

Municipal Center

Department of Labor

US (Federal) Court House

CONSTITUTION AVE NW

National Mall

Grand Army of the Republic Monument

Canadian Embassy

Newseum

Andrew Mellon Fountain

Sears House

Federal Trade Commission

National Archives

FEDERAL TRIANGLE

Department of Justice

Federal Bureau of Investigation

Internal Revenue Service

Old Post Office

Evening Star Building

Ariel Rios Building

EPA

Wilson Building

Ronald Reagan Building

DC Visitor Information Center

Franklin Statue

Pulaski Statue

Pershing Statue

Pershing Park

Freedom Plaza

National Theatre

National Place

Warner Theatre

Petersen House

Ford's Theatre

Riggs National Bank

International Spy Museum

National Portrait Gallery

Smithsonian American Art Museum

Madame Tussauds Wax Museum

Martin Luther King Jr Memorial Library

National Museum of Women in the Arts

New York Ave Presbyterian Church

Metropolitan Square

MCPHERSON SQUARE

K Street

I ST NW

NEW YORK AVE NW

METRO CENTER

G PLACE

Verizon Center

Surratt House Site

Arch

GALLERY PLACE-CHINATOWN

PENN QUARTER

Law Enforcement Officers Visitor Center

The Lansburgh (Shakespeare Theatre)

Market Square

Naval Heritage Center

ARCHIVES-NAVY MEMORIAL

FDR Memorial

National Aquarium

Department of Commerce

White House

3RD ST NW

I-395

CONSTITUTION AVE NW

INDIANA AVE NW

PENNSYLVANIA AVE NW

N

0   500 yds

A downtown developed in the diamond formed by Pennsylvania, New York, Massachusetts and Indiana avenues, and fashionable stores and restaurants existed alongside printing presses, shoeshine stalls, oyster sellers and market traders. Entertainment was provided by a series of popular theatres, including Ford's Theatre, where President Lincoln was shot.

By the late nineteenth century, Pennsylvania Avenue marked the southern limits of Washington society; the shops on its north side were as far as the genteel would venture – the south side was a notorious gambling and red-light district. The downtown area was given a new lease of life in the 1930s, when the stately buildings of the Federal Triangle were built to house the expanding bureaucracy, but by the 1960s downtown was a shambling, low-rent neighbourhood that was badly damaged by the 1968 riots. As established businesses fled to the developing area north of the White House, the dilapidated region was a potent visual symbol of the divide between the "two Americas", the glittering showpieces of the Mall and Capitol Hill set just blocks from some of the worst urban blight in the US.

In the 1980s, however, Downtown began to be rescued from years of neglect. Since then, an enormous amount of money has been pumped into renovations, especially in the Penn Quarter. With an agreeable swath of delis, restaurants, sports bars and galleries being grafted onto the existing historic buildings and cleaned-up streets, it's sure to remain one of the city's most rapidly evolving areas for years to come.

Along Pennsylvania Avenue NW

Defining the border between Downtown and the Federal Triangle (forming its hypotenuse), **Pennsylvania Avenue NW** is one of the District's most famous roads, connecting the Capitol with the White House. The avenue is the site of the president's triumphal January **Inaugural Parade** from the Capitol (site of the inauguration) to the White House. Thomas Jefferson led the first impromptu parade in 1805, James Madison made the ceremony official, and every president since then, except Ronald Reagan in 1985, has trundled up in some form of conveyance – though Jimmy Carter and Barack Obama (partly) walked the sixteen long blocks to the White House. In addition, the bodies of nine presidents have been taken from the Capitol to the White House, lying in state in both locations.

Pershing Park and Hamilton Place

Beginning at Downtown's northwestern section of Pennsylvania Avenue, closest to the White House, pleasant **Pershing Park** was named after the commander of the American forces during World War I, John J. Pershing. His statue stands alongside a sunken terrace that becomes a **skating rink** in winter (mid-Nov to mid-March Mon–Thurs 10am–9pm, Fri & Sat 10am–11pm, Sun 11am–9pm; $7, skate rental $3). Just to the west, **Hamilton Place** is named after Alexander Hamilton, first US Treasury secretary, but marks the spot where general William Tecumseh Sherman (also honoured by a statue) presided over the Grand Review of the Union Armies in May 1865; six weeks after Robert E. Lee's surrender, the victorious troops marched up Pennsylvania Avenue in one of the largest military parades ever seen in the capital.

Willard Hotel

Looming over the north side of Pershing Park at 14th Street is one of the grandest Washington hotels, the **Willard** (see p.194) – a Washington landmark for over 150 years. Although a hotel has existed on the site for nearly 200 years, it was after 1850, when Henry Willard gave his name to the place, that it became a haunt of statesmen, politicians, top brass and presidents – including Abraham Lincoln, who was smuggled in here before his first inauguration (during which snipers were placed on the roof). The *Willard*'s opulent public rooms attracted favour-seekers anxious to press their demands on political leaders; it's even believed that the hotel gave rise to the word "lobbyist" for all the deal making that took place in that hotel entryway. More inspiringly, Dr Martin Luther King Jr wrote the cadences of the "I Have a Dream" speech while in his hotel room shortly before the 1963 March on Washington.

Drop by the galleried lobby and tread the main corridor's plush carpets to get a feel for where DC's swells and well-heeled still hang out. If you can afford the pricey rates, it's also a very good place to stay.

Freedom Plaza and around

The large open space known as **Freedom Plaza** lies where Pennsylvania Avenue kinks into E Street (at 13th) and is the site of numerous festivals, protests and open-air concerts. Lined in marble, the square is inlaid with a large-scale representation of Pierre L'Enfant's city plan, crafted in bronze and coloured stone, and etched with various laudatory inscriptions.

On the plaza's south side, the Beaux-Arts **Wilson Building**, no. 1350, with its mighty caryatids, Corinthian columns and bold corner shield emblems, predates all other Federal Triangle edifices. Erected in 1908 to house city council offices, when it was known as the District Building, it escaped demolition in the 1920s and 1930s. It now houses the mayor's office and city council chambers, along with an **art collection** (Mon–Fri 9am–5pm; free) that arrays the work of some 200 city sculptors, painters, photographers and mixed-media artists on all six of the building's floors.

Across the street, at no. 1321, the **National Theatre** – on this site since 1835, though the current building dates from 1922 – has hosted numerous presidents in the audience for its theatrical works, which lately include a lot of off-Broadway toe-tappers (see p.235). At the northeastern corner of the plaza, the elegant **Warner Theatre** (at 13th and E) is a classic 1920s moviehouse that has been reborn as a performing-arts centre.

Old Post Office

Two blocks east of Freedom Plaza at 1100 Pennsylvania Ave NW is the steel-framed Romanesque Revival **Old Post Office** (Mon–Sat 10am–7pm, Sun noon–6pm, March–Aug closes an hour later; Ⓣ202/289-4224, Ⓦwww.oldpost officedc.com; Federal Triangle Metro). Built from 1899 to 1914, it has managed to survive the decades intact, with its towering granite walls, seven-storey atrium, restored iron support beams and burnished wood panelling. It provides a grand, out-of-proportion home to rather middling ethnic restaurants and shops, but it does feature daily jazz and r'n'b performances at lunchtime, making for an enjoyable stop on your way to or from the Mall.

The stunning **clock tower** is the centrepiece of the building, making it resemble an Old World church (summer Mon–Fri 9am–8pm, Sat 10am–8pm, Sun

10am–6pm; winter Mon–Fri 9am–5pm, Sat & Sun 10am–6pm; free; ☎202/606-8691, ⓦwww.nps.gov/opot); from here park rangers oversee short, free tours up to the **observation deck**, 270ft above Pennsylvania Avenue. The glass-elevator ride allows you to see the building in all its glory, and the viewing platform (three flights of stairs beyond the elevator) offers a stunning city panorama and information about the building's chequered history – including the inauspicious death of the local postmaster, who, during the opening celebration, fatally plummeted down an elevator shaft. More safely ensconced, on the way back down to the elevator you can see the **Congress Bells**, replicas of those in Westminster Abbey. A Bicentennial gift from London, they were installed here in 1983.

Back outside on the avenue, **Benjamin Franklin** – "Philosopher, Printer, Philanthropist, Patriot", as his statue has it – gives a cheery little wave. You can park yourself on a bench and look across to the Beaux-Arts facade of the 1898 **Evening Star Building**, no. 1101, with its attractive balconies, pediments and carvings; it used to house one of Washington's longest-lasting newspapers, until it went kaput three decades ago.

Market Square and around

In 1801 the city's biggest outdoor market opened for business at the foot of 7th Street. It backed onto the canal dividing the Mall from Downtown, where goods barges could be unloaded; out front, top-heavy carts and drays spilled across Pennsylvania Avenue and up 7th Street on the way out of the city. It was a notoriously noxious spot, and there was little clamour when it was demolished in 1870 to make way for the grand Victorian **Centre Market**, a colossus holding seven hundred vendors of meat, fruit and vegetables, and other produce, to be distributed locally and nationwide. By the Depression the market had outlived its usefulness and the **National Archives** building (see p.121) was erected on the site in 1935. The concave, colonnaded buildings of the development opposite, known as **Market Square**, are given over to café-restaurants and outdoor seating, while upper-floor apartments have sweeping views over the revitalized Penn Quarter.

US Navy Memorial

Market Square's 100ft-diameter circular plaza is covered by an etched representation of the world, circled by low-tiered granite walls lapped by running water. These elements are part of the **US Navy Memorial** (memorial 24hr; Heritage Centre daily 9.30am–5pm; Archives–Navy Memorial Metro), which also includes a statue of a lone sailor, kit bag by his side, and inscribed quotations from the likes of Themistocles, architect of the Greek naval victory during the Persian Wars, and naval aviator Neil Armstrong. Especially worth a look are the 26 bronze relief panels on the walls, which illustrate different aspects of the Navy's mission in various wars, though the imagery and captions can be off-kilter ("LSTs: Fondly Known as Large, Slow Targets"). In summer the **Navy Band** holds regular concerts at the memorial.

Directly behind the memorial, in the easternmost Market Square building at 701 Pennsylvania Ave NW, the **Naval Heritage Center** has changing exhibits. Films, presented in the Burke Theater, show the glories of sea and air battles. Portraits honour the US presidents who have served in the US Navy: JFK famously commanded a motor torpedo boat and was awarded the Navy and Marine Corps Medal for heroism, and Johnson, Nixon, Ford, Carter and Bush (the elder) all served with distinction, too.

Just west of the Memorial is the much less appealing **FBI Building**, a giant, Brutalist structure housing America's secretive national police force, which is about as welcoming as its fortress-like architecture would suggest.

FDR Memorial

Across Pennsylvania Avenue from here, in the green plot in front of the National Archives at 9th Street, a small marble memorial commemorates wartime president **Franklin Delano Roosevelt**. It was FDR's wish that any memorial to him erected after his death be "plain, without any ornamentation", and no larger than an office desk, and that's what he got – at first. Placed here in 1965 on the twentieth anniversary of his death, the monument is inscribed simply "In Memory of Franklin Delano Roosevelt 1882–1945". But despite his request, the much more elaborate FDR Memorial opened on the National Mall in 1997 (see p.48).

East of the memorials

A little further up on the north side of Pennsylvania Avenue, the turreted, pink-stone **Sears House**, at no. 633, once contained the studio of nineteenth-century photographer Matthew Brady, whose graphic photographs of the slaughter at Antietam in 1862 first brought home the full horror of the Civil War to the American people. A block northeast of the Navy Memorial on Indiana Avenue, small **Indiana Plaza** is taken up by the monument to the victorious Grand Army of the Republic, a triangular obelisk adorned with figures representing Fraternity, Loyalty and Charity. Back on the south side of Pennsylvania Avenue, the bronze, triple-layer fountain in the corner plot between 6th Street and Constitution Avenue commemorates former Secretary of the Treasury and art maven **Andrew Mellon**, fittingly sited across from the National Gallery of Art, which he funded and filled with paintings. The monument is also known as the **"Zodiac Fountain"** for its twelve relief images of the astrological signs that run around its middle course. Finally, just before 4th Street NW, the chic stone-and-glass **Canadian Embassy** presents a striking rivalry between Neoclassical and contemporary elements – though with its temple-like columns completely enveloped by aggressive modern angles, it's not much of a contest.

Newseum

Although some have described Washington journalism as being at a low ebb, with serious news traded out for entertainment and sharply declining reader- and viewership, you'd never know it by visiting the **Newseum**, 555 Pennsylvania Ave NW (daily 9am–5pm; adults $20, kids $13; Archives–Navy Memorial Metro). This "edutainment" colossus opened to the public in 2008 and provides a flashy look at the greatest hits of the news biz, loaded with pop-up headlines, electronic ticker tape, and refresher courses on the First Amendment, along with various props and outfits worn by media celebrities and investigative sections on supposed "liberal bias" in the news media.

There's certainly a lot of space to fill for the purpose: with a quarter of a million square feet and seven levels, the Newseum is chock-full of splashy graphics, easy-to-read banners, and a simplified approach to history and information, all of which it has in common with the newspaper whose parent company provided the financial impetus to open the place – *USA Today*. On the various levels, you'll see how modern news is gathered and transmitted, witness pivotal moments in journalism through docudrama re-enactment, bone up on freedom of speech and press, and get a look at the history of news as provided by the News Corporation, owner of FOX News. There's also a chunk of the Berlin Wall, a refresher on 9/11, and interactive kiosks where you can answer trivia questions and get to play reporter with your own camera-and-mic setup. Ultimately, if you have easily bored children in tow and need a break from the heavier institutions in Washington, the museum will provide ample entertainment for a few hours; those interested in actual nuts-and-bolts journalism can skip it.

The Federal Triangle

The wedge of land formed by 15th Street and Pennsylvania and Constitution avenues, the **Federal Triangle** is the massive zone linking the White House and US Capitol, with grand Neoclassical piles thrusting their imposing facades out towards passers-by. Most of these structures were erected in the 1930s in an attempt to graft instant majesty upon the capital of the Free World. The Triangle's nineteenth-century origins, however, were distinctly humble: it began as a canal-side slum known as Murder Bay. Hoodlums frequented its brothels and taverns, and on hot days the stench from the town market drifted through the ill-fitting windows of the district's cheap boarding houses. Few improvements came until the 1920s, after prostitution was controlled and The Triangle was bought and redeveloped in its entirety between 6th and 15th streets, following a classical plan that featured buildings opening onto interior courtyards. Although never fully realized, the plan made for a remarkably uniform area. Different architects worked on various projects, but all of the buildings have the same characteristics: granite facades, stone reliefs, huge columns, inhuman scale and ponderous inscriptions.

National Aquarium

Built in 1931, the 1000ft-long **Department of Commerce**, on 14th St, south of Pennsylvania Ave NW (daily 9am–5pm; $9; Federal Triangle Metro), was one of the first Federal Triangle buildings to be completed, and today it forms the western side of the Triangle, at 14th Street between E and Constitution. Its main points of interest are that it houses the White House Visitor Centre (see p.39), on the north side of the building, and the **National Aquarium**, on the east side, at 14th Street. Founded in 1873, this is the oldest aquarium in the country, and even though it's been here since 1932, the Department of Commerce's drab grey corridors still seem like a strange environment for fish. Despite its impressive-sounding name and central location, the aquarium is one of the city's most disappointing sights, with the fish tanks more resembling those of an elaborate pet store than a national-calibre institution. Visit the National Museum of Natural History instead, one long block south and east.

Ronald Reagan Building to the FTC

Heading east of the Commerce Department, the **Ronald Reagan Building**, 1300 Pennsylvania Ave, is the country's second-largest federal building after the Pentagon. Inside, along with the International Trade Centre and other offices, you'll find an immense, barrel-vaulted atrium containing a food court, restaurant and exhibition space on the west side. The irony is, of course, that this colossally expensive federal superstructure is named after the president who vowed to shrink the size of government (and in any case had little to do with the building's construction). The main reason you'll want to visit is to check out the **DC Visitor Information Centre** (summer Mon–Fri 8.30am–5.30pm, Sat 9am–4pm; winter Mon–Fri 9am–4.30pm; ☎1-866/324-7386, ⓦwww.itcdc.com), which provides maps and information. Across the courtyard to the east, and impossible to miss if you're heading toward the Federal Triangle Metro, is the gargantuan **Ariel Rios Building**, a Neoclassical, New Deal-era behemoth that houses the Environmental Protection Agency.

East across 12th Street, the 1930 **Internal Revenue Service** (IRS) building was the earliest federal structure to grace the Federal Triangle area. Its Neoclassical design is textbook material, though libertarians may take issue with the inscription

The Declaration of Independence

We hold these truths to be self-evident: that all men are created equal, that they are endowed by their Creator with certain unalienable rights, that among these are life, liberty, and the pursuit of happiness...

Declaration of Independence, Second Continental Congress, 1776

Revolutionary fervour was gaining pace in the American colonies in the early months of 1776, whipped up in part by the demagoguery of **Samuel Adams's** Sons of Liberty and other militant groups and the publication of **Thomas Paine's** widely read pamphlet *Common Sense*, which castigated monarchical government in general and **George III** of England in particular. In May, the sitting Second Continental Congress in Philadelphia advised the colonies to establish their own governments, whose delegates in turn increasingly harried the Congress to declare independence. The die was cast on June 7 when Richard Henry Lee of Virginia moved that "these United Colonies are, and of right ought to be, Free and Independent States". Four days later, while debate raged among the delegates, Congress authorized a committee to draft a formal declaration.

Five men assembled to begin the task: **Thomas Jefferson**, Benjamin Franklin, John Adams, Roger Sherman and Robert Livingston. Jefferson, an accomplished writer, was charged by the others to produce a draft, which was ready to be presented to Congress by June 28. Despite the evidence of most history books, though, Jefferson didn't simply rattle off the ringing declaration that empowered a nation. For a start, he lifted phrases and ideas from other writers – the "pursuit of happiness" was a common contemporary rhetorical flourish, while the concept of "unalienable rights" had appeared in George Mason's recent **Declaration of Rights for Virginia**, the most direct influence on Jefferson's work. Moreover, his own words were tweaked by the rest of the committee and other changes were ordered after debate in Congress, notably the dropping of a passage condemning the slave trade, in an attempt to keep some of the Southern colonies on board. However, by the end of June, Congress had a document that spelled out exactly why Americans wanted independence, whom they blamed for the state of affairs (George III, in 27 separate charges), and what they proposed to do about it. Read today, this product of considerable debate and negotiation is a model of political thought.

At this point, myths start to obfuscate the real chain of events. After a month of argument – not every delegate agreed with the proposed declaration – Congress finally approved Lee's motion on July 2, 1776. Technically, this was the day that America declared independence from Great Britain, though two days later, on **July 4, 1776**, Congress, representing the "thirteen United States of America", also approved Jefferson's document; within a couple of years, celebrations were being held on the anniversary of the fourth. The only man actually to sign the Declaration on July 4 was **John Hancock**, president of the Continental Congress, who appended his name with flourish so that the poor-sighted king wouldn't miss it – hence the colloquialism "John Hancock" for someone's signature; other signatures weren't added until August 2 and beyond, since many of the delegates had gone home as soon as the Declaration was drawn up. In any case, if the **War of Independence** didn't go well, those signatures were as good as death warrants and would allow the British to prosecute the signatories for treason and other crimes. The mood was best summed up by Ben Franklin, the oldest of the signatories, who declared, "Gentlemen, we must now all hang together, or we shall most assuredly all hang separately."

on the facade: "Taxes are what we pay for a civilized society". Across 10th Street is the Art Deco-influenced **Department of Justice**, in whose enclosed courtyard stands a bust of former US Attorney General **Robert F. Kennedy** by Robert Berks, who sculpted the 8ft-tall bronze bust of JFK in the Kennedy Centre. Across 9th Street, you'll see the National Archives, and across 7th Street sits the fittingly triangular **Federal Trade Commission** (FTC) building. Friezes over the building's doors on Constitution Avenue depict images of agriculture and the control of trade, symbolized by twin exterior statues (at the rounded 6th Street side) of a muscular man wrestling a wild horse.

National Archives

John Russell Pope's **National Archives**, 700 Pennsylvania Ave NW (research room Mon, Tues & Sat 9am–5pm, Wed–Fri 9am–9pm; rotunda and exhibit hall daily 10am–5.30pm, summer closes 7pm; last admission 30min before closing; Archives–Navy Memorial Metro), is by default the greatest building in the Triangle, representing high Neoclassicism with bells on, showing off 72 ornate Corinthian columns (each 50ft high), a dome that rises 75ft above floor level, and a sculpted pediment, facing Constitution Avenue, topped by eagles. The Archives is responsible for the country's federal records dating back to the 1700s, meaning it's stuffed with information, not just here but in dozens of satellite offices and warehouses around the country. When the department opened in 1935, its holdings were already formidable; today they are almost unfathomable. What everyone comes to see is the Holy Trinity of American historical records – the **Declaration of Independence**, the **US Constitution** and the **Bill of Rights** – but the National Archives also keeps hundreds of millions of pages of documents, from war treaties to slave-ship manifests; seven million pictures; hundreds of thousands of reels of film and sound recordings; eleven million maps and charts; and a quarter of a million other artefacts. If you're a researcher, you can apply for official ID to give you access to the collection; if not, you'll have to wait in line like all the other visitors.

The Charters of Freedom

The Archives' three key documents, called the **Charters of Freedom**, sit in the magnificent marble **rotunda** within state-of-the-art airtight containers filled with argon gas. The pages of these post-Colonial artefacts are written in elegant calligraphy in closely spaced lines – which, given their faded ink, makes them very hard to read under the low light of the display cases. It won't help to take a flash photo, or any other kind of photograph or camcorder image, since all have been banned as of 2010.

Perhaps the most popular of these documents is the **Declaration of Independence**. That it's survived at all since 1776 is rather amazing: not only was the document used as a political, social and educational tool for the first half-century of its existence – visiting one part of the country after another – but an engraving to make copies wasn't even struck until 1823. The following years didn't save the document from further wear and tear, though, as it was still moved around constantly, even within the city itself, until it was finally preserved with limited technology in the 1920s and more modern methods in the early 1950s. The two other documents here are also very important, if not quite as remarkable in their survival. The copy of the **Constitution** is the one signed at the 1787 Constitutional Convention in Philadelphia by twelve of the original thirteen states (Rhode Island signed three years later), while the first ten amendments to the Constitution became the articles of the **Bill of Rights**, and the one on display here is the federal government's official copy. Less familiar but still historically significant documents relating to Western US expansion, law and politics are often on view near the Charters of Freedom. Seeing any of these documents can involve a long wait in summer, as visitors pore over the words, trying to decipher the intricacies of eighteenth-century penmanship.

The 1936 **murals** along the rotunda's walls were created by Barry Faulkner and underscore the documents' significance with their harmonious neo-Renaissance balance and colours. Recently restored to their New Deal-era splendour, they show Thomas Jefferson handing the Declaration of Independence to John Hancock, while other founding figures look on with various states of interest, a few with their backs turned; and James Madison presenting the Constitution to Convention chair George Washington, resplendent in a cloak and sword and looking more like a king than a president.

The rest of the collection

Although the Charters are the only documents guaranteed to be on display, other historic documents that you may find on view are the Louisiana Purchase, with Napoleon's signature, the World War II Japanese surrender document, the Strategic Arms Limitation Treaty of 1972, and President Nixon's resignation letter. The Archives also hosts temporary exhibitions, lectures and films. A more recent arrival is the **Public Vaults**, which present a selection of about one thousand of the items the institution holds, made accessible through interactive exhibits and kiosks, as well as simple displays – the 1823 first printing plate of the Declaration of Independence and a draft of the Emancipation Proclamation holding pride of place.

To plunge deeper into the Archives' collection, a **shuttle bus** (free; on the hour Mon–Fri 8am–5pm) can take you to the Archives' College Park, Maryland depository (research hours same as National Archives main building), where you can track down records on military, bureaucratic, presidential and all kinds of other matters. Finally, it's a good idea to take one of the excellent **guided tours**, which show you more of the Archives' holdings, as well as its **genealogy centre**; indeed, the Archives' resources were of great help to Alex Haley, who spent many hours here tracing his ancestry, and led to the writing of his iconic *Roots* saga.

Judiciary Square

Since the city's earliest days, when storehouses served as rank jails for runaway slaves, **Judiciary Square** – east of 5th Street, between E and F streets – has been the central location for DC's local and federal government and judiciary, with the difference being that in the old days, a surrounding residential community existed of police officers, lawyers and judges, among others. The construction of the I-395 freeway ensured that those old homes were wiped out, and now almost all that remains are bleak, faceless modern towers, the stark emblems of justice in contemporary Washington.

The 1820 Greek Revival-style **Old City Hall** is on D Street between 4th and 5th, now occupied by the District of Columbia Court of Appeals, whose relocation coincided with the dubious decision to erect a modern glass-and-steel box atrium out front. Its outdoor statue of **Abraham Lincoln**, quickly erected in 1868, is said to be the first such honour bestowed after Lincoln's assassination.

Within a few blocks of here stand the US Tax Court, Department of Labor, Municipal Centre and Army Corps of Engineers buildings – all uniformly gloomy and monolithic. The **US Federal Courthouse** (main entrance on Constitution Ave) sees the most high-profile action, from the trial of various Watergate and Iran-Contra defendants to that of former mayor Marion Barry. Immediately west of the courthouse, off C Street, is **John Marshall Park**, whose eponymous bronze figure sits in a humble 5ft chair and extends his hand outwards to the viewer.

National Law Enforcement Officers Memorial

The impressive **National Law Enforcement Officers Memorial**, E St NW between 4th and 5th sts (memorial 24hr; visitor centre at 605 E St Mon–Fri 9am–5pm, Sat 10am–5pm, Sun noon–5pm; Judiciary Square Metro), dedicated in 1991, is in the centre of Judiciary Square. Walls lining the circular pathways around a reflecting pool are inscribed with the names of more than 19,000 police officers killed in the line of duty, beginning with US Marshal Robert Forsyth, shot dead in 1794, his killers never apprehended. More than the officers' names themselves, which are mostly unknown to the general public, the walls read like a who's who of historical miscreants responsible for such murders: gangsters like John Dillinger and Bonnie and Clyde; gunfighters like Billy the Kid; assassins such as Lee Harvey Oswald; and assorted militants and terrorists, including those responsible for 9/11.

By 2013 a new, underground **National Law Enforcement Museum** will open at 4th and E streets, and promises to give a more detailed look at the history of American police forces.

National Building Museum

Formerly the Pension Building, the imposing red-brick **National Building Museum**, 401 F Street NW (Mon–Sat 10am–5pm, Sun 11am–5pm; $5; ☏ 202/272-2448, ⓦ www.nbm.org; Judiciary Square Metro), was once home to a courthouse and various federal agencies; now it's an architectural museum with rotating exhibits on urban renewal, high-rise technology and environmental matters. The permanent exhibitions include designs and plans related to old Kress company five-and-dime stores, East Coast-oriented historic photography, an overview of terracotta use, and various "architectural toy" collections such as Lego and Lincoln Logs. Also worth a look is the Pension Commissioner's three-room office suite, with its fireplaces, decorative friezes and vaulted ceilings. Free **tours** (daily 11.30am, 12.30pm & 1.30pm) give you access to the otherwise restricted third floor – the best spot to view the building's towering columns and their intricate capitals.

As much as any exhibit, the building is of most interest for its architectural details and intriguing history. **Montgomery C. Meigs** was quartermaster general of the Union Army during the Civil War and, with his astounding logistical prowess, had as much as any general to do with winning the conflict. Afterwards, he sought to honour veterans of both sides of the war with a stunningly designed building. The exterior of the oversize Renaissance-style palazzo is enhanced by a 3ft-high terracotta frieze that runs around the building (between the first and second floors) and depicts various military images, including charging cavalry, wounded soldiers, and marines rowing in a storm-tossed sea. Inside, Meigs maximized the use of natural light in his majestic **Great Hall**, inspired by the generous proportions of Rome's Palazzo Farnese. The hall's centrepiece fountain is surrounded by eight **Corinthian columns** measuring 8ft across at the base and more than 75ft high; each is made up of 70,000 bricks, plastered and painted to resemble Siena marble. Above the ground-floor Doric arcade, the three open-plan galleried levels, 160ft high, were once aired by vents and clerestory windows –

opened each day by a young boy employed to walk around on the roof. Not surprisingly, this vast, striking space has been in regular demand since its inception. Grover Cleveland held the first of many presidential **inaugural balls** here in 1885 (when there was still no roof on the building), and in summer 2008 Hillary Clinton chose the Great Hall to announce to her disappointed supporters that she was suspending her presidential campaign.

⑤ The Penn Quarter

Not to be confused with Pennsylvania Avenue itself, which loosely acts as a south-western boundary, the **Penn Quarter** is the city's official designation for a cache of renovated buildings, engaging museums, stylish cafés and bars, and other sights between 5th and 12th streets, south of G Street. The **Verizon Center**, just north in Chinatown, has played an especially big role in the area's revitalization, beginning life as the MCI Centre and luring folks to spend money in an area that was once a blighted symbol of urban decay.

DC's downtown area was marred following the **1968 riots**, spurred by the assassination of Dr Martin Luther King Jr. White residents and institutions fled, and urban disinvestment, federal neglect and suburbanization contributed to the area's steep decline. It took the full development of the Metro system – connecting downtown with the rest of the city – and a new national attitude toward redeveloping urban cores to bring in the masses; now the Penn Quarter is a thriving downtown district that calls to mind some of the more frenetic activity of old Washington, though without the grime and chaos. Be sure to check out the area's better restaurants and notable attractions, including excellent **Smithsonian museums**, the **International Spy Museum** and **Ford's Theatre**, among many other, lesser-known, sights.

National Portrait Gallery

The **National Portrait Gallery** and **American Art Museum**, 8th and F sts NW (daily 11.30am–7pm; free; ☎202/633-8300, ⓦwww.npg.si.edu; Gallery Place–Chinatown Metro), are among the best and most enjoyable of all the Smithsonian's museums. The history of these institutions is a lengthy one: before the Smithsonian was founded, the federal government had its own art collection; this was later given over to the Smithsonian, which had yet to find premises for a planned "National Gallery" to house its expanding art collection. Not until the Patent Office building became available did the Smithsonian finally find a home for its 38,000 paintings, prints, drawings, sculpture, photographs, folk art and crafts – the seed of the largest collection of American art, colonial to contemporary, in the world.

Portraits of prominent citizens were the foundation of many early American art collections, but the **National Portrait Gallery** itself didn't open until the 1960s, and now occupies one-half of the space in the building. The permanent collection contains more than four thousand images of notables from every walk of life, but perhaps its best-known piece is **Gilbert Stuart**'s celebrated "Lansdowne" portrait of George Washington. In addition to paintings, the gallery contains numerous sculptures and photographs, including more than five thousand plate-glass negatives of the Civil War era by Matthew Brady. One of the most impressive sights, though, is also the newest – the Norman Foster-designed **Kogod Courtyard**, crowning the building's large internal space with a huge glass and

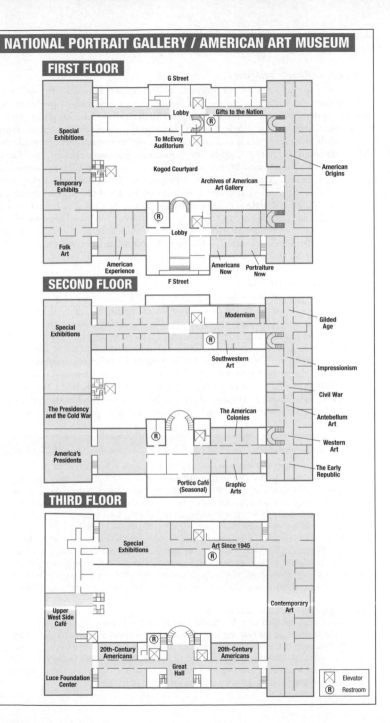

NATIONAL PORTRAIT GALLERY / AMERICAN ART MUSEUM

FIRST FLOOR

G Street

Lobby
Gifts to the Nation
Ⓡ

Special
Exhibitions

To McEvoy
Auditorium

American
Origins

Kogod Courtyard

Archives of American
Art Gallery

Temporary
Exhibits

Ⓡ

Lobby

Folk
Art

American
Experience

Americans
Now

Portraiture
Now

F Street

SECOND FLOOR

Modernism

Gilded
Age

Special
Exhibitions

Ⓡ

Southwestern
Art

Impressionism

Civil War

The American
Colonies

Antebellum
Art

The Presidency
and the Cold War

Ⓡ

Western
Art

America's
Presidents

The Early
Republic

Portico Café
(Seasonal)

Graphic
Arts

THIRD FLOOR

Special
Exhibitions

Art Since 1945

Ⓡ

Contemporary
Art

Upper
West Side
Café

Ⓡ

20th-Century
Americans

20th-Century
Americans

Great
Hall

Luce Foundation
Center

| ⊠ | Elevator |
| Ⓡ | Restroom |

aluminium canopy supported by steel columns, its dramatic effect heightened by tasteful ficus and olive trees.

Popular culture images

The most popular areas of the gallery's collection are labelled "**Bravo**" and "**Champions**" and comprise portraits of figures from the worlds of **performing arts** and **sports**. Notable works include **Paul Robeson** as Othello; photographs of **Gloria Swanson** and **Boris Karloff**; a rough-hewn wooden head of **Bob Hope**, with protruding nose; and an almost three-dimensional metallic study of **Ethel Merman** as Annie Oakley. Perhaps most striking, though, is Harry Jackson's terrific polychrome bronze sculpture of an aged **John Wayne**. American sports icons immortalized here include a pugnacious **Joe Louis** and a poignant **Arthur Ashe**, painted in the last few months of his life. Action paintings encompass **Mickey Mantle** watching as **Roger Maris** hits another homer in the 1961 season, and James Montgomery Flagg's depiction of the **Jack Dempsey–Jess Willard** heavyweight championship fight of 1919. Seated to the right of the struggling Willard (in black shorts) is the eager **Damon Runyon**, who was a sports reporter before he wrote humorous, streetwise stories.

Presidential portraits

As you might expect, the gallery has an impressive collection of **presidential portraits**. Gilbert Stuart's image of **George Washington**, an imperial study of a stalwart man, is one of the star attractions. It's known as the "Lansdowne" portrait after the person for whom it was commissioned: the Marquis of Lansdowne, who had earned American respect for defending the rebellious colonies in the British Houses of Parliament. Some of the other presidential studies are notable for the artists behind them: **Norman Rockwell** created an overly flattering portrait of Richard Nixon, while a bust of a relatively carefree, first-term **Bill Clinton** was the work of Jan Wood, a sculptor otherwise best known for her depictions of horses. Alexander Healy, who was commissioned for presidential portraits

Old Patent Office

Three blocks west of the National Building Museum and in the centre of the Penn Quarter, the Greek Revival **Old Patent Office**, begun in 1836 by Treasury Building and General Post Office architect **Robert Mills**, is among the oldest buildings in the city, though it wasn't completed for thirty years. It was designed to hold offices of the Interior Department and the Commissioners of Patents, and models of America's patented nineteenth-century inventions were on display – including Eli Whitney's cotton gin, Samuel Colt's pistol and Robert Fulton's steam engine, as well as items by Thomas Edison, Benjamin Franklin and Alexander Graham Bell. During the Civil War the building's halls were filled with over two thousand beds and used for emergency hospital services. In March 1865, just before the end of the war, Lincoln's second inaugural ball took place here, with four thousand people in attendance for a night of dancing and feasting. "Tonight", wrote Walt Whitman (himself a nurse at the building during the war), "beautiful women, perfumes, the violins' sweetness… then, the amputation, the blue face, the groan, the glassy eye of the dying".

Despite its heritage, the building was scheduled for demolition in the 1950s, before the Smithsonian stepped into the breach. Today the Old Patent Office building houses two of the city's major art institutions: the **National Portrait Gallery** and the **American Art Museum**. Note that some items not found in these museums may be on display in the Renwick Gallery's impressive Grand Salon (see p.104).

beginning in the 1850s, produced a moving portrayal of a pensive (and surprisingly handsome) **Abraham Lincoln**. Edmund Tarbell faced a unique challenge when painting **Woodrow Wilson**'s portrait; because the president was always too ill to pose, Tarbell was forced to work entirely from photographs. English portraitist Douglas Chandor's rather raffish **Franklin Delano Roosevelt** painting has FDR in a chic, fur-lined cape and sporting his trademark cigarette holder. This painting was to be part of an (unfinished) study of FDR with Churchill and Stalin at Yalta, which explains the alternative sketches of Roosevelt's hands holding cigarettes, glasses and pens. Finally, a notorious portrait of Lincoln, taken in February 1865 by war photographer Alexander Gardner, has a crack in the plate running across Lincoln's forehead. After his assassination, many observers saw this, in retrospect, as a terrible omen.

American Origins

The gallery's "**American Origins**" collection features portraits of both colonial figures and Native Americans, with several studies of braves and chiefs by George Catlin, a lithograph of **Sitting Bull**, and a painting of **Pocahontas** in English dress. A bust of **Geronimo** was sculpted by the Apache artist Allan Houser, a distant relative. Industrialists, inventors and businessmen are pictured alongside churchmen and feminists, so together with Bell, Edison and Carnegie there's **Belva Ann Lockwood**, the first woman to run for president (in 1884; she got 4149 votes), a bust of **Susan B. Anthony** by Adelaide Johnson (better known for her *Suffrage Monument* statue in the Capitol), and a stuffy portrait of feminist **Elizabeth Cady Stanton**.

Literature and the arts

Studies of personalities from literature and the arts include a touching early photograph by Man Ray of **Ernest Hemingway** and his young son, and the extraordinary bulky terracotta figure of **Gertrude Stein**, depicted by Jo Davidson as a tranquil seated Buddha. Fascinating, too, are Edward Biberman's creepy study of **Dashiell Hammett** in a horrible wool coat, and John White Alexander's depiction of a transfixed Samuel Clemens (better known as **Mark Twain**). Alexander painted **Walt Whitman** as a seated sage, with light streaming through his bushy beard. The collection's most prized piece, however, is Edgar Degas' severe portrait of his friend, Impressionist **Mary Cassatt**, hunched over a chair with a sneer on her face. Cassatt hated the image so much that she had it sold with the understanding that it wouldn't be allowed to go to an American collection where her family and friends might see it.

American Art Museum

The **American Art Museum**, 8th and F sts NW (daily 11.30am–7pm; free; ⊤202/633-7970, ⓦamericanart.si.edu; Gallery Place–Chinatown Metro), or technically, the National Museum of American Art, is the most recent appellation for an institution that has had many names over the years, from the "National Gallery" to the "National Collection of Fine Arts" to the "Smithsonian Art Collection". Whatever it's been called, there's always been a good collection of work here, with hundreds of items on display and thousands more on view in the **Luce Foundation Centre**. Here, you can spot works arranged cheek by jowl in cosy display cases, shelves and drawers, with more information on each item in the densely packed collection on view at computer kiosks around the centre. Although there are always plenty of temporary exhibitions going on, what follows is a selection of works from the permanent collection, some of which will usually be on display.

Western imagery

One of the museum's highlights is its selection of nineteenth-century art of the American West, including almost four hundred paintings by **George Catlin**, who spent six years touring the Great Plains, painting portraits and scenes of Native American life that he later displayed as part of his "Indian Gallery". His paintings were the first contact many white settlers had with the aboriginal peoples of America, and viewers were fascinated by his lush landscapes showing buffalo herds crossing the Missouri, or those featuring tribes at work and play. The contrast between cultures is best seen in Catlin's painting of a warrior named Pigeon's Egg Head arriving in Washington, DC in full traditional dress, only to return to his tribe in frock coat and top hat, sporting an umbrella and smoking a cigarette.

Catlin also produced many keenly observed domestic studies, like the painting of a woman with a child in an elaborately decorated cradle, while a **Joseph Henry Sharp** painting shows Blackfoot Indians making medicine by burning feathers over an open fire. One of Catlin's contemporaries, **John Mix Stanley**, primarily depicted Apache warriors, though one of his works captures a graphic *Buffalo Hunt*. There's a remarkable bronze statue, too, called *The Indian Ghost Dancer*, by **Paul Wayland Bartlett**, where the dancer is near exhaustion after hours of trancelike dancing.

Folk art

The museum's **folk art** collection includes some traditional pieces, notably Native American ceramics, but it's the contemporary works that really stand out. **Malcah Zeldis**'s exuberant *Miss Liberty Celebration* depicts the Statue of Liberty surrounded by a family group comprising Elvis, Einstein, Lincoln, Marilyn and Chaplin, and was completed to celebrate the artist's recovery from cancer. The most extraordinary piece here is perhaps **James Hampton**'s so-called *Hampton Throne*, a mystic, cryptic cluster of foil- and gilt-covered lightbulbs, boxes, plaques, wings, altars and furniture capped by the text "Fear Not". Hampton, a solitary figure who referred to himself as "Saint James", worked in a garage on N Street NW between 1950 and his death in 1964. It's believed that *Hampton Throne* is full of obscure religious references and was unfinished at the time of the artist's death. Incidentally, the work's full title is *The Throne of the Third Heaven of the Nations' Millennium General Assembly*.

Early American art

The heavyweights of **nineteenth- and early twentieth-century American art** include significant chunks of work by **Albert Pinkham Ryder**, whose dark, often nightmarish, paintings are full of symbolism, twisted landscapes and classical-fiction or mythical allegories rendered in small frames with thick paint. His best pieces here include *Jonah*, a swirling, abstract seascape; *Lord Ullin's Daughter*, poised amid tumultuous waves and perilous rocks; and *King Cophetua and the Beggar Maid*, a dark, surreal encounter in a dreamlike terrain. There's more general appeal in those works of **Winslow Homer**, whether it's the rural studies of his *Bean Picker* or *A Country Lad*, or the leisurely antics of female models in his dappled *Sunlight and Shadow* and *Summer Afternoon*, all executed in the same prolific period during the 1870s.

Other works by renowned artists include **Mary Cassatt**'s *Spanish Dancer*, showing little of her later Impressionist flair; accomplished society portraitist **John Singer Sargent**'s study of the beautiful, taffeta-clad *Elizabeth Winthrop Chanler*; and colonial master **John Singleton Copley**'s striking portrait of *Mrs George Watson*. There are also examples from the noted collection of sculptures and models by **Hiram Powers**. The surface of *America*, a plaster model of crowned Liberty, is punctured by the tips of a series of metal rods, inserted to act as a guide for carving the eventual marble version. *Thomas Jefferson* shows the same technique, making it look as if the frock-coated president has a severe case of acne.

Landscapes and portraits

The excellent collection of American **landscapes** includes *Among the Sierra Nevada Mountains*, a superb example of the dramatic power of **Albert Bierstadt**, whose three long trips to the American West between 1858 and 1873 provided him with enough material for the rest of his career. The painting's striking ethereal light illuminates distant ducks in flight, and snowcapped peaks. Likewise, there is no hint of human presence in the enormous **Thomas Moran** landscape *The Chasm of the Colorado*, alive with multifarious reds. Similar, though smaller, expressions of grandeur can be found in scenes of Lake Placid, the Colorado River and Niagara Falls painted by **Hudson River School** artists such as Jasper Francis Cropsey and John Frederick Kensett, who cast their sensuous eye across what Americans soon came to regard as their own backyard.

Charles Bird King powerfully portrays the original inhabitants of these landscapes in the images of five Pawnee braves wearing red face-paint and ceremonial bead earrings. The steady flow of Native Americans through the capital in the 1820s – there to sign away their land in a series of worthless treaties – prompted him to divert his attention to recording their likenesses instead. Also rather extraordinary, though in quite a different fashion, is his contemporaneous portrait of *Mrs John Quincy Adams*, obviously uncomfortable with the artist's suggestion that she sit at a harp in an ill-advised crown of feathers.

Twentieth-century art

The museum's **twentieth-century art** collection is usually displayed in the spectacular 260ft-long **Lincoln Gallery**, which runs down the east side of the building. It was here, amid the white marble pillars, that Abraham Lincoln and his entourage enjoyed his second inaugural ball. There are notable twentieth-century modern pieces, among them items by Robert Motherwell, Willem de Kooning, Robert Rauschenberg, Clyfford Still, Ed Kienholz and Jasper Johns, but none is more vibrant than Nam June Paik's jaw-dropping **Electronic Superhighway**, a huge neon-outlined map of the US with each state represented by TV screens pulsing with hypnotic images. The museum also owns a decent selection of abstract works by the artists of the **Washington Colour School** – primarily Gene Davis, Morris Louis, Kenneth Noland, Thomas Downing, Paul Reed and Howard Mehring – also known as colour-field painting. All tended to stain their canvases with acrylic paint to give greater impact to colour and form, methods that first came to public attention in 1965 at a groundbreaking exhibition of modern art in DC.

Along 7th and F streets

The core of the Penn Quarter lies at 7th and F streets, where spruced-up buildings that hark back to the post-Civil War era (notably 700–738 F St) form the hub of an arts district studded with boutiques, theatres and galleries. The Smithsonian museums and the 20,000-seat **Verizon Center**, 601 F St NW (☎202/628-3200, ⓦ www.verizoncenter.com), have had something to do with that transformation as well – it's the home of the NBA's mediocre **Wizards**, the WNBA **Mystics** and the NHL's **Capitals** (see p.247). Elsewhere, with the revival of the neighbourhood's fortunes, high-end chain retailers and chic restaurants have also migrated here, along with the requisite depositories for all that tourist loot; the most conspicuous such sight is **Madame Tussauds Wax Museum**, 1025 F St (summer daily 10am–6pm; winter Mon–Thurs 10am–4pm, Fri–Sun 10am–6pm; $20), which, along with the usual rash of frozen celebrities, provides a selection of political figures such as FDR and Churchill commiserating over World War II, J. Edgar Hoover scheming over the Cold War, and Lincoln getting assassinated for winning the Civil War.

Elsewhere, **The Lansburgh**, 420 7th St (between D and E), was once a grand department store, its soaring facade now providing a grand frame for the Shakespeare Theatre Company, while at 9th and F streets, the elegant Roman-esque Revival **Riggs National Bank Building** has been rescued as a *Courtyard by Marriott* hotel (see p.196) and still features its grand 1891 facade, with rough-hewn arches and brick-and-granite cladding. Best of all is the former **General Post Office**, 7th and F streets, which was inspired by the ancient Roman Temple of Jupiter; the city's first marble building, this Neoclassical masterwork dates back to 1842. Since the post office relocated later in the nineteenth century, the building has served as the site of the US Tariff Commission and, in its present form, the trendy *Hotel Monaco* (see p.198).

International Spy Museum

Without question, the **International Spy Museum**, 800 F St NW (usually daily 10am–7pm summer, 9am–7pm winter; $18; ☎202/207-0219, ⓦwww .spymuseum.org; Gallery Place–Chinatown Metro), is a big part of F Street's revival, residing in five nineteenth-century structures, including the Atlas Building, which, fittingly, was home to the US Communist Party from 1941 to 1948. Despite the steep entrance fee, the museum is one of DC's most popular sights (call ahead for entry information, as tickets can sell out days in advance in high season). Its success has even engendered the creation of a theme-park-like interactive game, **Operation Spy**, in which guests have an hour to find a nuclear weapon, a task that sends them scurrying through elevators and corridors and riding on motion simulators using their code- and safe-cracking abilities as well as video and audio surveillance. It's an extra $14 per person (12 and above only; $25 joint ticket) to play.

The museum proper is crammed full of the kind of Cold War-era gizmos, weapons and relics that will make readers of Robert Ludlum and Tom Clancy giddy with delight; it also has displays covering thousands of years of spycraft, beginning with a small model of the infamous Trojan Horse and moving on to ancient Rome, imperial China, Elizabethan England and Civil War-era America. Most of the museum is devoted to the US during the years 1939 to 1991, from the beginning of World War II to the end of the Cold War, with a sizeable assortment of multimedia exhibits, walk-through re-creations, dioramas and video clips. A series of interesting galleries covers topics like celebrities (notably Marlene Dietrich) fighting the Nazis through subterfuge, and allows you to view **re-creations** of a cramped East Berlin escape tunnel and a darkened "interrogation room" for captured spies.

Among these galleries, the standouts are the **artefacts** from the height of the Cold War in the 1950s and 1960s. Some of the many highlights include tiny pistols disguised as lipstick holders, cigarette cases, pipes and flashlights; oddments like invisible-ink writing kits and a *Get Smart!*-style shoe phone; a colourful and active model of James Bond's Aston Martin spy car; bugs and radio transmitters hidden in ambassadorial gifts (such as a Great Seal of the US given by Russians); ricin-tipped poison umbrellas used to kill Warsaw Pact dissidents; and a rounded capsule containing a screwdriver, razor and serrated knife – ominously marked "rectal tool kit". Also highlighted are the many personalities, real and imagined, that make up the colourful world of espionage: Whittaker Chambers and his microfilm-containing pumpkin are here, as are Mata Hari and **celebrity spies** like singer Josephine Baker and, more inexplicably, TV superchef Julia Child.

Ford's Theatre National Historic Site

On the west end of the Penn Quarter, the district north of Pennsylvania Avenue has been home to several theatres since the founding of the city, being little more than a stroll from the White House and mansions of Lafayette Square. In 1861, entrepreneur John T. Ford converted a church into an eponymous theatre that proved to be popular until April 14, 1865, when, during a performance of *Our American Cousin* (top ticket price, $1), actor and Southern sympathizer John Wilkes Booth shot President **Abraham Lincoln**. Following Lincoln's assassination, **Ford's Theatre** (daily 9am–5pm, closed during rehearsals and matinees; free, but tickets required; turn up when the site opens to book, or call ☎202/397-7328; ☎202/347-4833, ⓦwww.fordstheatre.org, www.nps.gov/foth; Metro Centre Metro) was draped in black as a show of respect, and it remained closed while the conspirators were pursued, caught and tried. Ford abandoned attempts to reopen the theatre after he received death threats, the government decreed that it could never again be used as a place of public entertainment, and the theatre was eventually converted into offices and storage space. It wasn't until the 1960s that it was restored to its former condition – not only using period furnishings but, defying the earlier decree, operating again as a working theatre.

A grand new renovation has brought the site back to vivid life, and within this surprisingly charming historic structure (which follows the smallish size and proportions of theatres of that era) you can see the damask-furnished and flag-draped presidential box in which Lincoln sat in his rocking chair, and which has been closed off to theatre-goers in honour of the slain president. Other eye-opening items include the actual murder weapon (a .44 Derringer), a blood-stained piece of Lincoln's overcoat, and Booth's knife, keys, compass, boot and diary. There are also mementoes on view of that fateful night, such as theatre tickets, instruments played by the house orchestra, and old playbills.

Also part of the historic site is the **Petersen House**, across the street at 516 10th Ave NW (same hours and entry; free), where, having been shot in Ford's Theatre, an unconscious President Lincoln was carried and placed in the back bedroom of a home owned by tailor William Petersen. Lincoln never regained consciousness and died the next morning. You can walk through the restored Petersen House's gloomy parlour rooms to the small bedroom, where there's a replica of the bed on which Lincoln died – he lay diagonally, since he was too tall to lie straight.

Chinatown and around

DC's version of **Chinatown**, north of the Penn Quarter, stretches no more than a handful of undistinguished city blocks along G and I streets NW, between 6th and 8th. The vibrant triumphal arch over H Street (at 7th), paid for by Beijing in the 1980s, is hopelessly at odds with the neighbourhood itself, since it heralds little more than a dozen restaurants and a few grocery stores. In fact, the city's first Chinese immigrants, in the early nineteenth century, didn't live in today's Chinatown (which began in the early twentieth century) but in the slums of **Swampoodle**, north of the Capitol. At that time, H Street and its environs were home to small businesses and modest rooming houses. In one of these, during the 1860s, **Mary Surratt** presided over the Lincoln assassination conspirators. A plaque marks the site of the house (then no. 541 H St), now a restaurant at 604 H St NW.

Elsewhere, **Mount Vernon Square**, which blocks the easy diagonal progress of Massachusetts and New York avenues, is the site of the grand, Neoclassical old **library**, 801 K St NW, now the site of the **Washington Historical Society** (daily 10am–5pm; free; ☎ 202/383-1800, ⓦ www.historydc.org), which presents regular exhibitions of local artists and the history of the District. Due north, the huge **Washington Convention Centre**, along N St between 7th and 9th, hosts big-ticket corporate events as well as political spectacles and the odd inauguration gala.

Around Metro Centre

Metro Centre, the downtown hub of the Metro system, has separate exits along G and 12th streets. To the east is the main public library, **Martin Luther King Jr Memorial Library**, 901 G St NW (Mon & Tues noon–9pm, Wed–Sat 9.30am–5.30pm, Sun 1–5pm), whose sleek lines of black steel and bronze-tinted glass announce it as the work of Mies van der Rohe. Inside, a large mural by Don Miller depicts the life and death of the esteemed civil rights leader. A few blocks north of Metro Centre is **1100 New York Avenue**, a 1939 former bus terminal with a sprightly Art Deco facade, now preserved within an office complex, its Streamline Moderne lobby open during daylight hours and offering the odd exhibit related to the golden age of bus stations.

Two blocks west of the terminal, the red-brick **New York Avenue Presbyterian Church**, 1313 New York Ave NW (daily 9am–1pm), offers a 1950s facsimile of the mid-nineteenth-century church in which the family of President Lincoln worshipped. The pastor at that time, Dr Gurley, was at Lincoln's bedside at the Petersen House when he died and conducted the funeral service four days later at the White House. Someone in the church's office (on the New York Avenue side) should be able to point out the president's second-row pew, while downstairs in the "Lincoln Parlor" you can see an early draft of his Emancipation Proclamation and portraits of Lincoln and Dr Gurley.

National Museum of Women in the Arts

Across the street from the church, the **National Museum of Women in the Arts** (Mon–Sat 10am–5pm, Sun noon–5pm; $10) houses the most important collection of its kind – more than four thousand works by around a thousand female artists, from the sixteenth century to the present day, as well as silverware, ceramics, photographs and decorative items. Even the building itself, a former Masonic lodge, is striking for its trapezoidal shape, brick-and-limestone facade and elegant colonnade.

Renaissance to Neoclassical art

The permanent collection starts with works from the Renaissance, such as those of **Sofonisba Anguissola**, who achieved fame as an accomplished portraitist before becoming court painter to Phillip II of Spain; her evocative *Double Portrait of a Lady and Her Daughter* is on display along with the engaging *Holy Family with St John* by her contemporary **Lavinia Fontana**. A century or so later, Dutch and Flemish women like **Clara Peeters**, **Judith Leyster** and **Rachel Ruysch** were producing still lifes and genre scenes that were equal to those of their more famous male colleagues – note the vivacity of Peeters's *Still Life of Fish and Cat*. On occasion, female artists broke out of their limited environment to paint non-traditional subjects: for example, German-born **Maria Sybilla Merian** crafted superb engravings of flora and fauna, inspired by her intrepid explorations in Surinam in 1699. Meanwhile, in France, women like **Elisabeth-Louise Vigée-Lebrun** held sway as court painters, depicting the royalty fluttering around Marie Antoinette, though she was denied the respect accorded her male contemporaries, and was kept out of the Académie des Beaux-Arts until the 1780s.

Nineteenth-century art

In the nineteenth century, American women artists began to enter the fray. **Lilly Martin Spencer** was inordinately popular as a producer of genre scenes: *The Artist and Her Family at a Fourth of July Picnic* is typically vibrant, despite the grim wartime period in which it was painted. As Impressionism widened the parameters of art, painters like **Berthe Morisot** and, particularly, **Mary Cassatt** produced daring (for the time) scenes of nursing mothers, young girls and mewling babies. Cassatt, like many of her contemporaries, was intrigued by the forms and colours of Asian art; *The Bath*, an etching of mother and baby created with crisp swatches of pale colour, was influenced by an exhibition of Japanese woodblocks she had seen in Paris, where she lived from an early age. **Cecilia Beaux**, also inspired by her stay in Paris, was sought-after for her rich, expressive portraits such as that of Ethel Page – so much so that she was honoured with a commission to paint Theodore and Mrs Roosevelt in 1903.

Twentieth-century art

The museum's twentieth-century collection includes classical sculptures by Camille Claudel, paintings by Georgia O'Keeffe and Tamara de Lempicka, linocuts by Hannah Höch, and a cycle of prints depicting the hardships of working-class life by the socialist **Käthe Kollwitz**, part of her powerful *A Weaver's Rebellion*. Insightful self-portraits reveal Kollwitz appearing drained by her work in an etching of 1921, and **Frida Kahlo**, dressed in a peasant's outfit and clutching a note to Trotsky, dedicating herself to the Revolution. The last gallery reaches into modern times, with striking photographs of figures from the entertainment and literary worlds by Louise Dahl-Wolfe, and contemporary work by sculptors Dorothy Dehner and Louise Nevelson, minimalist Dorothea Rockburne, and Abstract Expressionists Helen Frankenthaler, Lee Krasner and Elaine de Kooning, among others. One of the highlights is a series of studies for *The Dinner Party*, by **Judy Chicago**, a groundbreaking feminist work from the 1970s.

North of K Street

K Street, the axis of business and political lobbying, roughly divides the older section of Downtown to the southeast from the newer, blander section to the northwest. When companies first moved in during the 1970s, local building restrictions prevented them from aping New York's soaring urban landscape. Restricted to a maximum height of 130ft, the structures are generally production-line boxes of little distinction in which lobbyists, lawyers, brokers and bankers beaver away from dawn until dark. Between 13th and 20th streets there's barely a building to raise the pulse, though street vendors do their best to inject a bit of life, hustling jewellery, T-shirts, silk ties, hot dogs and bath salts.

DOWNTOWN: NORTH OF K STREET AND DUPONT CIRCLE

ACCOMMODATION

Aaron Shipman House	A
Beacon	I
Carlyle Suites	X
Chester Arthur House	B
DC Guesthouse	Z
Dupont at the Circle	D
Embassy Circle Guest House	C
Embassy Inn	H
Fairfax at Embassy Row	R
Hamilton Crowne Plaza	B
Helix	J
Holiday Inn Central	K
Jefferson	F
Madera	O
Mayflower	T
Palomar	N
Rouge	V
St Regis Washington	A
Swann House	P
Tabard Inn	Q
Topaz	Q
William Lewis House	D

CAFÉS & RESTAURANTS

Afterwords Café	9
Alberto's Pizza	29
Bistrot du Coin	4
Bombay Club	56
Café Asia	54
Café Citron	32
Café Promenade	T
City Lights of China	2
DC Coast	51
Firehook Bakery	14
Giovanni's Trattu	38
Grillfish	40
Java House	15
Julia's Empanadas	39
Komi	21
Loeb's Deli	55
Luna Grill & Diner	10
Malaysia Kopitiam	41
Marvelous Market	10
Mio	49
Moby Dick House of Kabob	36
Naan and Beyond	50
Nooshi	46
Obelisk	30
The Palm	37
Pizzeria Paradiso	20
Restaurant Nora	6
Siroc	52
Skewers	23
Stoney's	49
Sushi Taro	22
Tabard Inn	7
Teaism	5
Thai Chef	19
Urbana	43
Vidalia	43
Zorba's Café	13

BARS & CLUBS

Aura Lounge	41
Big Hunt	32
Black Fox Lounge	3
Brickskeller	16
Buffalo Billiards	35
ChurchKey	33
Eighteenth Street Lounge	42
FAB Lounge	1
Fox and Hounds	18
Gazuza	9
HR-57	12
Josephine	48
Logan Tavern	25
Madhatter	41
New Vegas Lounge	26
Ozio	44
Panache	53
The Park at Fourteenth	47
Recessions	47
Steve's Bar Room	34

GAY RESTAURANTS, BARS & CLUBS

Apex	31
Annie's Paramount Steakhouse	11
Cobalt	8
FAB Lounge	1
Green Lantern	45
JR's	17
MOVA Lounge	24
Omega	28
SoHo Tea & Coffee	27

Connecticut Avenue and around

Along with Pennsylvania Avenue NW, **Connecticut Avenue** NW is one of the two major roads through Washington, leading from Downtown to Dupont Circle and on to Upper Northwest. Indeed, it's also arguably the most appealing of all the District's thoroughfares, if only because it links so many interesting neighbourhoods – from chic and swanky to funky and bohemian – and takes you past all sorts of excellent restaurants, boutiques, bookshops, bars, clubs, museums and galleries along the way.

Mayflower Hotel

The double-bay-fronted **Mayflower Hotel**, 1127 Connecticut Ave NW (see p.195), has graced its location since 1925, when its first official function was to host President Calvin Coolidge's inaugural ball. Countless other official and unofficial events have taken place here – everything from high-profile diplomatic luncheons to off-the-record journalistic meetings. Designed by the New York architects responsible for Grand Central Terminal, the *Mayflower* is best known for its remarkable 500ft-long **Promenade** – effectively a lobby connecting Connecticut Avenue to 17th Street – which could comfortably accommodate an army division or two. It's rich in rugs, oils, sofas, gilt and mirrors, as is the hotel's **Grand Ballroom**, in which a dozen incoming presidents have swirled around the dance floor over the years. FDR lived in the *Mayflower* for a while after his inauguration, as did Truman while the White House was being renovated, and J. Edgar Hoover lunched here every day when he ran the FBI. The renovated hotel is an expensive night's rest, but you don't have to stay here to troop through the marvellous public spaces or watch the swells having lunch in the elite *Café Promenade* (see p.208).

Charles Sumner School

One long block north and east from the hotel at 1201 17th St NW, the **Charles Sumner School** (Tues–Fri 10am–5pm; free; ☎202/442-6060; Farragut North Metro) honours the nineteenth-century senator nearly clubbed to death in the Old Senate Chamber by pro-slavery Congressman Preston Brooks of South Carolina. Brooks violently objected to a speech Sumner had directed at his uncle, Senator Andrew Brooks, and it took three years for Sumner to recover from his injuries, but both he and Brooks became heroes to their respective sides.

To improve the education offered to black children, this one-time public high school – the first in the country for African American youth – was established in the city in 1870. A harmonious red-brick building with a handsome central clock tower, the school is today largely used for conferences, but a free onsite **museum** has a number of mildly interesting exhibits, which range from temporary shows by black artists to highlights of the life of Frederick Douglass to displays relating to the city's school system.

St Matthew's Cathedral

While not quite on the same level as the National Shrine of the Immaculate Conception further north (see p.151), **St Matthew's Cathedral**, 1725 Rhode Island Ave NW (Mon–Fri & Sun 6.30am–6.30pm, Sat 7.30am–6.30pm), is still monumental and replete with evocative neo-Gothic character. The centrepiece above the altar is a towering, 35ft **mosaic** of the church's namesake, the patron saint of civil servants; other features include a grand organ with seventy tin pipes, a white-marble altar and pulpit, and four more mosaics depicting the four Evangelists (Matthew, Mark, Luke and John). Beyond its striking appearance, the cathedral is perhaps best known as the place where **JFK**'s funeral Mass was held in 1963, and an inlaid plaque honouring the slain president lies in front of the altar (he was buried at Arlington National Cemetery). More surprisingly, in 2005 former Chief Justice William Rehnquist was eulogized here in a Lutheran ceremony, and Protestant presidents as well as just about every notable Catholic politician in Congress have also dropped by. If you want to peer at the bigwig worshippers, church services are open to all.

16th Street and around

Most of the area above K Street was scantily populated until well into the nineteenth century, but post-Civil War expansion changed **16th Street** completely, replacing ramshackle buildings in a predominantly black neighbourhood with large mansions, gentlemen's clubs and patrician hotels, all benefiting from their proximity to the White House. Heading north from the Executive Mansion, the old *Carlton Hotel*, 16th and K streets, has maintained its rich 1920s decor after transforming into the stylish *St Regis* (see p.195). Further along on 16th Street, the stately *Jefferson Hotel*, at no. 1220 (see p.195), was built in 1922 and has long been a favourite of presidential entourages for its nineteenth-century-styled charm.

About a block east, the **Metropolitan AME Church**, 1518 M St NW (Mon–Fri 9am–6pm), is a large, neo-Gothic, red-brick structure built and paid for in 1886 by former slaves. It hosted Frederick Douglass's funeral in February 1895, as he had often preached here. On the day of the funeral, crowds swamped the street outside, black schools closed for the day, and flags in the city flew at half-mast. This formidable edifice is one of the District's ecclesiastical high points, with its striking narrow arches and spires and handsome decorative granite trim, but is structurally deficient and may not last another 125 years without significant renovation. Nearby are the offices of the **Washington Post**, 1150 15th St NW, the second most famous daily in America after the *New York Times*, its reputation still based squarely on the investigative coup of its reporters Bob Woodward and Carl Bernstein, who exposed the Watergate scandal that led to the resignation of President Nixon in 1974. One block north of the *Jefferson Hotel*, **Scott Circle**, at Massachusetts and Rhode Island avenues, was once a fashionable nineteenth-century park but is today a traffic roundabout graced with a statue of Union commander General Winfield Scott astride his horse.

North of the circle, architectural highlights on 16th include the **Carnegie Institution**, at P Street, a pleasing Neoclassical monument from 1909, with grand Ionic columns and bronze doors that lead to a two-storey rotunda; the **Cairo**, at Q Street, an 1894 hodgepodge of Moorish, Romanesque and early-modern Sullivan-esque designs; the so-called **Green Door**, 1623 16th St, an 1886 Richardsonian Romanesque mansion with stone cladding, red-brick arches and turrets; and the **Chastleton**, no. 1701, a Gothic Revival apartment complex from the 1920s with arched windows, heraldry and gargoyles.

Scottish Rite Temple

John Russell Pope's **Scottish Rite Temple**, halfway between Downtown and the Shaw district at 1733 16th St NW (Mon–Thurs 8am–5pm; free), is one of DC's most eye-catching buildings; indeed, if you're anywhere in the vicinity, you can't possibly miss it, with its towering Ionic columns, ziggurat-like roof, huge base, and ancient-temple design inspired by the Mausoleum at Halicarnassus, one of the Seven Wonders of the Ancient World.

Built in 1915 of limestone and granite, this Masonic temple is loaded with arcane symbolism, striking imagery (notably the two sphinxes guarding the building),

The US capitol was designed, constructed and ruled by **Freemasons** from its inception through much of the twentieth century. While some have seen sinister implications in this secretive group – indeed, an actual Anti-Mason Party collected votes in early American elections – others have marvelled at the way it fostered a sense of inclusiveness among political leaders who might otherwise have had little to do with each other. The hallmarks of Masonry can be found almost everywhere in town, from the layout of the city streets, to the placement and physical shape of its major buildings, to the mysterious character of American currency. For a glimpse of Masonry in action you won't have to look far: many current institutions (such as the National Museum of Women in the Arts) occupy former Masonic temples, while gleaming icons such as the Scottish Rite Temple and George Washington Masonic Memorial are eye-popping architectural spectacles built around the symbols and emblems of the secret society.

and inscriptions hailing knowledge, truth and other values. Unlike many such temples, though, this one has long been accessible to the uninitiated. There's a **museum** that honours the works of selected Masons locally and nationally, and offers a selection of regalia that includes the ceremonial vestments of each degree of Masonhood (aprons, caps, jewels, rings and so forth), with each rank getting increasingly elaborate duds. Pride of place, though, goes to the replica of the foundation stone of the US Capitol, laid by George Washington (a Mason) in 1793, a near-perfect 18in cube. The **public library** also rewards a visit, housing a voluminous collection of works by Scottish Mason and poet Robert Burns, among other celebrated members of the order.

Logan Circle and 14th Street

In the early twentieth century, an influx of black middle-class residents began to fill the roomy Victorian houses around **Logan Circle**, between Downtown and Shaw. The houses have miraculously survived the neighbourhood's slow decline since the 1950s; turrets, terraces, balconies and pediments in various states of repair signal the fact that this is a protected historic district. Since the mid-1990s there's been a major rebound in housing prices, and the many theatre companies, trendy bars and restaurants, and chic boutiques signal that gentrification is well under way.

14th Street, half a block west, had many of its buildings burned in the 1968 riots but has since recovered and become a commercial axis for the neighbourhood, with various refurbishment projects regularly taking place. However, keep in mind that the closest Metro access is six long blocks away and the Logan Circle area is something of an island for redevelopment – there are plenty of dicey areas further north and east.

Bethune Council House

In one of the restored townhouses just off Logan Circle, the **Bethune Council House**, 1318 Vermont Ave NW (Mon–Sat 9am–5pm, last tour 4pm; ☏202/673-2402, ⓦwww.nps.gov/mamc; free), serves as a memorial to one of DC's most prominent African American residents, Mary McLeod Bethune, who founded the Daytona Educational and Industrial School for Negro Girls, later **Bethune-Cookman College**; worked under FDR as a special adviser on minority affairs and director of the Division of Negro Affairs (the first African American woman to head a federal office); and took part in the conference that established the United Nations. Administered by the National Park Service, the house serves as a research centre and archive, though you're welcome to tour the restored rooms, which contain a few of Bethune's mementos alongside period photographs and changing exhibitions. The memorial to Bethune in Lincoln Park (see p.86) records more of her legacy. The best way to get here is the fifteen-minute walk up Vermont Avenue from McPherson Square Metro, past Thomas Circle.

Dupont Circle

Dupont Circle is the great traffic roundabout formed at the intersection of Massachusetts, Connecticut and New Hampshire avenues with 19th and P streets, making for an elaborate two-ringed, ten-spoked wheel. The traffic circle also gives its name to the surrounding streets: a fun, relaxed neighbourhood alive with hipsters, yuppies and old-timers, plus the city's most densely packed choices for lodging, dining, drinking and clubbing.

Easily accessible on the Metro Red Line, it's also one of the city's best areas for a walk, loaded with gorgeous townhouses and mansions from the nineteenth and early twentieth centuries, as well as a number of museums, bookshops and galleries. Along with Connecticut Avenue NW, the other major stretches for night-time entertainment are P Street west of the Circle and 17th Street east of it. **Embassy Row**, just to the northwest along Massachusetts Avenue, is lined with historic Beaux-Arts mansions now stuffed with diplomats and staffers, with flags of their respective nations flying out front. One of the best times to visit Dupont Circle is the first weekend in June, when a consortium of museums sponsors the Dupont–Kalorama **Museums Walk Weekend** (Ⓦ www.dkmuseums.com), featuring free concerts, historic-house tours and craft fairs.

Some history

Until the Civil War, Pacific Circle – as Dupont Circle was first known – marked the western edge of the city, beyond which were farms, barns and slaughterhouses. After the war, however, streets were paved and a bridge was built across Rock Creek to nearby Georgetown. The **British Embassy** was built here in the mid-1870s, and subsequently lawyers and businessmen installed their families in grand Victorian houses. By the turn of the century, Dupont Circle was where all self-respecting industrial barons and high-flying diplomats built their city mansions. Massachusetts Avenue, northwest of the Circle, became so popular with foreign legations that it acquired the tag Embassy Row, while the even more secluded residences north of S Street developed into the exclusive neighbourhood of **Kalorama** (see p.142) – named in Greek for the "beautiful view" it afforded of the Rock Creek Valley.

Dupont Circle's golden age of soirées and socialites ended, however, as many of its wealthy residents were hit by the 1929 stock market crash and sold out; other mansions were torn down or became boarding houses for the post–World War II influx of federal workers. The Circle became solidly middle-class and, during the 1970s, even vaguely radical, as a younger hippie crowd moved in and gays and lesbians found the tolerant atmosphere to their liking. By the 1980s redevelopment money began to pour in and rampant gentrification took place, driving out the hippies and giving the formerly edgy neighbourhood an elite air that appealed to a more upscale market. At the end of the 2000s, Dupont Circle's course has become appropriately circular, and it's once more an upmarket address, full of designer coffeehouses and swanky restaurants – though few multi-millionaires and industrial barons.

The traffic circle and around

The traffic island of Dupont Circle is as much a hub as any roundabout in DC, and centres on a **fountain** whose frolicking nude allegorical figures – representing sea, stars and wind – were meant to honour the naval exploits of Civil War admiral Samuel Dupont. Although the site of the odd political protest, on the whole it's an easygoing hangout with chess players hogging the tables in the centre of the Circle and numerous cafés, bookshops and restaurants close by. There are Metro entrances to the northwest and south.

There are too many notable examples of historic architecture here to mention, but a few buildings stand out. The private Neoclassical **Washington Club**, 15 Dupont Circle NW at Massachusetts Ave, was formerly the Patterson House, built in 1901 by master Beaux-Arts architect Stanford White. It was here that the Coolidge family camped out during White House renovations and entertained Charles Lindbergh soon after his solo transatlantic crossing. Another members-only institution, the swanky **Sulgrave Club**, 1801 Massachusetts Ave, has an elegant Beaux-Arts design and terracotta details and was completed a year after the Patterson House, while at 1785 Massachusetts Ave, the **National Trust for Historic Preservation** (☎202/588-6000, ⓦwww.nationaltrust.org) occupies the towering edifice once known as the Andrew Mellon Building. The striking 1922 building has lovely period details, again of a late Beaux-Arts flavour; for a closer look, take one of the Trust's free tours, offered by reservation only. The turn-of-the-twentieth-century Neoclassical style influences almost every neighbourhood building of that vintage, holding up even by 1936, when petrol stations like the old **Embassy Gulf**, 2200 P St NW, were built to resemble Classical Revival banks.

Just outside the northwest-side Metro exit, the grand **Blaine Mansion**, at 2000 Massachusetts Ave, is a marvellous red-brick Victorian from 1881 that was once home to three-time presidential candidate James "Slippery Jim" Blaine, whose worst defeat was in 1884, when he became the first Republican nominee to lose a general election after the Civil War.

Heurich House

Although most of the grand old mansions are open only to club members, embassy employees and private owners, one historic residence is regularly open to the public. The wondrous **Heurich House**, 1307 New Hampshire Ave NW (tours Thurs–Sat 11.30am & 1pm, Sat also 2.30pm, Wed by reservation only; $5; ☎202/429-1894, ⓦwww.heurichhouse.org; Dupont Circle Metro), was built in 1894 for German-born brewing magnate Christian Heurich, and is a stunning, if extreme, example of the Richardsonian Romanesque style popular at the time. With its rough-hewn stone tower and castellations and richly carved wood-and-plaster interior, the mansion – known as "The Brewmaster's Castle" – resembles a miniature medieval fortress. The tours take you through many of the restored rooms and focus on the mansion's lavish decor and the lifestyle of its original occupants. On display are the formal parlour, drawing room and dining room, a music room with a mahogany musicians' balcony, some of the fifteen opulent marble and onyx fireplaces, and the basement *Bierstube* (beer room), carved with such Teutonic drinking mottos as "He who has never been drunk is not a good man".

Embassy Row

While there are many historic structures housing diplomatic missions in the vicinity of the circle, **Embassy Row** starts in earnest a few paces northwest up Massachusetts Avenue. Here, the Indonesian Embassy at no. 2020 occupies the magnificent **Walsh-McLean House**, built in the Second Empire style in 1903 for gold baron Thomas Walsh. It's a superb building – with colonnaded loggia, mansard roof and intricate, carved windows – that was once one of high society's most fashionable venues. Nearby, the **Cosmos Club**, 2121 Massachusetts Ave, was founded in 1878 by Western explorer John Wesley Powell, and is an exquisite private entity whose 1901 Beaux-Arts style has played host to numerous presidents, diplomats and scientists.

Along with the historic digs around here, there are a number of **statues**, too. A tall, brooding memorial to Czech president **Tomas Masaryk** stands at 22nd and Q streets; across from the Indian embassy, a skinny **Mahatma Gandhi** with a walking stick presides over a traffic island at Massachusetts, Q and 21st; and **Winston Churchill** flashes the victory sign outside the residence of the British ambassador, 3100 Massachusetts Ave, supposedly with one foot on DC (American) soil and the other on embassy (British) grounds. The residence itself is a lovely incarnation of an English country manor, designed in 1928 by Edward Lutyens, and in great contrast to the bleakly modern British embassy on the same property.

Although the diplomatic residences in the area are typically closed to the public, you can take a closer look inside some three dozen of them during May's free **Around the World Embassy Tour**, which also focuses on the food, dance, art and music of their respective cultures. For more information, visit the "Passport DC" section of Culture Tourism DC's website (Ⓦ www.culturaltourismdc.org).

Anderson House

The **Anderson House**, 2118 Massachusetts Ave NW (tours Tues–Sat 1.15, 2.15 & 3.15pm; free; Ⓣ 202/785-2040 ext 427, Ⓦ www.societyofthecincinnati.org; Dupont Circle Metro), is a veritable palace, built between 1902 and 1905 as the winter residence of Larz Anderson, who served as ambassador to Belgium and Japan, its Beaux-Arts grey-stone exterior sporting twin arched entrances with heavy wooden doors and a colonnaded portico. Inside, cavernous fireplaces, inlaid marble floors, Flemish tapestries, evocative murals and a grand ballroom provide a lavish backdrop for diplomatic receptions. Anderson bequeathed this wonderful house to the **Society of the Cincinnati**, as his great-grandfather was a founding member. Established in 1783, the society is the oldest patriotic organization in the country and maintains a small museum of Revolutionary War memorabilia here; if you can prove your lineage to an American officer in that conflict, you can apply to become a member. Appropriately enough, **George Washington** was its first president general, and there's a white marble bust of him in the entrance hall. The best time to visit the Anderson House is when it's offering one of its regular **free concerts** (see p.233), typically classical chamber-music recitals.

Sheridan Circle and around

Further northwest, at **Sheridan Circle**, the 1909 equestrian statue of Union general Phillip H. Sheridan commemorates this controversial figure of modern warfare, who was the innovator of "scorched earth" tactics in the Civil War and went on to mercilessly battle native tribes in the Indian Wars before, more surprisingly, advocating for the protection of what became Yellowstone National Park. On the south side of the circle, the **Residence of the Turkish Ambassador**, 1606 23rd St, is brimming with Near Eastern motifs; oddly, it wasn't commissioned by the Turks at all but by one Edward Everett, the man who patented the fluted bottle cap. From the circle you can duck down 23rd Street to see **Dumbarton Bridge**, guarded on either side by enormous bronze bison. The bridge provides the quickest route into northern Georgetown, emerging on Q Street by Dumbarton House, about twenty minutes from Dupont Circle.

The Phillips Collection

The **Phillips Collection**, 1600 21st St NW (Tues–Sat 10am–5pm, Sun 11am–6pm, Thurs closes at 8.30pm; Tues–Fri free, Sat & Sun $10, special exhibitions $12–15; ☏202/387-2151, ⓦwww.phillipscollection.org; Dupont Circle Metro), claims to be "America's first museum of modern art", based on its having opened eight years before New York's Museum of Modern Art. The oldest part of the Georgian Revival brownstone building was the family home of founder **Duncan Phillips**, who established a gallery in 1921 financed by the family's steel fortune. Phillips bought nearly 2400 works over the years; the collection is diverse, though it was initially guided primarily by Phillips's own enthusiasms, which included plenty of French Impressionists and modernists like Mark Rothko and other American Abstract Expressionists, as well as pre-modern artists like Giorgione and El Greco.

From its original building, the museum has expanded considerably, adding the **Goh Annex** on 21st Street in 1989 and a new underground wing, the Sant Building, to focus on more contemporary works. There's also a gift shop and a café on site. A full programme of **cultural events** includes classical music recitals, lectures, tours and other activities.

European works

The permanent collection is regularly rotated throughout the galleries, and arranged by non-historical themes, so you'll have to browse the art rather than zeroing in on a particular section. Wherever they're located, the **European** power-houses of the collection comprise a wistful Blue Period Picasso, *The Blue Room*; Matisse's modernist nude study *Studio, Quai St-Michel*, a Cézanne still life and enigmatic self-portrait, and no fewer than four Van Goghs, including the powerful *Road Menders*. Pierre Bonnard gets a good showing – you have to stand well back to take in the expansive, post-Impressionist scale of *The Terrace* and *The Palm*. Top billing generally goes to Renoir's *The Luncheon of the Boating Party*, where straw-boater-wearing dandies linger over a long and bibulous feast. Phillips bought the painting in 1923 as part of a two-year burst of acquisition that also yielded Cézanne's *Mont Saint-Victoire* and Honoré Daumier's *The Uprising*. There's an impressive selection of **Degas** works, too – from early scenes like *Women Combing Their Hair* to the late ballet picture *Dancers at the Bar*, in which the background and hair of the subjects collide in an orange frenzy.

Other **nineteenth-century works** include pieces by Gustave Courbet and Eugène Delacroix (note his wonderful painting of the violinist Paganini in full fiddle). Phillips's catholic taste comes to the fore with the two paintings of a repentant St Peter: one, fat and desperate, by Goya, the other a striking, eerie study by El Greco. Later modern pieces include thirteen Cubist works by Georges Braque; Jean Arp's striking *Helmeted Head II*; Mondrian's *Painting no. 9*; and **Paul Klee**'s kaleidoscopic maze of rectangles, triangles and trapezoidal shapes in *The Way to the Citadel*.

American works

Beyond French Impressionism, the collection's strength is **late nineteenth-** and **early twentieth-century American art**, featuring pieces like Winslow Homer's bleak *To the Rescue*; James McNeill Whistler's enigmatic *Miss Lilian Woakes*; and Albert Pinkham Ryder's moody and atmospheric *Macbeth and the Witches*. Also worth a look are Charles Sheeler's sleek ode to the modern age, *Skyscrapers*, a few colourful still lifes by Stuart Davis, and Jacob Lawrence's extracts from a powerful 59-piece series called *The Migration of the Negro*. **Edward Hopper**'s works include *Sunday*, featuring a man sitting alone on a bleak, empty street, and *Approaching a City*, viewed from the vantage point of sunken train tracks.

Abstract Expressionist works from the 1950s include a sweeping set of paintings by Mark Rothko, such as his *Orange and Red on Red*, in the Rothko Room of the Sant Building. Also on view are Philip Guston's phantasmagoric *The Native's Return*; Helen Frankenthaler's bloody red stain of *Canyon*; Sam Francis's jazzy and vivid *Blue*; Willem de Kooning's swirling and pulsing forms of *Asheville*; and Richard Diebenkorn's California beach abstraction *Ocean Park no. 38*.

Kalorama

North of Sheridan Circle, exclusive **Kalorama**'s quiet streets with manicured lawns stretch out to meet Rock Creek Park, and the diplomatic community thrives behind lace curtains and bulletproof glass in row after row of multimillion-dollar townhouse embassies, private homes and hibiscus-rich gardens. One of the best such examples, the **Hauge House**, lies on the neighbourhood's south end, at 24th and S streets. This sprawling French Renaissance limestone mansion housed the District's first Norwegian embassy in 1907, and today it's home to the Cameroon embassy.

If you head up 24th Street toward Kalorama Circle, you'll find spectacular views across Rock Creek Park to Georgetown and beyond. Just to the east, the **Residence of the French Ambassador**, 2221 Kalorama Rd NW, is a Tudor Revival country manor that was originally built for a mining magnate and sold to the French in 1936 for the then absurdly expensive sum of almost half a million dollars. Similarly impressive, the **Codman-Davis House**, 2145 Decatur Place NW, is a 1907 Beaux-Arts mansion built by museum founder William Corcoran in smart neo-Georgian style. More surprisingly, the grand Georgian estate known as **The Lindens**, 2401 Kalorama Rd NW, isn't a Revival structure at all, but an authentic 1754 Colonial mansion, built in Massachusetts when DC was still swampland, and relocated here as a preservation measure in the 1930s. Technically, it's the oldest building in Washington, though that title belongs more authentically to the Old Stone House in Georgetown (see p.164).

Woodrow Wilson House

Many commanders in chief lived in Washington, DC before moving into the White House; all but one of them left the moment they retired from public service. **Woodrow Wilson**, the 28th president, spent the last years of his life in a fine Waddy Butler Wood-designed Georgian Revival house at 2340 S St NW that is now open for **tours** (Tues–Sun 10am–4pm; $7.50; ⓣ 202/387-4062; ⓦ www.woodrowwilsonhouse.org; Dupont Circle Metro). It's a comfortable home – light and airy, with high ceilings, wood floors, a wide staircase and a solarium – which, despite his incapacitating stroke in 1919, Wilson aimed to use as a workplace where he could write political science books and practice law. However, Wilson lived here for only three years, and after he passed away was interred in Washington National Cathedral.

Visitors are first ushered into the front parlour, where Wilson liked to receive guests, and then continue on to see other parts of the house including the elevator, installed to help the enfeebled ex-president move between floors, and the bedroom, furnished by his wife Edith as it had been in the White House. The canvas-walled library of the scholarly president (he ran Princeton University before he ran the country) once held eight thousand books, but they were donated to the Library of Congress after his death; the only remaining ones are the 69 volumes of Wilson's own writings. In a separate room is a silent-movie projector and screen that were given to him after his stroke by Douglas Fairbanks Sr.

Textile Museum

Next door to the Woodrow Wilson House, in two equally grand converted residences, the **Textile Museum** (Tues–Sat 10am–5pm, Sun 1–5pm; $5; ☎202/667-0441, ⓦwww.textilemuseum.org; Dupont Circle Metro) presents exhibitions drawn from its 18,000-strong collection of textiles and carpets. The museum had its roots in the collection of George Hewitt Myers, who bought his first Asian rug as a student and opened the museum with three hundred other rugs and textile pieces in 1925. Based in his family home and designed by no less an architect than John Russell Pope, the museum soon expanded into the house next door; today both buildings and the beautiful gardens are open to the public. Displays might include pre-Columbian Peruvian textiles, Near and Far Eastern exhibits (some dating back to 3000 BC), and rugs and carpets from Spain, South America and the American Southwest. Other temporary exhibits might cover topics such as contemporary textile design and the intersection of art, craft and fashion, with objects designed as much to hang on a wall as on a body.

6

Adams Morgan, Shaw and Outer Northeast

U nlike Dupont Circle or Downtown to the south, **Adams Morgan** and **Shaw** offer little in the way of museums or official attractions, and are rarely visited by folks arriving into town on tour buses. However, for residents of the city, they offer some of the liveliest street culture, best independent shops, and richest blend of races and cultures in the region. Even better, these are the essential spots for freewheeling dance clubs, rock- and punk-music venues and cheap bars. With this authentic edge, however, comes a bit of diciness, and if you're coming at night it's best to take a taxi between the popular stretches, or use the DC Circulator, a shuttle that connects Adams Morgan and Shaw with Downtown at McPherson Square (see p.161).

Adams Morgan is one of the few areas in the city with an inexpensive **nightlife scene**, and you should dine out at least once here, since its range of ethnic restaurants is unparalleled in the District. In the historically black district of Shaw, to the east, the spectre of gentrification has loomed large in the last few years, and the area now boasts no end of new restaurants, bars and clubs, and developers have begun building condos for the expected next wave of (mostly white) yuppies.

Beyond Adams Morgan and Shaw, the **Outer Northeast** section of DC offers a handful of scattered attractions, like the marvellous **National Arboretum** and the awe-inspiring **National Shrine of the Immaculate Conception**; both are some distance from Northeast's more crime-ridden areas, and accessible in the daytime with few hassles. Several of the area's other sights are also within easy reach of the Metro system, while others will require a taxi or bus ride.

Adams Morgan

For the last decade DC's trendiest district, **Adams Morgan**'s various designer restaurants, stylish bars and hip stores share space with the traditional Hispanic

ADAMS MORGAN, SHAW & OUTER NORTHEAST

National Shrine and Takoma Park ▲

National Zoological Park ▲

Georgetown ▼

0 200 yds

CAFES & RESTAURANTS

Amsterdam Falafelshop	18
Bardia's	25
Ben's Chili Bowl	38
Bukom Café	17
Casa Oaxaca	32
Cashion's Eat Place	14
Coppi's	46
The Diner	10
Dukem	42
El Tamarindo	36
Florida Avenue Grill	30
Grill from Ipanema	9
Henry's Soul Café	35
La Fourchette	24
Lauriol Plaza	51
Mama Ayesha's	1
Meze	21
Napoleon	23
Pasta Mia	19
Perry's	20
Pizza Mart	15
Saki	6
So's Your Mom	16
Tabaq Bistro	39
Tryst	2
U-topia	44

GAY CAFES

Jolt 'n Bolt	50
L'Enfant	37

BARS & CLUBS

9:30 Club	A
Bedrock Billiards	C
Black Cat	D
Bohemian Caverns	G
Bossa	E
Bourbon	F
Chi Che Lounge	B

Chief Ike's Mambo Room	33	Latin Jazz Alley	41
Columbia Station	11	Looking Glass Lounge	49
District	52	Madam's Organ	22
Fatback	40	Millie and Al's	31
Habana Village	12	Red Room	34
Heaven & Hell	27	Rumba Café	26
African American Civil War Memorial	45	The Saloon	4
		Solly's Tavern	28
		Toledo Lounge	8
		Twins Jazz	5
		U Street Music Hall	48
		Velvet Lounge	3

ACCOMMODATION

Adam's Inn	
American Guest House	
Courtyard by Marriott	
Normandy	
Washington Hilton	
Windsor Inn	
Windsor Park	

Map labels

WOODLEY PARK-ZOO
Rock Creek Park
KALORAMA TRIANGLE
Woodward Apartments
Altamont Building
Lothrop Mansion
KALORAMA
Woodrow Wilson House Museum
Textile Museum
Phillips Collection
Anderson House
SHERIDAN CIRCLE
DUPONT CIRCLE
ADAMS MORGAN
Kalorama Park
DC Arts Center
Wyoming Building
STRIVERS SECTION
Frederick Douglass House
Meridian International Center
Meridian Hill Park
French Embassy Site
Pink Palace
Warder House
Ecuador Embassy
Tivoli Theatre
COLUMBIA HEIGHTS
Ontario Building
McMillan Reservoir
Howard University
Founders Library
Howard Hall
Howard University Hospital
LEDROIT PARK
Howard Theatre
Lincoln Theatre
African American Civil War Museum
Source Theatre
SHAW
CARDOZO

see inset
N

businesses that have thrived here since the 1950s. Spanish is still much in evidence, especially in signs along Columbia Road, and the neighbourhood certainly celebrates its heritage well at the annual shindig of **Adams Morgan Day** (mid-Sept; ⓦwww.adamsmorgandayfestival.com). Along Adams Morgan's **18th Street** strip are festive bars, restaurants, cafés and clubs, but keep in mind that late-night hours for bars and clubs can sometimes see college students battling it out with bouncers, and noisome drunks bothering passers-by. You shouldn't have any troubles, though, if you come for what the district is best known for – its **food**. There are some excellent ethnic restaurants here; Ethiopians are responsible for some of the most highly rated places, but you can devour anything here from Argentine to Vietnamese cuisine.

Adams Morgan is generally thought of as being bounded by Connecticut and Florida avenues and 16th and Harvard streets, though in practice most visitors see little more than the few blocks on either side of the central **Columbia Road/18th Street intersection**, where most of the bars and restaurants are situated; a popular **farmers' market** (May–Dec Sat 8am–1pm) occupies the southwestern plaza where the two arteries meet. The area's Hispanic legacy is at its strongest in the stretch of Columbia Road northeast of 18th Street, a good place to check out the street stalls, jewellery sellers and thrift stores.

The eastern boundary of the neighbourhood is marked by 16th Street and Meridian Hill Park – at night, don't stray further east than Ontario Road, beyond which it can get a little dodgy. To the west, the neighbourhood boundary is formed by the **National Zoo** and Connecticut Avenue NW, which is where you'll find the nearest **Metro**: from the Woodley Park–Zoo station on Connecticut Avenue, it's a fifteen-minute walk across the striking Neoclassical Duke Ellington Bridge to the Columbia Road/18th Street junction. From the Dupont Circle Metro stop it's a steep twenty-minute hike up 19th Street to Columbia Road. By **bus**, take the L1, L2 or L4, or the #42 or #43 lines from Downtown.

Some history

In the late nineteenth century, the area's hilly, rural reaches were colonized by wealthy Washingtonians looking for a select address near the power housing of Dupont Circle. Impressive apartment buildings were erected in the streets off Columbia Road, boasting expansive views and connected to Downtown by streetcar. Until World War II some of the city's most prominent politicians and business people lived here, and many of their mansions survive intact. After the war, the city's housing shortage meant that many of the area's signature **row houses** were converted into rooming houses and small apartments; well-to-do families moved further out into the suburbs and were replaced by a growing blue-collar population, black and white, and, crucially, by increasing numbers of Latin American and Caribbean immigrants in the 1960s. Concerned that the area was becoming too segregated, a local group fashioned a symbolic name from two local elementary schools: one all-white (John Quincy Adams), one all-black (Thomas P. Morgan). Nowadays the melange of peoples, colours and accents makes Adams Morgan one of DC's most diverse and engaging neighbourhoods.

Along 18th Street

South of Columbia Road, **18th Street** is the centre of DC's melting pot, and the broad mix of visitors is equalled by the wide range of restaurants and stores – including pizza joints, ethnic diners, Latin botanicas, junk emporia, bistros, astrologers and palm-readers, antiques sellers, vintage-clothing dealers, book and music shops, coffeehouses and fringe theatres. The scene is presided over by lines

The streets of the western side of Adams Morgan provide a generous amount of architectural interest. This is especially true in the **Kalorama Triangle**, between Connecticut Avenue and Columbia Road, which, a bit different from its neighbour to the southwest, Kalorama (see p.142), is a well-heeled district of high-rise historic-revival blocks, with many fine architectural examples built in the first three decades of the twentieth century. These are almost too numerous to mention, but for a quick glance, check out the Spanish Mission Revival block of the historic **Woodward Apartments**, 2311 Connecticut Ave, with its Baroque-flavoured ornament and bell tower; or, at the southern end of the Triangle, the condos of the **Wyoming Building**, 2022 Columbia Rd NW, an early twentieth-century gem with mosaic floor, moulded ceilings and marble reception room with graceful Ionic columns – a building that housed the Eisenhowers between 1927 and 1935.

By contrast, at 1919 Connecticut Ave NW, the **Washington Hilton** is a charmless modern block that became infamous as the spot where, in the driveway roundabout, John Hinckley Jr fired six shots at Ronald Reagan in a 1981 assassination attempt, leaving the president and three others seriously wounded and his press secretary, James Brady, permanently paralyzed. Across the street, the Neoclassicism of the 1911 **Lothrop Mansion**, no. 2001, somehow seems fit for the Russian trade delegation now occupying it, while just to the north, the Italian Renaissance-style **Altamont Building**, 1901 Wyoming Ave NW, at 20th St, is striking for its rooftop terrace and squat towers, barrel-vaulted and gilded lobby, and an adjoining parlour featuring Old English-style furniture. A little further from the Triangle, but most glamorous of all the Adams Morgan buildings, is the cupola-topped Beaux-Arts majesty of the **Ontario Building**, up north at 2853 Ontario Rd (at 18th), built between 1903 and 1906. Its roll call of famous former residents includes five-star generals Douglas MacArthur and Chester Nimitz, and *Washington Post* scribe Bob Woodward.

of **Victorian row houses** in various states of disrepair or renovation, with increasing numbers of artists' and yuppies' lofts adding more change and ferment to the neighbourhood. The architecture here is more eye-catching than histori-cally unique. (To see more classic buildings, venture a few blocks east toward Meridian Hill, preferably in the daytime.)

Columbia Heights

The hilltop precinct of **Columbia Heights**, roughly between Florida Avenue and Columbia Road along 16th Street NW, represents the creeping eastern edge of the gentrification shaping Adams Morgan. In the heart of the neighbourhood, at Columbia Road and 16th Street, the Columbia Heights Metro stop is largely responsible for the changing demographics of the area, with "urban pioneers" of all races coming in and refurbishing the historic structures into shops, condos and restaurants. The neighbourhood centrepiece is the **Tivoli Theatre**, just northeast of the Metro at 14th Street at Park Road, a 1924 movie palace built in the Italian Renaissance Revival style and still a considerable anchor to the area's street life. Recently restored, it's been reopened as the **GALA Hispanic Theatre** (T 1-800/494-8497, W www.galatheatre.org), presenting lively, Latin-themed productions.

Given that most other things worth seeing lie further south on or around **16th Street**, it may be tempting to take a lengthy stroll through this neighbourhood. But caution is advised after dark – what looks convenient on a map can involve treks through unexpectedly down-at-the-heel or dicey pockets. If you're not familiar with the turf, take a taxi or the Metro.

Meridian Hill Park and around

Although it might be hard to believe these days, the area around **Meridian Hill Park**, between Florida Avenue and Euclid Street, was, in the mid-twentieth century, one of the swankiest areas of DC – its townhouses and condos sought out by the swells of high society. The riots of 1968 led to blight and crime in later years, but there's been a rebound since then, especially evident in the graceful contours of this fetching space. Although the place has the informal moniker of Malcolm X Park, it gives a broad hint of what things were like in older days: here you'll find nothing less than a twelve-acre French-style **garden**, finished in 1930, with smartly designed greenery and pathways, well-balanced terraces, and a central series of thirteen stepped waterfalls. The park boasts a few other oddments – such as a strange set of **statues** depicting Joan of Arc, Dante and one of America's worst presidents, James Buchanan.

The streets around the park hold some stunning mansions. One such standout is the so-called **Pink Palace**, on the north side of the park at 2600 16th St, which has been painted many colours but still sports its original Venetian Renaissance windows and overall design. The **Benjamin Warder House**, across the street, is a stocky version of a Romanesque castle, designed by H.H. Richardson and now a luxury apartment building (for a look, call ☎202/332-1717 or visit Ⓦwww .wardermansion.com). The former **Embassy of France**, a block south at 2460 16th St, is a stunning 1908 version of a High Baroque palace, while the current **Ecuadorean Embassy**, 2535 15th St, is done up in smart French Second Empire attire. Further north, a trio of delightful historic-revival churches, from the 1920s and 1930s, clusters around the intersection of 16th Street and Columbia Road; **National Baptist Memorial Church** is the most arresting of the three, with its colonnaded combination of Baroque and Neoclassical elements.

Meridian International Center

The **Meridian International Center**, 1624–1630 Crescent Place NW (free; ☎202/667-6800, Ⓦwww.meridian.org; Columbia Heights Metro), regularly exhibits the work of global artists and has displays on international themes related to science, culture and education, as well as lectures and concerts by musicians from selected countries (call ☎202/939-5568 for hours and details). However, the interest really lies in the pair of historic-revival mansions that play host to the centre and its displays. **Meridian House**, designed by John Russell Pope, was the residence of Irwin Laughlin, a high-powered Spanish ambassador and steel heir who built a neo-Baroque home featuring limestone walls, formal European-style gardens, priceless antiques, sculpted Neoclassical busts, and assorted curiosities and treasures gathered from a lifetime's worth of globe-hopping. Next door, the English Georgian-style **White-Meyer House** is another revivalist work of Pope's for an ambassador (to France), its elegant symmetry and balance and Ionic columns lending it a vaguely Classical feel.

Shaw

East of Adams Morgan and Meridian Hill, the historic district of **Shaw** – roughly between U and M streets and 13th Street and New Jersey Avenue – is one of the oldest residential areas in DC. **U Street** is the area's hub, a good place for a festive night out or a stroll around some of the historic sights and landmarks. Well-scrubbed chain merchants coexist with storefront churches and businesses that have been around for decades, and the district is racially and ethnically as rich and diverse as any place in the city. But the hip and lively bars of U Street are just blocks from grim pockets of urban poverty, and fancy condos in remodelled row-house blocks sit near dilapidated wrecks. It's a strange blend, but only those truly interested in the Shaw environment or architecture need go exploring (in the daytime) beyond the tourist zone.

To visit the main section of Shaw, hop on the DC Circulator (see p.161), which links the district with Adams Morgan and McPherson Square downtown.

Some history

First settled by immigrant whites who built shanty housing along 7th Street after the Civil War, the area became majority black by the turn of the twentieth century, as thousands of black immigrants from the rural Southern states came here in search of work and to escape the grinding racism of the deeper South, some to be educated at the historic all-black **Howard University** (founded in 1867). Thereafter, 7th Street became one of the booming city's main commercial arteries and remained busy during the Depression with pool halls, churches, cafés, theatres and social clubs; a shopping strip developed on 14th Street; and **U Street** evolved into the "Black Broadway", with theatres putting on splashy vaudeville shows and jazz concerts, among many other kinds of entertainment. For years the neighbourhood was known simply as "14th and U", eventually taking the name "Shaw" after **Colonel Robert Gould Shaw**, the (white) commander of the Union Army's first black regiment (the Massachusetts 54th).

Segregation – entrenched in Washington since the late nineteenth century – ironically secured Shaw's prosperity, since black residents stayed within the neighbourhood to shop and socialize. However, news of the assassination of Dr Martin Luther King Jr in 1968 sparked three days of arson, rioting and looting that destroyed businesses and lives along 7th, 14th and H streets. A dozen people were killed, millions of dollars lost, and middle-class blacks fled to the suburbs, leaving behind a fringe of the poor and desperate.

A decade into the twenty-first century, the signs of revival are unmistakable: revitalized U Street has a Metro station and once again figures on the city's nightlife scene, while apartment blocks that once stood abandoned have re-emerged as smart (black and white) yuppie condos. The main source of friction, as ever in urban America, is between the African American old-timers who saw the neighbourhood through its worst days and typically white newcomers who have little knowledge of or interest in the historic character or culture of the place.

U Street and around

The only part of Shaw most visitors see is the thriving section of **U Street** in the blocks near the U Street–Cardozo Metro station. Between the world wars, U Street ranked second only to New York's Harlem as America's centre of black entertainment. Across from the Metro, at the splendid **Lincoln Theatre**, 1215 U St, built in 1921, vaudeville shows and movies were bolstered by appearances of the most celebrated jazz performers of the day: Count Basie, Billie Holiday, Cab Calloway, Ella Fitzgerald and DC's own Duke Ellington among them. The theatre now serves as a performing arts centre (see p.235).

The dashing **Howard Theatre**, several blocks east of the U Street scene at 624 T St (Ⓦ www.howardtheatre.org), opened in 1910 as the first theatre in DC built for black patrons. An unknown **Ella Fitzgerald** won an open-mike contest here; 1940s big bands filled the auditorium; and later artists such as James Brown, Smokey Robinson, Gladys Knight, and Martha and the Vandellas lined up to appear; in 1962 **The Supremes** played their first headlining gig here. It's now undergoing a lengthy renovation.

6 African American Civil War Memorial and Museum

Leave the Metro by the 10th Street exit and you'll emerge near the **African American Civil War Memorial**, where *The Spirit of Freedom* sculpture stands in the centre of a granite-paved plaza, partially encircled by a Wall of Honor, along which you'll find the names of the 209,145 United States Coloured Troops (and their 7000 white officers) who served. President Lincoln sanctioned the creation of African American regiments in 1862, and slaves, former slaves and freedmen joined the fight. Sadly, these brave troops were not included in the celebratory Grand Review of the Union Armies along Pennsylvania Avenue after the war's end, an early sign that the battle for equality had only begun.

Two blocks west of the memorial, in the 1903 Italianate **True Reformer Building** – which was designed, built and financed by African Americans – the associated **museum** (Mon–Fri 10am–5pm, Sat 10am–2pm; free) uses photographs and documents from African American history to describe the era, including the original bill of sale for an 11-year-old girl along with oral histories and war narratives, plus antique and replica uniforms and weapons. Other features include a "Descendants' Registry", where visitors can look up relatives who may have served with the US Coloured Troops, and a computer search service to identify individual troops along with the history of their regiments.

Note that in coming years the museum will be moving closer to the memorial, to 1925 Vermont Avenue NW, to display its collection in a more spacious and inspiring setting; contact the museum on ☎202/667-2667 or check Ⓦwww .afroamcivilwar.org for details.

Howard University

Prestigious **Howard University**, 2400 6th St NW (☎202/806-8009 for campus tours, Ⓦwww.howard.edu; Shaw–Howard University Metro) – named after General Otis Howard, commissioner of the Freedmen's Bureau – was established in 1867 by a church missionary society to provide a school for freed blacks after the Civil War. Its first faculties were in law, music, medicine and theology, though today hundreds of subjects are taken by almost 15,000 students from over a hundred countries. Famous alumni include Pulitzer Prize-winning author Toni Morrison, opera diva Jessye Norman, Supreme Court justice Thurgood Marshall, former mayor of New York City David Dinkins, UN ambassador Andrew Young, activist Stokely Carmichael and football goalkeeper Shaka Hislop.

Only one of the original campus buildings remains – **Howard Hall**, 607 Howard Place, a handsome French Second Empire-style structure built in 1867. Many of the other buildings are historic revivals from the 1930s, and few are better than the **Founders Library**, a gigantic edifice modelled after Philadelphia's Independence Hall. The library houses the **Moorland-Spingarn Research Centre** (Mon, Wed & Fri 9am–1pm & 2–4.30pm), which contains the country's largest selection of literature relating to black history and culture, with thousands of books, articles and other artefacts. In the library's Wesley Room, the university **museum** (Mon–Fri 9am–4.30pm; ☎202/806-7240) presents rotating exhibits of its holdings, which may include African icons and artefacts, memorabilia and antiques from the university's early days, and historic photos and recollections of the Shaw neighbourhood and the city in general.

LeDroit Park

As the rough triangle formed by W Street and Florida and Rhode Island avenues, **LeDroit Park** preserves some fifty historic neo-Gothic, French Second Empire and Victorian homes; alongside, row houses still exist in their original brick and terracotta state, and the neighbourhood has a whimsical flavour that has withstood decades of decay and indifference to be at least partially refurbished as a fascinating urban village. The best-preserved group of original houses is along the 400 block of U Street, though other pockets from the 300 to 500 blocks of T Street also exist. Prominent black citizens continue to be associated with the area – the family of DC's first black mayor, Walter Washington, owned a house here for years, along with Duke Ellington, Jesse Jackson and Nobel Prize winner Ralph Bunche. The area is accessible from a convenient **Metro station**, Shaw–Howard University, three blocks west.

Strivers' Section

Not part of Shaw per se, but rather standing as its own independent neighbourhood between Dupont Circle, Shaw and Adams Morgan (bounded by Florida Avenue and 16th and Swann streets), is another historically black area: the **Strivers' Section**. From the 1870s, these Victorian row houses attracted many notable African Americans, including poet **Langston Hughes**, who lived at 1749 S St and worked for the *Washington Sentinel* in the 1920s, and **Frederick Douglass**, who occupied three of the five Second Empire units at 2000 17th Street in the mid-1870s. Although not as architecturally distinguished as the homes of LeDroit Park, those in the section do convey a fetching Victorian-era style in several eye-catching forms, from Romanesque (2102 17th St) to Neoclassical (1830 17th St) – with a good number being historically protected and preserved.

Outer Northeast

Most visitors stick to the central DC neighbourhoods, but a number of unique, fascinating sites make it worth the effort to venture to some further-flung parts of the city. Spread across the Outer Northeast section of town are the expansive **National Arboretum**, the monumental **National Shrine of the Immaculate Conception**, the quaint and historic **Takoma Park**, and more. For some sights a car will be necessary, for others there's a Metro station within blocks. Keep in mind, though, that none of these spots is very near the others, and in between you may run across some of those down-at-the-heel neighbourhoods you've been warned to stay away from – so take heed.

National Shrine of the Immaculate Conception

Two of DC's most interesting spots are easily accessible by Metro heading north from Shaw (with a transfer at the Fort Totten station). The first is the largest Catholic church in the US, the **National Shrine of the Immaculate Conception** at 400 Michigan Ave NE (daily: April–Oct 7am–7pm; Nov–March 7am–6pm; free tours Mon–Sat 9am–11am & 1–3pm, Sun 1.30–3.30pm; Brookland Metro), which was built in the 1950s. Its grand Byzantine design, looming dome with multicoloured mosaics, and towering Roman arch above the entrance would alone make the site an eye-grabber, but added to these features are a sleek bell tower, lovely bas-relief panels, several large buttresses, and a huge circular Celtic *triqnetra*, symbolizing the Trinity – and that's just the exterior. Inside, the church is astoundingly big, with some 75 chapels or alcoves for statues, intricate mosaics showing a fight against a seven-headed serpent (among other scenes), a big pipe organ and even larger baldachin with four great marble columns, and, looming above it all – its eyes seeming to follow you around the church – a jaw-dropping mosaic of Jesus clad in a striking red robe, with jets of flame shooting out from his golden halo.

President Lincoln's Cottage at the Soldiers' Home

Near the National Shrine, just west across North Capitol Street, the awkwardly named **President Lincoln's Cottage at the Soldiers' Home**, 3700 N Capitol St (visitor centre Mon–Sat 9.30am–4.30pm, Sun 11.30am–5.30pm; tours Mon–Sat 10am–3pm, Sun noon–4pm; $12; ☎202/829-0436, ⓦwww.lincolncottage.org; Brookland Metro), is set among 250 acres largely devoted to serving the needs of retired soldiers. For visitors, though, its centrepiece is the Carpenter Gothic **Lincoln Cottage**, which dates from 1843. As much Colonial farmhouse as anything, it initially served to house veterans of the Mexican–American War in 1851. It got its current moniker due to its use by Abraham Lincoln as a presidential retreat: he summered here from 1862 to 1864, at the height of the Civil War, and even wrote a draft of the Emancipation Proclamation on the premises. The story of that famed document occupies pride of place in the second-storey Emancipation Room, filled with mementos of the president's career and legacy, including a reproduction of the desk where he wrote the monumental imperative. Elsewhere, you can get more information on the 16th president's role in the war and the history of this and other old soldiers' homes. Sited on one of Washington's highest peaks, the cottage was undoubtedly a source of inspiration for Lincoln, who was perhaps comforted by the irony that his arch-nemesis, Confederate president Jefferson Davis, had, as a US senator, been an ardent proponent of building such retreats in the 1850s and thus inadvertently funded the president's favourite spot during the war.

Takoma Park, MD

Take the northbound Red Line two stops from the Brookland station and you'll come to **Takoma Park, Maryland**, America's first planned suburb for urban commuters, as well as the one-time hub of the Seventh Day Adventist Church. Today it is one of the country's most avowedly progressive communities and is still largely intact with its original 1880s buildings and design. Some of the stylish historic homes worth checking out include the **Bliss House**, 7116 Maple Ave, an Italianate charmer made of wood but with a painted brick-and-stone facade; the Victorian bungalows along Willow Avenue north of Tulip Street; the **Zigzag Art Deco structure** at 7000 Carroll Ave; and the grand **Cady Lee Mansion**, Chestnut Ave at Eastern, the best of several Queen Anne buildings, rich with gables, ginger-bread detailing, a wraparound porch and slate roof, and which occasionally holds public events (☎202/207-3333, ⓦwww.cadylee.org). The Takoma Metro station is right in the middle of this area (on the border between DC and Maryland), which is an excellent spot for an hour or two of wandering. For neighbourhood maps and information, including a free homes tour the first Sunday in May, visit ⓦwww.historictakoma.org.

National Arboretum

Nestled along the Anacostia River roughly two miles northeast of the Capitol building, the sprawling **National Arboretum**, 3501 New York Ave NE (daily 8am–5pm; free; T202/245-2726, W www.usna.usda.gov), is an oasis of green amid an otherwise grim part of the District. The best time to visit is from mid-April to October, when plenty of plants are in bloom and **tram tours** are offered (April–Oct Sat & Sun 10.30am, 11.30am and on the hour 1–4pm; $4); these forty-minute journeys meander along the park's 9.5 miles of roadways past ponds, gardens and plant collections, taking in everything from colourful bursts of azaleas to the woodlands of Japan. The best way to get to the park is by car or taxi. At the entrance at 24th and R streets you'll find the **visitor centre**, where you can pick up a visitor's guide, which includes a map, seasonal plant information and descriptions of the gardens.

Well worth a visit, the surreal gathering of **"Capitol Columns"** stands in a meadow at the heart of the grounds, supporting open sky. Once part of the US Capitol, the sandstone pillars, crafted in the Neoclassical Corinthian style, presided over every presidential inauguration from Jackson to Eisenhower. They were effectively put out to pasture in the 1950s in order to correct a flaw in the Capitol's design, which caused the columns to appear mismatched relative to the size of the dome. Other arboretum highlights include the **Dogwood Collection**, best seen in bloom on a late spring afternoon; the **National Grove of State Trees**, a thirty-acre site where trees native to each state (plus the District of Columbia) grow on individual plots; and the clumsily named **Dwarf and Slow-Growing Conifer Collection**, basically a set of little pines, spruces and firs that make for an off-kilter hillside landscape. Also appealing is the so-called **Asian Collection** of variant natural landscapes that call to mind the features of East Asia with white pines, Japanese apricot, camellias and other evocative trees and flowers.

Those preferring a short, self-guided walking tour can take in the sights closest to the administration building. Here, in addition to the **National Herb Garden**, the largest of its type in the country, you'll find the arboretum's most popular destination, the renowned **National Bonsai and Penjing Museum** (daily 10am–4pm), which celebrates the ancient Chinese and Japanese art of growing tiny trees, with selections from Asia as well as North America. Even if you have no interest in this sort of thing, the odd, sprightly array of miniature plants is really worth a look, with some of the branches and blooms gnarled and twisted almost to a grotesque degree.

Kenilworth Aquatic Gardens

Well off the beaten path, **Kenilworth Aquatic Gardens**, 1550 Anacostia Ave NE (daily 7am–4pm; summer tours Sat & Sun 9am & 11am; free; Deanwood Metro), is a National Park on the eastern fringe of the District, and definitely worth a look if you're interested in horticulture or natural preserves. Set on seven hundred acres of protected marshlands, the twelve-acre gardens are rich with water lilies and lotuses, and you can take an up-close view of them on an elevated **boardwalk** that hovers over the waterline, or the (much) more adventurous can get here by way of canoe from the Anacostia River during high tide. Alternatively, there are several good paths for exploring this wet terrain, with its many ponds and pools, as you're able to see a pristine part of the river – hard to imagine in other parts of the District. The lilies are in bloom from May to September, but are at their best in late July. While the gardens are accessible by the I-295 freeway, you can also reach them by taking the Metro to Deanwood station a few blocks south.

7

Upper Northwest

I n the heights above Georgetown, running up to the District's border with Maryland, the smart neighbourhoods of **Upper Northwest** constitute some of the most exclusive territory in Washington. The upper- and upper-middle-class relocation up Connecticut, Wisconsin and Massachusetts avenues began when a number of nineteenth-century presidents made the cool reaches of rural **Woodley Park** – across Duke Ellington Bridge from Adams Morgan – their summer home; Grover Cleveland later bought a stone cottage further north in an area that today is called **Cleveland Park**. Within three decades both Woodley Park and Cleveland Park had become bywords for fashionable, out-of-town living, replete with apartment buildings designed by the era's top architects. The tone is no less swish today, with a series of ritzy suburbs stretching into Maryland – on the DC side of the border, **Tenleytown** and **Friendship Heights** have no proper attractions but offer a few shopping and dining options, notably a number of malls.

Elsewhere in the Upper Northwest you'll find the expansive **National Zoo**, part of the Smithsonian Institution; **Washington National Cathedral**, the sixth-largest cathedral in the world; and the wooded expanse of **Rock Creek Park**, the biggest and most enjoyable of the city's green spaces. Given the elevation of this area, and the rather strenuous effort you'll need to get around it, you're advised to take the **Metro Red Line**, which runs underneath the area in some of the country's deepest subway channels; those in the mood for a serious hike can hoof it up these slopes from Dupont Circle.

Woodley Park

The first Upper Northwest neighbourhood you'll encounter – either north from Georgetown on Wisconsin Avenue or west from Adams Morgan on Calvert Street – is **Woodley Park**, which can be quite lively along Connecticut Avenue with restaurant-goers and bar-hoppers, though there's only a handful of attractions in the neighbourhood proper. Near the intersection of Calvert Street and Connecticut Avenue is a pair of splendid hotels that give a hint of the serious money that lurks in the surrounding hills: the massive **Marriott Wardman Park Hotel**, Connecticut Ave NW and Woodley Rd (see p.197), a red-brick, vaguely Colonial Revival giant, which has a tower that still dominates the local skyline and attracts high-profile politicians and social butterflies; and, across on Calvert Street, the hybrid Art Deco-style **Shoreham** hotel (now an Omni; see p.197), which has hosted an inaugural ball or gala for every president from FDR to George W. Bush; here

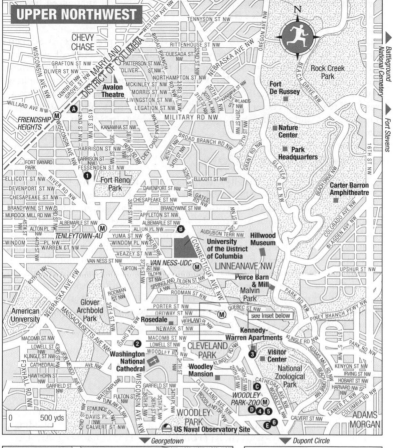

President Truman played poker, JFK courted Jackie, Nixon announced his first Cabinet, and, in the celebrated **Blue Room**, Judy Garland, Marlene Dietrich, Bob Hope and Frank Sinatra entertained the swells.

To check out where relatively staid nineteenth-century presidents passed their summers, head up Connecticut Avenue to Cathedral Avenue and walk west past 29th Street to the **Woodley Mansion**, now the elite Maret School. This white stucco Georgian was built in 1800 for Philip Barton Key, whose nephew Francis later penned "The Star-Spangled Banner". Its elevation meant that it was a full ten degrees cooler in the summer than downtown, and presidents Van Buren, Tyler and Buchanan needed no second invitation to spend their summers here.

US Naval Observatory

Half a mile southeast of Woodley Mansion, located where 34th Street reaches Massachusetts Avenue, the **US Naval Observatory**, Massachusetts Ave NW at Observatory Circle (tours every other Mon night 8.30–10pm; reserve several months in advance by fax at Ⓕ202/762-1489 or via the website; free; Ⓣ202/762-1467, Ⓦwww.usno.navy.mil; no close Metro), is built around a twelve-inch refracting telescope that dates from 1892 and has been recording and studying the position of celestial objects for over a century. The tours tell you more about the Observatory's overall mission of providing accurate astronomical and navigational information, as well as keeping time with an array of atomic clocks. You can get here from the guard gate at the end of the street called Observatory Circle. The observatory site also accommodates the official home of the vice president of the United States, an 1893 Queen Anne mansion.

Cleveland Park

Back on Connecticut Avenue and heading north past the zoo you'll soon reach **Cleveland Park**, a stylish suburb marked by a few eye-catching buildings, including the **Kennedy–Warren Apartments** (no. 3133), a soaring Art Deco evocation of 1930s (and twenty-first-century) wealth, and the **Broadmoor** (no. 3601), a residential development from 1928 with grand-scale and angular Art Deco versions of Classical motifs, the tallest apartment block in the area. However, it's further west into the hills, around Newark Street and Highland Place, where you'll see the really historic buildings that make this neighbourhood unique. These hills hold the area's highest concentration of upper-class residences, dating from its great turn-of-the-twentieth-century expansion, and it was on Newark Street that Grover Cleveland's (long-demolished) summer house – the one that prompted the whole influx – once stood.

You can get a closer view at esteemed estates like the **Rosedale**, 3501 Newark St NW, featuring the area's oldest structure – a weathered stone building, which dates from 1740 – amid later Colonial and early American additions; its rambling grounds are open daily (enter at Newark and 35th St; Mon–Fri 7am–dusk, Sat & Sun 8am–dusk; free). Also interesting, the **Tregaron**, 3100 Macomb Ave NW, is a stately Colonial Revival structure that sits on 13 acres of ponds, meadows and gardens, linked by a walking trail and well worth a brief journey (grounds Mon–Sat 8am–8pm, Sun 8am–5pm; free). For more on local highlights, contact the **Cleveland Park Historical Society** (Ⓣ202/363-6358, Ⓦwww.clevelandparkdc.org).

Washington National Cathedral

Set on the heights of **Mount St Alban**, unaffected by the city's building restrictions, **Washington National Cathedral**, at Massachusetts and Wisconsin aves NW (Mon–Fri 10am–5.30pm, Sat 10am–4.30pm, Sun 8am–5pm; tours Mon–Sat 10–11.30am & 12.45–3.30pm, Sun 1–2.30pm; $5 donation; ⊤202/537-6200 or 364-6616, Ⓦwww.nationalcathedral.org; Woodley Park–Zoo Metro), is the sixth-largest cathedral in the world, a monumental building so medieval in spirit it should surely rise from a dusty old European town plaza rather than a DC suburb. Built from Indiana limestone and modelled on the medieval English Gothic style, it's supported by flying buttresses, bosses and vaults, and shows off striking stained-glass windows, quirky gargoyles, massive columns and – an all-American touch – two rows of state flags hanging below the clerestory level.

Although a Protestant church, and the seat of the Episcopal Diocese of Washington, the cathedral hosts services for other denominations as well. Most prominently, it's held memorial services for the victims of 9/11 and a number of presidents: **Woodrow Wilson** was commemorated and interred here upon his death in 1924, which was appropriate since much of the work on the building took place during his presidency. **Gerald Ford** lay in state here most recently in 2007, while three years earlier **Ronald Reagan**, after first lying in state in the Capitol Rotunda, was honoured with a memorial service here before his body was flown back to California for burial. **Dwight Eisenhower** received similar honours, though as yet Wilson is the only president to be buried here (his house is just south in Kalorama; see p.142).

Visiting the cathedral

The centre portal in the west facade isn't always open; you may have to enter from the northwest cloister. For a floor plan and information, descend to the **Crypt**, where there's an **information desk** and a huge **gift shop**. Guided **tours** are available regularly, but phone ahead or check the website for schedules of the many **speciality tours**, which feature everything from the cathedral's gardens to its gargoyles to its stained glass. The 57-acre grounds, or **Cathedral Close** (virtually a small fiefdom), hold cathedral offices, three schools, a college, sports fields and a swimming pool. There is also a **Herb Cottage** that sells dried herbs and teas, a **greenhouse** with plants for sale, and the **Bishop's Garden**, a walled rose-and-herb garden laid out in medieval style.

It's easiest to reach the cathedral by **bus**, either from Woodley Park on the #96, #97 or #X3 lines (getting off at Woodley and Wisconsin aves), or the #N2, #N3, #N4 or #N6 from Dupont Circle. If you don't mind a twenty-minute walk, you can take the **Metro**. From the Woodley Park–Zoo station, turn left from Connecticut Avenue into Cathedral Avenue and right into Woodley Road to reach the lower-level information centre; the west door is around the corner on Wisconsin Avenue. For a longer, downhill walk, go up to the Tenleytown Metro station and head one and a half miles south along Wisconsin Avenue (a route also covered by bus lines #31, #32, #36 and #37).

The interior

Place yourself first at the west end of the **nave** to appreciate the immense scale of the building; it's more than a tenth of a mile to the high altar at the other end. Along the south side of the nave, the first bay commemorates **George Washington** with a marble statue, while five bays down is **Woodrow Wilson**'s sarcophagus. In the adjacent bay, look up to the **Space Window**, whose stained glass incorporating a sliver of moon rock commemorates the flight of *Apollo II*, while other stained-glass windows cover great moments in US history from the Lewis and Clark expedition to the landings at Iwo Jima. On the north side, across from Washington, the **Abraham Lincoln Bay** is marked by a bronze statue of Abe, with Lincoln-head pennies set into the floor. The last bay before the North Transept features a small likeness of **Dr Martin Luther King Jr** above the arch, inscribed "I Have A Dream". On Sunday, March 31, 1968, the reverend preached his last sermon here before heading for Memphis, where he was assassinated.

From the **High Altar** – adorned with a 6ft-tall gold cross – there's a splendid view back down along the carved vault to the west rose window. The beautifully intricate **reredos** features 110 figures surrounding Christ in Benediction. An elevator from the south porch at the west end of the nave ascends to the **Pilgrim Observation Gallery**, which affords stupendous city views. The 53 copper-and-tin bells of the cathedral's **carillon** ring out 150ft above the nave, and, even higher, its London-made **peal bells** boom out following weekly services; unlike the carillon, which is played with a keyboard, the peal bells are sounded in the medieval fashion, by tugging thick ropes.

National Zoological Park

The **National Zoological Park**, 3001 Connecticut Ave NW (April–Oct 10am–6pm, Nov–March 10am–4.30pm; free; parking $10–20; ☎202/633-4800, ⓦnationalzoo.si.edu; Cleveland Park or Woodley Park–Zoo Metro), is part of the Smithsonian Institution and, with its free admission, is always a popular draw for visitors who make it up this far. Sited between Woodley Park and Adams Morgan, the zoo sprawls down the steep sides of Rock Creek, with trails through lush vegetation leading past simulations of more than three thousand creatures' home environments. The main entrance on Connecticut Avenue is a ten-minute walk from either **Metro** station, but it's easiest to arrive at the Cleveland Park one; from there the zoo is a level stroll south along Connecticut Avenue; from Woodley Park you'll have to hike uphill. Just inside the gate you'll find the **visitor center**, where you can pick up a map and list of the day's events, including feeding times. From here, three trails loop downhill through the park to Rock Creek: the central **Olmsted Walk**, passing most of the indoor exhibits, the steeper **Valley Trail**, with aquatic exhibits, birds and "Amazonia", and the **Asia Trail**, which offers a grab bag of leopards, red pandas and sloth bears. Head down one and back up another, visiting the side exhibits on the way, and you'll walk more than two miles.

Park highlights

Along the **Olmsted Walk** are the **giant pandas** Mei Xiang and Tian Tian, who arrived from China in 2000 to fill the absence created by the recent deaths of Ling Ling and Hsing Hsing, the famous pair presented by Beijing during Richard Nixon's 1972 visit. The pandas are on view daily from 9am to 4.30pm and are a constant focus of media interest for their mating activity. The zoo's next major addition (due to open in 2012) is **Elephant Trails**, which will offer multiple habitat areas with a variety of terrains for the giant pachyderms, as well as a social-izing centre and an "Elephant Trek" that will allow them to get out on the trail and shake a little trunk.

Elsewhere, **Amazonia** is a re-creation of a tropical river and rainforest habitat – piranhas included – while the **Small Mammal House** showcases some of the zoo's lovable oddballs like golden tamarind monkeys, armadillos, meerkats and porcupines. Further along, orang-utans are encouraged to leave the confines of the **Great Ape House** and commute to the "**Think Tank**", where scientists and four-legged primates come together to hone their communications skills.

Between the Ape House and Think Tank is the **Reptile Discovery Center**, with a full roster of snakes, turtles, crocodiles, alligators and lizards. On the **Valley Trail**, seals and sea lions splash in an outdoor pool, and then it's a slow walk uphill to **Beaver Valley**, which has the titular scamp on view, as well as grey seals, otters, wolves and pelicans, not to mention a **Bald Eagle Refuge** that showcases the intense, snowy-domed raptor that became the country's national symbol, despite Ben Franklin's feeling that the turkey would be more appropriate.

Rock Creek Park and around

Dividing Upper Northwest from Adams Morgan and the north-central part of the District, the natural preserve of **Rock Creek Park** (daily dawn–dusk; free) was established in 1890, its 1800 acres spread out above the National Zoo to form a mile-wide tract of woodland west of 16th Street. Going by **car** is the easiest way to get around the park; by public transport, you can take the **Metro** to Cleveland Park, which provides access just north of the zoo via **bus** routes #H2, #H3 and #H4 (or a more lengthy slog on foot), or to Friendship Heights, from which **buses** #E2, #E3 and #E4 run up Western Avenue and McKinley Street before cruising along Military Road into the middle of the park. To reach the east side of the park or the amphitheatre, take bus #S1, #S2 or #S4, which run up 16th Street from Downtown. Alternatively, you can hop on a **bike** in Georgetown and ride north along the creek.

The park's wooded confines, craggy outcrops and rambling streams are peppered with historic features, including the old **Peirce Barn** and **grist mill** (under renovation). There are also fifteen miles of **trails and paths** that run along both sides of the creek and include tracks, workout stations, bridleways and a cycle route that runs from the Lincoln Memorial north through the park and into Maryland. On weekends (Sat 7am to Sun 7pm) and holidays, Beach Drive between Military and Broad Branch roads is closed to cars, as rollerbladers, cyclists, runners and walkers happily make the space their own. The park also has ballparks, thirty picnic areas and the **Carter Barron Amphitheatre**, 16th St and Colorado Ave NW, which hosts **summer concerts** (see box, p.230).

The **Nature Center**, 5200 Glover Rd, just south of Military Road (Wed–Sun 9am–5pm; ☎202/895-6070), acts as the park **visitor center**, with natural history exhibits and details of weekend **guided walks** and self-guided **nature trails**. There's also an on-site **planetarium** (45min shows Wed 4pm, Sat & Sun 1pm & 4pm; free) that presents the sky and its constellations as they will appear that night, and also allows for more in-depth views of longer-term phenomena; ask also about the stargazing sessions that occur monthly from April to November.

Fort Circle Parks

Just on the other side of Military Road from the Rock Creek Nature Center, the remains of Fort De Russey stand as a reminder of the network of defences that ringed the city during the Civil War, now known as the **Fort Circle Parks** (most daily dawn–dusk; free; ⓦwww.nps.gov/cwdw). Guarding against Confederate attack from the north, **Fort De Russey** was one of 68 forts erected around DC. The sites of others have been appropriated as small parks on either side of Rock Creek Park. East on Military Road from the park to 13th Street NW and north of Missouri Avenue, **Fort Stevens** marks the spot at which the city came closest to falling to Confederate troops during the Civil War. An army of 15,000 soldiers crossed the Potomac in July 1864 and got within 150 yards of the fort before the hastily reinforced Union defence drove them back under a barrage of artillery fire. Today, you can somewhat imagine the scene, with the earthen mounds, wooden works, and vintage cannons testifying to the site's importance.

Seven blocks further north, at 6625 Georgia Ave, is **Battleground National Cemetery** (daily dawn–dusk), which holds the remains of the Union soldiers killed in the battle to defend Fort Stevens. Buses #70, #71 and #79 run here, up 7th Street (which becomes Georgia Avenue NW) from the National Mall, but given Georgia Avenue's rather fearsome reputation you're advised to come and go by taxi.

Hillwood Museum and Gardens

Just west of Rock Creek and a short distance north of Peirce Mill at 4155 Linnean Ave NW, the 1923 neo-Georgian manor once known as Arbremont was acquired in the 1950s by **Marjorie Merriweather Post**, heir to the cereal-company fortune, and transformed into a showpiece she renamed Hillwood. These days, the red-brick mansion and its lovely grounds – thick with roses and French- and Japanese-style gardens – are part of the **Hillwood Museum** (Tues–Sat 10am–5pm; closed Jan; $12; by reservation only at ☎202/686-5807, ⓦwww.hillwood museum.org; Van Ness–UDC Metro), and while the site is handsome enough, what brings people out here is the cache inside. Through her Russian-ambassador husband, in the 1930s Post managed to collect a treasure trove of Fabergé eggs and boxes, Byzantine and Orthodox icons, eighteenth-century glassworks and other priceless items that today form the core of the museum's collection. There's also an array of French and English decorative-arts items, including tapestries, gilded commodes, porcelain cameos and parquet-inlaid furniture, arrayed in cases or on walls almost to the point of nausea.

The easiest way to get here is by **bus** (following the same routes as for the west side of Rock Creek Park) or **Metro** to the Van Ness–UDC station, from which it's a mile walk, first south on Connecticut Avenue and then east along Upton Street.

Georgetown

C alled by Jan Morris "the most obsessively political residential enclave in the world", **Georgetown** is both a tourist favourite and a bastion of entrenched wealth that sits at some remove from the rest of the District. The Kennedys moved here before JFK made it to the White House and were followed by establishment figures who have adopted Georgetown as their home (or, more usually, one of their homes): crusading scribbler Bob Woodward, *Washington Post* publisher Katharine Graham and her editor Ben Bradlee, first woman secretary of state Madeleine Albright, Senator John Kerry – the list goes on and on.

There is, of course, more to Georgetown than its upper-crust denizens. The area is at its vibrant best along the spine of **Wisconsin Avenue** and **M Street**, with bars, coffee shops, fashionable restaurants and boutiques in which Georgetown University students rub shoulders with staid old power brokers. Its history is diverting too, and many of the area's buildings date to the early eighteenth century, making it older than the capital itself. Federal-era and shuttered Victorian townhouses hung with flower baskets stud the streets, while a series of stately mansions and handsome parks, gardens and cemeteries lies north of Q Street. Down on the **C&O Canal**, below M Street, the odd horse-drawn boat fills the waterway, while the tree-shaded towpaths have been turned over to cyclists and walkers; to the north, upper Georgetown is home to the elite of the elite, and while you won't get to poke around any of the private mansions or Georgian row houses, there are a handful of historic homes that are open to the public.

Georgetown's most annoying feature is that it's not on the **Metro** (Rock Creek and its valley are in the way). The nearest station is Foggy Bottom–GWU, from which it's a fifteen- to twenty-minute walk up Pennsylvania Avenue and along M Street to the junction with Wisconsin Avenue. Alternatively, approach from Dupont Circle, a similar-length walk west along P Street (or over the Dumbarton Bridge and along Q St), which puts you first in the ritzier, upper part of Georgetown. **Buses** #32 and #36 run from the Mall and Downtown; #D1, #D3 and #D6 go via E St, 13th St, K St and Dupont Circle to Q St in Georgetown and return via M St; and #G2 runs from Dupont Circle to P and Dumbarton streets. At night you'll find **taxis** relatively easy to come by on the main drags; it's a $10–15 ride to and from most downtown DC locations. The best bet might be to take the **DC Circulator** bus (daily 7am–9pm; limited night service Sun–Thurs 9pm–midnight, Fri & Sat 9pm–2am; $1; Ⓦwww .dccirculator.com), which connects upper Georgetown to the lower part along Wisconsin Avenue and M Street, then heads east to the Foggy Bottom–GWU Metro stop and runs along K Street before its final leg on Massachusetts Avenue to Union Station. Another Circulator route runs between the Rossyln Metro station in Virginia and Dupont Circle via M Street in Georgetown (Sun–Thurs 7am– midnight, Fri & Sat 7am–2am).

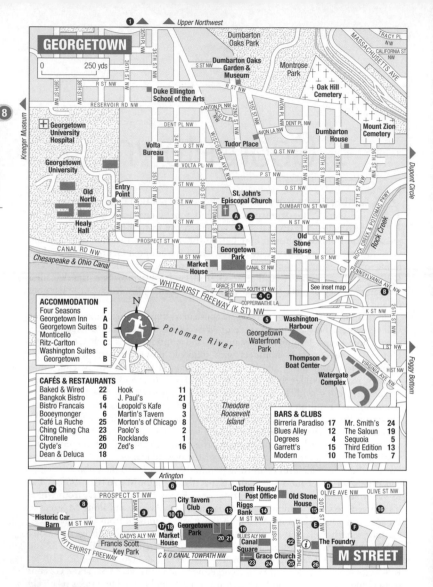

GEORGETOWN

GEORGETOWN

ACCOMMODATION

Four Seasons	F
Georgetown Inn	A
Georgetown Suites	D
Monticello	E
Ritz-Carlton	C
Washington Suites Georgetown	B

CAFÉS & RESTAURANTS

Baked & Wired	22	Hook	11
Bangkok Bistro	6	J. Paul's	21
Bistro Francais	14	Leopold's Kafe	9
Booeymonger	6	Martin's Tavern	3
Café La Ruche	25	Morton's of Chicago	8
Ching Ching Cha	23	Paolo's	2
Citronelle	26	Rocklands	1
Clyde's	20	Zed's	16
Dean & Deluca	18		

BARS & CLUBS

Birreria Paradiso	17	Mr. Smith's	24
Blues Alley	12	The Saloun	19
Degrees	4	Sequoia	5
Garrett's	15	Third Edition	13
Modern	10	The Tombs	7

Some history

In the early eighteenth century, when this area was part of Maryland, Scottish merchants began to form a permanent settlement around shoreside warehouses on the higher reaches of the Potomac River. Here they oversaw a thriving trade, exporting the plentiful **tobacco** from nearby farms and importing foreign materials and luxuries for colonial settlers. The merchants named their flourishing port either after their royal protector, George II, or after the town founders, both also named George.

Once George Washington had selected the Potomac region as the site of the new federal capital, it seemed logical that such a **port** be included in the plans. In 1791,

162

together with Alexandria in Virginia, the town was incorporated within the **federal district** but was still distinct as a township under its own name. By 1830 it had a population of nine thousand and was thriving with Georgian and Federal-style brick houses, fashionable stores, well-tended gardens and even an eponymous university (founded in 1789). By the time of the Civil War, though, Georgetown was in trouble. The tobacco trade had faltered due to soil exhaustion, while the steady growth of Baltimore and Washington itself badly affected the town's prosperity. The **Chesapeake and Ohio (C&O) Canal**, completed in 1850, represented an attempt to revive trade with the interior, and for a time Georgetown became a regional centre for wheat, coal and timber shipment. But the canal was soon obsolete: the coming of the railway was swiftly followed by the development of larger steamboats, which couldn't be accommodated by Georgetown's canal or harbour. Relegated to a mere **neighbourhood** in the District of Columbia after losing its charter in 1871, Georgetown experienced another blow in 1895 when most of its old street names – some in use for more than 150 years – were abandoned by order of Congress in favour of the numbers and letters of the federal city plan.

For much of the late nineteenth and early twentieth centuries, Georgetown was anything but a fashionable place to live. However, a mass influx of white-collar workers to DC during the New Deal era and World War II reversed Georgetown's rather down-at-heel image. Part of the charm for newcomers was that George-town's boundaries – southern river, eastern creek, western university and northern estates – had prevented indiscriminate development, leaving a collection of picture-perfect buildings still intact from the nineteenth century or earlier.

This character persists and is, of course, zealously preserved by Georgetown residents who have increasingly included DC's most fashionable and politically well-connected residents. Since 1967 Georgetown has been registered as a **National Historic Landmark**: new buildings and renovations (including house-paint colours) have to be sympathetic to their surroundings, and the canal has been landscaped and preserved as a historic park.

M Street and around

Cutting through the lower town before crossing Rock Creek into Foggy Bottom, **M Street** has been Georgetown's central artery for two centuries, and it still offers a good introduction to the area, providing you with a vibrant glimpse of Washington society amid old-fashioned row buildings packed cheek-by-jowl with scarcely an alley in between. As elsewhere in Georgetown, the street retains many of its original red-brick Georgian, Federal and later Victorian buildings, though the ground floors have all been converted for retail use. The area's **visitor centre**, 1057 Thomas Jefferson St (Wed–Sun 9am–4.30pm; ☎202/653-5190), has information on the buildings and on the C&O Canal.

Shops, restaurants and bars proliferate around the main M Street–Wisconsin Avenue junction, where the gold dome of the grand, Neoclassical **Riggs National Bank** stands as a useful landmark; its original owner, financier and later gallery owner William Corcoran, saw the bank become the sole depository of federal funds within Washington and later the dominant player on the local banking scene. The bank is now owned by PNC, which saw fit to cover the Riggs name above the portico with its own corporate logo. Even more historic, though a bit more discreet, is the **City Tavern Club**, nearby at 3206 M St, a sturdy brick Georgian building that was put up in 1796 and four years later became the staging ground for President John Adams's final review of the layout for the new capital city. It's survived the centuries well, and now hosts a private, members-only club (Ⓦwww.citytavernclubdc.org). Just beyond is **Georgetown Park**, 3222 M St, once a car park for horse-drawn omnibuses and now a shopping mall. A block west, at Potomac Street, the triple-arched, red-brick **Market House** has hosted a public market since 1795, the current version dating to 1865, though today the butchered carcasses and patent medicines have made way for a Dean & Deluca deli (see p.214).

At the junction with 34th Street, the **Francis Scott Key Bridge** (better known as just "Key Bridge") shoots off across the river to Rosslyn. The Key Bridge's namesake was the author of "The Star-Spangled Banner", who moved to Washington in 1805 and lived in a house here at M Street. His home was later demolished to make way for the **Whitehurst Freeway** – a sacrilege only belatedly atoned for by the establishment of **Francis Scott Key Park**, just off the street. The park contains a bronze bust of Key, a 60ft flagpole flying the Stars and Stripes, a wisteria-covered arbour, and a few benches from which to peer through the break in the buildings to the river.

The Old Stone House

The **Old Stone House**, 3051 M St NW (daily noon–5pm; free; tours by reservation at Ⓣ202/895-6070, Ⓦwww.nps.gov/olst), is the only extant pre-Revolutionary house in DC and sits, incongruously, in the centre of the M Street action. Built like a small fortress, it was constructed in 1765 by a Pennsylvania carpenter and retains its rugged, rough-hewn appearance. Its 3ft-thick walls are made of craggy blue fieldstone; its wooden beams are massive oak timbers; and its floor is hard with packed earth. The simple kitchen and carpenter's workshop are downstairs, with panelled parlours and bedrooms upstairs. It's certainly quaint enough, but it's unlikely that Pierre L'Enfant used it as a base while designing the federal city, as was suggested when it was rescued from demolition in the 1950s; it's of historical value mainly because it was lucky enough to survive the years. Today it's been restored to what it probably looked like in the late eighteenth century, with an attached English garden providing a nice respite from the Georgetown shopping hubbub.

N Street and around

Potomac Street, a few blocks west of the Old Stone House, is a good route to take you north to **N Street**, which contains some of Georgetown's finest Federal-era buildings. None is open to the public, but several particularly attractive facades appear between 29th and 34th streets. Robert Todd Lincoln (President Lincoln's son) lived out the last decade of his life at **no. 3014**; the house was later purchased by *Washington Post* stalwart Ben Bradlee. Four blocks west is **no. 3307**, which JFK and Jackie owned from 1957 to 1961; Jackie also lived briefly in **no. 3017** after JFK's assassination. There's a cluster of other historic houses on **Prospect Street**, one block south, where late eighteenth-century merchants built mansions like those at **nos. 3425** and **3508**; as the street name suggests, they once possessed splendid views down to the river from which they derived their wealth. Appropriately, in this vicinity sits the original **Custom House and Post Office**, 1221 31st St, which occupies a stately 1858 structure that once housed Treasury Department facilities for managing customs for the busy international trade along Georgetown's waterfront. That function is long gone, but a federal post office still occupies the ground floor.

Georgetown University

Before you leave lower Georgetown it's worth swinging by **Georgetown University**, located on the heights above the river; the **main gate** is at 37th and O streets. Founded in 1789 as the Jesuit Georgetown College, it's the oldest Catholic university in the country and the spawning grounds for numerous diplomats, Supreme Court justices and politicians – Bill Clinton foremost among them. Today, the university and its six thousand students give the neighbourhood much of its buzz. The architecture is a bit of a hybrid, ranging from the graceful porch entry and plain Georgian facade of the **Old North** building, which dates from 1795, to the spooky Romanesque details of **Healy Hall**, finished ninety years later, to a handful of modern buildings.

Just south of the university at 3600 M Street, the Romanesque Revival **Historic Car Barn** is a massive, four-storey brick structure with rooftop pavilion that represented the apex of mass transport when constructed in 1897 for the many trolley lines serving the city. Rich with black-iron decor, granite floors and panelled ceilings, the huge spaces were never filled to capacity and the building was an outsize emblem of the decline of mass transport by the 1950s. Amazingly, it was preserved instead of demolished, and now serves as office space for Georgetown University. Also in the area, 97 vertiginous **"Exorcist Steps"** connect M and Prospect streets and send shudders through the spines of moviegoers who remember the two violent deaths that took place here in that horror flick.

The Kreeger Museum

As one of Washington's most obscure cultural attractions, the **Kreeger Museum**, 2401 Foxhall Rd NW (Tues–Fri by reservation only 10.30am & 1.30pm, Sat without reservation 10am–4pm; tours Tues–Fri 10.30am & 1.30pm, Sat 10.30am, noon & 2pm; $10; ☏202/338-3552, ⓦwww.kreegermuseum.org), is sited in the hills northwest of Georgetown University (in the district of Foxhall), though it well rewards a visit for its splendid array of twentieth-century modernist art. Housed in an ultramodern white-walled home designed by Philip Johnson, the museum offers quite the stash: Impressionists such as Monet and Renoir, post-Impressionists like Van Gogh and Cézanne, early moderns such as Picasso, and Abstract Expressionists like Mark Rothko and Clyfford Still. Also worth a look are the jagged steel monoliths of David Smith; the lean metallic sculptures of Brancusi; James Rosenquist's huge Pop Art diptychs and triptychs; and Edvard Munch's disturbing Scandinavian brand of Expressionism. It's hard to predict exactly what will be on view at any one time, but the collection is large enough to ensure most modern art fans won't go away disappointed. Additionally, the museum has a number of works by Indian and African artists, and items from the pre-Columbian world.

Wisconsin Avenue and around

Georgetown's most bustling area is where M Street meets **Wisconsin Avenue**, the neighbourhood's cultural and commercial epicentre. Whereas M Street's offerings tend to be more mainstream chain stores and tourist-friendly boutiques, Wisconsin Avenue caters more to locals and those with a flair for independent shopping – anything from upstart DC designers and hometown coffeehouses to modernist galleries and engaging bars. The architecture in the vicinity has some highlights too, like **St John's Episcopal Church**, just off Wisconsin at O and Potomac, a quaint Federal structure built in 1806 by US Capitol architect William Thornton to house DC's oldest Episcopal congregation (dating to 1776). The blocky, Neoclassical **Volta Bureau**, three blocks west of Wisconsin at 1537 35th St, was built in 1893 as an institute for the deaf; the building was funded by Alexander Graham Bell with money he was awarded by the French government's Volta Prize after inventing the telephone. Finally, the **Duke Ellington School of the Arts**, at 35th and R streets, is a grand Greek Revival high school founded by the jazz great to serve as a magnet for artistically inspired DC youth.

The C&O Canal

On a clear summer's day there's no better spot to be in Georgetown than along the **Chesapeake and Ohio (C&O) Canal**, whose eastern extremity feeds into Rock Creek at 28th Street NW. The canal is overlooked on both sides by restored red-brick warehouses, spanned by small bridges, lined with trees and punctuated by occasional pastel-coloured towpath houses. The prettiest central stretch starts at **30th Street**, where the adjacent locks once opened to allow boatloads of coal, iron, timber and corn from the upriver Maryland estates to pass through.

Some history

The Potomac River had been used by traders since the earliest days of settlement in the region, but a series of rapids and waterfalls – like those at Great Falls, just fourteen miles from Georgetown – made large-scale commercial navigation all but impossible. A canal was proposed (George Washington was one of the shareholders) that would follow the line of the river and open up trade as far as the Ohio Valley, but when construction finally finished in 1850, the **C&O** reached only as far as Cumberland in Maryland, 184 miles and 74 locks away. The canal never attracted sufficient trade, mainly because of competition from the railways; the last mule-drawn cargo boat was pulled through in the 1920s, after which severe flooding from the Potomac destroyed much of the canal infrastructure. Although the stretch was under threat of being turned into yet another highway in the 1950s, the C&O's historical importance was recognized in 1971 when its entire length was declared a **National Historic Park**, and today scores of visitors hike, cycle and ride horses along the restored towpaths; canoeing and boating are allowed in certain sections, too, and the National Park Service offers passenger canal-boat services (see box opposite).

Along the canal

One of the most appealing stretches of the canal is the short section between **Thomas Jefferson Street** and **31st Street**, where artisan houses dating from the building boom of the mid-nineteenth century have been handsomely restored as shops, offices and, occasionally, private homes. Thomas Jefferson Street itself is lined with attractive brick houses, some in the Federal style, featuring rustic stone lintels, arched doorways with fanlights, and narrow top-floor dormers. On the south side of the canal, **The Foundry**, 1050 30th St, is just one of the many brick warehouses that line the canal; today it contains office and academic space. Other warehouses have received similar treatment, and frame either side of the waterway as far up as Francis Scott Key Bridge, five blocks west.

    Wisconsin Avenue, south of the canal, anchors the oldest part of Georgetown. This was the first road built from the river into Maryland during colonial times, and

Activities on the C&O Canal

It's 184 miles from Georgetown to the canal terminus at Cumberland, Maryland. Along the way, the canal wends its way through highly varied scenery: past waterfalls, through forests, and beside the ridges and valleys of the Appalachian Mountains.

Canal boats

To sign up for trips on the 90ft, mule-drawn **canal boats** – accompanied by park rangers in nineteenth-century costume who work the locks – stop in at the **C&O Canal Visitor Center**, 1057 Thomas Jefferson Street NW (Wed–Sun 9am–4.30pm; ☎202/653-5190, ⓦwww.nps.gov/choh). Tickets cost $5, and there are usually 3 or 4 departures per day Wednesday to Sunday mid-June to early September, with reduced service from April to mid-June and early September to late October.

Along the canal

A number of outlets **along the canal** rent boats, canoes and bikes, including several in the first twenty-mile stretch from Georgetown. For a day-trip by **bicycle**, Great Falls (see below) – an easy, flat fourteen miles away – is a reasonable destination. You'll need to observe a 15mph speed limit on the towpath, wear a helmet and give way to all pedestrians and horses. It takes most people a couple of hours to bike from Georgetown to Great Falls; the only slightly tricky part is just before Lock 15, going west, where you'll have to carry the bike for a couple of hundred yards. **Canoes** and **boats** are limited to specific areas (visitor centres and rental outlets can advise) and you shouldn't venture onto the Potomac River, which can be very dangerous, or swim in the canal itself. You can **picnic** anywhere you like, but light fires only in authorized fireplaces. First-come, first-served basic **campsites** are dotted along the entire length of the canal; the one closest to the city is at Swains Lock, at mile 16.6.

Great Falls Park

Great Falls Park (daily 7am–dusk; $3 per individual entry or $5 per vehicle), fourteen miles from Georgetown, is marked by the thrilling and majestic torrent of the Potomac falling 76ft over the course of a mile, through gorges and over rocky precipices, the entire spectacle encouraging death-defying kayakers to risk their necks taking it on. The **Great Falls Tavern Visitor Center**, 11710 MacArthur Blvd, Potomac, MD (daily 10am–5pm; ☎301/767-3714, ⓦwww.nps.gov/grfa), has a museum covering the history of the canal, built to get around the perils of the falls. This is the starting point for local tours, walks and canal boat trips (enquire at the visitor centre). Nearby, a boardwalk offers terrific views of the falls themselves. There is no access to the park by public transport. By car, take MacArthur Boulevard, signposted from Georgetown, or Exit 41W off the Beltway; outside rush hour, it's a 20-minute drive.

---

was a major route for farmers and traders who used the slope of the hill to roll their barrels down to riverside warehouses. Later, canal boatmen would be lured into the Gothic Revival **Grace Church**, 1041 Wisconsin Ave, by promises of salvation from the earthbound drudgery of hauling heavy goods from barge to warehouse.

The waterfront

South of the C&O Canal, **K Street** was once known as Water Street because it fronted the Potomac River, though land reclamation has now pushed the water a hundred yards or so further south. K Street's most noticeable feature is what's above it, namely the looming **Whitehurst Freeway** – the elevated road built in 1949 to relieve traffic congestion on M Street. Cross the road under the freeway and you reach the riverside development of **Washington Harbour** (east of 31st), its interlocking towers set around a circular, terraced plaza with spurting fountains, around which are various restaurants, shops and condos. The waterfront on either side has been landscaped as part of the new **Georgetown Waterfront Park,** which offers shady spots and arbours, and steps down to the waterfront, with construction on the park proceeding toward the west. There are views upriver to the Francis Scott Key Bridge and downriver to Theodore Roosevelt Island and Bridge, as well as across the river to the Watergate Complex and Kennedy Center. If you'd like to go for a **cruise,** several boat-rental shops offer the means to explore the calmer waters around the Key Bridge and Roosevelt Island (see box, p.167).

Northern Georgetown

Set on "The Heights" above Q Street, the grand mansions and estates of **northern Georgetown** sat out the upheavals that took place below during the nineteenth and twentieth centuries. Owned by the area's richest merchants, the land here was never exploited for new construction when Georgetown was in the throes of expansion. Today several of the fine homes and beautiful grounds are open to the public.

Tudor Place

Two blocks east of Wisconsin Avenue between Q and R streets at 1644 31st St NW, stately **Tudor Place** (tours on the hour Tues–Sat 10am–3pm, Sun noon–3pm; $8; T 202/965-0400, W www.tudorplace.org) was designed by William Thornton, who was also responsible for the US Capitol and Georgetown's St John's Episcopal Church. Completed in 1816 for Thomas Peter and his wife Martha Custis Peter (granddaughter of Martha Washington), the house displays an incongruity that was rare for the period – Thornton embellished the fundamentally Federal-style structure with a Classical domed portico on the south side. The exterior has remained virtually untouched since and, as the house stayed in the same family for more than 160 years, the interior has been spared the constant "improvements" wrought in Georgetown's other period homes by successive owners.

Guided tours show you furnishings lifted from the Washingtons' family seat at Mount Vernon and fill you in on how Martha Peter watched from her bedroom window in the then-unfinished house as British troops burned down the US Capitol in 1814. You're supposed to reserve in advance for the tours, but ringing the bell at the front gate gives you access to the five and a half acres of gardens during the day (Mon–Sat 10am–4pm, Sun noon–4pm; free). Walk up the path and bear to the right where a white box holds detailed maps of the paths, greens, box hedges, arbours and fountains. You can also request a garden tour (reserve at T 202/965-0400 ext. 115) to guide you through the fetching grounds.

Garden Day

Each May, the Georgetown Garden Club sponsors its annual **Garden Day,** when private patches of greenery are open to the public, some of them quite lovely and almost none regularly viewable behind the stoic facades of the Georgian and Federal townhouses that front them. You can expect to see anything from carefully tended pleasure gardens rich with roses and shrubs, to old-world fantasy plots dotted with pergolas, mosaics and gazebos, to simple groves adorned with ponds and fountains. Tickets cost $30 ($35 on day of tour) for the self-guided tour and raise funds for charity and conservation efforts. Check local listings magazines for details, call T 202/965-1950 or visit W www.georgetowngardentour.com.

Dumbarton Oaks

One long block east of Wisconsin Avenue, and just north of Tudor Place at 1703 32nd St, the grand estate of **Dumbarton Oaks** (gardens: mid-March to Oct Tues–Sun 2–6pm; Nov to mid-March Tues–Sun 2–5pm; $8; museum: Tues–Sun 2–5pm; free; ☎202/339-6401, Ⓦwww.doaks.org) encompasses a marvellous red-brick Georgian mansion surrounded by gardens and woods, a fine setting for the 1944 meeting of international delegates whose deliberations led to the founding of the United Nations the following year. Its ten acres of **formal gardens** (entrance at 3101 R St), with their beech terrace, evergreens, rose garden, brick paths, pools and fountains, provide one of DC's quietest and most relaxing retreats.

The estate's highlight, however, is its **museum**, which has a striking selection of **pre-Columbian** art, with countless gold, jade and polychromatic carvings, sculpture and pendants of Olmec, Inca, Aztec and Mayan provenance – among them ceremonial axes, jewellery made from spondylus shells, stone masks, and sharp jade "celts" possibly used for human sacrifice. Equally fascinating is the **Byzantine collection**, with the silver Eucharist vessels, ivory boxes and painted icons all standouts. Perhaps most extraordinary is the miniature fourteenth-century **mosaic icon** of the Forty Martyrs, which depicts a Christian martyrdom legend in cubes of enamel paste and semiprecious stone. Finally, the **Music Room** offers wondrous paintings and tapestries, walnut chests and credenzas, a decorative wooden ceiling, and vintage pianos and harpsichords.

Dumbarton House

A little further southeast at 2715 Q St NW, **Dumbarton House** (tours mid-March to mid-Dec Tues–Fri 10am–4pm, Sat & Sun 11am–3pm; mid-Dec to mid-March Tues–Sun 11am–3pm; $5; ☎202/337-2288, Ⓦwww.dumbartonhouse.org) is one of the oldest homes in Georgetown, built between 1799 and 1804. The construction of the bridge over Rock Creek in 1915 necessitated the house's removal, brick by brick, from further down Q Street to its present position. Known for a century as "Bellevue", the elegant Georgian mansion housed Georgetown's first salon. In 1814, as the British overran Washington, Dolley Madison watched the White House burning from Bellevue's windows (the house was the first refuge for the fleeing president and first lady). The **National Society of Colonial Dames of America**, now headquartered here, will provide the historical background and escort you slowly through period rooms filled with Federal furniture, early prints of Washington, DC and middling portraits. If you don't have an hour to spare or an insatiable interest in decorative porcelain that once, possibly, adorned the White House, content yourself instead with a seat in the quiet, restful garden.

Oak Hill Cemetery

Some of the most elite names from Georgetown history are interred at **Oak Hill Cemetery**, 3001 R St (Mon–Fri 9am–4.30pm). Endowed by banker and art collector William Corcoran, exclusive Oak Hill began receiving Georgetown's dead in 1849. Dating from that time is the brick **gatehouse** at 30th and R streets, where you enter the lovingly kept grounds that spill down the hillside to Rock Creek. Within the grounds, the diminutive brick-and-sandstone **Gothic chapel** is the sprightly work of James Renwick (architect of the Smithsonian Castle). Ask at the gatehouse for directions to the resting homes of the cemetery's most notable names, including Corcoran himself; Edwin Stanton, secretary of war under President Lincoln; and former Secretary of State Dean Acheson.

Northern Virginia

I n the city's early years, the boundaries of Washington, DC extended into
Northern Virginia, making the capital city a perfect diamond. In 1846, the
state asked for its part of DC back, and the District of Columbia hasn't
extended into Virginia since – at least officially. In reality, the region is a
fundamental part of the capital metroplex and is home to hundreds of thousands
of its employees, whether just across the Potomac or in further-flung suburbs
beyond the confines of the famed Beltway that ties together the region in one
vast, slow-moving freeway system.

Northern Virginia had a fundamental presence in the nascent United States, as a
hub for tobacco growing, slavery and politics, with many of Virginia's and the
country's most famous statesmen – Thomas Jefferson, George Washington and
James Madison – having a hand in all three. By the 1860s, though, the old plantation order was crumbling, and after Virginia chose the Confederate side in the
Civil War, it saw its farmsteads and economy wrecked for decades after. These
days, if you travel through the countryside, you can still find rolling green hills,
historic plantation manors and horse farms that provide a sense of the old "Cavalier"
spirit – though closer to Washington, DC itself, the area is largely suburban and
crossed by countless freeways.

Northern Virginia's most notable sights are well worth seeking out if you have a
few days to spare. Closest to Washington, DC, **Arlington** is best known for its
military sights – from the famous national cemetery to the Pentagon – while the
more agreeable **Alexandria**, with its old town full of attractive buildings and
low-key charm, seems at least two centuries removed from the modern whirl. To
the west, the Virginia heartland provides even more of a sense of tradition, with
its preserved Civil War battlefields, famous planter estates such as Mount Vernon
and Gunston Hall, and rolling agricultural land peppered with well-preserved
nineteenth-century villages.

Arlington

For many visitors, **Arlington** is synonymous with its **cemetery**, and little else.
However, this small city – which is technically a county – across the Potomac from
Washington has experienced an influx of urbanites in the past decade, and has
plenty to offer. While its southern neighbour, Alexandria, is still better for **dining**
and **shopping**, Arlington does boast a few major malls in the neighbourhoods of
Pentagon City and Crystal City (not themselves destinations), and much of the
nightlife scene is clustered around the Clarendon and Court House districts and

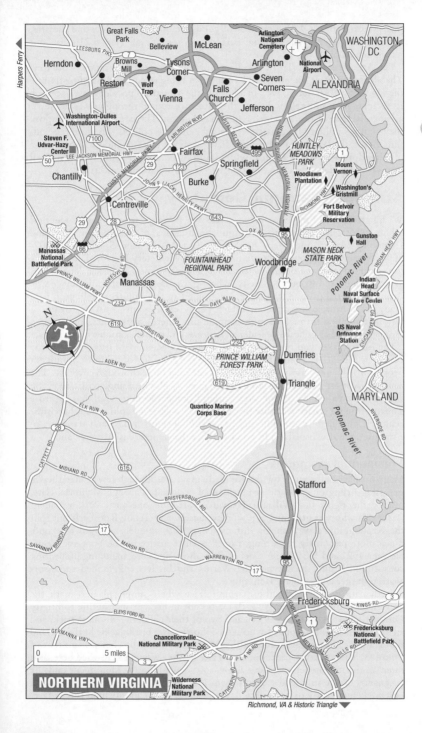

Richmond, VA & Historic Triangle ▼

their Metro stations. With a number of good restaurants, bars, clubs and theatres, sticking around for an evening isn't a bad idea at all (see p.216 for our recommendations).

The Arlington Memorial Bridge is one of four bridges (the Francis Scott Key, Theodore Roosevelt Memorial and 14th Street being the others) that directly link the suburb to Washington, DC; in addition, the **Metrorail** provides easy access on its Orange, Blue and Yellow lines – the latter two routed through DC's domestic **airport**, Reagan National, which is also in Arlington. The fact that the **Pentagon**, the country's military headquarters, is sited here only bolsters this close relationship. Across the Potomac to the immediate east is the pleasant and walkable refuge of **Theodore Roosevelt Island**, while south of here, the **Mount Vernon Trail** runs down to Alexandria and eventually to George Washington's estate.

Arlington National Cemetery

Washington's grand monuments sit across the Potomac from a sea of identical white headstones spreading through the hillsides of **Arlington National Cemetery** (daily: April–Sept 8am–7pm; Oct–March 8am–5pm; ℡703/607-8000, ⓦwww.arlingtoncemetery.mil; Arlington Cemetery Metro). The 624-acre site commemorates the deaths of some 300,000 US soldiers and their dependants, as well as John and Robert Kennedy, whose graves here make it a pilgrimage site. A military burial ground (the largest and oldest in the country), Arlington is in many ways America's pantheon, which partly excuses the constant stream of visitors trampling through on sightseeing tours. There's a restrained, understated character here that honours presidents, generals and ordinary soldiers alike.

The **Metro** takes you right to the main gates on Memorial Drive. The **visitor centre** by the entrance issues **maps** indicating the gravesites of the most prominent people buried here; various guidebooks on sale offer more thorough coverage. The cemetery is enormous (far too large to take in every plot on a single visit), so if you simply want to see the major sites without doing too much walking, board a **Tourmobile** for a narrated **tour** (see box, p.27); tickets are sold inside the visitor centre. (Combined Tourmobile tickets, including sights in DC and transport to Arlington, are also available.) In good weather the cemetery is busy by 9am.

Presidential memorials

Many people head straight for the Kennedy gravesites, though few realize they're bypassing Arlington's only other presidential occupant. Through Memorial Gate, just to the right, lies **William Howard Taft**, the one-term 27th president (1909–13) who was groomed as a worthy successor to Teddy Roosevelt but split the Republican Party with his intransigence. Taft uniquely enjoyed a second, much more personally rewarding, career as chief justice of the Supreme Court between 1921 and 1930. Later chief justices also reside here, including pioneering constitutional-rights archetype Earl Warren and his less enlightened successors Warren Burger and William Rehnquist.

Further up the hillside is the marble terrace where simple plaques mark the gravesites of **John F. Kennedy**, 35th US president, his wife **Jacqueline Kennedy Onassis** (laid to rest here in 1994), and two of their children – a son, Patrick, and an unnamed daughter, both of whom died shortly after birth. Jackie lit the **eternal flame** at JFK's funeral and ordered that the funeral decor be copied from that of Lincoln's, held a century earlier in the White House. When it's crowded here, as it often is, the majesty of the view across to the Washington Monument and the poignancy of the inscribed extracts from JFK's inaugural address are sometimes obscured; come early or late in the day if possible. In the plot behind JFK's grave,

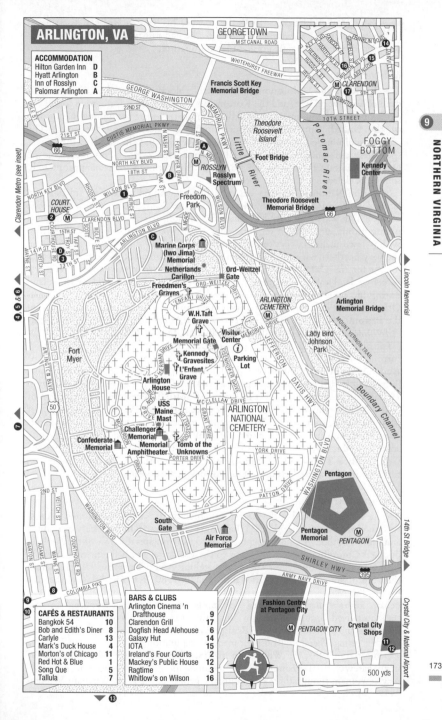

ARLINGTON, VA

ACCOMMODATION
Hilton Garden Inn   D
Hyatt Arlington   B
Inn of Rosslyn   C
Palomar Arlington   A

GEORGETOWN
M ST CANAL ROAD
WHITEHURST FREEWAY

Francis Scott Key
Memorial Bridge

GEORGE WASHINGTON
CUSTIS MEMORIAL PKWY

Theodore
Roosevelt
Island

Foot Bridge

Theodore Roosevelt
Memorial Bridge

FOGGY
BOTTOM

Kennedy
Center

FRANKLIN ROAD
KEY BLVD
HERNDON ST
HARTFORD ST
GARFIELD ST
DANVILLE ST
14
15
16
CLARENDON
9TH ST
17
WASHINGTON
10TH STREET

22ND ST
21ST ST
66
NORTH KEY BLVD
NORTH NASH ST
NORTH KENT ST

RHODES ST
NORTH KEY BLVD
18TH ST
OAK ST
FORT MYER DRIVE
WILSON BLVD
M
ROSSLYN
Rosslyn
Spectrum

Little River
MEMORIAL PKWY

Potomac River

66

Lincoln Memorial ▶

Arlington
Memorial Bridge

COURT
HOUSE
2
M
CLARENDON BLVD
15TH ST
COURT HOUSE RD
TAFT ST
SCOTT
ROLFE
PIERCE ST
1
Freedom
Park
WILSON BLVD
ARLINGTON BLVD

◀ Clarendon Metro (see inset)

C
Marine Corps
(Iwo Jima)
Memorial
Netherlands
Carillon
Freedmen's
Graves
Ord-Weitzel
Gate
ORD-WEITZEL DRIVE
ARLINGTON
CEMETERY
M

◀ 4, 5 & 6

WAYNE ST
VEITCH ST
13TH ST

L'ENFANT DRIVE
W.H.Taft
Grave
Memorial Gate
Kennedy
Gravesites
L'Enfant
Grave
Arlington
House
Visitor
Center
i
Parking
Lot

MEMORIAL DRIVE
JEFFERSON
EISENHOWER DRIVE
DAVIS HWY

Lady Bird
Johnson
Park

MOUNT VERNON TRAIL

Boundary Channel

Fort
Myer
50

ARLINGTON BLVD

SHERMAN DRIVE
GRANT DRIVE
McCLELLAN DRIVE
ARLINGTON
NATIONAL
CEMETERY

◀ 7

USS
Maine
Mast
Challenger
Memorial
Confederate
Memorial
Memorial
Amphitheater
Tomb of the
Unknowns
PORTER DRIVE
YORK DRIVE

WASHINGTON BLVD

Pentagon

2ND ST
VEITCH ST
WASHINGTON BLVD
PATTON DRIVE
South
Gate
Air Force
Memorial
Pentagon
Memorial
Pentagon
M
PENTAGON

BARTON ST
ADAMS ST
WAYNE ST
COURTHOUSE RD
COLUMBIA PIKE
8
SHIRLEY HWY
ARMY NAVY DRIVE
395

14th St Bridge ▶

BARS & CLUBS
Arlington Cinema 'n
Drafthouse   9
Clarendon Grill   17
Dogfish Head Alehouse 6
Galaxy Hut   14
IOTA   15
Ireland's Four Courts 2
Mackey's Public House 12
Ragtime   3
Whitlow's on Wilson 16

9
10
CAFÉS & RESTAURANTS
Bangkok 54   10
Bob and Edith's Diner 8
Carlyle   13
Mark's Duck House 4
Morton's of Chicago 11
Red Hot & Blue   1
Song Que   5
Tallula   7

Fashion Centre
at Pentagon City

M PENTAGON CITY

Crystal City
Shops
11
12

Crystal City & National Airport ▶

N

0   500 yds

13

an isolated, plain white cross marks the grave of his brother **Robert**, assassinated in the kitchen of LA's *Ambassador Hotel* after he had just won the 1968 California primary for the Democratic presidential nomination.

Military graves

The **Tomb of the Unknowns**, white marble blocks dedicated to the unknown dead of two world wars and the Korean and Vietnam wars, is guarded round the clock by impeccably uniformed soldiers who carry out a ceremonial **Changing of the Guard** (April–Sept every 30 minutes, otherwise on the hour). The circular, colonnaded **Memorial Amphitheater** behind the tomb is the site of special remembrance services, especially busy during key holidays like Memorial Day and Veterans Day, when the spartan marble columns form an appropriately sombre backdrop.

Arlington National Cemetery began as a burial ground for **Union soldiers**, on land taken from Robert E. Lee after he joined the Confederate army at the outset of the Civil War. As a national cemetery, though, it was subsequently deemed politic to honour the dead on both sides of the war; the **Confederate section**, with its own memorial, lies to the west of the Tomb of the Unknowns, while on the very northern edge of the cemetery are buried some 1500 **black troops** who fought for the Union during that war and 3800 **former slaves** who lived in a parcel of land called Freedmen's Village, who were removed from their land during the cemetery's creation. Most of their graves are marked without names. Other sections and memorials commemorate America's long list of conflicts, from the Revolutionary War to the current wars in Afghanistan and Iraq, with a few dozen markers for **foreign troops** from Britain, France, Italy and Canada.

The highest concentration of notable military graves is found in the myriad plots surrounding the Tomb of the Unknowns: with a map you'll find the graves of **Audie Murphy**, the most decorated soldier in World War II, and boxer **Joe Louis** (born, and buried here, as Joe Louis Barrow), world heavyweight champion from 1937 to 1949. Elsewhere are the graves of **John J. Pershing**, commander of American forces in World War I; Arctic explorer **Robert Peary**; civil rights leader **Medgar Evers**, shot in 1963 by rampaging racists in the Deep South; astronauts **Virgil Grissom** and **Roger Chaffee** of the ill-fated 1967 *Apollo* flight; tough-guy actor **Lee Marvin**; pioneering black lawyer and first African American Supreme Court justice **Thurgood Marshall**, among seven other associate justices; and thriller-writer **Dashiell Hammett**, a World War II sergeant.

Group memorials

The most photographed of the many group memorials is the one dedicated to those who died aboard the space shuttle **Challenger**; it is located immediately behind the amphitheatre, though a more recent marker commemorates the crew of the similarly doomed **Columbia** mission. Adjacent to the *Challenger* site is the memorial to the **Iran Rescue Mission**, whose failure in snatching American embassy workers from their captors doomed Jimmy Carter at the polls in 1980. Both stand close to the mast of the **USS Maine**, whose mysterious destruction in Havana harbour in 1898 – still debated more than a century later – prompted the rise of "yellow journalism" and the short-lived Spanish–American War; the war itself is commemorated by a memorial and a monument to the **Rough Riders**, a devil-may-care cavalry outfit in which a young Theodore Roosevelt made his reputation.

Dedicated in 1997, the **Women in Military Service** memorial, situated at the main gateway, is the country's first national monument to honour American servicewomen, though there's an honorary group statue at the Vietnam Veterans

Memorial, while the very recent **Pentagon Memorial** is a five-sided black-granite stone inscribed with the names of Washington's victims of the 9/11 attacks.

Arlington House

Immediately above the Kennedy gravesites, the imposing **Arlington House** (daily 9.30am–4.30pm; free) was the one-time home of Confederate commander Robert E. Lee, and where he was when, in 1861, he heard the news that his home state of Virginia had seceded from the Union. Soon after, Lee resigned his commission and left Arlington for Richmond, where he took command of Virginia's military forces, and the federal government eventually confiscated the estate. He never returned to Arlington, and as early as 1864 a **cemetery** for the Union dead was established on the grounds of the house, with the mansion itself used as an ad hoc **camp** for Union soldiers. After Lee's death, his family took their case to the US Supreme Court; they argued for the return of the family land and succeeded in getting it back in 1874. However, they ultimately had to sell it back to the government Lee had fought against because, despite their earlier wealth and prominence, the clan had fallen on hard times and needed the money – $150,000.

The house itself is a Greek Revival mansion that features six thick Tuscan columns and a stately Neoclassical style, adding grandeur to its position on the high ground above the Potomac. The principal bedroom is the place where Lee wrote his resignation letter from the US Army, and the family parlour the spot in which he was married; a fair number of the furnishings are original. On the estate's north side is a small **museum** that tells the family saga and recounts Lee's history, though the bent toward the heroic may be too much for visitors lacking ardour for the Confederate "Lost Cause".

From the grounds the views across the river to the Mall are stunning. No less a man than the **Marquis de Lafayette**, a guest at Arlington House in 1824, thought the aspect "the finest view in the world". Fittingly, the grave of Washington, DC designer **Pierre Charles L'Enfant** was belatedly sited here in 1909 after the US government forgave his feuding over pay for his services; there is a small memorial to him here as well, though the city itself still lacks a proper monument to his accomplishments.

Marine Corps Memorial and Netherlands Carillon

Lying to the north, just outside the cemetery walls on Arlington Blvd at Meade St, is the 78ft-high bronze **Marine Corps Memorial** (☎703/289-2500; Arlington Cemetery Metro). It's about a twenty-minute walk from the cemetery's main visitor centre to the **Ord-Weitzel Gate**, though the easiest approach is to take the **Metro** to the **Rosslyn** station, from which it's a ten-minute, signposted walk. The memorial commemorates the Marine dead of all wars – from the first casualties of the Revolutionary War to the fallen in Iraq – but it's more popularly known as the **Iwo Jima Statue**, after the bloody World War II battle for the small but strategically essential Pacific island where 6800 lives were lost. In a famous image – inspired by a contemporaneous photograph – half a dozen marines raise the Stars and Stripes on Mount Suribachi in February 1945; the site remains one of the few federal installations that allows Old Glory to fly around the clock, without a ceremonial raising or lowering. In summer (June–Aug), the US Marine Corps presents regular **parades** and **concerts**, and the annual **Marine Corps Marathon** (Ⓦwww.marinemarathon.com) starts here each October.

Nearby, to the south, rises the **Netherlands Carillon**, a 130ft-high steel monument dedicated to the Netherlands' liberation from the Nazis in 1945. Given by the Dutch in thanks for American aid, the tower is set in landscaped grounds featuring thousands of **tulips**, which bloom each spring. The fifty copper-and-tin bells of the carillon are rung on Saturdays and holidays (May–Sept), at which times you can climb the tower for superlative city views.

Air Force Memorial

South of Arlington National Cemetery at Fort Myer, off Washington Blvd, is the **Air Force Memorial** (daily: April–Sept 8am–11pm; Oct–March 8am–9pm), a long-delayed tribute to America's airmen dedicated in 2006. The site is immediately recognizable by its three giant steel arcs, which twist out 270ft into the sky and, by their placement, recall a missing fourth arc – the so-called "missing man" – a familiar manoeuvre at Air Force flight shows and exhibitions. The image is underlined further by the Contemplation Wall, which shows aircraft in such a display and salutes the dead of the service's twentieth-century wars. Elsewhere, granite entry walls are inscribed with names of the service's Medal of Honor winners and inspirational quotes, and a quartet of 8ft bronze statues recalls an honour guard with crisp, martial form.

The Pentagon

The locus of modern American war-making, the **Pentagon**, I-395 at Jefferson Davis Hwy (tours Mon–Fri 9am–3pm, by reservation only; ☎703/695-3325, ⓦpentagon.afis.osd.mil; Pentagon Metro), is the seat of the **US Department of Defense**, and one of the largest chunks of architecture in the world, with its five 900ft-long sides enclosing 17.5 miles of corridors and a floor area of 6.5 million square feet.

Terrorists left their mark on this massive structure on 9/11 when they crashed **American Airlines flight 77** into its western flank, tearing open a hole almost 200ft wide – an event remembered at the **Pentagon Memorial** outside the building (daily 24hr), featuring 184 benches that commemorate each person killed at the site. In the wake of the attack, the military suspended all general Pentagon **tours**, though they've since resumed, with direct access via the Pentagon Metro stop. If you're a US citizen, you can reserve a tour through your senator or representative; foreign nationals should contact their embassy; otherwise, you can make a reservation on the website. In any case, the tours mainly focus on the prosaic aspects of the building, among them its prodigious size – number of restrooms, pints of milk drunk daily by its employees, and so on.

The most interesting thing about the Pentagon is the structure itself, which was thrown together in just sixteen months during World War II to consolidate seventeen different buildings of what in those days was properly called the **War Department**. Efficiency dictated the five-storey, five-sided concrete design: with so many employees, it was imperative to maintain quick contact between separate offices and departments – it takes just seven minutes to walk between any two points in the building.

The Mount Vernon Trail and Theodore Roosevelt Island

If you've had enough of government sights and are interested in doing a little hiking or biking, you might consider taking on the 18.5-mile **Mount Vernon**

Wolf Trap

About ten miles west of Arlington via Route 7 is what some call the Kennedy Center of folk music. In 1966, Congress declared **Wolf Trap**, 1624 Trap Rd, Vienna, VA (☏703/255-1868 or 255-1900, ⊛www.wolftrap.org), a "National Park for the Performing Arts", meaning that it would be devoted to **American music** in all its native forms: bluegrass, jazz, ragtime, Cajun, zydeco, Native American and countless others. The space for this music could hardly be better – a pair of remodelled barns from the eighteenth century (moved here from upstate New York), which provide just the right weathered charm and echoey acoustics for instruments such as banjos, guitars, mandolins, gourds and washboards. The German barn is the larger of the two, giving you a chance to listen to the music on the "threshing floor" or in a hayloft above. Wolf Trap's other venues, on the same site, include the modern, less atmospheric Filene Center and a theatrical stage. **Prices** can vary widely, so check the website for detailed information. For directions on how to **get there** by public transport, call ☏202/637-7000 or visit ⊛www.wmata.com; Metro shuttle-bus service is available for most performances from the West Falls Church Metro station. The park has concession stands and a restaurant, but in summer it's nicer to bring a picnic and eat on the grass.

Trail, which runs parallel to the George Washington Memorial Parkway, from just south of Theodore Roosevelt Memorial Bridge a further seven miles to Alexandria and on to Mount Vernon. The trail sticks close to the Potomac for its entire length and runs past a number of sites of historic or natural interest. For more information, and a free **trail guide**, contact the National Park Service in Washington (☏202/619-7222, ⊛www.nps.gov). Those looking for a quieter place for a constitutional should head to **Theodore Roosevelt Island** (daily 6am–10pm; free), a nature park with 2.5 miles of trails that meander through marsh, swamp and forest, presided over by a statue of the eponymous 26th president. You can get to the island, which lies across a footbridge from the start of the Mount Vernon Trail, from the Arlington side of the Potomac, not far from the Rosslyn Metro station.

Alexandria

Six miles south of Washington, DC, across the Potomac, **Alexandria** is a historic gem thick with restored Georgian manors, Revolutionary-era taverns and churches, and other hallmarks of the region's rich past. Virginia was the first and biggest British colony on the continent, and Alexandria generated the bulk of its wealth through a tobacco industry that relied on thousands of imported slaves. What's now known as **Old Town Alexandria** – the compact downtown grid by the Potomac – was left to rot after the Civil War ended slavery. Many of the warehouses and wharves were abandoned, while other buildings became munitions factories during both world wars. Today, after decades of spirited renovation, the Colonial-era streets and converted warehouses are hugely popular attractions, making the town an intriguing relic just across the water from the nation's capital. It's also prime **shopping** territory, with antiques, crafts, ethnic folk-art, vintage-clothing and gift stores on every corner. Good hunting grounds are at the upper end of King Street (toward the Metro station), along Cameron Street (behind City Hall) and at the Torpedo Factory Arts Center (on the waterfront).

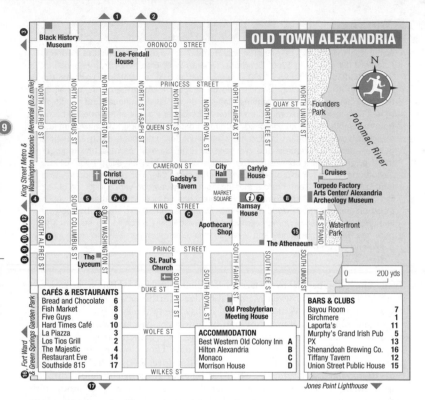

Although the main drags – particularly King Street – are heavy with traffic, it's not hard to find pockets of peace and quiet here. Cobbled, tree-lined streets with herringbone brick pavements are lined with pastel-washed houses featuring boot-scrapers and horse-mounting blocks outside the front door, and cast-iron drainpipes stamped "Alexandria, DC".

Old Town practicalities

The **Metro** station for Old Town Alexandria is King Street (Yellow and Blue lines; 25min from downtown DC), a mile or so from most of the sights. Outside King Street station, pick up the local **DASH** bus ($1.25; ☎703/746-3274, ⓦwww .dashbus.com), which runs down King Street, and get off at Fairfax Street; if you prefer, you can take the twenty-minute walk from the station instead. **Drivers** should follow the George Washington Memorial Parkway south from Arlington and take the East King Street exit. **Cyclists** or **walkers** can get here via the **Mount Vernon Trail** (see p.176); Big Wheel Bikes, 2 Prince St, Old Town Alexandria (☎703/739-2300, ⓦwww.bigwheelbikes.com; see also p.244), can rent you a bike to ride to and from Mount Vernon, ten miles away.

Old Town is laid out on a grid, and most of the sights lie within a ten-block area. Guided walks, ghost tours and river cruises (see p.181) operate during the high season. Note that many sights are closed on Mondays, and that opening hours are limited on Sundays.

Ramsay House

The town's **visitor centre**, in **Ramsay House**, 221 King St (daily 10am–8pm, Jan–March closes 5pm; ☎703/746-3301, Ⓦvisitalexandriava.com), provides pamphlets and information on countless historic sites and curiosities. The house itself is the oldest in town, built (though not originally on this site) in 1724 for **William Ramsay**, one of Alexandria's founding merchants and later its first mayor. Ramsay had the house transported upriver from Dumfries, Virginia, and placed facing the river, where his ships loaded up with tobacco. The water is now three blocks away: the bluff that the town was built on was excavated after the Revolutionary War, and the earth was used to extend the harbour into the shallow bay, which is why Ramsay House stands so high above the street, its foundations exposed.

Carlyle House and City Hall

When the town was established, Ramsay's fellow merchant **John Carlyle** bought two of the most expensive land plots and built Alexandria's finest Colonial-era home. In the 1750s, when all the town's other buildings were constructed of wood, the Georgian, white-sandstone **Carlyle House**, 121 N Fairfax St (tours Tues–Sat 10am–4pm, Sun noon–4.30pm; $5; ☎703/549-2997, Ⓦwww.carlyle house.org), made a powerful statement about its owner's wealth. Accounts of Carlyle's business dealings – he ran three plantations and traded numerous slaves – inform the half-hour **guided tour** of the restored house. Contrast the family's draped beds, expensively painted rooms and fine furnishings with the bare servants' hall, which has actually been over-restored – in the eighteenth century it would have had an earthen floor and no glass in the windows. To their credit, the displays in the mansion don't shy away from presenting the bare, disturbing details of the lives of slaves during the era. Aside from slavery and domestic matters, the tour discusses how Carlyle House played a role in intercontinental affairs: in August 1755, it was used as **General Braddock**'s headquarters during the planning of the French and Indian War. George Washington was on Braddock's staff, and after the war he frequently visited the house.

Across the way, **Market Square**, off King Street, has been the heart of Alexandria since its founding. The modern brick terrace around the square sounds one of the few discordant notes in the Old Town. The Georgian Revival **City Hall** facing the square at 301 King St – notable for its quaint steeple – looks rather sprightly for such an old building; not surprisingly, it's a post-Civil War reconstruction of an early nineteenth-century Benjamin Latrobe creation. A weekly **farmers' market** still sets up in the City Hall arcades (Sat 5–10.30am), as it has for some 250 years.

Gadsby's Tavern Museum and historic churches

Gadsby's Tavern Museum, 134 N Royal St (tours: April–Oct Tues–Sat 10am–5pm, Sun & Mon 1–5pm; Nov–March Wed–Sat 11am–4pm, Sun 1–4pm; $5; ☎703/838-4242, Ⓦwww.gadsbystavern.org), occupies two Georgian buildings: the City Hotel from 1792 and the tavern itself from 1785. Downstairs, *Gadsby's Tavern* is still a working restaurant, complete with Colonial-style food and costumed staff. In early American society, anyone who was anyone dropped by here for a visit – from the Marquis de Lafayette to Thomas Jefferson. Short **tours** of the complex by a knowledgeable guide lead you through the old tavern and hotel rooms; summer **lantern tours** offer the same perspective, bathed in a nocturnal romantic glow (June–Aug Fri 7–10pm; $5).

Three blocks west up Cameron Street, the English-style **Christ Church**, 118 N Washington St (Tues–Sat 10am–4pm), a working branch of the Episcopal diocese, contains the Washington family pew. Identified by a striking red-and-white bell tower and set in a legendary churchyard, the Georgian edifice was built of brick and finished just before the Revolution. During the Civil War, Union soldiers worshipped here, as did FDR and Churchill on one occasion eighty years later. Further south, the sedate 1808 **St Paul's Church**, 228 S Pitt St (Mon–Fri 9am–5pm, Sat & Sun 7am–7pm), has a simple facade graced by three gentle arches, and its interior is a pleasant mix of Gothic arches and classical columns. Its skilful designer was none other than Benjamin Latrobe, architect of the US Capitol.

Lee-Fendall House and Alexandria Black History Museum

The Washingtons weren't the only notable family with ties to Alexandria. A descendant of the Lees of Virginia, Phillip Fendall built his splendid clapboard mansion, the **Lee-Fendall House**, 614 Oronoco St (Wed–Sat 10am–4pm, Sun 1–4pm; $5), in 1785. Much of the furnishing dates from the antebellum era, and the house has been remodelled in Greek Revival style. Distinguished Revolutionary War general Henry "Light Horse Harry" Lee composed Washington's funeral oration here, and the home has had other famous residents in the years since. The most notable of these was powerful labour leader John L. Lewis, who moved in during 1937 as the head of the United Mine Workers, and soon created the Congress of Industrial Organizations as a rival to the American Federation of Labor, helping to merge both groups in the 1940s. Lewis lived here until his death in 1969.

A distinctly different view of town history is on view three blocks west at the **Alexandria Black History Museum**, 902 Wythe St (Tues–Sat 10am–4pm; $2), which details some two hundred years of slavery in the city in a once-segregated library building. Using household tools, implements, documents and photos, the museum traces local African American history back to the early eighteenth century, when Alexandria was a stopover for tens of thousands of African slaves on their way to the plantations of the New World. Displays examine the presence of slaves in the company and houses of prominent figures such as Lee, Carlyle and Washington, and recall the black soldiers, freedmen and activists who shaped the Civil War era. More in-depth analysis can be found in the museum's **Watson Reading Room**, which provides a scholarly angle on local history with thousands of books, articles and other materials.

Lyceum and Athenaeum

South of King Street, the **Lyceum**, 201 S Washington St (Mon–Sat 10am–5pm, Sun 1–5pm; $2; ☏703/838-4994, ⓦwww.alexandriahistory.org), houses the town's history museum in a magisterial, 1839 Greek Revival building that was designed to be a centrepiece for the town's cultural pretensions – the evocative name harkening back to classical hubs for learning, discussion and oratory. Although the place doesn't quite have the same role today, its changing displays, film shows and art gallery can put some flesh on the town's history; varied exhibits range from old photographs and Civil War documents to locally produced furniture and silverware (the latter an Alexandrian speciality in the nineteenth century).

Five blocks east along Prince Street, the **Athenaeum** (Thurs, Fri & Sun noon–4pm; Sat 1–4pm; free; ☏703/548-0035, ⓦwww.nvfaa.org), another

Classical-style edifice, with its mighty Doric columns and high pediment, was built as a bank in 1852, which happened to hold the money of Robert E. Lee and other notables. After a stint as a talcum-powder factory and a church, it's now an arts centre, where you can check out the latest modern art in a series of galleries, with periodic music, dance and theatre performances.

Old Presbyterian Meeting House and Stabler-Leadbeater Apothecary Shop

The tomb of prominent Alexandria merchant John Carlyle lies in the quiet graveyard of the **Old Presbyterian Meeting House**, 321 S Fairfax St (Mon–Fri 9am–4pm). From 1772, the Scottish town founders met here regularly – most prominently in December 1799 for George Washington's memorial service. Despite its historic pedigree and religious importance, the site closed for sixty years beginning in 1889, and was allowed to deteriorate until finally being restored in the 1950s. A similarly venerable property can be found nearby at 105 S Fairfax St, where patent medicines for Washington were concocted behind the tiny yellow windows of the **Stabler-Leadbeater Apothecary Shop** (April–Oct Tues–Sat 10am–5pm, Sun & Mon 1–5pm; Nov–March Wed–Sat 11am–4pm, Sun 1–4pm; $5), which was founded in 1792 and remained in business until the 1930s; it still displays its original furnishings, herbs, potions and medical paraphernalia – some eight thousand items in all, and well worth a look.

The waterfront

Eighteenth-century Alexandria wouldn't recognize its twenty-first-century waterfront beyond North Union Street, not least because the riverbank is several blocks further east, following centuries of landfill. Where there were once wooden warehouses and wharves heaving with barrels of tobacco, there's now a smart marina and boardwalk, framed by the green stretches of Founders Park to the north and Waterfront Park to the south.

Before this area was cleaned up in recent decades, the US government built a torpedo factory on the river, which operated until the end of World War II. Restyled as the diverting **Torpedo Factory Arts Center** (daily 10am–5pm; free; ☎703/838-4565, ⓦwww.torpedofactory.org), its three floors contain the studios of more than two hundred artists. All studios are open to the public, displaying sculpture, ceramics, jewellery, glassware and textiles in changing exhibitions. The centre also holds the **Alexandria Archaeology Museum** (Tues–Fri 10am–3pm, Sat 10am–5pm, Sun 1–5pm; free), where much of the town's restoration work was carried out. You can see ongoing preservation efforts in a laboratory open to the public, its specimens covering 250 years of town history and encompassing digs for relics as diverse as Civil War castoffs, freedmen's gravesites, nautical ruins, and lost coins and household implements.

Sightseeing cruises (call for hours; $12–40; ☎703/684-0580, ⓦwww .potomacriverboatco.com) are run by the Potomac Riverboat Company and depart in front of the Food Pavilion; longer trips run to DC or Mount Vernon and back. One particularly interesting sight to look out for is the **Jones Point Lighthouse**, a small wooden house with little to distinguish it beyond the fact that it's the oldest American lighthouse not sited directly on the ocean; dating from 1855, it has been out of use for more than eighty years. The lighthouse sea wall contains a stone **boundary marker** showing the southernmost point of the District of Columbia, laid in 1794, before Virginia regained its acreage in 1846.

The lighthouse is located nearly under the Woodrow Wilson Bridge off I-495 on Jones Point Road; the grounds, but not the house itself, are open in daylight hours as a park.

George Washington Masonic Memorial

In a town bursting with Washington mementos, none is more striking than the **George Washington Masonic Memorial**, 101 Callahan Drive (Mon–Sat 10am–4pm, Sun noon–4pm; free; ☎703/683-2007, ⓦwww.gwmemorial.org), whose 333ft tower – built on top of a Greek temple – looms behind the King Street Metro station, often disappearing into the low-hanging fog during the winter months. The Virginia Freemasons built the memorial in 1932 to honour a "deserving brother", and the tower was designed to resemble nothing less than the long-destroyed Lighthouse at Alexandria, one of the seven wonders of the ancient world. Inside, the glorious visual ode continues with a 17ft-tall bronze **statue** of the general and president, sundry memorabilia, and dioramas depicting events from his life. To see this, and the superb views from the observation platform, you'll have to take a forty-minute **tour**, which leaves from the building's main hall (Mon–Sat 10am, 11.30am, 1.30pm & 3pm, Sun noon, 1.30pm & 3pm; $5). But even from the steps outside, the views across the Potomac to the Washington Monument and Capitol dome in the distance are terrific.

Fort Ward

During the Civil War, the federal occupation of Alexandria brought an urgent need to defend it, and built expressly for this purpose was **Fort Ward**, seven miles west of Old Town at 4301 W Braddock Rd (park daily 9am–dusk; museum Tues–Sat 10am–5pm, Sun noon–5pm; free), which became one of the largest forts defending the capital region in the 1860s. Mainly staffed by black soldiers and liberated slaves, the fort featured rifle trenches, guard towers and artillery batteries, making for an impressive display to any would-be invaders. Ultimately, though, the Confederates didn't come near the place, choosing to approach Washington from the west instead of the south. In any case, these days there's enough here to get the idea of what wartime challenges were like, with bomb shelters, trenches, powder magazine, ammo room and various cannons setting the scene, and a replica officers' hut and on-site museum full of the usual military relics and memorabilia.

Green Spring Gardens Park

Several miles west of the city of Alexandria, the natural expanse of **Green Spring Gardens Park**, Braddock Rd at Little River Turnpike on Rte 236 (grounds daily dawn–dusk, house Wed–Sun noon–4.30pm; ☎703/941-7987, ⓦwww.fairfax county.gov/parks/gsgp), is a terrific spot for a respite from sightseeing (though badly served by public transport). Set on 27 acres, the park is based around the estate of eighteenth-century farmer John Moss. The 1760 red-brick Georgian manor house is the estate's centrepiece, while the grounds surrounding the mansion host farmers' markets, bonsai displays and seasonal events in the spring, summer and winter holiday seasons. The official purpose of the gardens – which hold native Virginian plants – is to educate people about the best ways to plant and maintain their trees and flowers (an on-site horticultural library helps, too). If you have an interest in this sort of thing, the display gardens can be impressive, and separate plots hold roses, herbs, shade plants, fruits and vegetables, mixed borders, and more. The periodic Sunday-afternoon tours include a **tea service** in the manor house ($27; call or see website for reservations).

The Virginia heartland

Further afield, the Virginia heartland of the landed gentry holds well-preserved historic estates, cottages, churches, barns and taverns tucked away along the quiet back roads. It's all very popular with tourists, nowhere more so than **Mount Vernon**, the longtime home of George Washington, and the related estates of **Woodlawn Plantation** and **Gunston Hall**. To the west, **Manassas**, the site of the bloody battles of Bull Run, provides a good jumping-off point for a tour of the many preserved Civil War battlefields in the area, while to the south, **Fredericksburg** is a town full of Civil War legend and lore, with a few appealing boutiques as well.

Mount Vernon

Set on a shallow bluff overlooking the broad Potomac River, sixteen miles south of Washington, DC at 3200 George Washington Memorial Pkwy, **Mount Vernon** (daily: April–Aug 8am–5pm; March, Sept & Oct 9am–5pm; Nov–Feb 9am–4pm; $15) is among the most attractive historic plantations in the country. George Washington lived on his beloved estate for forty years, during which he ran it as a thriving and innovative farm, anticipating the decline in Virginia's tobacco cultivation and planting instead grains and food crops with great success. When he died, it seemed only fitting that he be buried on its grounds, as his will directed; America's first president lies next to his wife, Martha, in the simple family tomb.

To reach **Mount Vernon**, go first to Huntington Metro (Yellow line) and then take Fairfax Connector Bus #101 ($1.50; ☎703/339-7200, ⓦwww.fairfax county.gov/connector). It's an easy enough route, and takes only half an hour. A taxi from the Metro station costs $25. Drivers can follow the George Washington Parkway from DC; there's free parking at the site. The Mount Vernon Trail (see p.176), starting in Arlington, 18.5 miles away, ends here, too.

It's only fifty minutes to Mount Vernon from Old Town Alexandria on **cruises** offered by the Potomac Riverboat Company (call for hours; $40 round-trip; ☎703/684-0580, ⓦwww.potomacriverboatco.com). The **Tourmobile** bus (mid-June to Aug daily 11am; $32; ☎202/554-5100, ⓦwww.tourmobile.com) also runs out here from Arlington National Cemetery – a four-hour round-trip that allows you about three hours at Mount Vernon. The prices of both cruise and Tourmobile trips include admission to the house and grounds.

Some history

George Washington's father, **Augustine**, built a house on his Washington estate in 1735. During the years before 1775 – when he was called away to be a general in the Continental Army – George himself came to know the place well. He tripled its size to eight thousand acres, divided it into five separate working farms, and landscaped the grounds; rolling meadows, copses, riverside walks, parks and even vineyards were all laid out for the family's enjoyment.

The lifestyle of an eighteenth-century **gentleman farmer** was an easy one, in Washington's case supported by the labour of more than two hundred slaves who lived and worked on the outlying farms. The modest house he inherited was enlarged and redecorated with imported materials; formal gardens and a bowling green were added; and the general bred stallions, hunted in his woods, and fished in the river. He studied scientific works on farming, corresponded with experts, and, introducing new techniques, expanded the farms' output to include the production of flour, textiles and even whiskey.

Washington spent eight years away from Mount Vernon during the Revolution War, and was prevented from retiring there for good at the end of the fighting: in 1787 he headed the Constitutional Convention in Philadelphia, and two years later he was elected to his first term as US president. He visited his house only another dozen or so times during his presidency, often for just a few days. When he finally moved back in 1797, at the end of his second term in office, he and Martha had just two and a half years together before his death on December 14, 1799. Out on one of his long estate inspections, he got caught in the snow and succumbed to a fever that killed him.

Slave quarters and museum

The path up to the mansion passes various outbuildings, including a set of former **slave quarters**. Ninety slaves lived and worked on the grounds alone, and typically lived lives of deprivation and overwork. Washington was quick to realize that the move away from tobacco cultivation to more skilled farming made slavery increasingly unprofitable. He stopped buying slaves in the late 1770s, allowing those he owned to learn occupations such as carpentry, bricklaying and spinning, and to be kept on and supported once they had reached the end of their working lives. After his death, his will freed all of Mount Vernon's slaves, much to the chagrin of his wife, who wanted to retain as much of the family's "property" as possible.

On the site, the fancy modern **Reynolds Museum** has interactive displays, sculptures of Washington at various points in his life, and assorted short films about the general. It also traces Washington's ancestry and displays porcelain from the house, as well as medals, weapons, silver, and a series of striking miniatures, by Charles Willson Peale and his brother James, of Martha and her two children by her first marriage. The clay bust of Washington was produced by French sculptor Jean-Antoine Houdon, who worked on it at Mount Vernon in 1785 before completing his famous statue for the Richmond capitol.

The house and grounds

Fronting the circular courtyard stands the **mansion** itself, with the bowling green stretching before it. It's a handsome, harmonious wooden structure, sporting stunning views from its East Lawn. The wooden exterior was painted white, bevelled and sand-blasted to resemble stone; inside, the Palladian windows and bright rooms follow the fashions of the day, while the contents are based on an inventory prepared after Washington's death. Fourteen rooms are open to the public, including portrait-filled parlours, cramped bedrooms and the chamber where Washington breathed his last on a four-poster bed still in situ. Curiosities in his study include a wooden reading chair with built-in fan and a globe he ordered from London, while in the central hall hangs a key to the destroyed Bastille, presented to Washington by Thomas Paine in 1790 on behalf of the Marquis de Lafayette.

In addition to the mansion, there's plenty to see in the **grounds**, including the separate kitchen (set apart from the house because of the risk of fire), storehouse, stables, smokehouse, washhouse, overseer's quarters, kitchen garden and shrubbery. There's also a forest trail, and you can take a stroll down to the tomb, where two marble **sarcophagi** for George and Martha are set behind iron gates.

The gristmill and distillery

Located three miles west of the estate along Highway 235, George Washington's **gristmill** (April–Oct daily 10am–5pm; $4 with distillery, $2 with Mount Vernon admission) provides a glimpse into the tedious labour involved with grinding grain to make it usable for other purposes. Guides in period costume demonstrate how waterpower drove the mill, which in turn produced flour from corn, wheat and other cereals. The on-site **distillery** features copper stills, a boiler and mash tubs, sometimes overseen by docents who give you a sense of the labour that went into making the potent drink. Upstairs you can look over relics and oddments associated with the ancient process, and a short film explaining what the distillery meant to Washington and the estate.

Woodlawn Plantation and Pope-Leighey House

Not far from the gristmill, near the intersection of highways 1 and 235, lie the sprawling grounds of **Woodlawn Plantation** at 9000 Richmond Hwy (April–Dec daily 10am–5pm; $8.50 each attraction, $15 combined ticket with Pope-Leighey House), which were part of the Mount Vernon estate until, after Washington's death in 1799, two thousand acres were ceded to his nephew, **Major Lawrence Lewis**, and Martha Washington's granddaughter, **Eleanor Custis Lewis**. An impressive red-brick Georgian manor house (finished in 1805) was built on the grounds by no less than US Capitol architect William Thornton, who used Palladian design elements and fashioned its decorative trim from local sandstone. However, much of the labour involved in building the house – all the bricks were fired in a kiln at the site – was provided by slaves. Looking around the estate, you can get a sense of the backbreaking work that was required; this lends an uncomfortable subtext to the graceful design, with its noble marble busts and elegant arched windows and doors.

Perhaps incongruously, Woodlawn Plantation is also the site of a structure designed by twentieth-century architect **Frank Lloyd Wright**, the **Pope-Leighey House**, in which he experimented with radical design concepts despite limitations of budget, space and labour. The house was not originally built here, but instead moved from another Virginia location when threatened with demolition. Luckily it survived, as this 1200-square-foot residence bears many of Wright's signature touches: the materials are limited to wood, brick, concrete and glass; the layout is strongly horizontal, with trellises to control direct sunlight; the clerestory windows employ unique cut-out patterns; the floor plan is open; and the ceilings are low – except for that of the living room, which rises to 13ft and occupies about half the overall space of the house.

Gunston Hall

A short drive south from Mount Vernon, and designed in a spirit similar to the area's other red-brick Georgian manors, **Gunston Hall**, 10709 Gunston Rd (daily 9.30am–5pm; $9), is a Colonial-era plantation once owned by **George Mason**, author of the Virginia Declaration of Rights, upon which the US Bill of Rights was largely based. In both its architecture and decor, Gunston Hall evokes primarily the Federal style, with its striking Neoclassical arches, original boxwood-lined walkway, lovely formal gardens (set on 550 acres that are mostly wooded), and all-around balance and symmetry. This was but one of Mason's many land speculations – the others encompassed some 24,000 acres of property – and like many other planters' estates, Mason's had its slaves; a veritable army of them managed the homestead, carefully trimmed the gardens, grew the crops, and worked in the laundry, smokehouse and dairy, which have all been reconstructed on the grounds.

Manassas National Battlefield Park

Manassas National Battlefield Park, 6511 Sudley Rd (daily 8.30am–5pm; park admission $3; ☏703/361-1339, ⓦwww.nps.gov/mana), extends over grassy hills at the western fringes of the Washington, DC suburbs, just off I-66. The first major land battle of the Civil War – known in the North as the **Battle of Bull Run** – was fought here on the morning of July 21, 1861. Expecting an easy victory, some 25,000 Union troops attacked a Confederate detachment that controlled a vital railroad link to the Shenandoah Valley. But the rebels proved powerful opponents, and their strength in battle earned their commander, **Thomas "Stonewall" Jackson**, his famous nickname. He and General Lee also masterminded a second, even more demoralizing, Union loss here in late August 1862, the battle of "Second Manassas" that came close to the high point of Confederate ascendancy. The **visitor centre** at the entrance describes how the battles took shape, and details other aspects of the war.

The Steven F. Udvar-Hazy Center

Just a few miles northeast of the battlefield, fervent devotees of aeroplanes and spacecraft can visit the **Steven F. Udvar-Hazy Center**, in the Virginia suburb of Chantilly, not far from Dulles Airport (daily 10.30am–5pm; free, parking $15). Everything that's too big to fit into the National Air and Space Museum (see p.65) on the Mall is here, spread across 400 million cubic feet. Among the eighty planes and sixty spacecraft are fighters from America's twentieth-century wars, transport craft, and planes used by the postal service, sports enthusiasts and commercial airlines. Highlights include the SR-71 **Blackbird**, a legendary spycraft that looks like a sleek black missile, and once travelled 80,000ft high in the atmosphere and provided intelligence to American forces in Vietnam; the B-29 **Enola Gay**, the plane that dropped the first atomic bomb on Hiroshima – though the exhibit features no discussion about the morality of nuking civilians; the colossal Air France **Concorde**, which in 1976 became the only supersonic jet to fly commercially; and the space shuttle **Enterprise**, a prototype for the first space shuttle, though this version has no engine.

Fredericksburg

Only a mile off the I-95 highway, halfway to Richmond from Washington, DC, **FREDERICKSBURG** is one of Virginia's prettiest historic towns, where elegant downtown streets are backed by residential avenues lined with white picket fences. In colonial days, this was an important inland port, in which tobacco and other plantation commodities were loaded onto boats that sailed down the Rappahannock River. Dozens of stately early-American buildings along the waterfront now hold antique stores and boutiques.

In the 1816 town hall, the **Fredericksburg Area Museum**, 907 Princess Anne St (Mon & Thurs–Sat noon–5pm, Sun 1–5pm; $7), has a range of displays tracing local history, from Native American settlements to the wartime era. The **Rising Sun Tavern**, 1304 Caroline St, was built as a home in 1760 by George Washington's brother, Charles. As an inn, it became a key meeting place for patriots and a hotbed

A visit to Harpers Ferry

Lying within West Virginia but a short hop from Washington, DC, the ruggedly sited eighteenth-century town of **Harpers Ferry** has been restored as a **national historic park**, clinging to steep hillsides above the rocky confluence of the Potomac and Shenandoah rivers. After suffering the ravages of the Civil War and torrential floods, the town was all but abandoned, but has since been reconstructed.

The place is most identified with **John Brown**, the zealous antebellum-era abolitionist and possible lunatic who seized a federal arsenal here in 1859 in hopes of raising a national black insurrection against slavery. It didn't work, and Brown's scattered forces were routed by US troops commanded by none other than Robert E. Lee. The town is still redolent of the era, and kept that way as a national historical park. Parking is virtually banned in the central area, though you can arrive via the shuttle buses that run from the large park **visitor centre** on US-340 (park and centre daily 8am–5pm; ☎304/535-6029, ⓦwww.nps.gov/hafe; park entry $4 per person, $6 per car).

Shuttle buses drop off at the end of gas-lit Shenandoah Street in the heart of the restored **Lower Town**, or Old Town, whose buildings include a blacksmith's shop, clothing and dry-goods stores, tavern and boarding house – as well as the **Master Armorer's House**, once occupied by the chief gunsmith. Museums housing exhibits on the Civil War and black history line both sides of High Street as it climbs away from the river. In the vicinity, a set of stone steps leads to the 1782 **Harper House**, the oldest in town. A footpath continues uphill, past overgrown churchyards hemmed in by dry-stone walls, to **Jefferson Rock**, a huge grey boulder affording a great view over the two rivers.

Harpers Ferry makes a popular excursion from Washington, DC and is served by several trains daily on the Maryland Rail Commuter network ($11; ☎1-800/325-7245, ⓦwww.mtamaryland.com) and by one daily Amtrak service, the Capitol Limited. Otherwise, you'll need to drive.

of sedition. It is now a small **museum** (March–Oct Mon–Sat 10am–5pm, Sun noon–4pm; Nov–Feb Mon–Sat 11am–4pm, Sun noon–4pm; $5), showcasing antique decor and a collection of pub games and pewter. Guides are on hand to explain eighteenth-century medicine at **Hugh Mercer's Apothecary Shop**, 1020 Caroline St (same hours; $5), which often involved treating patients with the likes of leeches and crab claws.

Fredericksburg's strategic location made it vital during the **Civil War**, and the land around the town was heavily contested. More than 100,000 men lost their lives in the major battles and countless bloody skirmishes. The **visitor centre**, 702 Caroline St (daily: summer 10am–6pm; winter 10am–5pm; ☎540/373-1776, ⓦwww.visitfred.com), has informative exhibits and can lead you out to **Fredericksburg and Spotsylvania National Battlefield Park** (hours vary, often Mon–Fri 9am–5pm, Sat & Sun 9am–6pm; ⓦwww.nps.gov/frsp; free), south of town. Contact the centre or the above website for information on the other major battlefields, **Wilderness** and **Chancellorsville**, as well as the various manors and shrines in the area.

Listings

Listings

Accommodation

Without a doubt, one of the highlights of staying in Washington, DC is cosying up in a swanky **hotel** in the historic centre and having the entire District at your feet, either literally or via the Metro system. Of course, for many this is far from a reality, and unless you're willing to shell out upwards of $350 a night, you'll probably be out of luck.

That said, great options abound beyond the big-name hotels: the handful of **B&Bs** offer historic charm at reasonable rates, particularly in spots like Dupont Circle; **chain hotels** and motels exist everywhere, with affordable rates unless they're in very popular areas; and **hostels** can be found here and there, allowing you to drop anchor in town for less than $40 a night.

Hotels and B&Bs

Standard DC **room rates** begin at around $150 a night, but many hotels dramatically discount their rates at **weekends** (Friday and Saturday nights), some by up to fifty percent. **Low season** runs from late autumn to winter, and throughout the year costs are cheaper when Congress isn't in session. The prices given in our listings are for the **cheapest double room in high season**. Since hotels charge by the room, three people can often stay in a double for the same price as two, though sometimes there's a small surcharge. A number of **agencies** (see box below) offer rooms in small inns, private homes and apartments, from around $80 per night; a luxury B&B, though, can be every bit as pricey as a hotel, with rates reaching as high as $300 a night. Also, don't forget to check international booking sites like ⓦtickets.priceline.com or www.hotwire.com, in which you can get a room at a fraction of the official rates quoted below.

There are hotels in all the main downtown areas, though accommodation near the White House, on Capitol Hill and in Georgetown tends to be business-oriented and pricey. Occasional **budget options** exist in Foggy Bottom and Adams Morgan, while most of the chain hotels and midrange places are downtown. Dupont Circle and Upper Northwest are also good spots in which to

---

Reservation services

Bed & Breakfast Accommodations Ltd ☎1-877/893-3233, ⓦwww.bedand breakfastdc.com

Capitol Reservations ☎202/452-1270 or 1-800/847-4832, ⓦwww.capitolreservations .com

WDCA Hotels ☎202/289-2220 or 1-800/503-3330, ⓦwww.wdcahotels.com

base yourself, though the latter is considerably more expensive and has fewer options. We've also listed a few options in Arlington and Alexandria.

You're more likely to find free **parking** in the outer neighbourhoods; garage parking is available at most downtown hotels, but you'll be charged $25–30 a night for the privilege. Very occasionally, an inn or hotel we list is on the edge of a dicey neighbourhood; where safety is an issue, we've noted it, and you're advised to take taxis back to your hotel at night in these areas.

Groups and families should consider the city's suite hotels, where you'll get a kitchen and possibly a separate living room, too. One other thing to keep in mind: in summer, DC is hot and humid, and **air-conditioning** is essential for getting a good night's rest.

Capitol Hill

See the **map** on p.75.

Capitol Hill Suites 200 C St SE ☎202/543-6000, ⓦwww.capitolhillsuites.com; Capitol South Metro. Converted apartments whose stylish units are equipped with kitchenettes or proper kitchens. Free continental breakfast and wi-fi. Busy when Congress is in session. At weekends the price drops down to $169; otherwise $299

George 15 E St NW ☎202/347-4200 or 1-800/576-8331, ⓦwww.hotelgeorge.com; Union Station Metro. Postmodern design and modern convenience meets 1928 Art Deco architecture, resulting in sleek lines, marble bathrooms, internet access, boutique furnishings with copious Washington imagery, in-room DVD players, and a trendy bar-bistro. Weekends $169, weekdays $299

Hyatt Regency Washington on Capitol Hill 400 New Jersey Ave NW ☎202/737-1234 or 1-800/233-1234, ⓦwww.washingtonregency .hyatt.com; Union Station Metro. Two blocks from the train station, this 800-room luxury hotel features a multistorey atrium, plus a pool and gym – and a few rooms with views of the Capitol. $249 weekends, weekdays $500

Liaison Capitol Hill 415 New Jersey Ave NW ☎202/638-1616, ⓦwww.affinia.com. The old *Holiday Inn* has been smartened up into a semi-boutique place with modern decor, rooms with iPod docks and flat-screen HDTVs, plus internet access, restaurant, gym and a rooftop pool. $249

🏃 **Maison Orleans** 414 5th St SE, Capitol South Metro ☎202/544-3694, ⓦwww .bbonline.com/dc/maisonorleans. This historic 1902 row house is now a pleasant B&B with a trio of functional rooms, plus a patio with fountains, a small garden, wi-fi and continental breakfast. It's within easy reach of the Capitol, too. $140

Phoenix Park 520 N Capitol St NW ☎202/638-6900 or 1-800/824-5419, ⓦwww.phoenixpark hotel.com; Union Station Metro. Irish-themed hotel near Union Station with chic decor, designer furnishings and flat-screen TVs. It's popular with politicos, who frequent its *Dubliner* pub (see p.219). There's a good restaurant, too, serving hearty breakfasts. Weekends $169, weekdays $279

Southwest Waterfront and around

See the **map** on p.89.

Holiday Inn Capitol 550 C St SW ☎202/479-4000 or 1-800/465-4329, ⓦwww.hicapitoldc .com; L'Enfant Plaza or Federal Center SW Metro. Within close walking distance of the Capitol and Smithsonian museums, this *Holiday Inn* includes a bar, restaurant and rooftop pool, though rooms are pretty basic. As with all of this chain's hotels in DC, weekend rates are attractive – (around $150). Weekdays $289

L'Enfant Plaza 480 L'Enfant Plaza SW ☎202/484-1000 or 1-800/635-5065, ⓦwww .lenfantplazahotel.com; L'Enfant Plaza Metro. Faded modern hotel a couple of blocks south of the Mall (and north of the Water-front itself), with easy access to the Metro. Spacious rooms have river or city views, plus there's a health club and rooftop pool. Rooms can be discounted by up to fifty percent at weekends; weekdays $300

Mandarin Oriental 1330 Maryland Ave SW ☎202/554-8588, ⓦwww.mandarinoriental .com; L'Enfant Plaza Metro. A dash of upscale colour to enliven the Waterfront's drab hotel scene, with exquisite decor and nice views of the riverfront and Tidal Basin, plus designer furnishings, indulgent spa facilities, whirlpool and sauna, as well as a tasteful garden and lounge. Weekends $259, weekdays $495

White House area and Foggy Bottom

See the **map** on p.97.

Fairmont 2401 M St NW ☏202/429-2400, ⓦwww.fairmont.com; Foggy Bottom–GWU Metro. Classy oasis with comfortable rooms, pool, health club, whirlpool and garden courtyard. Just north of Washington Circle, midway between Foggy Bottom and Georgetown. Weekends $179, weekdays $329

Hay-Adams 800 16th St NW ☏202/638-6600 or 1-800/424-5054, ⓦwww .hayadams.com; Farragut West or McPherson Square Metro. One of DC's finest hotels, from the gold-leaf and walnut lobby to the modern rooms with designer decor, to the suites with fireplaces, original cornices, high ceilings, marble bathrooms and balconies. Upper floors have great views of the White House. Breakfast is served in one of the District's better spots for early-morning power dining. $595

Lombardy 2019 Pennsylvania Ave NW ☏202/828-2600 or 1-800/424-5486, ⓦwww .hotellombardy.com; Foggy Bottom–GWU or Farragut West Metro. Red-brick, apartment-style hotel with modern furnishings, in a good location, close to two Metro stations. Spacious rooms, most with kitchenettes and internet access, plus café and gym. High season can bring a three-night weekday minimum. As low as $99 on off-season weekends, otherwise $189

Ritz-Carlton 1150 22nd St ☏202/835-0500, ⓦwww.ritzcarlton.com; Foggy Bottom Metro. Among the Ritz-Carltons in the area, this is the most convenient to central DC, with numerous top-of-the-line suites and smart rooms with designer decor and DVD players. Prices are very high, though they can halve at weekends. $649

River Inn 924 25th St NW ☏202/337-7600, ⓦwww.theriverinn.com; Foggy Bottom Metro. One of the area's best deals, offering decent weekend rates for clean and comfortable suites that have high-speed internet, micro-waves and kitchenettes, with designer decor and furnishings, plus a fine restaurant, *DISH* (see p.205). Weekends $129, weekdays $279

State Plaza 2117 E St NW ☏202/861-8200 or 1-800/424-2859, ⓦwww.stateplaza.com; Foggy

Bottom-GWU Metro. Comfortable, stylish suites with free internet access, kitchenettes and dining area, plus a rooftop sundeck, health club, spa and a good café. A three-night minumum stay is sometimes required. Weekends $129, weekdays $229

Downtown: Penn Quarter and Federal Triangle

See the **map** on p.114.

Courtyard Washington 900 F St NW ☏202/638-4600, ⓦwww.marriott.com; Gallery Place–Chinatown Metro. Stunning 1891 Romanesque Revival bank that has been converted into a truly original hotel. The lobby overflows with marble columns, elegant bronzework and grand archways, while the rooms (formerly smallish offices) have free wi-fi and varying, sometimes awkward, layouts. Also has an on-site spa and pool. $175 weekends, $349 weekdays

Grand Hyatt 1000 H St NW ☏202/582-1234, ⓦwww.grandwashington.hyatt.com; Metro Center Metro. With nearly 900 tastefully decorated rooms, this hotel also boasts an attractive twelve-storey atrium with lagoon, waterfalls and glass elevators, and includes a café, restaurant, sauna, spa, pool, gym and bar. Save $120–200 on weekends; weekdays $339

Hampton Inn 901 6th St ☏202/842-2500, ⓦwww.hamptoninn.com; Gallery Place–Chinatown Metro. Slightly north of the main attractions, but worth it to save (a little) money. No surprises, just clean and modern chain rooms spread over 13 floors, with gym, pool and jacuzzi. Complimentary breakfast and free wi-fi. You can save up to $100 by booking on weekends; weekdays $249

Harrington 1100 E St NW ☏202/628-8140 or 1-800/424-8532, ⓦwww.hotel-harrington.com; Metro Center or Federal Triangle Metro. One of the old and basic Downtown hotels, dating from 1914, with a prime location near Pennsylvania Ave. Although pretty worn around the edges, rooms (singles to quads) are air-conditioned and have TV, plus the prices are tough to beat for the area. $135

Henley Park 926 Massachusetts Ave NW ☏202/638-5200 or 1-800/222-8474, ⓦwww .henleypark.com; Mount Vernon Square–UDC Metro. Smart and stylish hotel with quasi-Tudor design a few blocks north of the Penn Quarter and right by the conference centre, though still in a borderline neighbourhood. Free wi-fi. Rates can drop to $119 on off-season weekends. $269

JW Marriott 1331 Pennsylvania Ave NW ☎202/393-2000 or 1-800/228-9290, ⓦwww .marriott.com; Metro Center or Federal Triangle Metro. Flagship Marriott in one of the best locations in the city, overlooking Freedom Plaza (ask for a room facing Penn. Avenue). Rooms are at the upper end of the corporate standard, plus there are good restaurants, a sports bar and a health club with indoor pool. Prices drop by as much as fifty percent at weekends. $449

Monaco 700 F St NW ☎202/628-7177, ⓦwww .monaco-dc.com; Gallery Place–Chinatown Metro. Once a grand Neoclassical post office designed by Robert Mills, nowadays ultra-chic accommodation complete with sophisticated modern rooms, minimalist contemporary decor, and public spaces with marble floors and columns, plus grand spiral stairways. $189, but weekday rates can reach $399

Morrison-Clark Inn 1015 L St NW ☎202/898-1200 or 1-800/332-7898, ⓦwww.morrisonclark .com; Mount Vernon Square–UDC Metro. Historic mansion one block from the conference centre and two from the Metro. Fifty-odd rooms in Victorian and other antique styles, with balconies overlooking a courtyard, and free wi-fi. Although the area can get dicey at night, this is still one of Downtown's better deals. Save $50 by booking on a weekend. $169

🏃 **Willard InterContinental** 1401 Pennsylvania Ave NW ☎202/628-9100 or 1-800/327-0200, ⓦwashington .intercontinental.com; Metro Center Metro. An iconic Washington hotel that dominates Pershing Park near the Treasury Building. In business on and off since the 1850s, it's a Beaux-Arts marvel with acres of marble, mosaics and glass; a stunning lobby and promenade; finely furnished rooms; and a top-drawer clientele thick with politicos, lobbyists and other honchos. See also p.116. Weekends $279, weekdays $429

Downtown: North of K Street

See the **map** on p.134.

Aaron Shipman House 13th St at Q St NW ☎413/582-9888, ⓦwww.aaronshipmanhouse .com; no Metro nearby. Just a block from

Logan Circle, this sturdy Victorian B&B hosts seven rooms and one suite with tasteful if reserved modern designs, in fetching surroundings with fountains, garden and patio. Very cosy and relaxing. Free wi-fi, and big discounts in low season. $185

Beacon 1615 Rhode Island Ave NW ☎202/296-2100 or 1-800/821-4367, ⓦwww.capitalhotel swdc.com; Dupont Circle or Farragut North Metro. Although the exterior is unpromising, this corporate spot offers a relaxed atmosphere inside with decent-size rooms, some with sofa beds and kitchenettes, plus flat-screen TVs and CD players. There's a bar and grill and a pool, too. Weekends $149, weekdays $269

🏃 **Chester Arthur House B&B 13th and P sts** NW ☎202/328-3510 or 1/877-893-3233, ⓦwww.chesterarthurhouse.com; no close Metro. There are several good B&Bs around Logan Circle, and this is one of the best: a lovely 1883 townhouse with elegant parlours, high ceilings, crystal chandeliers and numerous fireplaces. Two Victorian rooms and one suite come with antiques and fireplaces, and the suite also with a kitchenette. $175

DC Guesthouse 1337 10th St NW ☎202/332-2502, ⓦwww.dcguesthouse.com; Mt Vernon Square Metro. A few blocks east of Logan Circle, this handsome manse holds seven rooms themed mostly by colour, but with a real hodgepodge of styles ranging from Victorian chintz to modern minimalist. Rooms have DVD players and wi-fi, plus a tasty breakfast – which is what you would expect from one of the most expensive B&Bs in town. $200

Hamilton Crowne Plaza 14th and K St NW ☎202/682-0111 or 1-800/227-6963, ⓦwww .hamiltonhoteldc.com; McPherson Square Metro. A 1920s Beaux Arts-style hotel with swanky decor in the suites, fine city views and a central Franklin Square location. A bar, health club, sauna and high-speed internet add to the appeal. Weekends $149, weekdays $249

Helix 1430 Rhode Island Ave NW, near Logan Circle ☎202/462-9001, ⓦwww.hotelhelix.com; Dupont Circle or Farragut North Metro. A prime choice if you're after a young, convivial atmosphere. The bright and festive rooms include multicoloured furniture, and decor notable for its eye-popping details. Rooms also offer LCD TVs, CD players and free wi-fi. Rates can be cut by half at the weekend. $269

Holiday Inn Central 1501 Rhode Island Ave NW ☎202/483-2000 or 1-800/248-0016, ⊛www .inn-dc.com; Dupont Circle or Farragut North Metro. Don't let the grim, corporate exterior put you off: this is one of Downtown's better midrange options, located at Scott Circle, with basic, modern rooms, a rooftop pool, a bar and free breakfast. Prices can be halved at weekends. $199

Jefferson 1200 16th St NW ☎202/347-2200, ⊛www.jeffersondc.com; Farragut North Metro. This patrician landmark is a bit removed from the main action, but still a favourite since the 1920s for its antique-strewn interior with busts, oil paintings and porcelain at every turn, plus a fine restaurant and stylish guest rooms. Weekends $295, weekdays $500

Mayflower 1127 Connecticut Ave NW ☎202/347-3000, ⊛www.renaissancehotels .com/WASSH; Farragut North Metro. This sumptuous Washington classic has a promenade – a vast, imperial hall – and smart rooms with subtle, tasteful furnish-ings, the terrific *Café Promenade* restaurant is much in demand. Weekends $449, weekdays up to $600

🏃 **St Regis Washington** 923 16th St NW ☎202/638-2626 or 1-800/562-5661, ⊛www.starwood.com/stregis; McPherson Square Metro. The lobby of this 1920s Italian Renaissance classic just a few blocks north of the White House looks right out of a European palace, with antiques, chandeliers and carved wooden ceiling. One of DC's cosier luxury hotels, it features elegant rooms with stylish furnishings and LCD TVs. Weekends $275, weekdays $545

Topaz 1733 N St NW ☎202/393-3000, ⊛www .topazhotel.com; Dupont Circle Metro. This boutique hotel has vibrant rooms with padded, polka-dot headboards, striped wallpaper and funky furniture, plus LCD TVs. Several rooms have space for yoga – complete with workout gear and videos – or workout machines. Prices can be halved at weekends. $289

William Lewis House 1309 R St NW ☎202/462-7574 or 1-800/465-7574, ⊛www.wlewishous .com; McPherson Square Metro. Elegantly decorated, gay-friendly B&B set in two century-old townhouses north of Logan Circle. All ten antique-filled rooms have shared bath and internet access. Out back

there's a roomy porch and a hot tub garden. Breakfast included. It's ultra-cheap for what you get, so reservations are essential. $99

Dupont Circle

See the **map** on p.134.

Carlyle Suites 1731 New Hampshire Ave NW ☎202/234-3200 or 1-866/468-3532, ⊛www .carlylesuites.com; Dupont Circle Metro. An Art Deco-style structure with rooms that are more functional than fancy. Offers high-speed internet hookups, kitchenettes with fridges and microwaves, and an onsite café, business centre, gym and laundry. $159 weekends, but rates on weekdays can reach $315

Dupont at the Circle 1604 19th St NW ☎202/332-5251 or 1-888/412-0100, ⊛www .dupontatthecircle.com; Dupont Circle Metro. Nine handsome units – high ceilings, kitchenettes, marble bathrooms – in a Victorian townhouse near the Circle. Continental breakfast included. Offers higher-priced packages with romantic themes that include chocolate, truffles, massage, etc. Low season rates can dip as low as $175. $400

🏃 **Embassy Circle Guest House** 2224 R St NW ☎202/232-7744 or 1-877/232-7744, ⊛www.dcinns.com; Dupont Circle Metro. Great B&B choice in Kalorama, set in a restored 1902 Georgian mansion with eleven elegant, tastefully decorated rooms, with antique furnishings and high-speed internet. Few better deals for quality and location anywhere in the District. $290

Embassy Inn 1627 16th St NW ☎202/234-7800 or 1-800/423-9111, ⊛www.embassy-inn.com; Dupont Circle Metro. Welcoming B&B on a residential street in northeastern Dupont Circle, well placed for bars and restaurants. Free continental breakfast, wi-fi, coffee and papers, plus an early-evening sherry to speed you on your way. $169

Fairfax at Embassy Row 2100 Massachusetts Ave NW ☎202/293-2100, ⊛www.fairfaxhoteldc .com; Dupont Circle Metro. This smart property caters to clubby politicos, journal-ists and corporate types. Business chic, with on-site gym and pleasant rooms with flat-screen TVs, iPod docks and high-speed internet. Weekend rates can drop to $179; otherwise $349

Madera 1310 New Hampshire Ave NW ☎202/296-7600, ⊛www.hotelmadera.com;

Dupont Circle Metro. Attractive hotel with designer decor and amenities, high-speed internet, DVD players and plenty of space in the rooms. Other options include rooms with gym equipment or massage and spa services. Weekends $149, weekdays $329

Palomar 2121 P St NW, Dupont Circle ⓣ202/293-3100, ⓦwww.hotelpalomar-dc.com. Boutique hotel offering flat-screen TVs and CD players, on-site pool, fitness centre and stylish lounge, along with an evening "wine hour" for schmoozing with other guests. Plenty of arty touches, too, in the lobby and rooms. $269

Rouge 1315 16th St NW ⓣ202/232-8000, ⓦwww.rougehotel.com; Dupont Circle Metro. Dupont Circle's hippest hotel (though it's actually on nearby Thomas Circle), with a stylish party bar on site, and sleek rooms outfitted with flat-screen TVs, mod decor and postmodern art. The in-room massage services are a plus. Weekends $139, weekdays $260

Swann House 1808 New Hampshire Ave NW ⓣ202/265-4414, ⓦwww.swannhouse.com; Dupont Circle Metro. Elegant B&B in an 1883 Romanesque Revival mansion a 10-minute walk from both Dupont Circle and Adams Morgan. There are twelve individually decorated rooms – some with fireplaces, DVD players and whirlpool tubs – as well as porches and decks for reclining, and a private garden with fountain. $225

Tabard Inn 1739 N St NW ⓣ202/785-1277, ⓦwww.tabardinn.com; Dupont Circle or Farragut North Metro. Three converted Victorian townhouses hold forty unique, antique-stocked rooms – more snuggly than swanky, but an excellent deal. The fixtures and furnishings are far from sleek and modern (no elevators or TVs, and some rooms share bathrooms), but the affordable rates include breakfast and a pass to the facilities at the nearby YMCA. $113

Adams Morgan

See the **map** on p.145.

Adam's Inn 1744 Lanier Place NW ⓣ202/745-3600 or 1-800/578-6807, ⓦwww.adamsinn.com; Woodley Park–Zoo Metro. Simple B&B rooms in three adjoining Victorian townhouses near the zoo on a quiet residential street (just north of Calvert St). No TVs, but free wi-fi, continental breakfast, garden patio and laundry. Sharing a bathroom saves you $30. $139

American Guest House 2005 Columbia Rd NW ⓣ703/769-4244, ⓦwww.americanguesthouse.com; no close Metro. Centrally located B&B near Kalorama Triangle. Rooms come with free wi-fi, complimentary breakfast and a mix of Victorian and old American furnishings, and there's a library too. Good style and value all round. Heavily discounted in low season. $195

Courtyard by Marriott 1900 Connecticut Ave NW ⓣ202/332-9300 or 1-800/321-3211, ⓦwww.courtyard.com/wasnw; Dupont Circle or Woodley Park–Zoo Metro. Located at the southern tip of the Kalorama Triangle, the top-floor rooms of this hillside hotel have splendid views, and all enjoy free internet access, gym, outdoor pool, and a location that's a short walk from the heart of both Dupont Circle and Adams Morgan. Weekdays $289, weekends $189

Normandy 2118 Wyoming Ave NW ⓣ202/483-1350 or 1-866/534-6835, ⓦwww.doylecollection.com; Dupont Circle or Woodley Park–Zoo Metro. Quiet hotel in a smart neighbourhood, with smallish but comfortable rooms and free wi-fi. A decent fallback option, with nice touches like in-room DVD players and espresso machines. $259

Washington Hilton 1919 Connecticut Ave NW ⓣ202/483-3000 or 1-800/445-8667, ⓦwww.hilton.com; Dupont Circle Metro. Massive 1960s conference hotel midway between Dupont Circle and Adams Morgan, a few blocks north of the Metro, notorious as the place where Ronald Reagan was almost killed (see box, p.147). More than 1100 smallish rooms geared toward business types, but most have very good views. Facilities include pool, health club, tennis courts and bike rental. $199

Windsor Inn 1842 16th St NW ⓣ202/667-0300 or 1-800/423-9111, ⓦwww.windsor-inn-dc.com; no close Metro. Not too far from Dupont Circle, with simple but functional rooms in twin brick 1920s houses and spacious suites. Some rooms have fridges; ground-floor rooms look onto a terrace. Free wi-fi and continental breakfast. $145

Windsor Park 2116 Kalorama Rd NW ⓣ202/483-7700 or 1-800/247-3064, ⓦwww.windsorparkhotel.com; Dupont Circle or Woodley Park–Zoo Metro. Simple rooms with fridges, wi-fi and cable TV, just off Connecticut Avenue. Good value for the area, though pretty basic. Eight suites available. Continental breakfast included. $189

Upper Northwest

See the **map** on p.155.

Days Inn 4400 Connecticut Ave NW ☎202/244-5600 or 1-800/329-7466, ⓦwww.daysinn.com; **Van Ness UDC–Metro.** Near the university and a Metro stop, and within reach of Rock Creek Park, this hotel has a colourless, bunker-like exterior but offers clean, if smallish, rooms with all the usual chain-hotel conveniences. Big discounts in low season. $195

Embassy Suites at Chevy Chase Pavilion 4300 Military Rd NW ☎202/362-9300, ⓦwww .embassysuites.com; **Friendship Heights Metro.** Right on the Metro line, this is a good choice if you can't afford the Woodley Park big names, with nice two-room suites, free breakfast, high-speed internet, flat-screen TVs, plus spa, gym and pool. Also close to several malls. Weekends $149, weekdays $229–299

🏃 **Marriott Wardman Park 2660 Woodley Rd NW** ☎202/328-2000 or 1-800/228-9290, ⓦwww.marriott.com; **Woodley Park–Zoo Metro.** Woodley Park's historic, celebrity-filled monument is also the largest hotel in DC (and frequent site of political fund-raisers), with two pools, a health club, and restaurants bristling with attentive staff. Conference business keeps rooms full most weekdays. $299

Omni Shoreham 2500 Calvert St NW ☎202/234-0700 or 1-800/843-6664, ⓦwww.omnihotels .com; **Woodley Park–Zoo Metro.** Plush, grand Washington institution bursting with history (see p.154) and overlooking the south chasm of Rock Creek Park. Swanky, comfortable rooms, many with a view of the park, plus a fitness centre, pool, tennis courts, sauna, and the *Marquee Bar* for drinks. Weekends $179, weekdays $260

Woodley Park Guest House 2647 Woodley Rd NW ☎202/667-0218 or 1-866/667-0218, ⓦwww .dcinns.com; **Woodley Park–Zoo Metro.** Pleasant guesthouse on a residential Woodley Park side street offers a quiet refuge with 16 rooms and free continental breakfast. Well located near the Metro, the zoo and a swath of good restaurants along

Connecticut Avenue. Two-night minimum stay. $145

Georgetown

See the **map** on p.162.

Four Seasons 2800 Pennsylvania Ave NW ☎202/342-0444 or 1-800/332-3442, ⓦwww.fourseasons.com. This modern red-brick pile at the eastern end of Georgetown is one of DC's most luxurious hotels. Stars, royalty and high-rollers hanker for the lavish rooms and suites with views of Rock Creek Park or the C&O Canal. Service is superb, and there's a pool, fitness centre and full-service spa. Weekends $595, weekdays $795

Georgetown Inn 1310 Wisconsin Ave NW ☎1-888/587-2388, ⓦwww.georgetowninn.com. This red-brick hotel in the heart of Georgetown offers 96 tastefully appointed rooms and suites. Excellent deal for this pricey area, though it's looking a bit worn these days. Weekdays $249, weekends $169

Georgetown Suites 1111 30th St NW ☎202/298-7800 or 1-800/348-7203, ⓦwww .georgetownsuites.com. Affordable luxury in a central location. This all-suite hotel offers rooms with modern style and smart decor, with free wi-fi, fridges and microwaves, plus gym and laundry. There's a similarly priced facility on the same block, at 1000 29th St NW. Weekends $175, weekdays $225

Monticello 1075 Thomas Jefferson St NW ☎202/337-0900 or 1-800/388-2410, ⓦwww .monticellohotel.com. Though it could use a refurbishment, this is a good all-suite hotel in a decent spot near the historic C&O Canal; all rooms have free wi-fi, microwave and fridge, plus breakfast buffet. Summers see a small discount in price, as do some weekends. $249

Ritz-Carlton Georgetown 3100 South St NW ☎202/912-4100, ⓦwww.ritzcarlton.com. An ultra-chic luxury hotel rich with tasteful rooms and suites. Offers all the designer amenities you'd expect, including a great onsite spa, sauna and fitness room. Weekends $449, weekdays $699

Washington Suites Georgetown 2500 Pennsylvania Ave NW ☎202/333-8060, ⓦwww .washingtonsuitesgeorgetown.com. Spacious suites with kitchens and microwaves make this one of the better (and one of the few) bargains in Georgetown. Complimentary breakfast, free internet and gym. Weekends $129, weekdays $199

treatments. Discounts of up to $100 at weekends; weekdays $289

Arlington

See the **map** on p.173.

Hilton Garden Inn 1333 N Court House Rd ☎1-800/528-4444, ⓦhiltongardeninn1.hilton .com; **Court House Metro.** Among the best chain business hotels in the area, a block from the Metro with a business centre and gym. Suites have fridges, microwaves and free high-speed internet. Save $150 or more by coming on a weekend; otherwise $289

Hyatt Arlington 1325 Wilson Blvd ☎703/525-1234, ⓦwww.arlington.hyatt.com; **Rosslyn Metro.** Modern corporate property in a prime spot near a Metro station, as well as Georgetown and Arlington National Cemetery, with standard chain features plus gym and internet access. Huge rate drops on weekends, down to $129 or less; otherwise $289

Inn of Rosslyn 1601 Arlington Blvd ☎703/524-3400; **Rosslyn Metro.** Located near the northern edge of the cemetery and the Marine Corps Memorial, this is a basic but clean motel that's one of the few reasonably priced places in town. Rooms are nothing special, with somewhat dated furnishings, but they're clean and comfortable. $109

Palomar Arlington 1121 19th St North ☎703/351-9170, ⓦwww.hotelpalomar -arlington.com. An ultra-chic boutique hotel, and a welcome addition to the staid Arlington hotel scene. Along with smart decor, visitors can enjoy a stylish bar and Italian restaurant, fitness and business centres and the option of in-room spa

Alexandria

See the **map** on p.178.

Best Western Old Colony Inn 1101 N Washington St ☎703/739-2222, ⓦwww.bestwestern.com; **Braddock Road Metro.** Less than a mile from the Metro station on the north side of Old Town, this moderately priced choice with standard amenities (plus free breakfast, shuttle around Old Town and high-speed internet) is one of the better chain options in the historic centre. $189

Hilton Alexandria 1767 King St ☎703/837-0440, ⓦwww.hilton.com; **King Street Metro.** Located right by the Metro station, this solid corporate entry has clean and modern rooms, high-speed internet access, pool, gym and business centre. $255

Monaco 480 King St ☎703/549-6080, ⓦwww.monaco-alexandria.com; **King Street Metro.** One of the city's most appealing hotels, whose ultra-chic rooms have designer decor, plus jacuzzis, flat-screen TVs, in-room bars and other swanky amenities. There's also free wi-fi, and evening wine tastings. Rates drop by $70 at weekends. $289

Morrison House 116 S Alfred St, Old Town ☎703/838-8000, ⓦwww.morrisonhouse.com; **King Street Metro.** Faux Federal-era townhouse (built in 1985) complete with ersatz "authentic" decor like parquet floors, marble bathrooms and crystal chandeliers, yet with modern comforts like high-speed internet and designer linens. There's also an acclaimed restaurant, *The Grille*. Weekdays $319, weekends $229

Hostels

Washington, DC is hardly prime **hostel** territory, though there are a few cheapies scattered around if you know where to look. Except for the HI–Washington, DC, these are all pretty far afield, though not necessarily in the middle of nowhere. For rock-bottom alternatives, students can try contacting a **university** such as Georgetown (☎202/687-4560, ⓦhousing.georgetown.edu); George Washington, in Foggy Bottom (☎202/994-2552, ⓦliving.gwu.edu); Catholic, near the National Shrine (☎202/319-5277, ⓦconferences.cua.edu/housing); and American, in Upper Northwest (☎202/885-3370, ⓦwww.american.edu/ocl /housing). All offer a variety of dorms, doubles and apartments at budget rates in summer (June–Aug).

Capitol City Hostel 2411 Benning Rd NE ☎202/387-1328; no Metro. See map, p.75. If saving money is your paramount concern, consider this basic option located 25 blocks east of the Capitol in a grim neighbourhood – to which you'll absolutely have to take a taxi. Has computers for guests' use with high-speed internet, as well as amenities including a kitchen. Foreign guests must bring a passport. Dorms $24

HI–Washington, DC 1009 11th St NW, Downtown ☎202/737-2333, ⓦwww .hiwashingtondc.org; Metro Center Metro. See map, p.114. Large (270 beds), clean and very central hostel. Offers free continental breakfast, internet access and dorm rooms with shared bathrooms, plus kitchen, lounge, laundry and organized activities. Open 24hr, but take care at night around here. Dorms are as cheap as $29 in low season. $45

Hilltop Hostel 300 Carroll St NW, Takoma Park, MD ☎202/291-9591, ⓦwww.hosteldc .com; Takoma Park Metro. Right across from the Metro station, this hostel is a converted Victorian house that offers wi-fi and computer use, a games room with pool and table football, garden, laundry, kitchen and BBQ space. Six- to-nine-bed dorms $24, doubles $60

William Penn House 515 E Capitol St SE ☎202/543-5560, ⓦwww.williampennhouse.org; Capitol South or Eastern Market Metro. See map, p.75. One of the least expensive spots in town, in a prime location just blocks from the Capitol, this Quaker-run hostel doesn't require religious observance but does prefer that guests be active in progressive causes. Rooms hold four to ten people, and breakfast is included. There's no curfew, but also no booze allowed. Morning services available if you're interested. $40–50

Cafés and restaurants

n many ways, the Washington **dining** scene is an outlet of its power politics: fancy restaurants are constantly in demand by politicians, lobbyists and corporate heavyweights, and there's almost as much business conducted there as there is in the office corridors of K Street or Capitol Hill. The old-line stalwarts endure decade after decade, and some of them – most prominently the *Old Ebbitt Grill* – actually serve tempting dishes; others, though, get by on their deal-making atmosphere and leave the food as an afterthought. Our listings below focus on the best places to have an enjoyable meal, rather than the trendy, fly-by-night joints.

You're apt to find all manner of stylish Asian-fusion and New American restaurants here. Moreover, talented chefs and restaurateurs are not above cloning their successes, so you can expect new offshoots of DC's most popular eateries, both in the city and in the suburbs.

As for specific **cuisines**, good Southern and American food isn't hard to find, while Georgetown, in particular, has a rash of renowned restaurants that resemble nineteenth-century-style saloons, serving everything from oysters to strip steaks. Continental restaurants tend to be pricey, but there are some good bistros around, while Cajun, German, Greek and Spanish restaurants are thinner on the ground. The Chinese restaurants in Chinatown pale in comparison to Thai or Vietnamese places. There are also a comparatively large number of Ethiopian restaurants, especially in Adams Morgan, and it's possible to track down places serving food from countries as diverse as Argentina, Malaysia and El Salvador.

Finally, for a break from the high-pressure dining scene, DC's **cafés** are good spots to knock back a latte while reading the *Post* or surfing the internet. For a light meal or snack, they're also hard to beat, and of course can be found almost everywhere.

Neighbourhoods

The excellent Metro system and abundance of taxis mean that nowhere is really off limits when it comes to choosing a neighbourhood for a restaurant. There are also lots of opportunities to sit outside when the weather's agreeable – patios, pavement tables and open-front windows are common.

Downtown, **Chinatown** is the only central ethnic enclave with its own swath of restaurants, though the **Penn Quarter** has emerged as a dining centre with a rash of fine American and Continental eateries. **Georgetown** has the most varied selection – rowdy saloons, diners, ethnic restaurants, as well as some rather sniffy establishments – most of them in the few blocks on either side of the M Street/Wisconsin Avenue intersection. **Dupont Circle** (chiefly P St and Connecticut Ave) rivals Georgetown for its selection, with humble coffeehouses cheek-by-jowl with some of the best and trendiest eateries in town (such as *Komi*, *Restaurant Nora* and *Obelisk*). DC's most down-to-earth area for dining out is **Adams Morgan**, which also has the city's best bargains. 18th Street at Columbia Road is lined with scores of ethnic restaurants, all of which are still pretty good value. There are also pockets of worthwhile restaurants east of **Capitol Hill**, along Connecticut Avenue in **Upper Northwest**, in **Old Town Alexandria** and in scattered patches of **Arlington**.

The **listings** in this chapter correspond to the neighbourhoods in the Guide. Neighbourhood sections are in turn split into two divisions: "Cafés, snacks and light meals", detailing spots good for a quick burger, pizza or coffee, and "Restaurants". These two categories are not mutually exclusive; you can, of course, eat lunch or dinner at many of the diners, cafés and coffee shops we've listed, and also perhaps get a light meal at many of the restaurants. The most in-demand spots tend to be in Downtown and in Dupont Circle, and we've noted particularly popular restaurants in the reviews; you'll need to book well in advance to eat at the most renowned restaurants. For **listings by cuisine**, turn to the box on pp.202–203.

In terms of **price**, main dishes will cost less than $10 at inexpensive restaurants, $15–20 at midpriced ones, and more than $20 at expensive spots, with truly elite places charging much more. Often you'll be able to eat for less than we suggest; on the other hand, don't forget you have to add the price of drinks to your bill and, in most places, at least fifteen percent for service. If you're on a budget, look for set lunches (from as little as $5–8) and early-bird dinners (usually served before 7pm), in both inexpensive places and high-end restaurants

Capitol Hill

See the **map** on p.75.

Cafés, snacks and light meals

Au Bon Pain 50 Massachusetts Ave NE; Union Station Metro. Although there are better cafés than this chain in town, this is by far the most convenient and reliable spot to chow down on sandwiches, soups, cinnamon buns, croissants and salads while waiting for your train at Union Station – at any time of the day. Daily 24hr.

Le Bon Café 210 2nd St SE; Capitol South Metro. Good for a wholesome lunch of soup, quiche or a sandwich, or breakfast with pastries and waffles, and convenient for the Library of Congress. Mon–Fri 7.30am–5pm, Sat & Sun 8.30am–3.30pm.

Market Lunch Eastern Market, 225 7th St SE; Eastern Market Metro. Excellent spot for munch-and-go, market hall-counter meals, known for its pancakes, crab cakes and French toast, but also with fine sandwiches and assorted fish platters – served to a loyal band of shoppers and suit-and-tie congressional staffers. Tues–Sat 7.30am–3pm, Sun 11am–3pm.

Peregrine Espresso 660 Pennsylvania Ave SE; Eastern Market Metro. Inspired by Italian brewmaking, the espressos here pack an authentic punch. The "microbrewed" coffee is also worth a try. Also sells pastries and snacks. Mon–Sat 7am–9pm, Sun 8am–8pm.

Restaurants

Bistro Bis 15 E St NW ☎202/661-2700; Union Station Metro. Tasty French restaurant connected to a chic boutique hotel (the *George*; see p.192), with the requisite upmarket continental fare – onion soup, quiche, duck hash, grilled meats – with the occasional twist. Daily 7–10am, 11.30am–2.30pm & 5.30–10.30pm.

Café Berlin 322 Massachusetts Ave NE ☎202/543-7656; Union Station Metro. The perfect spot to fill up on your favourite gut-busting German food – from pork Jaegerschnitzel to potato pancakes to spiced herring with onions and apples. Cheap sandwiches, moderately priced main courses. Mon–Thurs 11.30am–10pm, Fri & Sat 11.30am–11pm, Sun 10am–10pm.

Johnny's Half Shell 400 N Capitol St NW ☎202/737-0400; Union Station Metro. Swanky seafood eatery where you can sample local specialities like crab cakes, oysters, pork ribs and seafood stew – go for the gumbo or, in summer, the soft-shell crabs. Also offers a good breakfast, lunch and happy hour. Mon–Fri 7–9.30am, 11.30am–2.30pm & 4.30–10pm, Sat 5–10pm.

Restaurants by cuisine

Las Placitas 517 8th St SE ☎202/543-3700; Eastern Market Metro. Great-value Mexican standards like burritos and quesadillas, plus pupusas and taquitos, and various Salvadoran specials pack the tables nightly at this fine and fun eatery. Mon–Fri 11.30am–3pm & 5–10pm, Sat 4–10pm, Sun 4–11pm.

The Monocle 107 D St NE ☎202/546-4488; Union Station Metro. If you want to get a glimpse of political powerbrokers stuffing their maws with delicious crab cakes, steaks, roasted oysters and trout, and sample a little of the fancy fare yourself (main courses $17–35), this is the place. Mon–Fri 11.30am–midnight.

Montmartre 327 7th St SE ☎202/544-1244, Eastern Market Metro. A handy and comfortable place to sample French bistro fare such as crêpes, pâté, quiche, seafood and traditional soups, with most main courses $15–22. Mon–Sat 11.30am–2.30pm & 5.30–10pm, Sun 11.30am–2.30pm & 5.30–9pm.

Mr Henry's 601 Pennsylvania Ave SE ☎202/546-8412; Eastern Market Metro. Saloon and restaurant with outside patio, grill, and a mixed gay and straight crowd. Except for the steak and seafood platters, most main courses – including some good burgers – are less than $10. Mon–Thurs & Sun 11am–midnight, Fri & Sat 11am–1am.

Pizza Boli's 417 8th St SE; Eastern Market Metro. For a quick bite on the way to the Hill, this spot right off the Metro is a great choice for its cheap, hot pizzas, including some good specials and white pizzas. Mon–Thurs & Sun 11am–1am, Fri & Sat 11am–2am.

Southwest Waterfront and around

See the map on p.89.

Cafés, snacks and light meals

Captain White's Seafood City 1100 Maine Ave SW; L'Enfant Plaza Metro. The kind of place that makes the Fish Wharf the city's best spot for fresh seafood, in this case a floating vendor hawking catfish, oysters, crab and other delicious choices, which you can get fresh to go or fried up in a tasty platter or sandwich. Mon–Thurs & Sun 11am–7pm, Fri & Sat 11am–9pm.

Restaurants

Cantina Marina 600 Water St SW ☎202/554-8396; Waterfront Metro. One of the few

serviceable restaurants in these parts, where you can get your fill of burgers, crawfish etouffee (stew with rice), muffuletta and crab-cake sandwiches for reasonable prices, while dining right on the water. Mon–Thurs & Sun 11.30am–10pm, Fri & Sat 11.30am–11pm.

CityZen 1330 Maryland Ave SW ☎202/787-6006; L'Enfant Plaza Metro. Lodged inside the chic Mandarin Oriental hotel (see p.192), this is a similarly upscale spot where for $110 you can sample a rotating six-course menu of French and Asian hybrids that may include items like white-corn falafel, veal loin, sweetbread scaloppine and crab tempura. Tues–Thurs 6–9.30pm, Fri & Sat 5.30–9.30pm.

Jenny's Asian Fusion 1000 Water St SW ☎202/554-2202; L'Enfant Plaza Metro. Upstairs from a yacht club, this is a fine spot for sampling Chinese staples like salt-and-pepper calamari and spicy aubergine, as well as crab cakes, beef Wellington, lobster tail and pan-seared fish. Most dishes $10–25. Mon–Thurs & Sun 11am–10pm, Fri & Sat 11am–11pm.

Phillips 900 Water St SW ☎202/488-8515; L'Enfant Plaza Metro. A popular seafood spot on the tour-bus circuit, not as good as Captain White's but a big draw for those looking to pack away giant helpings of fish and crab from the buffet menu. Near the Fish Wharf. Mon–Thurs & Sun 11am–9pm, Fri & Sat 11am–10pm.

White House area and Foggy Bottom

See the map on p.97.

Cafés, snacks and light meals

The Breadline 1751 Pennsylvania Ave NW; Farragut West Metro. DC's best sandwiches made with DC's best bread, stuffed with spicy chicken, pork sausage, prosciutto and other tasty fillings. This superb open bakery also offers pizza, empanadas, flatbreads, salads, smoothies, coffee and tea, using organic ingredients where possible. Mon–Fri 7.30am–3.30pm.

Capitol Grounds 1010 17th St NW; Farragut North or Farragut West Metro. A lively spot known for its gourmet sandwiches and breakfast staples, plus good coffee and a convivial atmosphere. Also at 2100 Pennsylvania Ave NW. Mon–Fri 7am–6pm, Sat 9am–4pm, Sun 9am–3pm.

Cosi 1700 Pennsylvania Ave NW; Farragut West Metro. Just a short hop from both the White House and Corcoran, this is better than your average chain restaurant for its often tasty, if a little pricey, sandwiches on freshly baked flatbread. There's another reliable branch downtown at 1001 Pennsylvania Ave NW. Mon–Fri 7am–7pm, Sat & Sun 9am–5pm.
Lawson's Deli 1776 I St NW; Farragut West Metro. Primo bagels, sandwiches and panini make Lawson's a local favourite; it's also good for salads, pastries and combination lunch boxes. Mon–Fri 6.30am–3pm.

Restaurants

Blue Duck Tavern in the Park Hyatt Hotel, 1201 24th St NW ☎202/419-6755; Foggy Bottom–GWU Metro. Designer-decorated finery provides the backdrop for this chic and pricey restaurant, offering steak, prawns, softshell crab, duck breast and delicious desserts to a crowd of business and diplomatic diners. Main courses $20–30. Mon–Fri 6.30–10.30am, 11.30am–2.30pm & 5.30–10.30pm, Sat & Sun 11.30am–2.30pm & 5.30–10.30pm.
DISH in the River Inn, 924 25th St NW ☎202/337-7600; Foggy Bottom–GWU Metro. Tasty American fare – from rockfish, crab cakes and flat iron steaks for mid-priced dinners to sandwiches, pasta and wraps for inexpensive lunches – served in posh surroundings. Given the restaurant's popularity with the chattering classes, its name is as much a verb as a noun. Mon–Fri 7am–10am, 11.30am–2.30pm & 5–10pm, Sat 8–10am & 5–11pm, Sun 8–10am & 5–10pm.
Kinkead's 2000 Pennsylvania Ave NW ☎202/296-7700; Foggy Bottom–GWU Metro. One of DC's favourite, and priciest, restaurants (around $50–70 for a multi-course meal), with a contemporary menu specializing in fish, from salmon and monkfish to seafood soups and stews, and a raw bar with oysters, lobsters, crab and mussels. It's very popular, so you'll need to book ahead. Daily 11.30am–2.30pm & 5.30–10pm.
Notti Bianche in the GW University Inn, 824 New Hampshire Ave NW ☎1-800/426-4455; Foggy Bottom–GWU Metro. Quality hotel restaurant serving up mid- to upper-end pasta and seafood – including the likes of grilled squid, pork chops and mushroom risotto. Also with pasta and panini for lunch, and omelettes and frittatas for breakfast. Not as

expensive as other fine restaurants in the area. Mon–Fri 7–10am, 11.30am–2.30pm & 5–10pm, Sat 8–11am & 5–11pm, Sun 8–11am & 5–10pm.
Primi Piatti 2013 I St NW ☎202/223-3600; Farragut West or Foggy Bottom–GWU Metro. Fine Italian restaurant with a knack for creating tasty, affordable gourmet pizzas – with ingredients such as goat's cheese and prosciutto – that at $10–15 are much cheaper than the meat and pasta dishes, for $20 and up. Mon–Fri 11.30am–2.30pm & 5.30–10.30pm, Sat 5.30–10.30pm.
Thai Coast 2514 L St NW ☎202/333-2460; Foggy Bottom–GWU Metro. Neighbourhood Southeast Asian restaurant with a convivial atmosphere that boasts the usual rolls, satays and curries, then throws in oddball items like crabmeat sausages and softshell crab. Cheap, filling and worth it. Mon–Thurs & Sun 11.30am–10.30pm, Fri & Sat 11.30am–11pm.

Downtown: Penn Quarter and Federal Triangle

See the **map** on p.114.

Cafés, snacks and light meals
Café Mozart 1331 H St NW ☎202/347-5732; Metro Center Metro. Worth seeking out if you have a yen for rib-stuffing German food. An eatery and deli with the requisite schnitzels, bratwursts, roasted meats and other favourites like Viennese goulash, plus sweets, cakes and desserts. On the pricey side, though, with main courses at $20–28. Mon–Fri 7am–10pm, Sat 9am–10pm, Sun 11am–10pm.
Corner Bakery 529 14th St NW; Metro Center Metro. Popular and busy bakery-café with a nice range of sandwiches, cookies, cakes, soups, salads and breakfast items like French toast and oatmeal – most of it good, though you'll have to wait if you come during rush hour. Mon–Fri 7am–7pm, Sat & Sun 8am–5pm.
Courtyard Cafe in the National Portrait Gallery, 8th at F St NW; Gallery Place–Chinatown Metro. A fine spot to take a break from the art, with nice outdoor views of the Penn Quarter and a reasonable range of wine, espresso, sandwiches and baked goods. Daily 11.30am–6.30pm.
Ebbitt Express 675 15th St NW ☎202/347-8881; Metro Center Metro. Takeaway place

next to the pricier *Old Ebbitt Grill* (see p.206). Excellent pastas, salads, grilled and cold sandwiches, and snacks to go, plus crab-cake or brisket platters and other delights, much of it affordable and tasty. Mon–Fri 7.30am–5pm.

Restaurants

Acadiana 901 New York Ave NW ☎202/408-8848; **Mount Vernon Square Metro.** Chic Cajun spot that serves up mid-priced muffaletta, poboys and crawfish for lunch, then saves the big-ticket scallops and bacon, veal medallions with grits, and grilled swordfish for dinner. Lunch dishes around $15, dinner main courses around $25. Also a fine Sunday brunch (11.30am–2.30pm). Mon–Sat 11.30am–2.30pm & 5.30–10.30pm, Sun 11.30am–2.30pm & 5.30–9.30pm.

Café Atlantico 405 8th NW ☎202/393-0812; **Archives–Navy Memorial Metro.** Classy nuevo Latino treat with spicy spins on traditional cuisine, but really best for its Minibar, a six-seat counter famed for its bizarre "molecular gastronomy" – the likes of beet "tumbleweeds", olive oil bonbons, and blue cheese and almond tarts. Only the adventurous need apply. Reserve at least a month in advance and expect to pay $120 a head. Minibar: two, six-person seatings per night, Tues–Sat 6pm & 8.30pm; otherwise Tues–Thurs & Sun 11.30am–2.30pm & 5–10pm, Fri & Sat 11.30am–2.30pm & 5–11pm.

District Chophouse & Brewery 509 7th St NW ☎202/347-3434; **Gallery Place–Chinatown Metro.** Classy joint with a buzzing atmosphere and an enticing grillhouse menu. A bit on the pricey side, but there are plenty of hunger-crushing options. Order a burger (with a house salad) or go for steak, lamb chops, lobster or crab cakes. Sun & Mon 11am–10pm, Tues–Sat 11am–11pm.

Ella's Pizza 901 F St NW ☎202/638-3434; **Gallery Place–Chinatown Metro.** There's tasty tapas at this nouveau Italian spot, but most people just come for the designer pizzas: wood-fired, thin-crusted delights topped with wild mushrooms, meatballs, prosciutto, shrimp and artichokes (though not all at once). Mon–Sat 11am–10pm, Sun noon–9pm.

Haad Thai 1100 New York Ave NW ☎202/682-1111, entrance on 11th St; **Metro Center Metro.** Business-oriented Thai restaurant featuring coconut-milk curries, tasty steamed fish and shrimp, roasted duck and wonton soup – all

good staples, well made and not too pricey. Mon–Fri 11.30am–2.30pm & 5–10.30pm, Sat noon–10.30pm, Sun 5–10.30pm.

J&G Steakhouse In the W Hotel, Pennsylvania Ave at 15th St NW ☎202/661-2440; **Metro Center Metro.** Catering to a crowd of politicos and theatre-goers, this is upper-end dining with attitude, featuring rack of lamb, lobster, steak and short ribs for $25–40. The fixed-price menu is a better deal, for $35 or $68. Breakfast and lunch are also available. Mon–Thurs 7am–2.30pm & 5–10pm, Fri 7am–2.30pm & 5–11pm, Sat 8am–2.30pm & 5–11pm, Sun 8am–2.30pm & 5–10pm.

Jaleo 480 7th St NW ☎202/628-7949; **Gallery Place–Chinatown Metro.** Upscale tapas bar-restaurant with tempting options such as sautéed shrimp, chicken fritters and *patatas bravas*, plus supreme paella. Limited reservation policy makes for long waits during peak hours. Sun & Mon 11.30am–10pm, Tues–Thurs 11.30am–11.30pm, Fri & Sat 11.30am–midnight.

🏃 **Old Ebbitt Grill 675 15th St NW** ☎202/347-4801; **Metro Center Metro.** In business in various locations since 1856, this is a plush re-creation of a nineteenth-century tavern featuring a mahogany bar, gas chandeliers, leather booths and gilt mirrors. Politico clientele indulges in everything from burgers and steaks to seafood and oyster platters ($14/half-dozen), breakfasts to late dinners. Mon–Fri 7.30am–1am, Sat & Sun 8.30am–1am; bar open until 2am or 3am.

The Source 575 Pennsylvania Ave NW, in the Newseum ☎202/637-6100; **Archives–Navy Memorial Metro.** LA-based wunderchef Wolfgang Puck takes DC by the lapels with this expensive fusion eatery – doling out curiosities from pork-belly dumplings to "lacquered" Chinese duckling – and attracts a range of celebrities, including President Obama himself. Mon–Fri 11.30am–2pm & 5.30–10pm, Sat 11.30am–3pm & 5.30–11pm.

Ten Penh 1001 Pennsylvania Ave NW ☎202/393-4500; **Federal Triangle Metro.** High-profile Asian-fusion restaurant serving up pricey meals like honey-and-soy-marinated duck, citrus-glazed salmon, grilled octopus and the estimable Chinese smoked lobster. Most dishes are well worth the cost (main courses at lunch $15–20, at dinner $25–30). Mon–Thurs & Sun 11.30am–2.30pm &

5.30–10.30pm, Fri 11.30am–2.30pm & 5.30–11pm, Sat 5.30–11pm.

Tosca 1112 F St NW ☎202/367-1990; **Metro Center Metro.** Expensive Northern Italian eatery with terrific seafood, lamb and veal dishes and pasta staples, with dishes like *fettuccine* with wild boar and lobster risotto, plus tasty desserts. Mon–Thurs & Sun 11.30am–2.30pm & 5.30–10.30pm, Fri 11.30am–2.30pm & 5.30–11pm, Sat 5.30–11pm.

Zaytinya 701 9th St NW ☎202/638-0800; **Gallery Place-Chinatown Metro.** This stylish, mid-priced Turkish and Middle Eastern restaurant serves a range of inventive meze plates, ranging from Lebanese beef tartare to pork-and-orange-rind sausage and veal cheeks. Good cheeses, too. Sun & Mon 11.30am–10pm, Tues–Fri 11.30am–11.30pm, Sat 11.30am–midnight.

Zola 800 F St NW ☎202/654-0999; **Gallery Place–Chinatown Metro.** Don't be deterred by this elite eatery's location in the Spy Museum; instead, enjoy a lunch that may include salmon pastrami, lobster mac and cheese, or leg of lamb sandwich, or a three-course dinner ($39) that may include lobster rolls, quail, and pork and peaches. Mon–Fri 11.30am–midnight, Sat 5pm–1am, Sun 5–10pm.

Downtown: Chinatown

See the **map** on p.114.

Restaurants

Eat First 609 H St NW ☎202/289-1703; **Gallery Place–Chinatown Metro.** You should scour the menu first at this wide-ranging, somewhat divey Cantonese diner, which has an array of solid Asian selections such as shrimp dumplings, roast duck, squid, pan-fried noodles and much more. Daily 11am–2am.

Full Kee 509 H St NW ☎202/371-2233; **Gallery Place–Chinatown Metro.** Known for its shrimp and other kinds of dumplings, egg drop and wonton soups, roasted meats and pan-fried seafood, this is a Cantonese staple with a following. Most dishes are $5–10 for lunch, $12–18 for dinner. Mon–Thurs & Sun 11am–10pm, Fri & Sat 11am–1am.

Kanlaya Thai 740 6th St NW ☎202/393-0088; **Gallery Place–Chinatown Metro.** A nice, cheap break from the Chinese fare around (not all of it good), with delicious Thai soups,

curries and stir-fried noodles, a wild-pork dish, and steamed curry chicken – here called "Rama in Jacuzzi". Daily 11.30am–10pm.

Matchbox 713 H St NW ☎202/289-4441; **Gallery Place–Chinatown Metro.** The gourmet pizzas are the undeniable high point, but the seafood and smallish hamburgers are tasty too. A range of prices depending on the dish, usually $10–25. Also on Capitol Hill at 521 8th St SE. Mon–Thurs 11am–11pm, Fri & Sat 11am–1am.

Proof 775 G St NW ☎202/737-7663; **Gallery Place–Chinatown Metro.** A delicious, upscale grab bag of flavours and styles, with a fine wine selection to boot. Try the charcuterie plates to start, then move on to a huge range of cheeses, sashimi, seafood and steak. A four-course set-price menu is $56. Sun & Mon 5.30–9.30pm, Tues–Fri 11.30am–2pm & 5.30–10pm, Sat 5.30–11pm.

Zengo 781 7th St NW ☎202/393-2929; **Gallery Place–Chinatown Metro.** Truly eclectic spot for international flavours from Japanese to Indian to Latin American, with the likes of duck tacos and pork tortas for lunch (plus noodles, sandwiches, sushi and dim sum) and pricey dinners of hoisin lamb chops, chicken tandoori, wonton tacos and Kobe beef. Mon–Fri 11.30am–2.30pm & 5–10pm, Sat 5–11.30pm.

Downtown: North of K Street

See the **map** on p.134.

Cafés, snacks and light meals

Julia's Empanadas 1221 Connecticut Ave NW; **Dupont Circle Metro.** Tasty Mexican turnovers stuffed with the likes of Chilean beef, chorizo, and spinach and mozzarella, and so cheap you'll barely notice the money leaving your wallet. Mon–Thurs 11am–2am, Fri & Sat 11am–4am, Sun 11am–7pm.

Loeb's Deli 832 15th St NW; **McPherson Square Metro.** Classic New York-style delicatessen, operating locally since 1959 and at this site since 1979. One of the better places in the District to get a decent pastrami or corned-beef sandwich, or a drippy cheesesteak, plus all the usual blintzes and bagel-and-lox staples. Mon–Fri 6am–4pm, Sat 8am–2pm.

Naan and Beyond 1710 L St NW; **Farragut North Metro.** Highlights among the cheap and tasty Indian dishes are baked naan

⑪

sandwiches filled with the likes of tandoori chicken, shrimp tikka and lamb, all for under $8 – handy alternatives to traditional sandwiches for the Farragut lunch crowd and Friday-night clubbers. Vegan options available. Mon–Fri 11am–9pm, Sat 11am–5am.

Nooshi 1120 19th St NW ☎202/293-3138; **Farragut North Metro.** Lovers of "noodles and sushi" looking for a cheap and hearty meal should sample the serviceable offerings at this lunch favourite, with good sushi, dumplings, drunken and fried noodles, spicy soups and tofu fries, among other curious and tempting choices. Mon–Sat 11.30am–11pm, Sun 5–10pm.

Teaism 800 Connecticut Ave NW ☎202/835-2233; **Farragut West or Farragut North Metro.** Pleasant spot for a pick-me-up chai or a dose of pan-Asian cuisine after a White House tour. The light fare includes salads, sandwiches and bento boxes; afternoon tea service as well. Also in the Penn Quarter at 400 8th St NW, which includes a tea shop (see opposite). Mon–Fri 7.30am–5.30pm.

Restaurants

Bombay Club 815 Connecticut Ave NW ☎202/659-3727; **Farragut North or Farragut West Metro.** Sleek but affordable Indian restaurant a block from the White House, with Raj-style surroundings, piano accompaniment and dishes that are a little out of the ordinary, like mango fish tikka, lobster curry and mulligatawny soup. Mon–Fri 11.30am–2.30pm & 5.30–10.30pm, Sat 5.30–11pm, Sun 5.30–9pm.

Café Asia 1720 I St NW ☎202/659-2696; **Farragut West Metro.** Breezy pan-Asian restaurant that's a good mid-priced choice for sushi and sashimi, or try the lemongrass-grilled chicken soup, crab wontons, lime chicken or Thai noodles. Altogether, something of a grab bag, though well worth a try. Mon–Thurs 11.30am–10pm, Fri 11.30am–midnight, Sat noon–midnight, Sun noon–9pm.

Café Promenade in the Mayflower hotel, 1127 Connecticut Ave NW ☎202/347-2233; **Farragut North Metro.** A scrumptious Mediterranean menu sets the tone in this elegant hotel restaurant, where you can expect to see all types of political heavyweights at nearby tables; the steaks, swordfish and lobster are among many other reliable dishes. Delectable breakfasts cost $15–20, lunchtime

sandwiches about the same, and dinner main courses $20–30. Daily 6.30am–10.30pm.

🏃 **DC Coast** 1401 K St NW ☎202/216-5988; **McPherson Square Metro.** Smart and characterful seafood haunt that has affordable lunches – crab sandwiches, brook trout, rockfish – and for dinner, upscale cuisine such as crispy fried oysters, Chinese smoked lobster, crawfish hush puppies, Blue Point oysters and crab with polenta. Mon–Fri 11.30am–2.30pm & 5.30–10.30pm, Sat 5.30–9.30pm.

Giovanni's Trattu 1823 Jefferson Place NW ☎202/452-4960; **Farragut North Metro.** Terrific mid- to high-priced Italian fare that delivers all the essential elements: fresh ingredients, delicate textures and flavours, and Old World staples done very well – octopus carpaccio, gnocchi, and a full range of pastas among the many fine options, most $18–30. Mon–Thurs 11.30am–3pm & 5.30–10.30pm, Fri 11.30am–3pm & 5.30pm–midnight, Sat 5.30pm–midnight.

Grillfish 1200 New Hampshire Ave NW ☎202/331-7310; **Dupont Circle or Foggy Bottom–GWU Metro.** Chic restaurant offering casual dining and prime grilled seafood. The daily catch might include trout, rockfish, snapper, Arctic char, mahi-mahi, swordfish, shark or calamari – grilled, over pasta or served in a sauté pan. Most dishes are under $20. Mon–Thurs 11.30am–10pm, Fri 11.30am–11pm, Sat 5–11pm, Sun 5–10pm.

Malaysia Kopitiam 1827 M St NW ☎202/833-6232; **Dupont Circle or Farragut North Metro.** The no-frills decor will hardly draw you in, but if you like eclectic pan-Asian fare, the extensive selection of Indian, Malaysian and Chinese dishes will do the trick. Tuck into a bowl of noodles (some with gravy) or, for tastier fare, try the spicy beef crêpes, chili shrimp or lamb satay. Mon–Thurs 11.30am–10pm, Fri & Sat 11.30am–11pm, Sun noon–10pm.

Mio 1100 Vermont Ave NW ☎202/955-0075; **McPherson Square Metro.** Self-consciously chic eatery that has a wide range of inventive cocktails and desserts, though its fans come for dishes like chicken croquettes, shrimp stew, calamari with plantains and other modern Latin fare. Lunch specials $12–15, and dinner mains $20–25. Also set-price lunches and dinners at varying prices. Mon–Thurs 9am–2.30pm & 5–10pm, Fri 9am–2.30pm & 5–11pm, Sat 5–11pm.

Moby Dick House of Kabob 1300 Connecticut Ave NW ☎202/833-9788; Farragut North Metro. Delicious and cheap Middle Eastern fare that includes delicious, spicy gyros, chicken and lamb sandwiches, boneless chicken in pomegranate sauce, braised beef with aubergine, and other delights. Another branch at Dupont Circle (see p.210). Mon–Thurs 11am–10pm, Fri 11am–11pm, Sat noon–11pm.

The Palm 1225 19th St NW ☎202/293-9091; Dupont Circle or Farragut North Metro. This classy "power meatery" is renowned for its New York strip and lobster – and for the power players and celebrities who wine and dine here both at lunch and dinner. Reservations are required for this DC branch of a New York institution. Mon–Fri 11.45am–10pm, Sat 5.30–10pm, Sun 5.30–9.30pm.

Siroc 915 15th St NW ☎202/628-2220; McPherson Square Metro. Stylish Italian dining that includes a range of old favourites, such as spinach *fettuccine* and gnocchi with duck *ragù*, combined with more inventive dishes like *agnolotti* stuffed with braised ribs or black cod in cauliflower puree. Pasta is around $20, main courses $25. Also has good, affordable panini and pasta lunches. Mon–Fri 11.30am–2pm & 5.30–10.30pm, Sat 5.30–10.30pm, Sun 5–9.30pm.

Stoney's 1307 L St NW ☎202/347-9163; McPherson Square Metro. Down-to-earth saloon and bar that's more than three decades old, and continues to serve up a hefty range of comfort food – burgers, fries, chili, grilled chicken and especially grilled cheese sandwiches. Revel in its large, inexpensive portions, but be ready to wait cheek-by-jowl with the other hungry (and thirsty) patrons for the privilege. Mon–Thurs & Sun 11am–2am, Fri & Sat 11am–3am.

Tabard Inn 1739 N St NW ☎202/785-1277; Dupont Circle Metro. The restaurant of this mellow Victorian inn (see p.196) rotates its creative and expensive ($25–30 main courses) New American fare – you might find anything from pan-seared salmon to mushroom *ragù* to jumbo lump crab cakes. Its very pleasant garden is the perfect spot for brunch when the weather's right. Mon–Fri 7–10am, 11.30am–2.30pm & 5.30–10.30pm, Sat 11am–2pm & 5.30–10.30pm, Sun 11am–2pm & 5.30–9.30pm.

Vidalia 1990 M St NW ☎202/659-1990; Dupont Circle or Farragut North Metro. The New American cuisine dished up with a decidedly Southern twang has garnered this pricey restaurant a reputation as one of the District's best. Check the menu for delicious takes on swordfish, shrimp and grits, and a halibut steamer pot. Mon–Thurs 11.30am–2.30pm & 5.30–10pm, Fri 11.30am–2.30pm & 5.30–10.30pm, Sat 5.30–10.30pm, Sun 5–9pm.

Dupont Circle

See the **map** on p.134.

Cafés, snacks and light meals

Afterwords Café 1517 Connecticut Ave NW; Dupont Circle Metro. This spot in the back of Kramerbooks serves breakfast and brunch, coffee, and full meals – salad, pastas, grills and sandwiches, with the crab-cake version among the best. Mon–Thurs & Sun 7.30am–1am, Fri & Sat 6am–6pm.

Alberto's Pizza 2010 P St NW; Dupont Circle Metro. Little more than a basement-level takeaway stand, Alberto's nevertheless draws major queues on weekend nights for its excellent deals on thin crust pizza: a "slice" is one quarter of an entire pie, for $5. Also in Adams Morgan at 2438 18th St NW. Mon & Tues 11am–11.30pm, Wed & Sun 11am–12.30am, Thurs–Sat 11am–2am.

Firehook Bakery & Coffeehouse 1909 Q St NW; Dupont Circle Metro. Decent bakery-café serving up sandwich specials and a huge range of breads (also pies, desserts and cookies), plus good coffee at reasonable prices. Nearby branch at Farragut Square, 912 17th St NW, Downtown (Mon–Fri 6.30am–6.30pm). Mon–Fri 6.30am–7pm, Sat & Sun 7am–7pm.

Java House 1645 Q St NW; Dupont Circle Metro. A local favourite with a fine range of coffees – grab a cup to go or scramble for a sunny seat on the packed patio. A good spot to read a book, have an afternoon chat or fire up the laptop for wi-fi access. Desserts, bagels, salads and sandwiches are on offer throughout the day. Daily 7am–9pm.

Marvelous Market 1511 Connecticut Ave NW; Dupont Circle Metro. Pleasant takeaway deli with ready-made sandwiches and croissants, cheeses and olives, fresh produce, and good brownies and bread. Mon–Fri 7am–9pm, Sat 8.30am–8.30pm, Sun 8.30am–7pm.

Teaism 2009 R St NW ☎202/667-3827; Dupont Circle Metro. Serene Dupont Circle teahouse serving Japanese bento boxes, Thai curries, scones and, of course, lots of good tea, as well as a fine brunch. If you're looking to stock up on tea leaves, you'll find dozens of types on offer, as well as teapots and mugs. Mon–Thurs 8am–10pm, Fri 8am–11pm, Sat 9am–11pm, Sun 9am–10pm.

Restaurants

Bistrot du Coin 1738 Connecticut Ave NW ☎202/234-6969; **Dupont Circle Metro.** Classic bistro with a superb bar, boisterous atmosphere and genuine French food that actually tastes like it's supposed to – goat's cheese salad, steamed mussels, *tartines*, smoked duck breast and other choice offerings – all at reasonable prices. Mon–Wed & Sun 11.30am–11pm, Thurs–Sat 11.30am–1am.

Café Citron 1343 Connecticut Ave NW ☎202/530-8844; **Dupont Circle Metro.** Trendy restaurant serving tasty Caribbean-influenced Latin food, with dishes at $10–15; try the shrimp curry, habanero steak or Jamaican goat stew. By 10pm, the dining crowd gives way to meat-marketing partiers who come to grind to tunes provided by DJs or live Brazilian or salsa/merengue bands – and to fuel up on some of the best *mojitos* in town. Mon–Thurs 4pm–2am, Fri & Sat 4pm–3am.

City Lights of China 1731 Connecticut Ave NW ☎202/265-6688; **Dupont Circle Metro.** Mid-priced Chinese fare such as Szechuan and Hunan specialities and a strong emphasis on seafood, including dishes like spicy Szechuan squid and fried scallops. One of the few Chinese spots that gets vegetarian food right – standouts include the steamed dumplings and garlic aubergine. Mon–Fri 11.30am–11pm, Sat noon–11pm, Sun noon–10.30pm.

Komi 1509 17th St NW ☎202/332-9200; **Dupont Circle Metro.** One of the city's top restaurants, for which you should reserve well in advance, to enjoy fixed-price menus ($90 and $120) that may include suckling pig, pasta and *spanakopita* (spinach pie) – though you really never know. Tues–Sat 5.30–10pm.

Luna Grill & Diner 1301 Connecticut Ave NW ☎202/835-2280; **Dupont Circle Metro.** Inexpensive diner with bright decor and wholesome daily specials, "green plate" (vegetarian) dishes, and organic coffees and teas. The crab cake sandwich, pork chops, sirloin and veggie burgers are all worth a taste. An outdoor patio adds to the allure. Mon–Thurs & Sun 8am–10.30pm, Fri & Sat 8am–midnight.

Moby Dick House of Kabob 1300 Connecticut Ave NW ☎202/833-9788. Delicious and cheap Middle Eastern fare that includes spicy and savoury gyros, chicken and lamb sandwiches, boneless chicken in pomegranate sauce, braised beef with aubergine, and other cheap delights. Mon–Thurs 11am–10pm, Fri 11am–4am, Sat noon–4am.

Obelisk 2029 P St NW ☎202/872-1180; **Dupont Circle Metro.** Elite dining with flair. This trendy restaurant appeals for its delicious pasta, European cheeses and main courses such as lamb chops, quail and duck sausage, and suckling pig – all in a fixed-price menu for $75. Tues–Sat 5.30–10pm.

Pizzeria Paradiso 2003 P St NW ☎202/223-1245; **Dupont Circle Metro.** Arguably DC's best pizzeria, with favourites such as the gut-busting Siciliana, potato-and-pesto Genovese, and ultra-peppery and spicy Atomica. Also branches in Georgetown at 3282 M St NW and in Alexandria at 124 King St. Mon–Thurs 11.30am–11pm, Fri & Sat 11.30am–midnight, Sun noon–10pm.

Restaurant Nora 2132 Florida Ave NW ☎202/462-5143; **Dupont Circle Metro.** One of DC's finest eateries (with prices to match), set in a converted store with folk-art designs. The all-organic fare includes delicious choices like wild mushroom risotto, Spanish octopus, Amish pork roast and veal osso buco. Mon–Sat 5.30–10pm.

Skewers 1633 P St NW ☎202/387-7400; **Dupont Circle Metro.** This mid-priced restaurant is worth seeking out for its rich and tasty kebabs, aubergine salad and seafood, and even oddball items like ravioli and angel-hair pancakes – not to mention the belly dancing. Mon–Thurs 11.30am–11pm, Fri & Sat 11.30am–midnight.

Sushi Taro 1503 17th St NW ☎202/462-8999; **Dupont Circle Metro.** One of DC's best Japanese restaurants, with plenty of fine sushi, sashimi, tempura and teriyaki, at moderate to expensive prices. If raw fish isn't your thing, choose from the selection of steak and pork cutlets. Mon–Fri 11.30am–2pm & 5.30–10pm, Sat 5.30–10pm.

Thai Chef 1712 Connecticut Ave NW ☎202/234-5698; **Dupont Circle Metro.** Zesty and modern mix of Thai soups, seafood, pork and beef staples (along with a great Crying Tiger marinated beef dish) combined with excellent sushi; the Thai dishes are affordable; the pricier sushi is cheaper at happy hour. Mon–Thurs 11.30am–10.30pm, Fri & Sat 11.30am–11pm, Sun noon–4.30pm.

Urbana in the Palomar Hotel, 2121 P St NW ☎202/956-6650; **Dupont Circle Metro.** Colourful hotel restaurant that offers continental cuisine along with fine designer pizzas; it's also good for its pasta, seafood and rack of lamb. Not as expensive as you might think; fixed-priced menu $32 per person. Mon–Fri 6.30am–2pm & 5–10pm, Sat 11am–3pm & 5.30–11pm, Sun 11am–3pm & 5–10pm.

Zorba's Café 1612 20th St NW ☎202/387-8555; **Dupont Circle Metro.** Filling and cheap Greek and Middle Eastern combo platters, kebabs, pizzas and pitta-bread sandwiches, as well as daily specials and traditional dishes like bean casserole and spinach pie. Wash down one of the very good gyro sandwiches with pitchers of draught beer. Mon–Sat 11am–11.30pm, Sun noon–10.30pm.

Adams Morgan

All the places listed in Adams Morgan are within a few blocks of the junction of 18th Street and Columbia Road; the nearest Metro stops (noted below) are a good 15-minute walk away. See the **map** on p.145.

Cafés, snacks and light meals

Amsterdam Falafelshop 2425 18th St NW; Woodley Park–Zoo Metro. Among the finest falafel spots around, this unassuming eatery doles out piping-hot, seriously yummy falafel with a broad range of garnishes, and pretty good fries and brownies, too. Sun & Mon 11am–midnight, Tues & Wed 11am–2.30am, Thurs 11am–3am, Fri & Sat 11am–4am.

Casa Oaxaca 2106 18th St NW ☎202/387-2272; **no close Metro.** Not as flashy as some other Latin joints in the area, but among the best – great for its wide range of *mole* dishes, grilled steak and sautéed shrimp, at mid-range prices. Mon–Thurs & Sun 5–10.30pm, Fri & Sat 5–11.30pm.

The Diner 2453 18th St NW; Dupont Circle or Woodley Park–Zoo Metro. More a stylish café than a grungy dive, good and greasy

classics adorn the burger-, egg-, pancake- and sandwich-rich menu nonetheless. Daily 24hr.

Pizza Mart 2445 18th St NW; Woodley Park–Zoo Metro. Clubbers mop up an evening's worth of drinks with the hefty slices at this hole-in-the-wall pizzeria, one of several decent choices on this major Adams Morgan strip. Daily 11am–4am.

So's Your Mom 1831 Columbia Rd NW, ☎202/462-2666; **Woodley Park–Zoo Metro.** More than fifty types of sandwiches and heaping helpings of tuna salad, bagels, chicken livers and pastrami make this Jewish deli a hub of activity, not least for its cheap prices. Mon–Fri 7am–8pm, Sat & Sun 8am–7pm.

Tryst 2459 18th St NW ☎202/232-5500; **Dupont Circle or Woodley Park–Zoo Metro.** Very popular hangout where you can enjoy decent pastries, sandwiches and gourmet drinks, but also slurp down wine, beer and even morning cocktails. Also has internet access. Mon–Wed 6.30am–midnight, Thurs 6.30am–2am, Fri & Sat 6.30am–3am, Sun 7am–midnight.

Restaurants

Bardia's 2412 18th St NW ☎202/234-0420; **Woodley Park–Zoo Metro.** Unassuming little spot that has some of the District's best Creole fare, including beignets, seafood omelettes, po' boy sandwiches, and other Delta faves – all for cheap prices. Daily 10am–10pm.

Bukom Café 2442 18th St NW ☎202/265-4600; **Dupont Circle or Woodley Park–Zoo Metro.** Serves delicious West African dishes like spicy "beer meat", oxtail or okra soup, *egusi*, a broth of goat meat with ground melon seeds and spinach, and chicken *yassa*, with onions and spices, for $10–12. Daily 4pm–2am.

Cashion's Eat Place 1819 Columbia Rd NW ☎202/797-1819; **Dupont Circle or Woodley Park–Zoo Metro.** New Southern cuisine, with hickory-smoked lamb, rabbit meatloaf, corn cakes, grits, sweet potatoes, and fruit and nut pies – at mid- to high prices. Brunch dishes are about half-price. Tues & Sun 5.30–10pm, Wed–Sat 5.30–11pm.

El Tamarindo 1785 Florida Ave NW ☎202/328-3660; **Dupont Circle Metro.** A sizeable menu of Salvadoran-inspired rellenos, burritos, pupusas and other favourites, with many locals heading here to enjoy a late-night

Latin-food blowout. Mon–Thurs & Sun 10am–2am, Fri & Sat 24hr.

Grill from Ipanema 1858 Columbia Rd NW ☎202/986-0757; Woodley Park–Zoo Metro. Brazilian staples highlighted by meat stews, shrimp dishes and a solid weekend brunch. Try the mussels and watch your caipirinha intake. Mon–Thurs 4.30–11pm, Fri 4.30pm–midnight, Sat & Sun noon–midnight.

La Fourchette 2429 18th St NW ☎202/332-3077; Dupont Circle or Woodley Park–Zoo Metro. The brasserie's been here forever, and the food – affordable French classics including duck, steak and crêpes, served at closely packed tables – is good and reliable, if not particularly surprising. The main bonus is the pavement patio. Mon–Fri 11.30am–10.30pm, Sat 4–11pm, Sun 4–10pm.

Lauriol Plaza 1835 18th St NW ☎202/387-0035; Dupont Circle Metro. Serves scrumptious Tex Mex staples and grilled meats, shrimp and fajitas, plus Cuban steak and roasted chicken. The place frequently gets mobbed with tourists and partiers, and the service can be patchy in such a cramped and busy atmosphere. Mon–Thurs & Sun 11.30am–11pm, Fri & Sat 11.30am–midnight.

Mama Ayesha's 1967 Calvert St NW ☎202/232-5431; Woodley Park–Zoo Metro. Middle Eastern favourites like kibbeh, kabobs, grape leaves and the rest, with a lamb shank you can really sink your teeth into, plus spicy garlic lamb and chicken staples. Come for dinner, and be prepared to bust a gut without busting your wallet. Mon–Thurs & Sun noon–9.30pm, Fri & Sat noon–10.30pm.

Meze 2437 18th St NW ☎202/797-0017; Dupont Circle or Woodley Park–Zoo Metro. A wide array of delicious Turkish meze, both hot and cold, at cheap prices. Kebabs, grape leaves, shrimp cakes and crispy anchovy salad are among the highlights. Mon–Thurs 5.30pm–1.30am, Fri 5.30pm–2.30am, Sat 11am–2.30am, Sun 11am–1.30am.

Napoleon 1847 Columbia Rd NW ☎202/299-9630; Woodley Park–Zoo Metro. Tasty French cuisine that covers lamb and veal stew; fine ham, mushroom and beef crêpes; and rack of lamb, duck confit and other traditional dishes, mostly for affordable prices. Mon–Wed 5.30–11pm, Thurs 5.30pm–2am, Fri 5.30pm–3am, Sat 10am–3am, Sun 10am–midnight.

Pasta Mia 1790 Columbia Rd NW; Woodley Park–Zoo Metro. Expect a long wait at this no-frills, family-run *pasteria*, an authentic Italian eatery whose tasty selections of pasta, sausage, beef and fish are offered at prices so low it's worth the wait. Tues–Sat 6.30–10pm.

Perry's 1811 Columbia Rd NW ☎202/234-6218; Woodley Park–Zoo Metro. In-crowd restaurant serving a mid- to high-priced grab bag of sushi, lamb chops, mussels, swordfish steak and grilled salmon, much of it tasty. Rooftop tables are always at a premium. Mon–Thurs 5.30–10.30pm, Fri 5.30–11.30pm, Sat 11am–3pm & 5.30–11.30pm, Sun 10am–2.30pm & 5.30–10.30pm.

Saki 2477 18th St NW ☎202/232-5005; Woodley Park–Zoo Metro. Cheap happy-hour sushi and sashimi are the big draw here, along with other affordable Japanese selections. Downstairs is a festive club room. Mon–Thurs & Sun 5pm–1am, Fri & Sat 5pm–2.30am.

Shaw

See the **map** on p.145.

Restaurants

Ben's Chili Bowl 1213 U St NW; U Street–Cardozo Metro. Venerable U Street hangout across from the Metro, serving chili dogs, burgers, milkshakes and cheese fries at booths and counter stools – though at steeper prices than you might expect for fast food. The reason: politicians and celebrities love this place, as photos on the wall attest. Mon–Thurs 6am–2am, Fri 6am–4am, Sat 7am–4am, Sun 11am–11pm.

Coppi's 1414 U St NW ☎202/319-7773; U Street–Cardozo Metro. Very chic and trendy little pizza palace with a brick oven doling out organic pies with a range of fancy ingredients – prosciutto, goat's cheese, lamb sausage and the like – along with spicy calzones. Around $18–25 per pie. Mon–Thurs 6–11pm, Fri & Sat 5pm–midnight, Sun 5–10pm.

Dukem 1114 U St NW ☎202/667-8735; U Street–Cardozo Metro. One of the many great Ethiopian restaurants in Shaw, offering a fine, inexpensive sampling of traditional fare from the Horn of Africa – *gored gored* (cubed beef with butter, onion and jalapeno), *kwanta firfir* (beef jerky stew) and *minchet abesh* (ginger and garlic beef) are among the better options. Mon–Thurs & Sun 11am–2am, Fri & Sat 11am–3am.

Florida Avenue Grill 1100 Florida Ave NW
℡ 202/265-1586; U Street–Cardozo Metro. This
Southern-style diner has been serving
cheap and hearty meals for more than sixty
years to locals and stray political celebs.
Especially known for its biscuits and gravy,
eggs, ham and grits. Tues–Sat 8am–9pm,
Sun 8am–4.30pm.

🏃 **Henry's Soul Café 1704 U St NW**
℡ 202/265-3336; U Street–Cardozo
Metro. One of the District's hotspots for
authentic soul food, with the fried chicken
wings, baked trout, meatloaf, beef liver and
chitterlings giving a delicious taste of the
Deep South for under $10. There's also a
signature sweet potato pie or peach cobbler
for dessert. Mon–Fri 10.30am–9pm, Sat
7.30am–9pm, Sun 7.30am–8pm.

Tabaq Bistro 1336 U St NW ℡ 202/265-0965;
U Street–Cardozo Metro. Mediterranean fare
served with dash and spice, illuminated by
the usual lamb shanks and beef kotfe, plus
flavourful beef medallions, sautéed octopus,
risotto and marinated chicken. Also with
good weekend brunch options. Mon–Thurs
5–11pm, Fri 5pm–midnight, Sat 10am–
midnight, Sun 10am–4pm.

U-topia 1418 U St NW ℡ 202/483-7669; U Street–
Cardozo Metro. Arty, romantic bar-restaurant
with regular live blues and jazz, art exhibits,
good veggie dishes and affordable prices.
Eclectic main courses include Norwegian
salmon, blackened shrimp, veggie couscous
curry, burgers and pasta. There's also a fine
Sunday brunch. Mon–Wed & Sun
11am–11.30pm, Thurs 11am–midnight, Fri
11am–1am, Sat 5pm–1am.

Upper Northwest

See the **map** on p.155.

Cafés, snacks and light meals

Morty's Deli 4620 Wisconsin Ave NW; Tenley-
town Metro. This Jewish deli-diner is a long
way from anywhere, but devotees consider
the trek worth it for the true tastes of hot
corned beef, lox and bagels, whitefish and
sablefish platters, stuffed cabbage,
pastrami, chicken or matzo-ball soup, and
the rest. Daily 8am–9pm.

🏃 **Vace 3315 Connecticut Ave NW; Cleveland**
Park Metro. Grab a slice of the
excellent designer or traditional pizzas –
some of DC's best – and tasty sub
sandwiches, focaccia or pasta, or pack a

picnic from the selection of sausages, salads
and olives, then head to the zoo. Mon–Fri
9am–9pm, Sat 9am–8pm, Sun 10am–5pm.

Restaurants

Ardeo 3311 Connecticut Ave NW ℡ 202/244-6750;
Cleveland Park Metro. Ultra-trendy but not
too expensive spot (dishes $15–25), offering
fine short ribs, scallops, fresh oysters,
pan-roasted shrimp and garlic sausage, and
other mid-Atlantic specialities. Has a
delicious, affordable brunch that shouldn't be
missed either, with Belgian waffles, squid-ink
risotto and Scottish salmon. Mon–Thurs
5.30–10.30pm, Fri & Sat 5.30–11.30pm, Sun
11am–2.30pm & 5.30–10.30pm.

Cactus Cantina 3300 Wisconsin Ave NW
℡ 202/686-7222; no nearby Metro. A cheap
and festive Tex-Mex treat for Cathedral-
goers, with a great veranda and fine eats
like fajitas, *carne asada*, spicy chips and
salsa, and other staples, and new twists on
old favourites. Mon–Thurs 11am–11pm, Fri
& Sat 11am–midnight, Sun 10.30am–11pm.

Indique 3512 Connecticut Ave NW ℡ 202/244-
6600; Cleveland Park Metro. Chic and stylish,
mid-priced Indian cuisine that will either
make your tastebuds dance (the shrimp
curry or seafood masala) or attack them
with vigour (the piquant lamb vindaloo). Ask
for a towel to wipe away the sweat. Mon–
Thurs 5.30–10.30pm, Fri & Sat noon–3pm
& 5.30–11pm, Sun noon–3pm &
5.30–10.30pm.

Lebanese Taverna 2641 Connecticut Ave NW
℡ 202/265-8681; Woodley Park–Zoo Metro.
Delicious, mid-priced Middle Eastern joint
with soothingly dark, authentic decor.
Sample something from the assortment of
kebabs and grilled-meat platters, or go
straight for the leg of lamb. Mon–Fri
11.30am–2.30pm & 5–11pm, Sat
noon–11pm, Sun noon–9pm.

New Heights 2317 Calvert St NW ℡ 202/234-
4110; Woodley Park–Zoo Metro. Fashionable,
new-wave American restaurant serving an
inventive seasonal menu that is likely to
include anything from Georgia quail to wild
boar chops to trout salad, with upper-end
prices (main courses $24–32). Mon–Thurs &
Sun 5.30–10pm, Fri & Sat 5.30–10.30pm.

Open City 2331 Calvert St NW ℡ 202/332-2331;
Woodley Park–Zoo Metro. Centrally located,
zoo-accessible coffeehouse and diner
where you can enjoy a hefty breakfast of
omelettes and scrambles, as well as

sandwiches, burgers and seafood at lunch or dinner, plus a nice selection of cocktails and dessert treats. Plenty of vegetarian offerings, too. Mon–Thurs & Sun 6am–midnight, Fri & Sat 6am–1am.

Sabores 3435 Connecticut Ave ☎202/244-7196; **Cleveland Park Metro.** Smart and elegant tapas restaurant that will enliven your palate with its crab-stuffed avocado, Serrano ham, croquettes, crispy potatoes and *churrasco*, not to mention a mean *ropa vieja* (shredded beef). Desserts are also good, and the place offers a tasty brunch, too. Mon–Wed 6–10pm, Thurs–Sat 6–11pm, Sun 10.30am–2.30pm & 5–10pm.

Siam House 3520 Connecticut Ave ☎202/363-7802; **Cleveland Park Metro.** Terrific Thai favourites at this Cleveland Park standout, including drunken noodles and pad thai, but also clay-pot shrimp, a range of spicy curries and "spinach on fire". Mon 4.30–10pm, Tues–Thurs 11am–10pm, Fri 11am–11pm, Sat noon–11pm, Sun noon–10pm.

Spices 3333 Connecticut Ave NW ☎202/686-3833; **Cleveland Park Metro.** Stylish pan-Asian place serving creative, cheap to mid-priced spicy-crunchy tuna, crab-claw wontons, ginger salad and ultra-spicy "suicide curry" in a spacious, high-ceilinged dining room, complete with sushi bar. Mon–Fri 11.30am–3pm & 5–11pm, Sat noon–11pm, Sun 5–10.30pm.

Georgetown

See the **map** on p.162.

Cafés, snacks and light meals

Baked & Wired 1052 Thomas Jefferson St NW. Among the city's finest bakeries, where you can sample great pies and delicious coffee cakes, brownies, cookies and especially large and moist cupcakes. There's a nice selection of coffee and tea, too. Mon–Thurs 7am–8pm, Fri 7am–9pm, Sat 8am–9pm, Sun 9am–8pm.

Booeymonger 3265 Prospect St NW. Despite the unappetizing name, this deli/coffee shop at the corner of Prospect and Potomac streets is really worth seeking out for its signature sandwiches like the Gatsby Arrow (roast beef and Brie) and the Patty Hearst (turkey and bacon with Russian dressing), plus good breakfast selections. Daily 8am–midnight.

Ching Ching Cha 1063 Wisconsin Ave NW ☎202/342-2500. This bright and pleasant

tearoom transports tea-totallers to Old Asia with 70 kinds of black and green teas and herbal infusions, delicious hot or iced, a menu of tasty items like curry beef rolls, marble tea eggs (eggs cooked in tea) and dumplings, and an array of snazzy collectibles for sale. Daily 11am–9pm.

Dean & Deluca 3276 M St NW ☎202/342-2500. Superior self-service café and market in one of M Street's most handsome and historic red-brick buildings, the Market House. Croissants and cappuccino, designer salads, pasta and sandwiches, with a Southern bent evident in the buttermilk fried chicken, corn pudding and barbecued ribs. Daily: café 7am–8pm, market 9am–8pm.

Restaurants

Bangkok Bistro 3251 Prospect St NW ☎202/337-2424. In a stylish, often crowded dining room, this mid-priced gem has old favourites (tom yum, pad thai, shrimp cakes and satay) alongside coconut shrimp, duck noodles, spicy beef curries and fish in chili sauce. Mon–Thurs & Sun 11.30am–10.30pm, Fri & Sat 11.30am–11.30pm.

Bistro Français 3128 M St NW ☎202/338-3830. Notable for its (moderately priced) French cooking, from simple *steak frites*, baked mussels, onion soup and beef tenderloin to tuna steaks and liver mousse. Early-bird (5–7pm) and late-night (10.30pm–1am) set dinners for $25. Mon–Thurs & Sun 11am–3am, Fri & Sat 11am–4am.

Café la Ruche 1039 31st St NW ☎202/965-2684. Relaxing, inexpensive bistro with patio seating in warmer weather. Sample the mussels, quiches, *escargots*, croque monsieur and other fine sandwiches, or drop by for pastries and espresso. Also has a good weekend brunch. Mon–Thurs 11.30am–11.30pm, Fri 11.30am–1am, Sat 10am–1am, Sun 10am–10.30pm.

Citronelle in the Latham Hotel, 3000 M St ☎202/625-2150. Huge player on the DC dining scene, serving up French-inspired cuisine with California flair, and set-price food and wine pairings starting at $350. Reserve in advance, dress chic and bring plenty of attitude. Mon–Thurs 7.30–10.30am, 11.30am–2pm & 6.30–10pm, Fri 7.30–10.30am, 11.30am–2pm & 6.30–10.30pm, Sat 7.30–10.30am & 6.30–10.30pm, Sun 7.30–10.30am & 6.30–10pm.

Clyde's 3236 M St NW ☏202/333-9180.
Classic New York-style saloon-restaurant featuring clubby wood interior, plus a menu of crab cakes, steak, burgers, pasta and French dips. One of a dozen in a mid-priced local chain. Mon–Thurs 11.30am–midnight, Fri 11.30am–1am, Sat 10am–1am, Sun 9am–11pm.

Hook 3241 M St NW ☏202/625-4488. Hard to do better for the catch of the day than this centrally located seafood favourite, which serves up a mean tuna tartare for around $25, as well as meat dishes like *porchetta*. Also affordable lunch specials and a tempting weekend brunch. Mon–Wed 5–10pm, Thurs & Fri 11.30am–2.30pm & 5–11pm, Sat & Sun 10am–3.30pm & 5pm–midnight.

J. Paul's 3218 M St NW ☏202/333-3450. A "dining saloon" that offers the standard grill/barbecue menu, with some tasty crab cakes and a good raw bar, plus micro-brews. Good enough to fill you up after a long day of M Street shopping, and open long after comparable saloons close. Mon–Thurs 11.30am–2am, Fri & Sat 11.30am–3am, Sun 10.30am–2am.

Leopold's Kafe 3315 M St NW ☏202/965-6005. European-chic café that doles out mid- to high-priced continental fare like sweet onion tarts, veal schnitzel, bratwurst and smoked fish, as well as delicious desserts and pastries. Breakfast can be particularly good here. Mon, Tues & Sun 8am–10pm, Wed 8am–11pm, Thurs–Sat 8am–midnight.

Martin's Tavern 1264 Wisconsin Ave NW ☏202/333-7370. Four generations have run this place and counted politicos from JFK to Dubya among their regulars. The old-fashioned, clubby saloon serves up steaks and chops, great burgers, linguine with clam sauce and other pasta meals, and oyster stew, for around $15–25. It's also known for its popular Sunday brunch. Mon–Thurs 11am–1.30am, Fri 11am–2.30am, Sat 9am–2.30am, Sun 9am–1.30am.

Late-night eats

At the following places you'll be able to order a meal at or after midnight on at least one night of the week (usually Fri and/or Sat).

Afterwords Café (24hr Sat & Sun), Dupont Circle, p.209
Alberto's Pizza Dupont Circle, p.209
Amsterdam Falafelshop Adams Morgan, p.211
Au Bon Pain Union Station, p.201
Ben's Chili Bowl Shaw, p.212
Bistrot du Coin Dupont Circle, p.210
Bistro Français Georgetown, p.214
Bob and Edith's Diner Arlington, p.216
Booeymonger Georgetown, p.214
Bukom Café Adams Morgan, p.211
Café Asia Downtown, p.208
Café Citron Dupont Circle, p.210
Café La Ruche Georgetown, p.214
Clyde's Georgetown, p.215
Coppi's Shaw, p.212
The Diner (24hr), Adams Morgan, p.211
Dukem Shaw, p.212
Eat First Chinatown, p.207
El Tamarindo Adams Morgan, p.211
Fish Market Alexandria, p.217
Giovanni's Trattu Downtown, p.208
Hook Georgetown, p.215
J. Paul's Georgetown, p.215
Jaleo Downtown, p.206
Leopold's Kafe Georgetown, above
Luna Grill Dupont Circle, p.210
Martin's Tavern Georgetown, above
Mark's Duck House Arlington, p.216
Matchbox Chinatown, p.207
Meze Adams Morgan, p.212
Moby Dick House of Kabob Downtown, p.209 & p.210
The Monocle Capitol Hill, p.204
Mr Henry's Capitol Hill, p.204
Naan and Beyond Downtown, p.207
Napoleon Adams Morgan, p.212
Old Ebbitt Grill Downtown, p.206
Open City Upper Northwest, p.213
Paolo's Georgetown, p.216
Pizza Boli's Capitol Hill, p.204
Pizza Mart Adams Morgan, p.211
Proof Downtown, p.207
Sabores Upper Northwest, p.214
Saki Adams Morgan, p.212
Stoney's Downtown, p.209
Tabaq Bistro Shaw, p.213
Tryst Adams Morgan, p.211
U-topia Shaw, p.213

Morton's of Chicago 3251 Prospect St NW
℡202/342-6258. The premium steak-house
chain's Georgetown branch serves a
fabulous porterhouse. Pick your cut – and
make sure you've come with a huge
appetite – or go for main courses ($25 and
up) that range from chicken to seafood. One
of several local branches, including one in
Arlington (see below). Mon–Sat 5.30–11pm,
Sun 5–10pm.

Paolo's 1303 Wisconsin Ave NW ℡202/333-
7353. Mid-level Italian dining with a few
coveted tables open to the pavement.
Gourmet pizzas ($10) and even better
pastas ($10–15) are specialities, though the
main courses cost around $20. Mon–Thurs
& Sun 11am–11.30pm, Fri
11.30am–12.30am, Sat 11am–12.30am.

🏃 **Rocklands** 2418 Wisconsin Ave NW
℡202/333-2558. A bit north of the
main action, almost in Upper Northwest, but
still worth the trek to enjoy some of DC's
best pork sandwiches, ribs, beans, sausage
and other staples of the Southern barbecue
scene, all for cheap prices. Mon–Sat
11am–10pm, Sun 11am–9pm.

Zed's 1201 28 St NW ℡202/333-4710. This
intimate spot is the best place for Ethiopian
food in Georgetown. The set lunch is cheap
but so are the dinner mains. The *doro wot*
(chicken stew in a red pepper sauce) is a
good, spicy choice, as are the tenderloin
beef cubes. There are also plenty of veggie
options. Mon–Thurs & Sun 11am–10pm, Fri
& Sat 11am–11pm.

Arlington and around

See the **map** on p.173.

Restaurants

Bangkok 54 2919 Columbia Pike ℡703/521-
4070; no close Metro. Upscale Thai food you
won't forget – among DC's best – with a
broad selection of spicy pork, drunken
noodles, green papaya or beef salad, duck
curry and a fine roasted-noodle soup.
Mon–Thurs & Sun 11am–10pm, Fri & Sat
11am–11pm.

Bob and Edith's Diner 2310 Columbia Pike; no
close Metro. Thumbs up to the tasty,
gut-busting diner fare at this cheap and
alluring breakfast joint. It's open round the
clock, so you can get your fill of country
ham, eggs, hash, grits, omelettes and home
fries whenever you're hungry. Daily 24hr.

Carlyle 4000 Campbell Ave ℡703/931-0777; no
close metro. Mid-level steak and seafood
with a nouveau twist, mixing in more exotic
flavours to create Tex Mex egg rolls,
jambalaya pasta, Mongolian lamb chops
and crab fritters. Mon–Thurs 11am–11pm,
Fri & Sat 11am–midnight, Sun
9.30am–10.30pm.

Mark's Duck House 6184 Arlington Blvd
℡703/532-2125, Falls Church, VA, west of
Arlington; East Falls Church Metro. More good
Asian fare in the 'burbs – this midpriced
restaurant, located in a mini mall, offers primo
Chinese food, such as roasted duck, salty
shrimp and lunchtime dim sum. Mon–Thurs &
Sun 10am–11pm, Fri & Sat 10am–midnight.

Morton's of Chicago 1631 Crystal Square Ave
℡703/418-1444; Crystal City Metro. Local
branch of this chic steakhouse chain, with
the standard array of delicious cuts of beef,
veal and lobster, most for $30 and up, plus
a clubby atmosphere conducive to boozing.
Mon–Sat 5–11pm, Sun 5–10pm.

Red Hot & Blue 1600 Wilson Blvd; Court House
Metro; Clarendon Metro. Memphis barbecue
joint that spawned a chain, serving the best
ribs in the area. A rack, with coleslaw and
beans, costs just $10. Mon–Thurs & Sun
11am–10pm, Fri & Sat 11am–11pm.

🏃 **Song Que** 6769 Wilson Blvd ℡703/536-
7900, Falls Church, VA, west of Arlington
off Arlington Blvd; East Falls Church Metro. It's
worth venturing out to this affordable,
popular spot for delicious Bahn Mi
sandwiches, Asian ice cream, green papaya
salad and other Vietnamese favourites. Daily
9am–9.30pm.

Tallula 2761 Washington Blvd ℡703/778-5051;
no close Metro. Chic modern American
restaurant six blocks west of the cemetery
that serves up expensive Amish chicken,
Peking duck breast and braised young goat,
as well as affordable small plates of blue
crab sausage and risotto fritters.
Mon–Thurs 5.30–10pm, Fri 5.30–11pm,
Sat 11am–2.30pm & 5.30–11pm, Sun
10am–2pm & 5.30–10pm.

Alexandria

See the **map** on p.178.

Cafés, snacks and light meals

Bread and Chocolate 611 King St; King Street
Metro. Popular bakery and coffeehouse with
good sandwiches and an array of omelettes

Best for brunch

Weekend **brunch** – especially Sunday brunch – is a Washington institution. The city's most prestigious hotels offer the best spreads, and provide visitors and locals with a relatively inexpensive way to experience their dining rooms. But many non-hotel restaurants also pride themselves on their brunches. The places listed below may not offer the swanky surroundings and free champagne refills of the hotels but are still, in their own way, excellent.

Acadiana p.206
Afterwords Café p.209
Ardeo p.213
Café La Ruche p.214
Cashion's Eat Place
   p.211

Clyde's p.215
Grill from Ipanema p.212
Hook p.215
Kinkead's p.205
Martin's Tavern p.215
Perry's p.212

Sabores p.214
Tabaq Bistro p.213
Tabard Inn p.209
Teaism p.208 & p.209
U-topia p.213

and eggs Benedict dishes, and comfort food like pot pie, pizza and French dips. Mon–Wed 7am–7pm, Fri & Sat 7am–9pm, Sun 8am–6pm.

Five Guys 107 N Fayette St; King Street Metro. This branch of a regional chain is an Old Town greasy spoon that cooks its juicy hamburgers to order and piles on the fixins. And don't forget the fries – the fresh, hand cut, boardwalk-style chips boast their own loyal following. Daily 11am–10pm.

La Piazza 535 E Braddock Rd; Braddock Road Metro. Straightforward Italian fare, and an especially good choice if you're craving a hot sub sandwich, with the chicken cheesesteak, meatball *parmigiana* and veal-and-peppers among the favourites. Mon–Sat 11am–3pm & 5–10pm.

Restaurants

Fish Market 105 King St ☎703/836-5676; King Street Metro. Midpriced, brick-walled restaurant with a terrace, a block from the water, serving oysters and chowder at the bar and fried-fish platters, adequate stews and pastas, but good Maine lobster and Maryland crab cakes. Mon–Thurs & Sun 11.30am–11pm, Fri & Sat 11.30am–midnight.

Hard Times Café 1404 King St ☎703/837-0050; King Street Metro. Four styles of cheap and fiery chili, from classic Texas to Greek-style Cincinnati to spicy-as-hell Terlingua, plus a veggie option. Good wings, rings and fries, too, and delicious microbrews. One of many in a local chain. Mon–Thurs & Sun 11am–11pm, Fri & Sat 11am–2am.

Los Tios Grill 2615 Mount Vernon Ave ☎703/299-9290; Braddock Metro. Good Latin American cuisine a mile and a half north of Old Town, with a bent toward Salvadoran. The Veracruz chicken, tortilla soup, fried yucca and fajitas are among the inexpensive favourites. Mon–Thurs & Sun 11am–10pm, Fri & Sat 11am–11pm.

The Majestic 911 King St ☎703/837-9117; King Street Metro. Down-home American favourites in this classic diner, with the Chesapeake Bay stew, rib chops, meatloaf and Amish chicken among the more piquant offerings, and fried green tomatoes, crab cakes and oyster po' boy driving the point home. Mon–Sat 11.30am–2.30pm & 5.30–10pm, Sun 1–9pm.

Restaurant Eve 110 S Pitt St ☎703/706-0450; King Street Metro. The buzz attached to this warm and cosy nouveau American bistro is fairly spot-on. Choices include five- to nine-course meals drawn from a rotating menu of seafood, game, cheese and desserts from $110 or $150, or expensive bistro fare such as pork belly, rabbit, rockfish and the like. Mon–Fri 11.30am–2.30pm & 5.30–9.30pm, Sat 5.30–10pm.

Southside 815 815 S Washington St ☎703/836-6222; King Street Metro. Moderately priced Southern cooking just the way you like it, with good old-fashioned favourites like biscuits with ham gravy, thick and buttery cornbread, succotash (corn and bean stew), BBQ shrimp, ribs, crab fritters, and straight-up crawdads and catfish. Mon–Thurs & Sun 11.30am–10.30pm, Fri & Sat 11.30am–11pm.

12

Bars and clubs

Nightlife in the District is not always the staid affair you might imagine – crowds of lawyers and lobbyists swilling Martinis as they hunt for the biggest power brokers in the room. Although this does occur, typically in the dreary hotel bars and corporate-dominated watering holes around K Street, in other areas you're likely to find a much livelier scene, attracting all types, from beer-guzzling students and funky hipsters to sprightly club kids. Some of the most notable **areas** to drop in for a drink or a dance include Capitol Hill, near Union Station and along Pennsylvania Avenue SE, buzzing with interns looking to cut loose from the suit-and-tie grind; Downtown around the Penn Quarter, for its mix of tourists and locals; Georgetown, at M Street and Wisconsin Avenue, a college-oriented scene; Dupont Circle, along 17th Street and Connecticut Avenue, a gay-and-straight mash-up with the District's broadest range of choices; Shaw, along U Street near the Metro, and Adams Morgan, at 18th Street and Columbia Road, for a hearty blend of beats and brews. Across the river, you can find assorted hangouts in Arlington, along Wilson and Clarendon boulevards, and in Alexandria, around Old Town. There's also a thriving – if relatively small – **gay scene**, with most of the action in Dupont Circle, especially on P Street (between 21st and 22nd) and 17th Street (between P and R); for more on these spots, turn to Chapter 14.

While there's plenty of crossover between bars, lounges, clubs and live-music venues – a well-soaked watering hole may have DJs on some nights, rock bands the next – we've categorized the following selections according to the main strength of each. If you're mostly interested in drinking and need little more than background music (live or canned), look under "**Bars**", below; if DJs and a frenetic social scene are the draw, try "**Clubs**" (p.224); and if you really want to groove on live jazz, rock or anything else and don't care much about cocktails or DJs, try "**Live music**" (p.226).

Bars

As in other American cities, Washington, DC has gone **smoke-free**, with rare exceptions granted for cigar bars. The listings below offer a spectrum of watering holes aimed at several different types of drinkers, from the chic yuppie palaces, offering brushed steel and glass surfaces and $15 cocktails, to the lower-end hangouts where well drinks (cheap house alcohol) go for as little as $2 and the atmosphere is convivial.

Most bars are **open** daily from 11am or noon until the legal closing time of 2.30am weekends, 1.30am weekdays. Virtually all have **happy hours** during which drinks are two-for-one or at least heavily discounted; the optimum time for

Brew horizons

Don't want to settle for just another Bud? **Microbrews** are big business these days, and you'll be able to get a decent selection of beers in many bars. For the best choice, hit one of the city's brewpubs – *Capitol City Brewing Company* (below & p.220), *District Chophouse & Brewery* (p.220) or *Shenandoah* (p.224) – or the beer specialists *Brickskeller* (p.221), *Birreria Paradiso* (p.223), *The Saloon* (p.222) or *D.A.'s RFD Washington* (p.220). Elsewhere, keep an eye out for the following local brews: Foggy Bottom Ale from DC, Virginia's Old Dominion; from Maryland, Heavy Seas and Wild Goose; and from Delaware, Dogfish Head.

these is weekdays between 4pm and 6pm. Some bars also offer free snacks to happy-hour drinkers – usually the standard pub grub of chicken wings and mozzarella sticks – while a few offer gourmet treats as well.

Capitol Hill

See the **map** on p.75.

18th Amendment 613 Pennsylvania Ave SE; Eastern Market Metro. Speakeasy-themed bar with Art Deco decor and cast of lobbyists and staffers out to party. Pricey but good cocktails are modern vodkatinis and the like (rather than hyper-sweet 1920s concoctions), though food prices are a bit steep for what you get. Mon–Thurs 4pm–2am, Fri & Sat 4pm–3am, Sun 11am–2am.

Argonaut 1433 H St NE; no Metro. Zesty grog house with a fun patio, where you can munch on bar fare like jalapeno hush puppies, or shrimp and grits, while slurping a rum cocktail, including the "Dark & Stormy" – rum-drenched ginger beer. Take a taxi, since the neighbourhood's on the dicey side. Mon–Fri 5pm–2am, Sat & Sun 11am–2am.

Bullfeathers 410 First St SE; Capitol South Metro. Politician-watchers may catch sight of a famous face or two at this old-time Hill institution, a dark and clubby spot with affordable beer and good burgers and bar food, and named after Teddy Roosevelt's favourite term for bullshit during his White House days. Not surprisingly, it's got a solid Republican bent. Mon–Sat 11.30am–midnight.

Capitol City Brewing Company 2 Massachusetts Ave NE; Union Station Metro. Prime microbrewing turf offering average pub food but good handcrafted beer, highlighted by the Amber Waves Ale, a rich and succulent beverage, and German-style Capitol Kolsch and Prohibition Porter. Another branch Downtown, 1100 New York Ave NW (see p.220). Both Mon–Thurs 11am–1am, Fri & Sat 11am–2am, Sun 11am–10pm.

Capitol Lounge 229 Pennsylvania Ave SE; Capitol South Metro. Brick-walled saloon on the Hill with so-so food but well-priced beer, plus three bars on two levels, and lots of Congressional staffers looking to get wasted thanks to generous happy hours. Mon 4pm–2am, Tues 11am–2am, Fri & Sat 11am–3am, Sun 10am–2am.

The Dubliner in the Phoenix Park Hotel, 520 N Capitol St NW ☏ 202/737-3773; Union Station Metro. A wooden-vaulted, good-time Irish bar catering to visiting business and lobbying types, with draught Guinness, boisterous conversation, rib-stuffing food like shepherd's pie and live Irish music. The patio is a nice summer hangout. Mon–Thurs & Sun 11am–2am, Fri & Sat 11am–3am.

Kelly's Irish Times 14 F St NW ☏ 202/543-5433; Union Station Metro. Colourful weekend folk music sets the stage at this lively, youth-oriented pub, which also features club music on the downstairs dancefloor and pints of Guinness. Mon–Thurs & Sun 11am–2am, Fri & Sat 11am–3am.

Pour House 319 Pennsylvania Ave SE; Capitol South Metro. Hill rats pour into this three-bars-in-one hangout for the food and drink specials. There are pool tables downstairs, plus an unexpected ode to the glories of Pittsburgh, with western Pennsylvania teams on some of the 15 TVs and Iron City beer on tap. Mon–Fri 4pm–2am, Sat & Sun 10am–2am.

The Pug 1234 H St NE; no Metro. Comfortable, boxing-themed neighbourhood bar that's not as in-your-face as some of the more frenetic bars and clubs in the vicinity but still appeals for its inexpensive drinks, pool table and convivial atmosphere. Given the dicey neighbourhood, you should take a taxi here. Daily 5pm–2am.

Tune Inn 331 Pennsylvania Ave SE; Capitol South Metro. Old-line neighbourhood dive bar that's been around forever and has a mix of grizzled regulars and wide-eyed newbies. Settle down in a booth, munch on the burgers and feed the jukebox. Mon–Thurs & Sun 10am–2am, Fri & Sat 10am–3am.

White House area and Foggy Bottom

See the **map** on p.97.

51st State Tavern 2512 L St NW; Foggy Bottom–GWU Metro. A neighbourhood fave for cheap beer, decent cocktails and spirits, tasty sandwiches and bar fare, and a pool table and pair of jukeboxes. Comfortable, friendly, and well worth stopping by for a draught. Mon–Thurs & Sun 4pm–2am, Fri & Sat 4pm–3am.

Froggy Bottom Pub 2142 Pennsylvania Ave NW; Foggy Bottom–GWU Metro. Colourful, three-level bar catering to students at nearby GWU. A good place if you're interested in shooting pool, munching on decent pizza and pub grub, and knocking back a good brew or two (or many more). Mon–Fri & Sun 7pm–2am, Sat 5pm–2am.

Lindy's Red Lion 2040 I St NW; Foggy Bottom–GWU or Farragut West Metro. No gimmicks, few frills – just a GWU student hangout doing a roaring trade in cheap beer and an array of good burgers. Have a few drinks and make a new friend or two on the patio. Mon–Thurs 11am–1.30am, Fri & Sat 11am–2.30am.

Marshall's 2524 L St NW; Foggy Bottom–GWU Metro. Good brews like Red Hook and classics like Guinness, plus a decent menu of steak, pasta and seafood, make this smart bar-and-grill a good spot. The kitchen serves till 1am (2am at weekends). Daily 11.30am–2am.

Downtown: Penn Quarter and Federal Triangle

See the **map** on p.114.

Capitol City Brewing Company 1100 New York Ave NW, entrance at 11th and H; Metro Center Metro. Copper vats, pipes and gantries adorn this microbrewery, serving a changing menu of home-brewed beers like Pale Rider

Ale, Capitol Kolsch and Prohibition Porter. There's also a branch at Union Station, 2 Massachusetts Ave NW (same hours). Mon–Thurs 11am–1am, Fri & Sat 11am–2am, Sun 11am–10pm.

District Chophouse & Brewery 509 7th St NW; Gallery Place–Chinatown Metro. This stunningly converted Downtown bank lends a dash of style to the Penn Quarter. The busy bar serves its own brews and offers good food (see p.206). Sun & Mon 11am–10pm, Tues–Sat 11am–11pm.

Fadó 808 7th St NW; Gallery Place–Chinatown Metro. DC outpost of a national Irish-pub chain – with Victorian and Celtic decor – that's a good spot for a Guinness and a bite to eat, though more authentic haunts can be found on Capitol Hill near Union Station. Mon–Thurs 11.30am–1am, Fri & Sat 11.30am–2am, Sun 11.30am–10pm.

Gordon Biersch Brewery 900 F St NW; Gallery Place–Chinatown Metro. Friendly chain bar in the Penn Quarter, whose extravagant setting, in a restored 1891 Romanesque Revival bank that's a historic landmark, merits a visit. The beers are decent, too (though the food isn't). Mon–Thurs & Sun 11am–11pm, Fri & Sat 11am–midnight.

Iron Horse Tap Room 507 7th St NW; Gallery Place–Chinatown Metro. One of the newest DC scene bars, where a mix of hipsters and politicos imbibe from a nice selection of mainstream beers, microbrews and cocktails and a notable array of bourbons. The food isn't as great, but it'll do for sustenance, and they even have skee ball. Mon–Thurs & Sun 11am–2am, Fri & Sat 11am–3am.

RFD Washington 810 7th St NW; Gallery Place–Chinatown Metro. One of the better DC microbreweries, with hundreds of bottled beers and locally crafted and international brews on tap – though the food tends to be mediocre. Located near the Verizon Center, so watch out for heavy post-game crowds. Mon–Thurs 11am–2am, Fri & Sat 11am–3am, Sun noon–midnight.

Rocket Bar 714 7th St NW; Gallery Place–Chinatown Metro. Self-consciously divey bar with minimal signage that's something of a hotspot for its cheap drinks, skee ball and shuffleboard, and upbeat atmosphere with a jukebox and cheerfully plastered patrons. No food, though. Mon–Thurs 4pm–2am, Fri 4pm–3am, Sat noon–3am, Sun noon–2am.

Round Robin Bar in the Willard Hotel, 1401 Pennsylvania Ave NW; Federal Triangle Metro.

Saloons

DC has a wealth of traditional saloon-restaurants, bristling with checked tablecloths, wood panelling, good-value food and attentive waiters. The list below singles out those where the bar action is pretty good as well.

Brickskeller Dupont Circle, p.221
Capitol Lounge Capitol Hill, p.219
Clyde's Georgetown, p.214
District Chophouse and Brewery Downtown, p.220

J. Paul's Georgetown, p.214
Martin's Tavern Georgetown, p.215
The Monocle Capitol Hill, p.204
Mr Henry's Capitol Hill, p.208
Stoney's Downtown, p.209

If you tire of drunken tourist antics in the Penn Quarter, this chic old-time bar is a nice refresher. Packed with political types in suits, it's worth a try for its expensive but well-made classic cocktails (notably the mint julep), decent sandwiches and burgers, and historical setting (see p.116). Mon–Sat 11am–1am, Sun 11am–midnight.

Downtown: North of K Street

See the **map** on p.134.

ChurchKey 1337 14th St NW, Logan Circle; no close Metro. As you might guess from the bottle-opener name, this place is very strong on beer – microbrews, foreign labels, you name it – whether on tap or from the voluminous selection of bottles. The tasty charcuterie plates and fine cheeses don't hurt, either. If you like thoughtful drinking and a relaxed atmosphere this is the spot. Mon–Fri 5pm–midnight, Sat & Sun noon–midnight.

Logan Tavern 1423 P St NW; Dupont Circle Metro. Festive Logan Circle watering hole that actually serves fine food – wasabi meatloaf to crab cakes to flat-iron steak, plus tasty desserts – to go with the nice selection of cocktails and spirits (including a potent bloody Mary). Mon & Tues noon–10.30pm, Wed & Thurs noon–11pm, Fri noon–midnight, Sat 11am–midnight, Sun 11am–10.30pm.

Ozio 1813 M St NW; Farragut North or Dupont Circle Metro. Ritzy cigar bar, lounge and club popular with the District's well-polished and -varnished scenesters during the week, and various club kids at the weekend. More fun if you love to pose. Mon–Thurs 5pm–2am, Fri 5pm–3am, Sat 6pm–3am.

Panache 1725 DeSales St NW ☎ 202/293-7760; Farragut North Metro. Tapas bar and restaurant that's almost as good for its food as for its drinks – which aren't bad, either, with

piquant cocktails and a full bar. Regular live entertainment and DJs on weekends. Mon–Thurs 11am–10pm, Fri 11am–2am, Sat 5.30pm–3am.

Recessions 1823 L St NW; Farragut North Metro. Convivial joint with festive atmosphere and a good happy hour, plus regular karaoke, as well as a full lunch and dinner menu of decent pasta and seafood. Pool, darts and a digital jukebox add to the appeal. Mon–Thurs 11.30am–midnight, Fri 11.30am–2am, Sat 5pm–2am.

Dupont Circle

See the **map** on p.134.

Big Hunt 1345 Connecticut Ave NW; Dupont Circle Metro. As well known for its eccentric decor as for its beer, which is fairly cheap for the area. A few dozen brews are on tap, including a fair selection of Belgian ales, and it has a good jukebox and a groovy crowd. Always happy during happy hour. Mon–Thurs 4pm–2am, Fri 4pm–3am, Sat 4pm–3am, Sun 5pm–2am.

Black Fox Lounge 1723 Connecticut Ave; Dupont Circle Metro. Engaging restaurant and bar with decent food (crab cake mac and cheese is a highlight) and an inventive array of cocktails, including a fine sidecar and the "Black Fox" – a potent mix of cacao, orange and rye. Mon–Thurs & Sun 4pm–1.30am, Fri & Sat 4pm–2.30am.

Brickskeller 1523 22nd St NW; Dupont Circle Metro. Brick-lined, divey basement saloon serving "the world's largest selection of beer" – though only a small fraction is typically available. Knowledgeable bar staff can advise, or you can try your luck from the colossal menu. Mon & Tues 5pm–2am, Wed & Thurs 11.30am–2am, Fri 11.30am–3am, Sat 6pm–3am, Sun 6pm–2am.

Buffalo Billiards 1330 19th St NW; Dupont Circle Metro. Happening basement hangout with dozens of HDTVs for sports viewing, as well as pool tables, darts, shuffleboard, a good selection of beers on tap, and tasty pub grub. Mon–Thurs 4pm–2am, Fri 4pm–3am, Sat noon–3am, Sun noon–2am.

Fox and Hounds 1537 17th St NW; Dupont Circle Metro. Friends of this small and easy-going dive bar smack in the middle of the 17th Street action mostly kick back and enjoy the very stiff (and very cheap) drinks. Mon–Thurs & Sun 11am–2am, Fri & Sat 11am–3am.

Gazuza 1629 Connecticut Ave NW; Dupont Circle Metro. This Middle Eastern-flavoured hookah joint serves adequate sushi, and also has a fair array of cocktails and an outdoor balcony, whose perch above Connecticut Avenue attracts an eclectic mix of boozers, smokers and music-lovers. Mon–Thurs & Sun 5pm–2am, Fri & Sat 5pm–3am.

Madhatter 1319 Connecticut Ave NW; Dupont Circle Metro. Comfortable saloon with a well-selected range of beers. An after-work crowd comes for the convivial happy hour, later giving way to a meat-marketing crowd. Mon–Thurs & Sun 11.30am–2am, Fri 11.30am–3am, Sat 10am–3am.

Steve's Bar Room 1337 Connecticut Ave NW; Dupont Circle Metro. Trendy little spot that attracts refugees from local dance clubs for its chic decor, buzzing social scene, regular DJs who play retro-80s schlock, and even a vending machine for Pabst Blue Ribbon. Mon–Thurs & Sun 9pm–2am, Fri & Sat 9pm–3am.

Adams Morgan

See the **map** on p.145.

Bedrock Billiards 1841 Columbia Rd NW; Dupont Circle or Woodley Park–Zoo Metro. A lively subterranean setting with quality bartenders and quirky art set this funky pool hall apart from Adams Morgan's more frenzied club scene. Mon–Thurs 4pm–2am, Fri 4pm–3am, Sat 1pm–3am, Sun 1pm–2am.

Bourbon 2321 18th St NW; Dupont Circle or Woodley Park–Zoo Metro. Happening spot serving decent food in the first-floor restaurant, with a few tasty items like crab cakes, but the upper-storey bar, loft and patio are the choice spots for thoroughly pleasant socializing and lubricating. Mon–Thurs 6pm–2am, Fri 5pm–3am, Sat 9.30am–3am, Sun 9.30am–2am.

Looking Glass Lounge 3634 Georgia Ave NW; Georgia Avenue–Petworth Metro. Murky lounge

with decent burgers and sandwiches, and spirits that include some twenty varieties of whiskey. One drawback: its location in a grim neighbourhood north of Columbia Heights. Luckily, there's a Metro stop a block north. Mon–Thurs & Sun 5pm–1.30am, Fri & Sat 5pm–2.30am.

Millie and Al's 2440 18th St NW; Woodley Park–Zoo Metro. The dive tavern that locals dig and visitors avoid – plenty of cheap beer, not much attitude, and folksy regulars adept at guzzling. Mon–Thurs 4pm–2am, Fri & Sat 4pm–3am.

Toledo Lounge 2435 18th St NW; Woodley Park–Zoo Metro. Cramped and bare-bones café-bar with attitude, with windows looking out on the local street life. The patio seats (best spot for hanging out) are great in summer and the beers and cocktails are cheap, so you can get your brain pickled with ease. Mon–Thurs 6pm–2am, Fri & Sat 6pm–3am.

Shaw

See the **map** on p.145.

Red Room Bar 1811 14th St NW; U Street–Cardozo Metro. Independent, no-cover bar attached to the *Black Cat* music club (see p.227) with red decor, pool, pinball, draught beers, a good jukebox, and amiable, punky clientele. Mon–Thurs & Sun 8pm–2am, Fri & Sat 7pm–3am.

The Saloon 1205 U St NW; U Street–Cardozo Metro. If you want some good Old World beer, this is the spot for you, with plenty of Belgian, German and Austrian brews on offer, and a crowd consisting mostly of beer lovers rather than drunken frat rats or pre-clubbing students. Tues–Thurs 11am–11pm, Fri 11am–2am, Sat 2pm–2am.

Solly's Tavern 1942 11th St ☎202/232-6590; U Street–Cardozo Metro. Convivial neighbour-hood bar that offers cheap beer, regular live music, and soccer and other TV sports, in an area quickly gentrifying with pricier and snootier lounges. Mon–Thurs & Sun 4pm–2am, Fri & Sat 4pm–3am.

Velvet Lounge 915 U St NW ☎202/462-3213; U Street–Cardozo Metro. Schmooze and booze (cheaply) in this relaxed spot, with nightly live music upstairs, including performances by some of DC's brashest and thrashiest up-and-comers. Mon–Thurs 8am–2am, Fri & Sat 8am–3am, Sun 8am–midnight.

Upper Northwest

See the **map** on p.155.

Atomic Billiards 3427 Connecticut Ave NW; Cleveland Park Metro. If you're not interested in chowing down (no food here) but do want to try your hand at darts, pool or shuffleboard, while getting blessedly buzzed, this is a fine spot. Good regular beers and microbrews on tap, sports on TV, and a fine jukebox round out one of the better (basement) bars in Upper Northwest. Mon–Thurs 4pm–2am, Fri & Sat 4pm–3am, Sun 4pm–2am.

Ireland's Four Fields 3412 Connecticut Ave NW ⊕ 202/244-0860; **Cleveland Park Metro.** Rollicking Irish music from Tuesday to Saturday draws a crowd to this otherwise uneventful Irish bar. There are outdoor seats in summer, the usual stews and pies, around a dozen beers on tap, and a friendly neighbourhood-bar atmosphere. Mon–Thurs & Sun 4pm–2am, Fri & Sat 4pm–3am.

Nanny O'Brien's 3319 Connecticut Ave NW ⊕ 202/686-9189; **Cleveland Park Metro.** The other Irish tavern in Cleveland Park, this is a smaller, more personable joint, but with the same successful mix of heavy drinking and live music (usually no cover) without much attitude. Also good for watching sports. Mon–Thurs & Sun noon–2am, Fri & Sat noon–3am.

Zoo Bar 3000 Connecticut Ave NW ⊕ 202/232-4225; **Woodley Park–Zoo Metro.** Timeless dive saloon across from the zoo, with Guinness and microbrews and weekend performances by blues, jazz and Dixieland acts. They also serve food, but it's better to stick with the suds. Mon–Thurs & Sun 11am–2am, Fri & Sat 11am–3am.

Georgetown

See the **map** on p.162.

Birreria Paradiso 3282 M St NW. Downstairs at a branch of Dupont Circle's famed *Pizzeria Paradiso* (see p.210) this supreme touchstone for beer lovers — who come not to get wasted but to sample some eighty bottled beers and various US and European brews, among them some excellent Belgian ales, lambics, stouts and porters. Mon–Thurs 11.30am–11pm, Fri & Sat 11.30am–midnight, Sun noon–10pm.

Degrees 3100 South St, in the Ritz Carlton Hotel (see p.197). A sleek and stylish lounge in a smart hotel whose patrons come for the well-prepared classic cocktails and to nibble on duck spring rolls and foie gras sliders. None of this comes cheap, but it's enough to put swagger in your stagger. Mon, Tues & Sun 2.30–11pm, Wed & Thurs 2.30–11.30pm, Fri & Sat 2.30pm–1.30am.

Garrett's 3003 M St NW. A dive bar geared toward a collegiate crowd, *Garrett's* features a pumping jukebox that keeps the crowd in a party mood, aided by nightly drink specials, along with a few microbrews. Mon–Thurs 11.30am–1.30am, Fri 11.30am–2.30am, Sat noon–2.30am, Sun noon–1.30am.

Mr Smith's 3104 M St NW. Cheap pub grub and a splendid garden drinking-and-eating area, sing-along piano bar (Wed–Sat), and cheap drinks during weekday happy hour make the regulars here give a slurry cheer. Mon–Thurs & Sun 11.30am–2am, Fri & Sat 11.30am–3am.

Sequoia 3000 K St NW. Popular restaurant-bar with one of the best locations in the area – at the eastern end of Washington Harbor – with fine drinks but overpriced and merely adequate food. The main draw is the outdoor terrace seating nicely overlooking the river. Mon–Thurs 11.30am–midnight, Fri & Sat 11.30am–1am.

The Tombs 1226 36th St NW ⊕ 202/337-6668. Busy student haunt adorned with rowing blades. Good for catching college football on Saturday afternoons in autumn or just soaking up the Georgetown vibe. Occasional live bands and club nights. Mon–Thurs 11.30am–1am, Fri & Sat 11am–2am, Sun 9.30am–1am.

Arlington and Northern Virginia

See the **map** on p.173.

Arlington Cinema 'n' Drafthouse 2903 Columbia Pike ⊕ 703/486-2345. A place to take in mid-level national comedy acts and second-run movies, as well as guzzle some decent brews and serviceable pub grub. Daily 11am–2am.

Clarendon Grill 1101 N Highland St; Clarendon Metro. This old favourite is a convenient spot to get plastered since it's right by a Metro stop. Weekend music selections include earnest acoustic strummers, retro cover bands and occasional DJs – but the real focus is drinking and the sport on the HDTV screens. Mon–Thurs 11am–1am, Fri & Sat 11am–2am.

Dogfish Head Alehouse 6220 Leesburg Pike ☎503/534-3342, **Falls Church, VA.** Headquartered in Delaware but with a pub west of Arlington in Falls Church, this is one of the nation's best microbrewers – with regular live music and delicious favourites like the 90-Minute IPA, spicy Raison d'Etre, and the redoubtable Lawnmower summer ale. Mon–Thurs 11.30am–11pm, Fri & Sat 11.30am–midnight, Sun 11.30am–10pm.

Ireland's Four Courts 2051 Wilson Blvd, at N Courthouse Rd ☎703/525-3600; **Court House Metro.** One of the nicest of the area's Irish bars, drawing a cheery Arlington crowd for the live music, dozen beers on tap, decent whiskey selection and filling Irish food. The Metro stop is but a short stagger away. Mon–Sat 11am–2am, Sun 10am–1am.

Mackey's Public House 23rd St and Crystal Drive; Crystal City Metro. A relaxed bar in a prime shopping strip, with hefty Irish food like lamb stew and shepherd's pie, and good old Emerald Isle beers such as Guinness and Harp, plus darts and pool. Also in Downtown DC at 1823 L St NW (Mon–Fri 11.30am–2am, Sat 11.30am–2am). Mon–Sat 11am–2am, Sun 11am–1am.

Whitlow's on Wilson 2854 Wilson Blvd, ☎703/726-9693; **Clarendon Metro.** Neighbourhood retro lounge with good happy-hour drinks and food, plus pool and wraparound bar. Also good for its nightly live music and a better-than-average Sunday brunch. Mon–Fri 11am–2am, Sat & Sun 9am–2am.

Alexandria

See the **map** on p.170.

Bayou Room 219 King St; King Street Metro. You can hear a mix of DJs spinning old-school pop hits from the 80s as well as Latin dance tunes at this divey hangout, but it's best for its cheap beers and cocktails and Cajun-style pub grub in a comfy environment filled with workaday drinkers and only a few hipsters. Above, in *Two Nineteen*, they serve Creole food in a more stylish setting. Mon–Thurs 11am–10.30pm, Fri & Sat 11am–11pm.

Murphy's Grand Irish Pub 713 King St; King Street Metro. Old Town's nightlife buzzes at this boisterous pub, which pours the city's best pint of Guinness. Local solo acts perform upstairs, while a central fireplace and chow like Irish stew and fish and chips add Emerald Isle-style atmosphere. Mon–Thurs & Sun 11am–1am, Fri & Sat 11am–1.30am.

PX 728 King St; King Street Metro. If you're looking to booze in a swanky setting, visit this "speakeasy", where you knock on the blue-lighted door for entry and proceed into the elegant confines of a 1920s-style lounge. The space is cosy (three dozen people max), the prices are outrageous (upwards of $15 per cocktail), but the classic and contemporary cocktails verge on the divine. Wed & Thurs 6pm–midnight, Fri & Sat 7pm–1am.

Shenandoah Brewing Co. 652 S Pickett St ☎703/823-9508; **King Street Metro.** Fine pub and brewing academy, where you can learn how to make your own beer (by appointment) as well as sample good brews like Skyland Red Ale, Stony Man Stout and Old Rag Mountain Ale. Thurs & Fri 4–11pm, Sat 10am–8pm.

Union Street Public House 121 S Union St; King Street Metro. It's hard to miss this sturdy red-brick building with gas lamps: a steak-and-seafood joint that's just as nice for drinking as eating, with its own handcrafted and hearty microbrews. Very popular at weekends. Mon–Thurs 11am–1am, Fri & Sat 11am–1.30am.

Clubs

DC's **club** scene moves at a frenetic pace; check out the *Washington City Paper* or the *Washington Post*'s "Weekend" section for calendars, reviews and ads. Although clubs come and go in all neighbourhoods, DC's trendiest **areas** are up in Shaw, Downtown near the intersection of Connecticut Avenue and 18th Street, and around Dupont Circle. At many places the music and clientele can change radically on different nights, so you might want to call to confirm the line-up before heading out.

Plenty of spots have low **cover charges**, generally between $5 and $20 (highest on weekends), and some have none at all. Upscale lounges and clubs are most likely to charge a steeper cover, and more often than not they have vague and at times completely arbitrary dress codes; if you avoid athletic gear, sneakers, flip-flops and baseball caps, you'll greatly enhance your standing with the guardians of the velvet ropes – though at some places, merely being male may be enough to keep you out on evenings when the club decides to enforce a female-leaning two-to-one ratio, or more.

Opening hours vary wildly from night to night, and can change randomly from month to month. Generally, clubs are open from Thursday to Sunday, don't get going until well after 11pm and stay open until at least 2am, with some continuing (especially at weekends) until 5am. If you're going to be out this late, have a taxi number with you, since some clubs are in dubious parts of town where walking around in the wee hours invites trouble. Also remember to take **photo ID** or your passport with you; you won't get into many places without one. Lastly, you must be at least 21 to drink alcohol in DC; if you're younger than that, check the local listings for an all-ages club – they do open occasionally, though usually without much success.

Downtown

See the **map** on p.134.

Eighteenth Street Lounge 1212 18th St NW ☎202/518-9820; Dupont Circle or Farragut North Metro. Ultra-cool, multi-level spot housed in Teddy Roosevelt's former mansion, behind an unmarked door. While the attitude can be a bit much, the DJs on the dancefloor level are a big draw, along with weekend live jazz. Dress smart and come early (before 10pm) to avoid the cover and queue.

Josephine 1008 Vermont Ave NW ☎202/347-8601; McPherson Square Metro. Fun club with highly stylized decor (like an antique furniture store on LSD) and a broad blend of patrons and hip-hop, pop and electronica. You do pay for the arty design, though, as the cover and price of drinks are among the highest in the area.

The Park at Fourteenth 920 14th St NW, ☎202/737-7275; McPherson Square Metro. Diverse crowd, smart decor and a good happy hour and decent food make this club-lounge one of the chicer places to enjoy an evening of dancing and boozing. Four floors and a variety of soundscapes add to the appeal (though cover can reach $20 at weekends).

Dupont Circle

See the **map** on p.134.

Aura Lounge 1837 M St NW ☎703/850-4619; Dupont Circle Metro. Fairly new and pricey club that offers sofas and cabanas to its guests and serves up a range of retro, hip-hop and the like indoors, with an outdoor patio offering ambient and other electronica, with some live music too.

FAB Lounge 1805 Connecticut Ave NW, ☎202/797-1122; Dupont Circle Metro. North of the main Dupont action, this neighbourhood club offers nightly dancing and a mixed gay and straight crowd. Eclectic music includes retro-pop, hip-hop and electronica. One of the better (among the few) choices for clubbing near the Kalorama Triangle.

Adams Morgan

See the **map** on p.145.

District 2473 18th St NW ☎202/725-0502; Woodley Park–Zoo Metro. More attitude than usual at this Adams Morgan club on the south side of the area, which is a velvet-rope scene where the beautiful people go to dance to chart music. Despite the name, this is more LA than DC, but worth a visit to see the local honeybees abuzz.

Heaven & Hell 2327 18th St NW ☎202/667-4355; Woodley Park–Zoo or Dupont Circle Metro. While Hell (downstairs) would have trouble making Dante's hit list, Heaven features techno and other dance music, and the entire place is a fairly libidinous, cologne-drenched affair.

Shaw

See the **map** on p.145.

Chi Cha Lounge 1624 U St NW ☎202/333-9232; U Street–Cardozo Metro. Swanky candlelit lounge oozing atmosphere, with DJs spinning house, pop, hip-hop and retro sets and regulars toking on fruit-cured tobacco from Middle Eastern-style hookahs. Sink into a sofa and sample some decent Andean tapas, too.

 Fatback 2001 11th St NW ☎202/299-0801; **U Street-Cardozo Metro.** Sweaty, crowded showcase for some of the city's best dancers, who can gyrate to nearly everything the DJ can throw at them. The young crowd and intense vibe, plus the pounding electronica, funk and hip-hop, make this a mainstay on the DC club scene, and well worth a visit if you have plenty of energy.

U Street Music Hall 1115 U St NW ☎202/588-1880; **U Street-Cardozo Metro.** Frenetic, youth-oriented club where the DJs spin your techno and hip-hop favourites with a top-notch sound system. Great fun, especially if you can keep up with the club kids.

Georgetown

See the **map** on p.162.

Modern 3287 M St NW ☎202/338-7027. If you're young and looking for a fun meat market, this smart lounge and club will do, boasting a stylish bar and mod decor as well as a mix of hip-hop, house and other beats.

Third Edition 1218 Wisconsin Ave NW ☎202/333-3700. Gung-ho college scene with second-floor dance club featuring DJs playing hip-hop and electro-pop, and periodic live music. It's a frenzied under-25 cattle market on weekends, when you'll probably have to wait in line and pay a cover.

Live music

The **live music** scene in Washington may surprise outsiders expecting an uninspiring selection of piano bars and lacklustre concert halls. If you want to see the "official" side of culture in the District, there are plenty of opportunities at spots like the Kennedy Center and Constitution Hall (see box, pp.230–231), but if you're really interested in head-banging, slam-dancing or otherwise shaking your ass with abandon, the city has plenty of good choices. It isn't New York or LA, but DC is cool enough to have venues run by indie-rock superstars (like Dave Grohl of the Foo Fighters) and a number of classic joints that have left a mark on rock, jazz and even punk history. **Jazz and blues** clubs are the most common across the city, while **country and folk** venues are mainly found across the water in Virginia; **rock and pop** in Arlington, Adams Morgan and Shaw; and **salsa and Latin** offerings in the latter two neighbourhoods. Check local listings for opening times, cover charges and ticket prices, which can vary widely depending on the night and the act.

Jazz and blues

 Blues Alley 1073 Wisconsin Ave NW (at Blues Alley), Georgetown ☎202/337-4141, ⓦbluesalley.com. See map, p.162. This small, celebrated Georgetown jazz bar has been in business for over forty years and attracts top names in R&B, blues and mainstream jazz. Two shows a night, plus one at midnight some weekends; cover can run to $50. Book in advance.

Bohemian Caverns 2003 11th St NW, Shaw ☎202/299-0800, ⓦwww.bohemiancaverns.com. U Street–Cardozo Metro. See map, p.145.

Legendary DC jazz supper club. The jazz happens in a basement grotto, below the stylish ground-level restaurant. Cover runs to $20 or more, with a limited number of reserved tickets for bigger acts.

Columbia Station 2325 18th St NW, Adams Morgan ☎202/462-6040, ⓦwww.columbia stationdc.com; Woodley Park–Zoo or Dupont Circle Metro. See map, p.145. One of the better places in the area to listen to live jazz and blues, presented nightly in a sophisticated supper-club setting.

HR-57 1610 14th St NW, Logan Circle ☎202/667-3700, ⓦwww.hr57.org; Dupont Circle Metro. See map, p.134. Small but authentic club where jazz in many of its manifestations – classic, hard bop, free and avant-garde – is performed by ardent professionals as well as newcomers on their way up. Also jam nights on Wed, Thurs & Sun. One of the essential cultural spots in this gentrifying neighbourhood.

Laporta's 1600 Duke St, Alexandria ☎703/683-6313, ⓦwww.laportas.net; King Street Metro. See map, p.178. Classy seafood restaurant with a good range of jazz acts performing nightly, everything from Dixieland and big band to bebop and scat to fusion and even a bit of gospel.

Madam's Organ 2461 18th St NW, Adams Morgan ☎202/667-5370, ⓦwww.madams organ.com; Woodley Park–Zoo Metro. See map, p.145. Notable three-level club that has a fine rep for showcasing a variety of live blues, grinding, raw R&B, and the odd bluegrass band, plus some rib-sticking soul food and generous cocktails. Upstairs, there's a pool table and a rooftop bar.

Ragtime 1345 N Courthouse Rd, Arlington ☎703/243-4003, ⓦragtimerestaurant.com; Court House Metro. See map, p.173. Relaxed bar-and-grill offering live music several nights a week, often in the blues and soul or New Orleans jazz vein.

The Saloun 3239 M St NW, Georgetown ☎202/965-4900. See map, p.162. Cosy bar with a huge range of bottled beers and nightly jazz trios or bands, plus occasional r'n'b and soul acts. Cheap drinks mean the college kids swarm to this joint.

Takoma Station Tavern 6914 4th St NW, Takoma Park, MD ☎202/829-1999, ⓦwww .takomastation.com; Takoma Metro. Laid-back club with live jazz and blues Wed–Sun, showcasing mostly local acts to an older crowd. On some evenings reggae

acts, comedians or other acts take the spotlight.

Twins Jazz 1344 U St NW, Shaw ☎202/234-0072, ⓦwww.twinsjazz.com; U Street–Cardozo Metro. See map, p.145. Celebrated jazz haunt drawing talented musicians most nights and for its free-spirited, regular jam sessions. Also serves decent Ethiopian, American and Caribbean food.

Rock and pop

9:30 Club 815 V St NW, Shaw ☎202/265-0930, ⓦwww.930.com; U St–Cardozo Metro. See map, p.145. If you have even the slightest interest in seeing an indie rock concert in the District, you'll probably find yourself at this top-shelf venue for national names. Tickets cost anything from $5 to $50. There's also a good upstairs bar – one of three in the complex.

Black Cat 1811 14th St NW, Shaw ☎202/667-7960, ⓦwww.blackcatdc.com; U St–Cardozo Metro. See map, p.145. Part-owned by Foo Fighter Dave Grohl, this all-ages indie institution provides a showcase for veteran alternative acts and up-and-coming rock, punk and garage bands alike, plus a sprinkling of world beat and retro-pop performers. Also check out the attached *Red Room Bar* (see p.222).

Chief Ike's Mambo Room 1725 Columbia Rd NW, Adams Morgan ☎202/332-2211, ⓦwww .chiefikes.com; Woodley Park–Zoo or Dupont Circle Metro. See map, p.145. Ramshackle mural-clad bar with live bands playing rock, reggae and r'n'b or DJs hosting theme nights of the retro-pop or hip-hop variety.

Clarendon Grill 1101 N Highland St, Arlington ☎703/524-7455, ⓦwww.cgrill.com; Clarendon Metro. See map, p.173. Old favourite for boozing, and something of a pick-up joint. Musical offerings include earnest acoustic strummers, alternative rockers and pop tribute bands.

Galaxy Hut 2711 Wilson Blvd, Arlington ☎703/525-8646, ⓦwww.galaxyhut.com; Clarendon Metro. See map, p.173. A regular line-up of interesting local indie rockers takes the stage nightly at this tiny neighbourhood hangout, with a bevy of beers on tap.

IOTA 2832 Wilson Blvd, Arlington ☎703/522-8340, ⓦwww.iotaclubandcafe.com; Clarendon Metro. See map, p.173. One of the area's best choices for music, this warehouse-style joint has nightly performances by local and national indie rock, folk and blues bands.

BARS AND CLUBS | Live music

There's a great bar and attached restaurant, too. Cover usually $12–20.

Rock and Roll Hotel 1353 H St NE, east of Capitol Hill ☎ 202/388-7625, ⓦ www .rockandrollhoteldc.com; no close Metro. See map, p.75. Midsize concert venue that hosts a variety of regional rockers (who can crash in the few overnight rooms), with a good sound system and cool crowd. It's in a rather dicey neighbourhood two miles east of Union Station, so take a taxi.

Folk, country and eclectic

Birchmere 3701 Mount Vernon Ave, Alexandria ☎ 703/549-7500, ⓦ www .birchmere.com; no nearby Metro. See map, p.178. Excellent, long-standing club with some of the region's (and nation's) best names in acoustic, folk, and mainstream and alternative country music, as well as some up-and-comers.

J.V.'s Restaurant 6666 Arlington Blvd, Falls Church, VA ☎ 703/241-9504, ⓦ www .jvsrestaurant.com. Favourite honky-tonk joint that's a local haunt for its mix of live folk, country, bluegrass and rock, and some open-mic nights – though located some way from DC.

New Vegas Lounge 1415 P St NW, Logan Circle ☎ 202/483-3971, ⓦ www.newvegasloungedc .com; Dupont Circle Metro. See map, p.134. Neighbourhood favourite that offers jazz, blues, raunchy Chicago R&B, 1970s soul and other favourites in a decidedly funky setting. Cover can go up to $15 for some acts.

State Theatre 220 N Washington St, Falls Church, VA ☎ 703/237-0300, ⓦ www.thestate theatre.com. Suburban venue in a stylish former moviehouse that rewards a drive out if you like country, folk or blues. Sometimes it mixes things up with 1980s pop-rockers and novelty acts as well.

Tiffany Tavern 1116 King St, Alexandria ☎ 703/836-8844, ⓦ www.tiffanytavern.com; King Street Metro. See map, p.178. This Old Town haunt hosts open-mic nights during the week, but at weekends it's all about bluegrass and its folk-flavoured local and regional performers.

Salsa and Latin American

Bossa 2463 18th St NW, Adams Morgan ☎ 202/667-0088, ⓦ www.bossaproject.com; Woodley Park–Zoo Metro. See map, p.145. A range of terrific salsa, samba, bossa nova and other Latin genres, along with jazz from traditional to modern, is the main draw at this engaging club (which also offers an upstairs lounge where DJs spin hip-hop and electronica tunes), together with a menu of decent tapas.

Habana Village 1834 Columbia Rd NW, Adams Morgan ☎ 202/462-6310, ⓦ www.habanavillage .com; Woodley Park–Zoo or Dupont Circle Metro. See map, p.145. Intoxicating Latin-dance joint spread over two floors with the eclectic spirit of the Adams Morgan of old. Cuban and Afro-Cuban rhythms are prominent, and tango and salsa too (with dance lessons available), and a good downstairs lounge/ bar serves a fine mojito.

Latin Jazz Alley 1721 Columbia Rd NW, Adams Morgan ☎ 202/328-6190; Woodley Park–Zoo Metro. See map, p.145. Smallish spot where you can set your groove to the rhythms of salsa, merengue, rumba or bossa nova, with Latin jazz at weekends and dancing lessons nightly.

Rumba Cafe 2443 18th St NW, Adams Morgan ☎ 202/588-5501, ⓦ www.rumbacafe.com; Woodley Park–Zoo Metro. See map, p.145. A Latin oasis, this sliver of a café-bar, its walls crammed with paintings and photo-graphs, is a good bet for a night of sipping caipirinhas and grooving to live Brazilian bossa nova and Afro-Cuban rhythms.

Performing arts and film

Washington's **high culture** is supported by a formidable institutional regime second only to New York's in government funding, prestige and media exposure. Indeed, the city's cultural beacons – from its concert halls to its award ceremonies – regularly make appearances on public television and radio, giving the impression that after a performer makes it in DC, he or she is a living legend on the road to national canonization.

The city's most prominent institution is the **John F. Kennedy Center for the Performing Arts** – popularly known as the Kennedy Center – encompassing a concert hall, opera house, theatres and other elements. Home to the National Symphony Orchestra, it stages seasonal productions by the city's top opera and ballet companies, and also hosts national and international artists, companies and ensembles. The other main artistic promoter in town is the **Washington Performing Arts Society** (WPAS; ☎202/833-9800, ⓦwww.wpas.org), which sponsors classical music, ballet and dance productions across the city.

A host of **smaller theatres** and **performance spaces** dedicated to contemporary, experimental, ethnic or offbeat productions offers a good alternative to these

Tickets

Prices vary considerably according to the event or production. You can expect to shell out a lot for the high-profile events at the Kennedy Center, National Theatre and the like, but many places offer half- or cut-price tickets on the day of the performance if there's space. In all instances it's worth a call to the box office; students (with ID), senior citizens, military personnel and people with disabilities qualify for **discounts** in most theatres and concert halls. You can also buy tickets over the phone from various **ticket agencies**, which sell advance-reserved, full-price tickets (plus surcharge). Usually no changes or refunds are allowed.

Tickets.com ☎1-800/955-5566, ⓦwww.tickets.com. Full-price tickets for events, by phone or online, with a service charge.

Ticketmaster ☎1-800/551-7328, ⓦwww.ticketmaster.com. Full-price tickets for events, by phone or online, with a service charge.

TicketPlace, 407 Seventh St NW, Downtown ☎202/393-2161, ⓦwww.ticketplace .org. On-the-day, **half-price** (plus ten percent surcharge) cash-only tickets for theatre and music performances. Not all tickets are available online — some are walk-in only. Ticket booth sales Wed–Fri 11am–6pm, Sat 10am–5pm, Sun noon–4pm.

establishment venues, as tickets tend to be cheaper (and more readily available). **Comedy clubs** have made some headway in the District in recent years, while the city's **moviehouses** present a range of interesting fare – foreign to indie to avant-garde – that you might not find in the blander suburban multiplexes.

To find out **what's on** in any of these categories, consult the Friday edition of the *Washington Post* (Ⓦwww.washingtonpost.com), the monthly *Washingtonian* (Ⓦwww.washingtonian.com) or the free, weekly *City Paper* (Ⓦwww.washington citypaper.com). Look out too for flyers and posters in bookshops and cafés.

Classical music, opera and dance

Classical music, **opera** and **dance** are well represented in the nation's capital: Symphonic classical music is performed at the Kennedy Center and at other big concert halls, while concerts and ensembles take place in a variety of major venues (see box below) in and outside the city.

Tickets for these big-name concerts tend to be pricey ($25–100) and need to be purchased in advance, either direct from the venues or from one of the major ticket agencies (see box, p.229). Because costs tend to vary considerably, you're

---

Major concert venues

The big-name **concert venues** in DC and beyond are scattered all over the place. If you plan on squeezing a lot of shows into your itinerary, be sure to factor in ample time for travel and traffic. Prices vary broadly according to the venue and the nature of the programme. For more details, call the box office numbers listed below, or Ticketmaster, Tickets.com or TicketPlace (see box, p.229).

In the District

Carter Barron Amphitheater 4850 Colorado Ave NW, Upper Northwest ☎202/426-0486; no close Metro. Popular summer amphitheatre in Rock Creek Park that offers a mix of free and ticketed events, including rock, pop and blues concerts, dance, theatre and classical-music performances, and much more.

DAR Constitution Hall 1776 D St NW, Foggy Bottom ☎202/628-4780, Ⓦwww .dar.org/conthall; Farragut West Metro. Widely known as the best concert hall in the city, before its title was usurped in the 1960s by the Kennedy Center. Now the 4000-seat auditorium mostly hosts mainstream concerts of pop, country and jazz acts.

Kennedy Center 2700 F St NW, Foggy Bottom ☎202/467-4600, Ⓦwww.kennedy -center.org; Foggy Bottom–GWU Metro. The National Symphony Orchestra performs in the 2800-seat Concert Hall, the Washington Opera in the Opera House, and opera, ballet and dance troupes in the Eisenhower Theater; there are less expensive chamber recitals in the Terrace Theater. See also p.229.

Lincoln Theatre 1215 U St NW, Shaw ☎202/328-6000, Ⓦwww.thelincolntheatre .org; U Street–Cardozo Metro. Renovated movie/vaudeville house featuring touring stage shows; pop, jazz, soul and gospel concerts; and dance, with a focus on multicultural productions.

Lisner Auditorium George Washington University, 730 21st St NW, Foggy Bottom ☎202/994-6800, Ⓦwww.lisner.org; Foggy Bottom–GWU Metro. A 1500-seat auditorium with regular classical and choral concerts on campus. Comedy, rock, pop and indie acts also take the stage, along with popular lecturers.

National Theatre 1321 Pennsylvania Ave NW, Downtown ☎202/628-6161, Ⓦwww .nationaltheatre.org; Metro Centre Metro. One of the country's oldest theatres, on this

encouraged to visit each site's or company's website to check ticket prices for each event. As a rule, performances at the major venues will cost $25 or more for anything resembling a decent seat. However, free shows at other DC concert halls – just like exhibitions at DC museums – often tend to be free, and where this is the case we've noted it below.

Classical music

The Concert Hall of the Kennedy Center (see box below), home of the National Symphony Orchestra, is the most prestigious spot in town for **classical music**, and DAR Constitution Hall (see box below) is another long-standing favourite. The **armed forces** have their own ensembles, which tend to be quite accomplished and more varied in their repertoire than you might expect. Groups play weekly during the summer in front of the US Capitol; the big names (Navy and Marine bands) are listed below, but the Army (☎703/696-3399, ⓦwww .usarmyband.com) and the Air Force (☎202/767-5658, ⓦwww.usafband .af.mil) also have a solid reputation, and perform throughout the region.

Aside from the **major companies**, there are any number of **small venues**, hosting all manner of classical performers, from virtuosi-in-training on college campuses to church choirs

site (if not in this building) since 1835. Today, it features flashy premieres, pre- and post-Broadway productions and musicals. In the summer, it also hosts movie revivals.

Verizon Center 601 F St NW, Downtown ☎202/628-3200, ⓦwww.verizoncenter .com; Gallery Place–Chinatown Metro. This 20,000-seater hosts big-name rock, pop and country gigs.

Warner Theatre 1299 Pennsylvania Ave NW, Downtown ☎202/783-4000, ⓦwww .warnertheatre.com; Metro Center Metro. Glorious 1920s movie palace that's been remodelled and is now staging post-Broadway productions, musicals and major concerts.

Outside the District

FedEx Field 1600 FedEx Way, Landover, MD ☎301/276-6050. The 91,000-seat football stadium hosts the Washington Redskins and occasional summer pop and rock concerts.

Jiffy Lube Live 7800 Cellar Door Drive, Bristow, VA ☎703/754-6400, ⓦwww.livenation .com. Outdoor summer stadium (25,000 seats) plays host to many of the major summer tours, though a bit removed from DC out near Manassas, VA.

Merriweather Post Pavilion 10475 Little Patuxent Parkway, Columbia, MD ☎410/715-5550, ⓦwww.merriweathermusic.com. Mid-level and major pop, jazz, country and mainstream rockers perform in spring and summer only. There's pavilion and open-air seating.

Patriot Center George Mason University, Fairfax, VA ☎703/993-3000, ⓦwww .patriotcenter.com. A 10,000-seat venue for big concerts and family entertainment.

Strathmore Music Center 10701 Rockville Pike, North Bethesda, MD ☎301/581-5100, ⓦwww.strathmore.org; Grosvenor-Strathmore Metro. This striking multi-building venue includes a nineteenth-century mansion, and is the occasional home to the Baltimore Symphony Orchestra and National Philharmonic, as well as performances of musicals and pop, folk, jazz and world-beat concerts.

Wolf Trap Farm Park 1624 Trap Rd, Vienna, VA ☎703/255-1868 or 255-1900, ⓦwww.wolftrap.org. US Park Service gem plays host to a variety of jazz, country, folk, zydeco and pop acts. See box, p.177.

(Washington National Cathedral; see p.157), to chamber musicians giving concerts in museums (Corcoran Gallery of Art; see p.104), historic houses (Dumbarton House; see p.169) and embassies. For details about Smithsonian Institution concerts, call ☎202/357-2700, or check ⓦwww.si.edu.

Major companies

Choral Arts Society of Washington 5225 Wisconsin Ave NW, Suite 603 ☎202/244-3669, ⓦwww.choralarts.org. The District's major choir, performing at the Kennedy Center, Wolf Trap and other region-wide locations. Offers traditional pieces (mainly classical and Romantic) and seasonal favourites, especially at Christmas.

Friday Morning Music Club 2233 Wisconsin Ave NW, Suite 326 ☎202/333-2075, ⓦwww.fmmc .org. Long-standing cultural group (est. 1886) that gives performances of classical, Romantic and contemporary pieces by major composers. Performs primarily at the Charles Sumner School (see p.135) and Strathmore Center, as well as at churches and Dumbarton House (see p.169).

National Symphony Orchestra 2700 F St NW ☎1-800/444-1324, ⓦwww.kennedy-center.org /nso; Foggy Bottom–GWU Metro. Performs in the Kennedy Center, serving up the big names in classical music under the baton of conductor Christoph Eschenbach, along with guest conductors. Tickets to perform-ances run from $20 to $95, though the orchestra also performs free outside the Capitol on the West Terrace on Memorial Day, July 4 and Labor Day.

US Marine Band 8th and I St SE, Marine Barracks ☎202/433-4011 or 433-6060, ⓦwww .marineband.usmc.mil. The oldest professional music organization in the country (dating from 1798) and an accomplished vehicle for all kinds of classical music – John Philip Sousa was a legendary director. Smaller ensembles perform folk and jazz, and there are also autumn and winter chamber recitals. All concerts are free, though advance tickets are required.

US Navy Band 617 Warrington Ave, Navy Yard SE ☎202/433-2525, ⓦwww.navyband.navy.mil. Offers free weekly summer concerts at the US Capitol and Navy Memorial (see p.117), with six different performing groups and eight chamber ensembles. Genres range widely, from sea shanties and drum-corps pieces to jazz, big-band, country and bluegrass – even rock and R&B. The classical-oriented Concert Band has been going strong for 85 years and receives the most publicity.

Washington Performing Arts Society 2000 L St NW, Suite 510 ☎202/833-9800, tickets ☎202/785-9727, ⓦwww.wpas.org. Coordinator of high-cultural events that puts together shows at DC's most prominent venues and offers ticket packages based on the buyer's interests. Categories (and prices) range widely from jazz to world beat to dance, and the schedule usually includes at least three to five classical shows per month.

Small venues

Arts Club of Washington 2017 I St NW, Foggy Bottom ☎202/331-7282, ⓦwww.artsclubof washington.org; Foggy Bottom–GWU Metro. Based in a historic Federal house where President James Monroe lived briefly in 1817, the club presents free Friday concerts at noon (Feb–July), tending toward chamber music and solo recitals.

Coolidge Auditorium Ground floor of Jefferson Building, Library of Congress, 1st St and Independence Ave SE, Capitol Hill ☎202/707-5502, ⓦwww.loc.gov; Capitol South Metro. Chamber music concerts in a historic venue (see p.84). Free, advance tickets are required.

Folger Shakespeare Library 201 E Capitol St SE, Capitol Hill ☎202/544-7077, ⓦwww.folger.edu; Capitol South Metro. Medieval and Renais-sance music in the Library's Elizabethan Theatre from the Folger Consort ensemble. Usually performs one series of concerts per month.

National Academy of Sciences 2101 C St NW, Foggy Bottom ☎202/334-2436, ⓦwww .nationalacademies.org/arts; Foggy Bottom–GWU Metro. Appealing 700-seat auditorium with free chamber recitals, often monthly from October to April. Building renovation means concerts have been put on hold until 2012.

National Gallery of Art West Building, West Garden Court, Constitution Ave NW at 7th St ☎202/842-6941, ⓦwww.nga.gov; Archives–Navy Memorial Metro. Free concerts every Sunday at 6.30pm (Sept–June) in the lovely West Garden Court, with seats available on a first-come, first-served basis. Also jazz performances in summer.

Phillips Collection 1600 21st St NW; Dupont Circle ☎202/387-2151, ⓦwww.phillips collection.org; Dupont Circle Metro. Classical music concerts in the museum's Music Room (Oct–May Sun 4pm); free with museum admission (see p.141). Arrive early.

Society of the Cincinnati at Anderson House 2118 Massachusetts Ave NW, Dupont Circle ☎202/785-2040, ⓦwww.societyofthecincinnati .org; Dupont Circle Metro. Free chamber recitals once a month (usually Sat at 1.30pm) in fine mansion surroundings (see p.140).

Opera

The District's version of **opera** involves one institutional heavyweight supported by a few smaller companies.

Bel Cantanti 6126 Montrose Rd, Rockville, MD ☎301/266-7546, ⓦwww.belcantanti.com. Affordable, minor-league troupe devoted to resurrecting lesser-known pieces by major composers and dusting them off for a rapt group of fans. Tickets are a bit cheaper than at Washington National Opera, though you'll have to go to the Maryland suburbs to take in a show.

Opera Camerata 1819 Shepherd St NW, Suite 100 ☎202/380-0008, ⓦwww.operacamerata .org. Small institution that offers thrice-yearly concerts of mostly the German and Italian warhorses of the genre. Rotating venues.

Victorian Lyric Opera Company ☎301/576-5672, ⓦwww.vloc.org. If it's operetta you're after, consider this regional troupe that principally highlights the works of Gilbert and Sullivan, as well as the frothier works of Donizetti, Mozart and other classical composers. Three operettas performed per year, in rotating venues in Rockville, MD.

Washington National Opera ☎202/295-2400 or 1-800/876-7372, ⓦwww.dc-opera.org. Tickets for one of the country's finest resident opera companies sell out well in advance, though you may get standing-room tickets at the box office. Performances are mainly Romantic European heavyweights, staged in the Opera House and the other Kennedy Center theatres. The season runs from September to June.

Dance

You can find **dance** in any number of good Washington venues, from ballet to hip-hop and from international stylings at the various Smithsonian institutions (check ⓦwww.si.edu) to avant-garde pieces put on by modern-art galleries and museums.

Dance Institute of Washington 3400 14th St NW ☎202/371-9656, ⓦwww.danceinstitute.org. Presents monthly performances at major venues in DC, Maryland and Virginia, and offers a range of dance classes.

The Dance Place 3225 8th St NE, Brookland ☎202/269-1600, ⓦwww.danceplace.org; Brookland Metro. Contemporary and modern dance productions, mainstream and

Free open-air concerts

Summer is a good time to catch a free **open-air concert** in Washington, though certain locations host events all year round. Ask at the visitor centre (see p.38) and see DC's festival calendar (Chapter 15) for more information.

Freedom Plaza Pennsylvania Ave NW. Year-round venue for folk events and music festivals.

National Zoological Park Connecticut Ave NW. Summer concerts featuring a variety of performances.

Netherlands Carillon Marine Corps (Iwo Jima) War Memorial, Arlington. Regular performances of rousing patriotic tunes and summer concerts by US Marine Band.

Sylvan Theatre Washington Monument grounds. Army, Air Force, Navy and Marine Corps bands perform during the summer.

US Capitol Armed forces bands perform in summer on the East Terrace, and the National Symphony Orchestra puts on concerts on the West Terrace on Memorial Day, July 4 and Labor Day.

US Navy Memorial 701 Pennsylvania Ave NW. Spring and summer concert series featuring Navy, Marine Corps, Coast Guard and high-school bands.

experimental, with a bent toward African- and African American-themed shows.
EDGEWORKS Dance Theater ☏ 202/483-0606, ⓦ www.hjwedgeworks.org. Pioneering, highly regarded troupe of African American men exploring racial, emotional, social and sexual topics in rotating venues around town, notably at the Kennedy Center.
Momentum Dance Theatre 651 E St NE, Capitol Hill ☏ 202/785-0035, ⓦ www.momentumdance theatre.com. Small troupe presenting inventive spins on the classics (such as a

jazz hip-hop *Nutcracker*) and jazz- and modern-oriented productions, often with a satiric twist. Irregular shows take place throughout the year at regional venues.
Washington Ballet 3515 Wisconsin Ave NW ☏ 202/362-3606 or 467-4600, ⓦ www .washingtonballet.org. Classical and contemporary ballet performed in rep by the city's major ballet company at the Kennedy Center. Every December *The Nutcracker* is performed at the Warner Theatre.

Theatre

As with other performing arts, **theatre** in the District has proven to be a revitalizing force for many formerly down-at-heel neighbourhoods, with areas from Adams Morgan to Logan Circle to the Penn Quarter experiencing a cultural boost that is at least partially thanks to the presence of independent theatres and troupes. Major-league shows also have a presence, with most Broadway productions either previewing or touring in Washington. Either way, there's often something engaging playing on any given night, and usually at a Metro-accessible location. As with other arts, ticket prices and policies vary depending on the event and location; call for details.

National Mall and around

Discovery Theater at Ripley Center, 1100 Jefferson Drive SW, National Mall ☏ 202/633-8700, ⓦ www.discoverytheater.org; Smithsonian Metro. Children's theatre (see box, p.250).

Capitol Hill and around

Atlas Performing Arts Center 1333 H St NE ☏ 202/399-7993, ⓦ www.atlasarts.org; no close Metro. A fascinating grab bag of theatre, dance, music, comedy and cabaret helps this performing-arts venue enliven an up-and-coming, if still seedy, part of town east of Capitol Hill.
Folger Shakespeare Library 201 E Capitol St SE ☏ 202/544-7077, ⓦ www.folger.edu; Capitol South Metro. A programme of three or four annual works is presented at the Elizabethan Theatre (Sept–June), not solely Shakespeare, but often including his contemporaries and later playwrights as well.
H Street Playhouse 1365 H St NE ☏ 1-866/811-4111, ⓦ www.hstreetplayhouse.com. A stately little gem from 1928 that used to be a car showroom, with a dramatic mix of topical and contemporary offerings from a variety of troupes. Take a taxi since it's not far from a down-and-out quarter.

Southwest Waterfront

Arena Stage 1101 6th St SW, Southwest Waterfront ☏ 202/488-3300, ⓦ www.arenastage.org; Waterfront Metro. One of the most popular and well-respected of DC's major theatrical institutions. In many ways the dramatic juggernaut in town, especially since reopening in a sleekly modern and inspiring building in late 2010. Multiple stages, events and troupes.

Foggy Bottom

Kennedy Center 2700 F St NW, at Virginia and New Hampshire Ave, Foggy Bottom ☏ 202/467-4600, ⓦ www.kennedy-center.org; Foggy Bottom–GWU Metro. The institutional heavyweight in town offers three dedicated theatres: the Eisenhower (drama and Broadway productions), the Terrace (experimental/contemporary works) and the smallish Theater Lab (eclectic).

Downtown

Ford's Theatre 511 10th St NW ☏ 202/347-4833, ⓦ www.fordstheatre.org; Metro Center Metro. The legendary site of Lincoln's assassination (see box, pp.266–267), this

(13)

restored nineteenth-century theatre stages mainstream musicals and dramas; newly renovated and well worth a visit.

GALA Hispanic Theatre 3333 14th St NW ☎ 202/234-7174, ⓦ www.galatheatre.org; Columbia Heights Metro. Specializes in works by Spanish-language playwrights, performed in Spanish or English, as well as performance art and poetry. Operates out of the classic Tivoli Theatre in Columbia Heights; see p.147.

National Theatre 1321 Pennsylvania Ave NW ☎ 202/628-6161, ⓦ www.nationaltheatre.org; Metro Center Metro. A classic American theatre dating to 1835. Expect to see premieres, pre- and post-Broadway productions and musicals.

Shakespeare Theatre in the Lansburgh building, 450 7th St NW ☎ 202/547-1122, ⓦ www .shakespearetheatre.org; Gallery Place–Chinatown Metro. Seven annual plays by Shakespeare and his contemporaries, along with the odd newer work. Each June the company stages free, outdoor performances at the Carter Barron Amphitheatre in Rock Creek Park (see box, p.230).

Source Theatre 1835 14th St NW ☎ 202/462-1073, ⓦ www.sourcedc.org; U Street–Cardozo Metro. New and contemporary works and classic reinterpretations. Promotes the Source Festival, a showcase for new, ultra-short works (10 minutes or so), every summer. Take a taxi here at night.

Studio Theatre 1501 14th St NW ☎ 202/332-3300, ⓦ www.studiotheatre.org. Independent theatre with two stages presenting classic and contemporary drama as well as comedy.

Warner Theatre 1299 Pennsylvania Ave NW ☎ 202/783-4000, ⓦ www.warnertheatre.com; Metro Center Metro. Beautifully renovated 1920s movie palace now staging

post-Broadway plays, musicals and major concerts.

Woolly Mammoth Theatre 641 D St NW ☎ 202/289-2443, ⓦ www.woollymammoth.net; Archives–Navy Memorial Metro. Popular theatre troupe that stages budget- and mid-priced productions of contemporary and experimental plays.

Adams Morgan and Shaw

DC Arts Center 2438 18th St NW, Adams Morgan ☎ 202/462-7833, ⓦ www.dcartscenter.org; Woodley Park–Zoo Metro. Performance art, drama, poetry, dance, and a whole range of multicultural activities are held in this space, which includes an art gallery and small theatre.

Lincoln Theatre 1215 U St NW, Shaw ☎ 202/328-6000, ⓦ www.thelincolntheatre.org; U Street–Cardozo Metro. Renovated movie/ vaudeville house features touring stage shows, concerts and dance, with a focus on musicals and multicultural productions.

Arlington

Gunston Arts Center 2700 S Lang St ☎ 703/228-1850, ⓦ www.arlingtonarts.org. Featuring two theatres – a proscenium stage and smaller "black box", hosting a range of drama, novelties and cultural events from local and regional troupes.

Rosslyn Spectrum 1611 N Kent St ☎ 703/276-6701; Rosslyn Metro. A good venue for theatre, concerts and cultural events, offering a mix of classics and new plays.

Signature Theatre 4200 Campbell Ave ☎ 703/820-9771, ⓦ www.signature-theatre.org. Theatrical group putting on premieres of new works, as well as revivals of classics and musicals, and irreverent adaptations of them.

Comedy

When it comes to **comedy**, several clubs offer the usual mix of big-name stand-up acts, improv, local or regional circuit appearances, and open-mic nights. Keep an eye out, too, for comedy troupes that appear in cabaret or improv shows at various venues around town, including big hotels.

Performances can be expensive, since there's often a drinks-and-food minimum charge on top of the ticket price. A big weekend show can cost as much as $50, though tickets for basic stand-up and improv nights are more like $15. Reservations for the big names are essential.

Capitol Steps Ronald Reagan Building and International Trade Center, 1300 Pennsylvania Ave NW, Downtown ☎202/408-8736 or 683-8330, ⓦwww.capsteps.com; Metro Center Metro. Well-established political satire by a group of Capitol Hill staffers on Fri and Sat nights at 7.30pm. It's a tourist favourite, so book well ahead.

The Comedy Spot 4238 Wilson Blvd, Arlington ☎703/294-5233, ⓦwww.comedyindc.com; Ballston Metro. Serves up a range of comedy, from family-friendly hijinks to "blue" adult entertainment, in two theatres. Can be amusing, depending on the troupe performing.

Improv 1140 Connecticut Ave NW ☎202/296-7008, ⓦwww.dcimprov.com; Farragut North Metro. DC's main comedy stage, part of a nationwide chain. Draws both up-and-coming performers and the occasional veteran from the TV comedy circuit.

Film

While the great majority of **moviehouses** in Washington show the same tired Hollywood schlock and teen sex comedies you can see anywhere, a few cinemas boasting a historic pedigree or inventive programming do exist, offering a good reason to venture beyond the mainstream.

Although **tickets** for night-time screenings are increasingly pricey, you can often still get a bargain at afternoon matinees, while museums and galleries often put on free films. If you happen to be here in April, look out for screenings tied to DC's annual **Filmfest** (ⓦwww.filmfestdc.org), which premieres national and international movies in cinemas across town.

American Film Institute 8633 Colesville Rd, Silver Spring, MD ☎301/495-6720, ⓦwww.afi.com/silver; Silver Spring Metro. Major film institution whose Silver Theatre offers regular programmes of art, foreign and classic films, usually built around certain directors, countries and themes, often with associated lectures and seminars. Located two blocks from the Metro stop.

Arlington Cinema 'n' Drafthouse 2903 Columbia Pike, Arlington ☎703/486-2345, ⓦwww.arlingtondrafthouse.com. Grab a brew or munch on food while you watch a second-run movie or mid-level comedy at this combination pub-theatre, with one screen showing half a dozen different flicks during the week.

Avalon Theatre 5612 Connecticut Ave NW, Upper Northwest ☎202/966-6000, ⓦwww.theavalon.org; Friendship Heights Metro. Near the Maryland border (a 10–15min walk from the Metro), this is a marvellously refurbished 1930s movie palace with handsome lobby, lovely ceiling mural and plenty of old-fashioned charm, showing independent films and Hollywood classics.

E Street Cinema 555 11th St NW, Downtown ☎202/452-7672, ⓦwww.landmarktheatres.com; Metro Center Metro. Independent film stalwart with eight screens showing indie, foreign, documentary and classic movies in a comfortable, stylish setting.

Mary Pickford Theater Madison Building, 3rd Floor, Library of Congress, 1st St and Independence Ave SE, Capitol Hill ☎202/707-5677, ⓦwww.loc.gov; Capitol South Metro. Free classic and foreign historic movies from the library's voluminous archives, in this small 64-seat theatre.

Uptown Theater 3426 Connecticut Ave NW, Upper Northwest ☎202/966-5400; Cleveland Park Metro. Along with the Avalon, this is the District's other 1930s moviehouse, with one large screen, plenty of balcony seating, and a slate of mainstream movies.

Gay DC

For a smallish East Coast city, Washington, DC's **gay and lesbian scene** is surprisingly vibrant. Though you'll find it a bit more buttoned-down than the ones in New York, LA and San Francisco, times have certainly changed in the nation's capital since 1975, when gay federal employees risked being fired from their government jobs for engaging in "immoral conduct".

The heart of DC's gay community is **Dupont Circle**, where the greatest concentration of shops, bars and restaurants catering to a gay clientele can be found – though the neighbourhood has largely gentrified since its gay heyday in the 1970s. Most of the action takes place along P Street, just west of the Circle between 21st and 22nd streets, and on 17th Street between P and R streets. Across town in **Capitol Hill**, a handful of gay-friendly spots are clustered in the vicinity of the Eastern Market Metro station, near the intersection of Pennsylvania Avenue and 8th Street.

For up-to-date **listings**, pick up a copy of the *Washington Blade* or the *Metro Weekly* (see below). Note that most **hotels** in Washington are gay friendly, so we haven't listed any specifically gay-oriented establishments; however, *Carlyle Suites* (see p.195), *Dupont at the Circle* (see p.195) and the *William Lewis House* (see p.195) are known for being particularly welcoming.

Organizations and resources

Metro Weekly Ⓦwww.metroweekly.com. Free magazine that makes an excellent guide to DC's gay nightlife scene, stuffed with ads and listings about the latest spots and specials. Available at various Dupont Circle and Capitol Hill bars and clubs.
Rainbow History Project Ⓣ202/907-9007, Ⓦwww.rainbowhistory.org. Preserves and promotes community history through exhibits, talks and archives, and publishes web-based DC timeline and database of gay and lesbian "places and spaces" from the 1920s to the present. Also offers downloadable walking-tour brochures of neighbourhoods such as Capitol Hill and Dupont Circle.

Washington Blade Ⓦwww.washingtonblade .com. News, listings and classified ads are featured in this free weekly paper, available at bookshops, restaurants and cafés around town.
Whitman-Walker Clinic at Elizabeth Taylor Medical Center, 1701 14th St NW, Logan Circle Ⓣ202/745-7000, Ⓦwww.wwc.org; U Street–Cardozo Metro. Nonprofit community health organization for the gay and lesbian community, providing accessible health care and services, including AIDS information. Check website for information on other regional facilities.

Festivals and events

The District's gay community hosts any number of freewheeling **parties** and **festivals** (as well as more sober-minded fund-raisers) throughout the year, usually packed with throngs of locals, and sometimes with the odd politico dropping in for a peek.

Capital Pride Early June; @www.capitalpride.org. Week-long festival still going strong after thirty years that features cultural, political and community events, including films, pageants, a parade and a street festival along Pennsylvania Avenue NW.

Reel Affirmations Late April–early May; @www.reelaffirmations.org. One of the nation's largest gay and lesbian film festivals, held at various venues. Inquire also about monthly gay-film screenings and cinema events.

High-Heel Race Tues before Halloween. Colourful street festival featuring a carnival-like atmosphere, drag queens in all manner of mind-blowing outfits, and a mad dash down 17th Street in three- to six-inch heels.

Restaurants and cafés

While more than a few places reviewed in the "Cafés and restaurants" chapter (see Chapter 11) have won loyal gay followings – including *Pizzeria Paradiso* in Dupont Circle (see p.210), and *The Diner* and *Perry's* in Adams Morgan (see p.211 & p.212) – the handful of spots below have become fixtures on the capital's gay and lesbian scene.

Annie's Paramount Steakhouse 1609 17th St NW ☎202/232-0395, Dupont Circle; Dupont Circle Metro. See map, p.134. A local institution, in business since the 1940s, serving mid-priced steaks, fried chicken, burgers and brunch – including a midnight brunch on weekends – to a spirited late-night crowd. Mon–Wed 10am–11pm, Thurs 10am–1am, Fri–Sun 24hr.

Banana Café & Piano Bar 500 8th St SE ☎202/543-5906, Capitol Hill; Eastern Market Metro. See map, p.75. Affordable Tex-Mex staples alongside Caribbean standouts such as codfish fritters and plantain soup, the house speciality. Stop by the upstairs *Piano Bar* from 4pm daily. Mon–Thurs 11am–10.30pm, Fri & Sat 11am–11.30pm, Sun 10am–10pm.

Jolt 'N Bolt 1918 18th St NW, Adams Morgan; Dupont Circle Metro. See map, p.145. Townhouse tea- and coffeehouse with side-alley patio tucked away up 18th Street. Wraps and sandwiches, pastries and fresh juices are served, and there's free wi-fi. Daily 7am–8pm.

L'Enfant 2000 18th St NW ☎202/319-1800, Adams Morgan; Dupont Circle Metro. See map, p.145. A French favourite known for its affordable savoury and sweet crêpes and offerings like quiche and croque monsieur. Mon–Thurs 6pm–midnight, Fri 6pm–1am, Sat 10am–1am, Sun 10am–midnight.

Mr Henry's 601 Pennsylvania Ave SE ☎202/546-8412, Capitol Hill; Eastern Market Metro. See map, p.75. Easy-going saloon and restaurant with tasty steak, seafood and burgers, plus outside patio and charcoal grill. See also p.204. Mon–Thurs & Sun 11am–midnight, Fri & Sat 11am–1am.

SoHo Tea & Coffee 2150 P St NW, Dupont Circle; Dupont Circle Metro. See map, p.134. Trendy late-night hangout for P Street clubbers refuelling on coffee, cakes and sandwiches. Occasional entertainment, plus free wi-fi. Mon–Wed & Sun 7am–1am, Thurs 7am–2am, Fri & Sat 7am–3am.

Bars and clubs

The focus of gay **bars and clubs** in DC is unquestionably Dupont Circle, though Capitol Hill Southeast has scattered points of interest, too. With the latter area, though, try to take a taxi around at night, as some of the backstreets can get rather dodgy.

Capitol Hill

See the **map** on p.75.

Phase One 525 8th St SE ☎202/544-6831,
🌐www.phase1dc.com; **Eastern Market Metro.**
Long-standing neighbourhood lesbian bar
with relaxed and convivial atmosphere, DJs,
dancing and a pool table. Wed events
sometimes feature jello wrestling. Wed,
Thurs & Sun 7pm–2am, Fri & Sat 7pm–3am.

Remington's 639 Pennsylvania Ave SE
☎202/543-3113, 🌐www.remingtonswdc.com;
Eastern Market Metro. Signature gay country
& western club with four bars and two
dancefloors; events include singing
competitions, spirited hoedowns, and
cowgirl-themed drag pageants. Mon–Thurs
4pm–2am, Fri 4pm–3am, Sat 8pm–3am,
Sun 6pm–2am.

Downtown and Dupont Circle

See the **map** on p.134.

Apex 1415 22nd St NW ☎202/296-0505,
🌐www.apex-dc.com; **Dupont Circle Metro.**
Centrally located dance club with DJs
spinning pop, hip-hop and electronica for a
mostly male party crowd, plus karaoke; the
insanity is at its height on Fri and Sat nights.
Thurs 9pm–2am, Fri & Sat 9pm–3am.

Cobalt 1639 R St NW ☎202/232-4416, 🌐www
.cobaltdc.com; **Dupont Circle Metro.** A fixture
on the gay scene. The first floor has an
engaging bar, and upstairs there's a frenetic
club with theme nights and yuppie types
gyrating to house and trance tunes. Mon–
Thurs 5pm–2am, Fri 5pm–3am, Sat & Sun
11am–3am.

FAB Lounge 1805 Connecticut Ave NW
☎202/797-1122, 🌐thefablounge.com; **Dupont**

Circle Metro. North of the Circle, this is a
spirited Kalorama club that draws a wide
variety of people, including women, who
come for the uncommon (for DC) lesbian
nights at this relaxed but still dance-oriented
club. Mon–Thurs 5pm–1am, Sat & Sun
5pm–2am.

Green Lantern 1335 Green Court NW ☎202/347-
4533, 🌐www.greenlanterndc.com; **McPherson
Square Metro.** Broad selection of regulars at
this casual bar that's a bit removed from the
posier Circle scene to the north; regular
karaoke nights and weekend video jockeys
as well. Mon–Thurs & Sun 4pm–2am, Fri &
Sat 4pm–3am.

JR's 1519 17th St NW ☎202/328-0090,
🌐www.jrswdc.com; **Dupont Circle Metro.**
A young, mostly male professional crowd
packs into this narrow saloon-bar, which
boasts a great location along the 17th
Street cruise strip. The place to be seen for
cocktails. Mon–Thurs & Sun 2pm–2am, Fri
& Sat 2pm–3am.

MOVA Lounge 1435 P St NW ☎202/797-9730,
🌐www.movalounge.com; **no close Metro.** Self-
consciously ultra chic lounge in Logan Circle
that is one of the District's pinnacles of gay
posing, with a variety of high-flying club
nights for the young and well heeled. To buy
in to this social challenge, wear a new shirt,
look smart and don't let the pretension get
you down. Mon–Thurs & Sun 5pm–1.30am,
Fri & Sat 5pm–2.30am.

Omega 2122 P St NW, in the rear alley
☎202/223-4917, 🌐www.omegadc.com; **Dupont
Circle Metro.** Friendly spot with four bars,
pool tables and a dark video room upstairs.
Stop in for happy hour or for a kickoff drink
at weekends. Mon–Thurs 4pm–2am, Fri
4pm–3am, Sat 8pm–3am, Sun 7pm–2am.

Festivals and events

W ashington has a huge variety of annual **festivals and parades**, many of them national in scope: America's Christmas Tree is lit each December on the Ellipse between the White House and the National Mall; the grandest Fourth of July Parade in the country takes place along and around the Mall; and every four years in January the newly inaugurated president rides in a triumphal parade up Pennsylvania Avenue, from the US Capitol to the White House. Many of the national holidays are celebrated with special events and festivities in the city – for a comprehensive list contact the Washington, DC Convention and Tourism Corporation (see p.39) or check the events calendar at ⓦwww.washington.org.

For a list of **national public holidays**, see box, p.36. For a list of **gay-oriented festivals**, see box, p.238.

January

Dr Martin Luther King Jr's Birthday 15th; ☎202/619-7222. Wreath-laying at the Lincoln Memorial, a reading of the "I Have a Dream" speech, concerts and speeches, plus activities at Martin Luther King Jr Memorial Library downtown (see p.132).

February

Black History Month Special events, exhibits and cultural programmes. Information from Martin Luther King Jr Memorial Library (☎202/727-1101) or the Smithsonian or National Park Service (see box below).
Chinese New Year Date varies; ☎202/638-1041. Dragon dancers, parades and fireworks light up H Street NW in Chinatown.
Abraham Lincoln's Birthday 12th; ☎202/619-7222. Wreath-laying and reading of the

Gettysburg Address at the Lincoln Memorial; honorary events at Ford's Theatre and other Lincoln-related sites.
Frederick Douglass's Birthday 14th; ☎202/426-5961. Wreath-laying, history exhibits and music at Douglass's home (and now National Historic Site) in Cedar Hill, Anacostia (see p.95).
George Washington's Birthday Parade 22nd; ☎703/991-4474, ⓦwww.washingtonbirthday.net. Spectacular parade and events in Old Town Alexandria. Also, concerts and wreath-laying at Mount Vernon (☎703/799-5203).

March

St Patrick's Day 17th; ☎202/637-2474, ⓦwww.dcstpatsparade.com. Big parade down Constitution Avenue NW on the Sunday before the 17th (call for grandstand seats) and another through Old Town Alexandria

---

Information lines

National Park Service ☎202/619-7222
Post-Haste (*Washington Post*) ☎202/334-9000
Smithsonian ☎202/357-2700
Washington, DC Convention and Visitors Association ☎202/789-7000

on the first Saturday of the month (☎703/237-2199, ⓦwww.ballyshaners.org).
Smithsonian Kite Festival Late March/early April; ☎202/633-3030, ⓦwww.kitefestival.org. Kite-flying competitions on the National Mall, with assorted games and prizes.

April

National Cherry Blossom Festival Early April; ☎877/442-5666, ⓦwww.nationalcherry blossomfestival.org. The famous cherry trees around the Tidal Basin bloom in late March/early April; celebrated by a massive parade down Constitution Avenue NW, the crowning of a festival queen, free concerts, lantern-lighting, dances and origami-making events.
Blessing of the Fleet Second Sat; ☎202/737-2300. Nautical celebrations and services at the US Navy Memorial, including sailors serving a famous navy bean soup. Boat-related displays and races at Southwest Waterfront marina.
White House Easter Egg Roll Easter Monday; ☎202/456-2200, ⓦwww.whitehouse.gov /eastereggroll. Great kids' event with entertainment and egg rolling (eggs provided) on the White House South Lawn. US citizens can enter for tickets through a national lottery on the website.
Smithsonian Craft Show mid-April; ☎202/633-5006 or 1-888/832-9554, ⓦwww.smithsonian craftshow.org. Fascinating craft exhibitions by regional artists and artisans at the National Building Museum (see p.123).
Filmfest DC Late April; ☎202/234-3456, ⓦwww.filmfestdc.org. Two-week festival premiering national and international movies in theatres and museums across the city.
William Shakespeare's Birthday 25th; ☎202/544-7077. The Bard is praised in song, word and food at the Folger Shakespeare Library (see p.83).
Duke Ellington's Birthday 29th; ☎202/337-4825, ⓦwww.smithsonianjazz.org. Music and events at Freedom Plaza on Pennsylvania Avenue NW. Music and lectures are given at some Smithsonian museums.

May

Garden Day Early May; ☎202/965-1950, ⓦwww.georgetowngardentour.com. Self-guided tours to see private patches of lush greenery at Georgetown's houses and mansions. Tickets go for $30 (or $35 on day of tour).

Mount Vernon Wine Festival/Sunset Tour Mid-May; ☎703/799-5203, ⓦwww .mountvernon.org. George Washington's estate hosts this celebration of early America's home-grown wine-making, featuring music, food and a trip to the first president's own cellar vaults. $30.
Memorial Day Last Mon. Wreath-laying, services and speeches at Arlington Cemetery (☎202/685-2851), the Vietnam Veterans Memorial (☎202/619-7222) and the US Navy Memorial (☎202/737-2300). The National Symphony Orchestra performs on the Capitol's West Lawn on the preceding Sunday.

June

Dupont-Kalorama Museum Walk First weekend; ☎202/387-4062 ext 12, ⓦwww.dkmuseums .com. Music, food and historic displays provide the backdrop to tours of museums and private homes and estates in Dupont Circle, Embassy Row and Kalorama.
DC Jazz Festival Early to mid-June; ☎202/232-3611, ⓦwww.dcjazzfest.org. Free musical events around town with many good local bands and singers, putting on more than a hundred jazz-oriented concerts and programmes.
DC Caribbean Carnival Late June; ☎202/726-2204. Caribbean-style parade spread over consecutive weekends, with masqueraders and live music, from Georgia and Missouri avenues to Banneker Park near Howard University.
National Capital Barbeque Battle Late June; ☎301/860-0630, ⓦwww.bbqdc.com. Get your fill of gut-busting, rib-stuffing barbecue at this celebration of the greasy and the grilled, which culminates with the awarding of the National Pork Barbeque Champion. Held along Pennsylvania Ave NW. $10.
Smithsonian Festival of American Folklife Late June/early July; ☎202/633-6440, ⓦwww .festival.si.edu. One of the country's biggest festivals, loaded with American music, crafts, food and folk heritage events on the Mall.

July

National Independence Day Celebration 4th; ☎202/619-7222. Reading of the Declaration of Independence at the National Archives; parade along Constitution Avenue NW; free concerts at the Sylvan Theatre near the Washington Monument; National Symphony Orchestra performance on west steps of the Capitol; finishing with a superb fireworks display.

Capital Fringe Festival Mid- to late July; ☎1-866/811-4111, ⓦwww.capfringe.org. Two weeks full of classic, modern, offbeat and avant-garde theatre performances, more than a hundred in all, hosted by galleries and theatres Downtown.

August

Arlington County Fair Mid-Aug; ☎703/228-1853, ⓦwww.arlingtoncountyfair.org. Traditional fair with rides, crafts, entertainment, food stalls, concerts and racing pigs at Thomas Jefferson Community Center, 3501 South 2nd St, Arlington.

DC Blues Festival Late Aug or early Sept; ☎202/962-0112, ⓦwww.dcblues.org. Free music, from folky acoustic blues to Chicago electric, at Rock Creek Park's Carter Barron Amphitheatre.

September

Adams Morgan Day First Sun after Labor Day; ☎202/232-1960, ⓦwww.adamsmorganday festival.com. One of the best neighbourhood festivals, with live music, crafts and cuisine along 18th Street NW – always packed and great fun.

Virginia Scottish Festival Early Sept; ☎703/912-1943, ⓦwww.vascottishgames.org. The "Great Meadow" near Manassas is the spot for the wearing of kilts, playing of bagpipes and eating of haggis. Also features Highland dancing and fiddling. $18.

Constitution Day 17th; ☎1-866/272-6272, ⓦwww.archives.org. The US Constitution is displayed at the National Archives to celebrate the anniversary of its signing, with naturalization ceremonies, a parade and concerts.

Oktoberfest Late Sept/early Oct; ☎1-800/830-3976, ⓦwww.dasbestoktoberfest .com. Although events take place around the region, the closest celebration to DC is just south of town at National Harbor, MD, where "Das Best Oktoberfest" has all the beer and sausage vendors you could want, plus singing, dancing and accordions.

October

White House Fall Garden Tours Mid-Oct; ☎202/208-1631, ⓦwww.whitehouse.gov. Free garden tours and military band concerts. Reserve well in advance for this popular event; check website on how to book.

Marine Corps Marathon Late Oct; ☎1-800/786-8762, ⓦwww.marinemarathon.com. The city's key distance event, beginning and ending at the Iwo Jima Monument and leading runners (all kinds, not just military members) past Georgetown, Capitol Hill, the National Mall and Pentagon along the way. $75 entry.

Halloween 31st; ☎703/549-2997. Unofficial block parties, costumed antics and fright-nights in Georgetown, Dupont Circle and other neighbourhoods. Carlyle House in Alexandria presents "haunted tours" of that city (ⓦwww.carlylehouse.org).

November

Seafaring Celebration Date varies; ☎202/433-4882. The Navy Museum hosts a family-oriented event with maritime activities, food, arts and children's performances.

Veterans Day 11th. Solemn memorial services and wreath-laying at 11am at Arlington Cemetery (usually with the president in attendance), African American Civil War Memorial, Vietnam Veterans Memorial and US Navy Memorial, among other military sites in town.

December

Candlelight Tours Date varies. Call well in advance for reservations at these extremely popular evening events, which take place at Mount Vernon (☎703/780-2000) and Old Town Alexandria (☎703/838-4242). Prices vary.

Christmas Tree Lightings Early Dec; ☎202/619-7222. Separate ceremonies for the lighting of the Capitol (west side) and National (Ellipse) Christmas trees – the latter lit by the president.

Christmas Services All month; ☎202/537-6200, ⓦwww.nationalcathedral.org. Carols, pageants, choral performances and bell-ringing at Washington National Cathedral. There is also much ceremony and ritual at the National Shrine of the Immaculate Conception (☎202/526-8300, ⓦwww .nationalshrine.com).

16

Sports and outdoor activities

T he nation's capital is one of the greenest cities on the East Coast, with easy access to a multitude of woodsy trails and a major waterway, the Potomac River. Thanks to these natural attributes, DC is a great place for people who like to cycle, sail, hike, paddle, skate, run, or just stroll in the great **outdoors** – all a welcome relief from pounding the pavement between monuments and museums.

The capital also has a lot to offer those who prefer to enjoy their **sports** from the sidelines. Unfortunately, the biggest name in town, football's Washington Redskins, has a waiting list for tickets that is at least ten years long – and they don't even play in the District. The situation isn't remedied by the area's other teams, basketball's Wizards and baseball's Nationals – both of them mediocre at best – though the Washington Capitals have experienced a resurgence in the last few years, making hockey, perhaps unexpectedly, your best choice for watching a winning team in the District.

Outdoor activities

The green expanse of **Rock Creek Park** – which stretches from the city's northern edge to the Potomac River (see p.159) – and the network of trails heading out from the capital to Virginia and Maryland together offer miles of routes for biking, walking and rollerblading. Downtown, the **Mall** and the **Ellipse** provide the city with a central playground, particularly in summer when softball season swings into gear, and are good spots to go for a run.

Forming DC's southwestern boundary, the Potomac offers everything from whitewater rapids to guided tours for novice paddlers to sunset sails, making it easy to take in spectacular views of DC from the water.

Cycling

For a pleasant outdoor excursion, the best option might be to **rent a bike** for short rides along the **Potomac River** or the **C&O Canal towpath**. Bicycle rentals (vendors listed below) cost anywhere from $5 per hour for a simple cruiser to $75 per day for a flashy mountain bike; the average price is $7 per hour and $35 per day, sometimes with a three-hour minimum.

Among DC's cycle paths are one in Rock Creek Park, the 18.5-mile **Mount Vernon Trail** (see p.176), and the 184-mile-long C&O towpath (see

243

box, p.167), starting in Georgetown and heading deep into Maryland. The Washington and Old Dominion Trail (Ⓦ www.wodfriends.org) starts a bit further out, in Vienna, VA, but offers 45 miles of tarmac following the route of an old-time railway, heading westward into northern Virginia.

The eleven-mile **Capital Crescent Trail** (Ⓣ 202/234-4874, Ⓦ www .cctrail.org), starting at Thompson Boat Center, branches off the C&O towpath after three miles and follows the course of an old railway line up into Bethesda and on to Silver Spring, both in Maryland. Once in Bethesda, cyclists can turn this trip into a 22-mile loop by returning via Rock Creek Park – follow the signs to the unpaved Georgetown Branch Trail, which cuts across Connecticut Avenue, to find the park. On the southern end, the trail links up with the Mount Vernon Trail (via the Key Bridge) and the Rock Creek Trail (via K St).

Many trails and bicycle paths crisscross the Metrorail system, giving you the option of cutting short a trip or avoiding backtracking. Keep in mind that while bikes are permitted on the Metro at any time during the weekend, they are prohibited during weekday rush hours (7–10am & 4–7pm) and on major holidays.

Rentals

Big Wheel Bikes 1034 33rd St NW, Georgetown Ⓣ 202/337-0254; 2 Prince St, Alexandria Ⓣ 703/739-2300; 3119 Lee Hwy, Arlington Ⓣ 703/522-1110; 6917 Arlington Rd, Bethesda, MD Ⓣ 301/652-0192; Ⓦ www .bigwheelbikes.com. Georgetown location (closed Mon) convenient to C&O Canal and Capital Crescent trails; Alexandria location near Mount Vernon Trail.
Fletcher's Boat House 4940 Canal Rd NW, Georgetown Ⓣ 202/244-0461, Ⓦ www.fletchers cove.com. Located on the C&O Canal.
Thompson Boat Center 2900 Virginia Ave NW, Georgetown Ⓣ 202/333-9543, Ⓦ www.thompson boatcenter.com. Starting point of the Capital Crescent Trail.
Washington Sailing Marina 1 Marina Drive, George Washington Memorial Parkway,

Alexandria Ⓣ 703/548-9027, Ⓦ www.washington sailingmarina.com. Located along the Mount Vernon Trail (see also p.176).

Tours and resources

Bike and Roll Ⓦ www.bikethesites.com. 1100 Pennsylvania Ave NW, Downtown Ⓣ 202/842-2453; One Wales Alley, Alexandria Ⓣ 703/548-7655; Union Station, 50 Massachusetts Ave NE Ⓣ 202/962-0206. Three- to four-hour guided bike tours of the major sights (most $40–48, including bike and helmet), plus tours of Mount Vernon and other customized tours. Also rents bikes from $10 per two hours or $25–70 per day. Tour reservations required.
Bike Washington Ⓦ www.bikewashington.org. Online recreational bicycling guide loaded with insider tips on local routes and trails.
Washington Area Bicyclist Association 2599 Ontario Rd NW Ⓣ 202/518-0524, Ⓦ www.waba .org. Advocacy group whose website offers info on trails, gear and local events.

Rollerblading

The Capital Crescent and Mount Vernon trails are both travelled by **rollerbladers** as well as cyclists, but one of the best spots for inline skaters at weekends is forested **Beach Drive** in Rock Creek Park (see p.159), which is closed to traffic from 7am on Saturday to 7pm on Sunday, and on holidays. Other good areas include the Tidal Basin south of the National Mall, and selected parts of Southwest Waterfront, East and West Potomac parks, and the riverside sections of Georgetown and Alexandria. The **Washington Area Roadskaters** (Ⓦ www.skatedc.org) is a local club that organizes group skates of varying lengths, as well as free weekly skate clinics (April–Oct Sat noon) in Rock Creek Park.

Jogging and walking

You can walk or jog on any of the trails described under "Cycling" or "Rollerblading", though many choose simply to put on their running shoes and hit the Mall, where the imperial buildings and monuments provide an inspiring backdrop for a workout. The sand and gravel paths circumscribing the mammoth front lawn of the city centre provide a surface easier on the knees than your typical city pavement.

Merely wandering around DC itself provide a workout of sorts, especially taking on the hill from Dupont Circle to Upper Northwest along Connecticut Avenue, and from there (for the truly in-shape) hoofing it all the way up to the Maryland border at Friendship Heights – a five-mile trek in total. Those looking for a quieter place for a constitutional should head to **Theodore Roosevelt Island** (see p.177), a nature park with 2.5 miles of trails that meander through marsh, swamp and forest. Other relaxing spots in the daytime include the **National Arboretum** (see p.153), **Rock Creek Park** (see p.159) and **Arlington National Cemetery** (see p.172).

Water activities

The **Potomac River** provides plenty of chances to get out on the water. Near Georgetown, several boat rental shops offer the means to explore the calmer waters on either side of the Key Bridge and around Roosevelt Island, a stretch of the river that provides a worthy afternoon retreat. From here, it's easy enough to paddle your way into the **Tidal Basin**, an outing especially pretty in spring, when the cherry blossoms are in bloom. Those keen on staying closer to shore can rent a **paddle boat** at the Tidal Basin Boat House, 1501 Maine Ave SW (mid-March to Aug daily 10am–6pm; Sept & Oct Wed–Sun 10am–6pm; two-seaters $12/hr; four-seaters $19/hr; ☎202/479-2426, ⓦwww.tidalbasinpaddleboats.com).

Going south, the river widens as it flows past Alexandria toward the Wilson Bridge, an area popular with sailors, windsurfers and sea-kayakers. South of the bridge on the Virginia side, you can glide into **Dyke Marsh Wildlife Preserve** (ⓦwww.nps.gov /gwmp/dyke-marsh.htm), a freshwater wetland home to osprey, blue heron and many other birds.

Rentals, as you'd expect, vary in price with the size and type of boat, with discounted rates offered for booking an entire day. Kayaks, canoes and rowing boats go for $10–20 per hour and $22–50 per day. **Sailing boats** range from $10 to $20 per hour (though you may find that there's a two-hour minimum rental) to $150 per day. As rental service tends to be seasonal (March to Nov), you'd do well to call in advance in early spring or late autumn.

Boat rentals

Fletcher's Boat House 4940 Canal Rd NW, Georgetown ☎202/244-0461, ⓦwww.fletcherscove .com. Rents rowing boats, canoes and bikes, and sells bait and tackle to the fishing crowd.

Thompson Boat Center 2900 Virginia Ave NW, Georgetown ☎202/333-9543, ⓦwww .thompsonboatcenter.com. Single and double kayaks, canoes and recreational and racing rowing shells, plus bikes.

Canoeing and kayaking

Atlantic Kayak Company ☎301/292-6455 or 1-800/297-0066, ⓦwww.atlantickayak.com. Kayak tours of DC monuments near the water and sights along the Potomac, including tours of Piscataway Creek, a Potomac tributary, and the Dyke Marsh Wildlife area (April–Oct; $45–50 each). Also moonlight tours, full-day trips, and overnight excursions to wildlife areas. No experience necessary; all equipment included.

Outdoor Excursions Boonsboro, MD ☎1-800/775-2925, ⓦwww.outdoorexcursions .com. Located below Great Falls, MD, with rafting and tubing trips (most $40–70), whitewater kayaking and sea-kayaking instruction, and canoe and kayak rentals.

Sailing

Mariner Sailing School at Belle Haven Marina off George Washington Parkway, Alexandria ☎703/768-0018, ⓦwww.saildc.com. Rentals include canoes, kayaks and rowing boats, plus Flying Scot and Sunfish sailing boats. A 34ft C&C sloop is available for charter ($90/hr including captain). Also offers sailing instruction.

Washington Sailing Marina 1 Marina Drive, George Washington Memorial Parkway, Alexandria ☎703/548-9027, ⓦwww.washingtonsailing marina.com. Seasonal sailing boat rentals (by reservation only). Also rents bikes. Located along the Mount Vernon Trail.

Spectator sports

Although they're not as rabid as the red-blooded fanatics in New York and Philadelphia, DC's fans still make a good show – the Redskins have sold out their games for years to come and even get politicians begging for tickets. Recent years have brought other new franchises as well: the Nationals (baseball), DC United (soccer) and Mystics (women's basketball) have given the capital something new to cheer – or boo, this being the East Coast.

An outing to a sporting event can be expensive, however, once the cost of tickets, snacks and beer is tallied, with football the most expensive proposition (but also the least likely for which you'll be able to find a ticket). Buy **tickets** through Ticketmaster (☎202/432-7328, ⓦwww.ticketmaster.com) or directly through the team's or stadium's box office.

Baseball

The capital was without a **baseball** team after the Washington Senators packed their bags for Texas in 1971. However, local politicians and business leaders clamoured for a team for many years, and in 2005 succeeded in acquiring the Montreal Expos – now rechristened the **Washington Nationals** (☎202/675-6287, ⓦnationals.mlb.com; April–Oct). The team has an impressive stadium, Nationals Park, south of Capitol Hill on the Anacostia waterfront, and tickets ($12–95) are regularly available since the team's not very good.

Basketball

Now that basketball legend Michael Jordan's days of playing with, and partly owning, the **Washington Wizards** (☎202/661-5050, ⓦwww .nba.com/wizards; Nov–April) are over, the capital is left with just another mediocre sports squad. Simply put, the best reason to show up is to catch one of the NBA's powerhouses rolling into the Verizon Center (☎202/628-3200, ⓦwww.verizoncenter.com; Gallery Place–Chinatown Metro) to push the team around. For this you can expect to pay extra; tickets average $10–125, but cost more when there's a very good or nationally popular (Lakers, Celtics, etc) team on the hardwood. In summer, the focus swings to the **Washington Mystics** (☎202/661-5050, ⓦwww .wnba.com/mystics; June–Aug), DC's pro women's team. Despite struggling since the inception of the WNBA in 1997, the Mystics draw one of the largest crowds in the league to the Verizon Center; tickets go for $10–65.

If you're really interested in seeing a solid b-ball squad take to the floor, you'll have to look beyond the pro ranks to the **Georgetown Hoyas** (☎202/687-4692, ⓦwww.guhoyas .com; tickets $8–62), the dominant team from the mid-1980s, which plays at the Verizon Center. Up the road in College Park, Maryland, just beyond the DC border, the **Maryland Terrapins** (☎301/314-7070, ⓦwww .umterps.com; tickets $8–55) put on a fine show for their young student fans and alumni at the **Comcast Center**.

Football

The **Washington Redskins** (☎301/276-6050, ⓦwww.redskins .com; Sept–Dec; tickets $65–100+) are the dominant obsession of the capital's sports fans. One of American football's oldest franchises, the team has also been one of the most successful since arriving in DC in 1937, with a total of five championships under its belt – the most recent in 1992. Redskins games, played at 91,000-seat FedEx Field in Landover, MD (☎301/276-6050, ⓦwww.redskins.com), remain among DC's hardest tickets to snag – indeed, tickets are sold by the season only and the waiting list is a decade long. So, unless you're prepared to pay ridiculous prices to touts, or know someone in DC with an extra ticket, chances are slim that you'll see the 'Skins in action except on TV.

Hockey

The Verizon Center's other main tenant, hockey's **Washington Capitals** (☎ 202/397-7328, ⓦ capitals.nhl.com; Oct–April; tickets $15–95), have a lengthy tradition of mediocrity, but looked to be turning things around in the 2010 season, when they secured a division title – before losing in the playoffs. However, with their improved play of late, the team has at least given fans at the Verizon Center the opportunity to see a pro sports team win more games than it loses.

Soccer

The city's major-league soccer team, **DC United**, plays at the RFK Stadium (☎ 202/587-5000, ⓦ www.dcunited .com; March–Nov; Stadium–Armory Metro; $22–55) and is among the most successful in the United States. Since the inaugural MLS season in 1996, the team has won the title four times (last in 2004). Average home attendance is around 25,000.

Kids' DC

For **children**, there may be no friendlier or more accommodating major city in the nation, or perhaps the world, than Washington, DC. Unlike some cities, such as Orlando, Florida, that offer designated family-friendly attractions such as theme parks but are otherwise hit-and-miss, there are practically no significant areas, outside of bars and clubs, where **children** are off limits in DC. Indeed, you can take a tot to practically any museum, historic mansion, art exhibit, memorial, monument or institution without the staff batting an eyelid. In fact, the District is accepting of children to such a degree that you might sometimes find some of its major sights – especially the natural history museum on the National Mall – unbearable because of it.

What follows is an overview of the best and most appropriate places to bring kids in DC, keeping in mind that almost every sight listed in the book could technically qualify.

Museums

The hub of activity for kids in DC is undoubtedly the **National Mall**, and in some stretches school groups, huge families and assorted toddlers are so thick on the ground you can barely wade through them – especially during the high season. That said, there's a definite delineation between Mall museums aimed at inquisitive young learners and those designed more as giant playpens. In the former category, institutions like the **National Gallery of Art**, the **Hirshhorn Museum** and the national museums of **Asian Art**, **African Art** and the **American Indian** are excellent spots to educate the mind and get a sense of American and international art and culture; some even provide pamphlets or guides aimed at young patrons. Misbehavers will be asked to leave, promptly and firmly. By contrast, the national museums of **Natural History**, **American History** and **Air and Space** are chaotic environments where ill-behaved youngsters often run amok with the interactive exhibits and hands-on displays.

Away from the Mall, the other major sight that attracts all kinds of young enthusiasts is the **International Spy Museum**, which entices visitors with its displays of Cold War gizmos and exotic weaponry; unlike the Mall museums, though, this one isn't free, and is among the priciest in town. Also around the Penn Quarter, the **Newseum** may capture some kids' imagination with acres of TV screens and various interactive gadgets and colourful kiosks. Only older kids may be able to sit still for the uber-educational **National Building Museum** or **National Postal Museum**, however. At other scattered locations around DC, the museums are aimed at even more mature children, or at least those with an appreciation or sense of history and art. The **Renwick** and **Corcoran** galleries and the **National Portrait** and **American Art museums**

Practicalities

Given the broad scope of children's activities in the nation's capital, it's not too surprising that kids are easily accommodated when it comes to actually staying in and visiting the city. At **hotels**, you may find that children of 12 years and under are sometimes allowed to stay in their parents' room for free or at a reduced rate; these and other facilities may even put on special games or entertainment for their apple-cheeked guests.

Kids are generally accepted in Washington **restaurants**, though such tolerance may be contingent on their maturity level and the time of night – badly behaved children will be accorded little slack at a quality restaurant or lounge at 10pm. In many cases, though, restaurants may offer reduced-rate meals to children, or even a separate menu filled with all kinds of kid-friendly, if not exactly healthy, favourites like peanut butter and jelly sandwiches and macaroni cheese.

One of the reasons DC is so popular with families and others with kids in tow is because so many **sights and attractions** are free. The Smithsonian is noted for charging no admission at its facilities, as are places like the US Capitol, government parks, the White House, National Gallery of Art, and countless other museums, galleries and parks. Where admission is charged at major attractions, it's usually under $10 (except for the Newseum and the International Spy Museum). The same is true when it comes to **transport** in and around the District, with many operators charging lower rates for kids; the Metro, for example, allows two very young kids (age 4 and under) to ride free with an adult; see ⓦ www.wmata.com for details.

will be enjoyed most by kids whose parents or guardians guide them through the displays.

Historic sites

Most **historic sites** – be they mansions, monuments or memorials – can be appreciated by a young audience, and as with the museums, many of these big names are located on the Mall. Typically, the **presidential memorials** (Jefferson, Lincoln and FDR) are fairly wide-open, so children's behaviour can be less inhibited than it would be inside.

There are countless other historic sites in the city appropriate for well-behaved kids with an interest in learning – these include **Dumbarton Oaks**, **Tudor Place** and the **C&O Canal** in Georgetown; the **Woodrow Wilson** and **Anderson** houses around Dupont Circle; the **US Supreme Court** and **Folger Shakespeare Library** on Capitol Hill; **Ford's Theatre** Downtown; and, further afield, **Mount Vernon** and **Old Town Alexandria**. Almost all children and their parents will want to visit the US

Capitol and the **White House** – especially during the annual Easter Egg Roll (see p.100) or the lighting of the National Christmas Tree (see p.100).

Parks and gardens

Aside from the National Mall itself, the District's assorted **parks and gardens** afford a welcome respite from an overdose of history, art and culture. Here, kids can run wild amid forested surroundings, or spread out on undulating lawns and hillsides once they've tired themselves out. The city's park squares near the White House are not the best places for this sort of activity, so you'll have to venture further out. Good choices for nature-based activity – which may involve cycling, hiking, boating or even Frisbee-playing, depending on the site – include **West and East Potomac parks**, the **Ellipse**, **Theodore Roosevelt Island**, the **Mount Vernon Trail** and especially **Rock Creek Park**. Other locations are less suited for burning off energy than taking in the natural splendour; these include the

Discovery Theater

The **Discovery Theater** (☎202/633-8700, ⓦwww.discoverytheater.org; Smithsonian Metro), at the Ripley Center, 1100 Jefferson Drive SW, in the Smithsonian, puts on year-round daytime children's entertainment, staging musicals and puppet shows at budget prices.

⑰

National Arboretum, which has the added historical attraction of the Capitol Columns; **Kenilworth Aquatic Gardens**; and the **US Botanic Garden**.

Another outdoor spot children will inevitably want to see is the splendid **National Zoological Park**, which has

the added benefit of free admission, as with all Smithsonian facilities. The National Aquarium, however, is best avoided – the cramped fish tanks and bureaucratic hallways of the Commerce Building are hardly the best places to show off nature in all its glory.

Shops and galleries

No one really comes to DC to **shop**, and most visitors content themselves with buying a few trinkets or T-shirts at museum stores or government buildings. For those who really want to spend, though, there are **malls** in **Friendship Heights**, on the border with Maryland, among other places (see box, p.253). Beyond this, the best areas for browsing are Adams Morgan, Dupont Circle, Georgetown and around **Eastern Market**, where arts-and-crafts shops coexist with speciality book and music stores and student-oriented hangouts. **Adams Morgan** has a strong ethnic flair, while in **Shaw** and **Logan Circle** a number of hip boutiques sit amid the funky bars, clubs and theatres. Across the river, **Alexandria** has its fair share of stores, many specializing in antiques and arts and crafts, and **Arlington** has a few malls.

The shopping heart has been ripped out of Downtown, however, as almost all the major **department stores** have given up the ghost. This situation is slowly improving with new shops around the Verizon Center, but for the foreseeable future you're best off at one of the mega-malls on the outskirts of the city, where you'll find Nordstrom, Saks Fifth Avenue, Bloomingdale's and Macy's. Only Filene's Basement has maintained its bargain-priced main outpost in the city, at 1133 Connecticut Ave NW, Downtown (☎202/872-8430), with a few other locations in the malls as well.

Usual **opening hours** are Monday to Saturday 10am to 7pm, though malls are open longer hours (see box, p.253). In Georgetown, Adams Morgan and Dupont Circle many stores open on Sunday, too.

Arts, crafts and antiques

The only indigenous local craft is politics, but specialist **arts-and-crafts** stores in DC let you take home a piece of historic memorabilia or American Victoriana if you wish. The richest pickings are in Dupont Circle; Georgetown, which also has a run of antiques shops; and Old Town Alexandria, loaded with antiques and bric-a-brac places aimed at the weekend visitor market. Another great spot to poke around for arts, crafts and other funky finds is the weekend flea market held at Eastern Market (see p.85). For commercial art galleries, see box, p.257.

Appalachian Spring 1415 Wisconsin Ave NW, Georgetown ☎202/337-5780; Union Station Metro; 50 Massachusetts Ave NE, Capitol Hill ☎202/682-0505; Union Station Metro. A colourful array of handmade ceramics, jewellery, rugs, glassware, kitchenware, quilts, toys and other eclectic examples of American craftwork.

Artcraft Collection 132 King St, Alexandria ☎703/299-6616; King Street Metro. A strange and impressive collection of handcrafted artefacts, such as painted furniture, exquisitely detailed jewellery, oddball sculptures, anthropomorphic teapots and iridescent vases.

(18)

Arts Afire 1117 King St, Alexandria ☏703/838-9785; King Street Metro. Major dealer in art glass, with a full complement of work from regional and national designers on display, everything from jewellery and home decor to kaleidoscopes, vases and trinkets.

Beadazzled 1507 Connecticut Ave NW, Dupont Circle ☏202/265-2323; Dupont Circle Metro. New and antique beads from all over the world, for which you'll pay a premium, plus ethnic jewellery, folk art and related books.

Ginza 1721 Connecticut Ave NW, Dupont Circle ☏202/332-7000; Dupont Circle Metro. Long-standing neighbourhood favourite for all things Japanese, including books, toys, screens, woodblock prints, kimonos and sandals.

Indian Craft Shop Department of the Interior, 1849 C St NW, Foggy Bottom ☏202/208-4056; Farragut West Metro. One of the city's best gift boutiques in a rather bleak stretch for shopping, selling rugs, crafts, beadwork, jewellery and pottery by artisans from native tribes in the US.

Old Print Gallery 1220 31st NW, Georgetown ☏202/965-1818. A favourite local seller of historic landscapes, antique maps, old charts and prints, plus political cartoons, DC scenes and early-American artisan work.

Pulp 1803 14th St NW, Shaw ☏202/462-7857; U Street–Cardozo Metro. Eye-popping, purple-fronted shop thick with trinkets and souvenirs, but best for its wide selection of greetings cards – from the mundane to the freakish – which it allows you to make, too, if you have the zeal for it.

Village on Capitol Hill 705 North Carolina Ave SE ☏202/546-3040; Eastern Market Metro. Oddball set of art-related items, from abstract paintings to quirky sculptures made by international artisans to colourful hats and jewellery.

Wake Up Little Suzie 3409 Connecticut Ave, Upper Northwest ☏202/244-0700; Cleveland Park Metro. Trinket emporium with a broad range of interesting items, including home-made jewellery and ceramics, arty novelty items, curious puppets and more.

Books

Washington's array of **bookshops** is one of the high points of its shopping scene; you'll find a place to suit you whether you're looking for discounted new novels or political science tomes, superstores with coffee bars or cosy secondhand shops. That said, the internet has crippled some independent sellers; the larger dealers such as *Borders* and *Barnes & Noble* can be found everywhere (and aren't listed here). The weekly *City Paper* and Friday's *Washington Post* list bookshop **events** such as lectures, concerts and readings.

General

Books a Million 11 Dupont Circle NW ☏202/319-1374; Dupont Circle Metro. Dupont Circle bookseller that's handy for its central location to the tourist hotels, though it's a chain and the selection, though broad, is not very adventurous. Also has toys and arty doodads.

Bridge Street Books 2814 Pennsylvania Ave NW, Georgetown ☏202/965-5200. Excellent independent seller offering volumes on politics, literature, history, philosophy, music and film, with author readings of fiction and poetry.

Kramerbooks 1517 Connecticut Ave NW, Dupont Circle ☏202/387-1400; Dupont Circle Metro. Esteemed city institution, as well as a fun place to hang out on the liveliest part of the Circle, with a very good and broad general

selection and a great café-restaurant, *Afterwords Café* (see p.209), and late-night hours at weekends.

Politics & Prose 5015 Connecticut Ave NW, Upper Northwest ☏202/364-1919; no close Metro. Located in the northern reaches of the District, this is a good independent bookshop/coffee shop with one of the best programmes of author appearances and readings in the city. If you love politics, this should be your first (literary) stop.

Secondhand

Bartleby's Books 1132 29th St NW, Georgetown ☏202/298-0486. Focuses on American history, law and politics, with a strong antiquarian bent, and with a good array of art, literature, poetry, and other books as well.

Malls

The **malls** around downtown DC are all pretty uninspiring; for better ones (and lower sales taxes) you'll have to head for the suburbs. There's direct Metro access to the stores at Friendship Heights, Crystal City and Pentagon City that are listed below. **Opening hours** are usually Monday to Saturday from 10am to 8pm, Sunday from noon to 6pm.

Downtown
Old Post Office Pavilion 1100 Pennsylvania Ave NW ☎202/289-4224; Federal Triangle Metro; see also p.116.

Union Station Mall 50 Massachusetts Ave NE ☎202/371-9441; Union Station Metro; see also p.86.

Georgetown
Shops at Georgetown Park 3222 M St NW ☎202/298-5577; Foggy Bottom–GWU Metro or DC Circulator (see p.161).

Out of town
Chevy Chase Pavilion 5345 Wisconsin Ave NW ☎202/686-5335; Friendship Heights Metro.

Crystal City Shops Crystal Drive at Jefferson Davis Hwy, Arlington ☎703/922-4636; Crystal City Metro.

Fashion Centre at Pentagon City 1100 S Hayes St, Arlington ☎703/415-2400; Pentagon City Metro.

Landmark Mall 5801 Duke St, Alexandria ☎703/354-8405.

Mazza Gallerie 5300 Wisconsin Ave NW ☎202/966-6114; Friendship Heights Metro.

Potomac Mills Outlet Mall 2700 Potomac Mills Circle, Prince William, VA ☎1-800/826-4557.

Tysons Corner Center 1961 Chain Bridge Rd, McLean, VA ☎703/847-7300. Biggest mall in the region.

Tysons Galleria 2001 International Drive, McLean, VA ☎703/827-7700.

White Flint Mall 11301 Rockville Pike, Bethesda, MD ☎301/468-5777.

Books for America 1417 22nd St NW ☎202/835-2665; Dupont Circle Metro. Broad selection of often ultra-cheap books, many of them recent releases, with some of DC's best bargain books. Also has a decent music selection.

Kulturas 1728 Connecticut Ave NW ☎202/588-1270; Dupont Circle Metro. A truly eclectic selection, including oddball artworks and vintage clothing, as well as a broad selection of used books. Also in the Upper Northwest neighbourhood of Tenleytown at 4918 Wisconsin Ave NW (☎202/244-0224; Friendship Heights or Tenleytown Metro).

The Lantern: Bryn Mawr Bookshop 3241 P St NW, Georgetown ☎202/333-3222. This rare and vintage book dealer has a great general selection of secondhand titles, all donated – though it's open only in the afternoon, and you should call in advance.

Idle Time Books 2467 18th St NW, Adams Morgan ☎202/232-4774; Woodley Park–Zoo Metro. Local favourite for a well-selected array of used and vintage titles, with a bent toward fiction, left-leaning politics, science and the offbeat.

Red Sky Books 4318 Fessenden St NW, Upper Northwest ☎202/363-9147; Friendship Heights Metro. This bookshop has a fascinating grab bag of material, and has an eclectic selection: music and songbooks, art and architecture (especially African art), craftworks, photography, travel and other topics.

Second Story Books 2000 P St NW, Dupont Circle ☎202/659-8884; Dupont Circle Metro. Large range of used books, antiques and records; the prices tend to be cheap and the staff knowledgeable.

Specialist interest

AIA Bookstore 1735 New York Ave NW, Foggy Bottom ☎202/626-7475; **Farragut West Metro.** Operated by the American Institute of Architects, this is a spot to visit if you're interested in local or national architecture of a wide variety of styles.

InfoShop in the World Bank, 701 18th St NW, Foggy Bottom ☎202/458-4500; **Farragut West Metro.** An excellent institutional bookshop with fine volumes on finance, education, international relations, the developing world and the environment, with many educational videos, too.

Library of Congress Shop 101 Independence Ave SE, Jefferson Bldg ☎1-888/682-3557; **Capitol South Metro.** The esteemed institution's own worthy bookseller, which offers volumes on the nation's art, folklore, history, geography and culture, as well as glossy books about the presidents.

US Government Bookstore 710 N Capitol St, Downtown ☎202/512-0132; **Union Station Metro.** Official tomes and publications loaded with all the facts and figures you could ever want, at the central government printing-office bookshop. Newly remodelled and reopened, too.

Clothing

The best areas for browsing for **clothing** are in Downtown, along Connecticut Avenue and Dupont Circle, also along Connecticut. Tucked among the ubiquitous Gaps and Banana Republics, you'll find a handful of unique boutiques worth a look. Gentrifying Adams Morgan has begun to get in on the act, with a growing number of ultra-hip clothing shops appearing along 18th Street, amid the trendy bars and restaurants.

But nearly every serious shopper winds up in **Georgetown**, the District's retail epicentre. Along Wisconsin Avenue and M Street you'll find the greatest concentration of the national chains, as well as local boutiques and more exclusive shops.

Women's boutiques

American in Paris 1225 King St, Alexandria ☎703/519-8234; **King Street Metro.** One of the top spots in town to get your fix of fashionable European clothing, as well as unique garments from local designers, with a serious French bent and plenty of attitude.

Betsey Johnson 3029 M Street, Georgetown ☎202/338-4090. The good-quality but whimsical creations of this well-known manic-pixie designer of women's fashions call out from behind a colourful facade.

Betsy Fisher 1224 Connecticut Ave, Downtown ☎202/785-1975; **Farragut North Metro.** Sophisticated women's attire, from conservative to hip, comes with sage advice from the owner herself. Popular with urban professionals on the prowl for chic designer names.

Donna Lewis 309 Cameron St, Alexandria ☎703/548-2452; **King Street Metro.** Hip yet classy women's clothes, and a handful of Italian bags and shoes. Prices are at the upper end, but with an in-house tailor, the clothes are sure to fit.

Imagine Artwear 1124 King St, Alexandria ☎703/548-1461; **King Street Metro.** Eclectic fashions bridging the gap between the aesthetic and the functional, including brightly coloured garments that could pass for tapestries, handcrafted jewellery and more.

Kenneth Cole 1100 S Hayes St, Fashion Centre at Pentagon City, Arlington ☎703/415-3522; **Pentagon City Metro.** Big name for upper-end men's and women's shoes, belts, sunglasses, jewellery and jackets.

Muleh 1831 14th St NW, Shaw ☎202/667-3440; **U Street–Cardozo Metro.** An essential stop for those living the elite DC dream, this store has a select range of the latest designer fashions (at stiff prices) as well as smart housewares and furniture.

Nuevo Mundo 313 Cameron St, Alexandria ☎703/549-0040; **King Street Metro.** Globetrotting mother-daughter team offers stylish clothes, unique "wearable art" from around the world (jewellery, accessories, etc), and other mildly exotic apparel.

Proper Topper 1350 Connecticut Ave NW, Downtown ☎202/842-3055; **Farragut North**

Metro. A sleek spot with a hip and stylish assortment of dresses, purses, bags, make-up, hats, watches, knick-knacks and jewellery. There's a second location in Georgetown at 3213 P St NW (T202/333-6200).

Pua Naturally 701 Pennsylvania Ave NW, Downtown T202/347-4543; **Archives–Navy Memorial Metro.** This classy boutique brings a splash of Nepalese and Indian flair to DC, with handwoven skirts, jackets and scarves, all made from natural fibres and dyes.

Sugar 1633 Wisconsin Ave NW, Georgetown T202/333-5331. As the name suggests, stock includes girlish and precocious skirts, tops, jeans and dresses from a range of big-name and up-and-coming designers.

Costumes, lingerie and accessories

Backstage 545 8th St SE, Capitol Hill T202/544-5744; **Eastern Market Metro.** For a Halloween get-up or an elaborate disguise, this costume shop teems with wigs, feather boas, tiaras and cat suits. Also sells make-up, masks, dance shoes and books on theatre.

Coup de Foudre 1001 Pennsylvania Ave NW, Downtown T202/393-0878; **Federal Triangle Metro.** Top-shelf lingerie with a French cut and attitude, with European-style bikinis, bridal underwear, and accessories also on offer.

Leather Rack 1723 Connecticut Ave NW, Dupont Circle T202/797-7401; **Dupont Circle Metro.** A bevy of chaps, waistcoats and boots, plus fetish items and sexual accessories too bizarre to describe.

Men's clothing

Caramel Boutique 1603 U St, Shaw T202/265-1930; **U Street–Cardozo Metro.** Well-selected array of men's (and women's) clothing, with an emphasis on clean lines and crisp designs; nothing too trendy or outlandish, but a good bet if you want to look smart.

Commonwealth 1781 Florida Ave NW, Adams Morgan T202/265-1830; **Dupont Circle Metro.** Smart streetwear that includes some of the region's top brands, with hip sneakers and

hats, leather wallets, and a full range of T-shirts and jeans.

Dash's of Old Town 1114 King St, Alexandria T703/299-4015; **King Street Metro.** You'll look better than any politician after a visit to this splendid, one-of-a-kind DC specialist in Italian menswear, with suits, jackets, ties and everything else you need to look like a diplomat.

Fleet Feet 1841 Columbia Rd NW, Adams Morgan T202/387-3888; **Woodley Park–Zoo Metro.** Provides the proper shoes for different sports, and lets you test-drive the pair outside. An assortment of sports clothes and accessories is also on hand.

Reiss 1254 Wisconsin Ave NW, Georgetown T202/944-8566. Fashion from England for men and women, all of it fairly chic and pricey, with tasteful suits and dresses to help you keep up with the DC in-crowd.

Secondhand and vintage

Annie Creamcheese 3279 M St NW, Georgetown T202/298-5555. A fun seller of vintage wear that offers countless items from various decades, including grand-motherly frocks, ultra-mod jackets and boots, stylish cocktail dresses, and retro T-shirts and jewellery.

Meeps Vintage Fashionette 2104 18th St NW, Adams Morgan T202/265-6546; **Woodley Park–Zoo Metro.** A neighbourhood favourite that offers a cool selection of men's and women's vintage attire, some of which dates as far back as the 1940s.

Nana 1528 U St NW, Shaw T202/667-6955; **U Street–Cardozo Metro.** Quality U Street retailer with a pleasing blend of new and vintage dresses, hats, jewellery and acces-sories, some of it at affordable prices.

Secondhand Rose 1516 Wisconsin Ave NW, Georgetown T202/337-3378. A fine spot to pick up the swanky designer dresses, suits and sunglasses you've seen the DC political glitterati wearing – for a fraction of the price they paid when the clothes were new.

Secondi 1702 Connecticut Ave NW, Dupont Circle T202/667-1122; **Dupont Circle Metro.** Agreeable selection of high-flying designer names, marked down to a more affordable level.

Museum and gallery stores

Any self-respecting museum or gallery has its own elaborate **gift shop**. However, a few truly inspired merchandisers – selling goods you may only find in the District – are worth a visit even if you haven't visited their associated museum or gallery, and the highlights of these select few are listed below. See also the Indian Craft Shop on p.252.

Bureau of Engraving and Printing 14th and C sts SW, south of the Mall ☎1-800/456-3408; **Smithsonian Metro.** Just the place for that ideal DC gift: presidential engravings, prints of the city, copies of famous texts, even bags of shredded cash.

International Spy Museum 800 F St NW, Downtown ☎1-866/779-6873; **Gallery Place–Chinatown Metro.** A full array of Cold War-style gadgets and devices to help you play spy, as well as toys, books, games and trinkets based around the espionage trade, or at least the James Bond version of it.

National Air and Space Museum Independence Ave and 6th SW, National Mall ☎202/357-1387; **Archives–Navy Memorial Metro.** Fantastic array of air- and space-related goodies, from science-fiction books to ray guns and spaceman "ice cream".

National Gallery of Art Constitution Ave, between 3rd and 7th St NW, National Mall

☎202/842-6002 or 1-800/697-9350; **L'Enfant Plaza Metro.** Perhaps DC's best art shop, with thousands of books, prints, slides, posters and postcards.

National Museum of African Art 950 Independence Ave SW, National Mall ☎202/786-2147; **Smithsonian Metro.** Rich and splendid displays of African arts and crafts, including fine fabrics, icons and jewellery.

National Museum of Natural History 10th St NW and Constitution Ave, National Mall ☎202/633-1000; **Federal Triangle Metro.** Though crawling with kids, worth a visit for its huge selection of tomes relating to science, geology, biology, paleontology and other fields.

Textile Museum 2320 S St NW, Kalorama ☎202/667-0441; **Dupont Circle Metro.** Unique T-shirts, ethnic fabrics, textile books, silks, cushion covers, ties, kimonos and jewellery.

Music

CD Cellar 2614 Wilson Blvd, Arlington ☎703/248-0635; **Court House Metro.** Thousands of CDs, DVDs, vinyl records and even VHS tapes in stock, most of them used and affordable, with some rare and

unexpected titles. Also at 709 West Broad St, Falls Church, VA (☎703/534-6318).

Crooked Beat 2116 18th St NW, Adams Morgan ☎202/483-2328; **Woodley Park–Zoo Metro.** Fine music dealer that tries to bring back the

Food and drink

Washington isn't exactly known for its emporia of **food and drink**, though a few good places do stand out. Tasty **coffee**, at least, isn't hard to find – many of the coffee bars listed in the "Cafés and restaurants" chapter can sell you the beans. For quality **tea**, try one of *Teaism*'s branches (p.209 and p.208) or *Ching Ching Cha* (p.214) in Georgetown.

Old-style **markets** are thin on the ground: Eastern Market (p.85) is your best bet, while the Fish Wharf (p.93) has a great selection of Chesapeake Bay seafood. There are weekend farmers' markets in Adams Morgan and Dupont Circle in DC, and various close locations in Maryland and Virginia (⊛www.freshfarmmarkets.org lists a number of these).

For bread, you can't beat *The Breadline* (p.204) or *Firehook Bakery & Coffeehouse* (p.209). The best general deli is the splendid *Dean & Deluca* (p.214) in Georgetown, although Dupont Circle's homespun *Marvelous Market* (p.209) is a great local find; other great delis are Loeb's (p.207), Morty's (p.213) and *Café Mozart* (p.205).

Galleries

Most of the District's commercial art **galleries** host rotating exhibitions that you can view at no charge. The galleries listed below are some of the more notable; call for details of current shows or check the *City Paper* or the *Washington Post*'s "Weekend" section. There's also a monthly listings guide called *Galleries* (Ⓦwww .galleriesmagazine.com), available in bookshops. Most are closed on Monday and many are also closed on Tuesday.

Downtown and Foggy Bottom

406 7th Street NW Archives–Navy Memorial or Gallery Place–Chinatown Metro. A group of galleries featuring the works of DC-area artists – paintings, sculpture, photographs and mixed media.

Arts Club of Washington 2017 I St NW Ⓣ202/331-7282; Foggy Bottom–GWU or Farragut West Metro. Eclectic exhibits of works by local artists; see also p.232, for its occasional classical-music concerts.

Irvine Contemporary Art 1412 14th St NW, Logan Circle Ⓣ202/332-8767; no close Metro. Broad, interesting selection of modern or contemporary paintings, prints and other visual art.

Long View Gallery 1234 9th St NW Ⓣ202/232-4788; Mount Vernon Square–UDC Metro. Tasteful, somewhat austere modern sculpture, painting and photography, with pieces mostly by regional names.

Dupont Circle

Aaron Gallery 2101 L Street NW Ⓣ202/234-3311; Farragut North Metro. Abstract Expressionism is alive and well at this showcase for local artists devoted to using composition, colour and line in a variety of media

Gallery 10, Ltd. 1519 Connecticut Ave NW Ⓣ202/232-3326; Dupont Circle Metro. A bevy of unusual and experimental pieces that span all kinds of media, from installations and video art to mixed-media sculptures and collage.

Jane Haslem Gallery 2025 Hillyer Place Ⓣ202/232-4644; Dupont Circle Metro. One of the brasher galleries, showcasing artists willing to experiment with form, colour and content in eye-opening ways, using a wide variety of media.

Studio Gallery 2108 R St NW Ⓣ202/232-8734; Dupont Circle Metro. Established gallery that appeals for its landscapes and abstracts (both painting and sculpture) by local artists.

Georgetown

Addison/Ripley Fine Art 1670 Wisconsin Ave NW Ⓣ202/333-5180. Contemporary and tasteful fine art – oil paintings, photography, sculpture and prints.

Cross Mackenzie Ceramic Arts 1054 31st St NW Ⓣ202/333-7970. Art pottery, from whimsical and bizarre to austere and abstract, at this must-see gallery for fans of modern ceramics.

Prada Gallery 1030 Wisconsin Ave NW Ⓣ202/342-0067. Contemporary art from local and regional artists working in a variety of media, with a bent toward abstraction.

Other locations

Kathleen Ewing Gallery 3615 Ordway St NW, Upper Northwest Ⓣ202/328-0955; no close Metro. Highly regarded gallery featuring nineteenth- and twentieth-century photography, plus some multimedia works.

Torpedo Factory Art Center 105 N Union St, Alexandria Ⓣ703/838-4565, Ⓦwww .torpedofactory.org; King Street Metro. The place for art in the Alexandria area, with three floors of galleries showcasing contemporary work by more than eighty regional artists.

Washington Printmakers Gallery Pyramid Atlantic Art Center, 8230 Georgia Ave, Silver Spring, MD Ⓣ301/273-3660; Silver Spring Metro. Original prints by contemporary artists, plus monotypes, relief works and other inventive uses of the print medium.

golden days of record stores, with expert staff able to recommend good indie, alternative and even mainstream music, and suggest the best choices in CD and vinyl.

Melody Record Shop 1623 Connecticut Ave NW, Dupont Circle ☎202/232-4002; **Dupont Circle Metro.** Well-selected array of CDs and DVDs, with an accent on classical, jazz and indie music, several listening stations, and a number of rarities and oddments. Also offers new vinyl.

Red Onion 1901 18th St NW, Adams Morgan ☎202/986-2718; **Dupont Circle Metro.**

Easy-to-miss basement store with a small but very well-chosen group of LPs, CDs and books; the kind of place you can have a proper browse, without hunting through too much rubbish.

Som Records 1843 14th St NW, Shaw ☎202/328-3345; **U Street–Cardozo Metro.** Essential stop for vinyl in the District, where you can grab everything from long-forgotten rock and jazz LPs up to the latest electronica platters. Aspiring DJs can also rent gear here.

Contexts

Contexts

History

I n the two centuries since Washington, DC was founded, it has been at the heart of American government, a showcase city embodying the ideals and aspirations of the United States. Among the mighty institutions, monuments and memorials, however, it's often easy to forget it's also a city where people live and work. The **history** below briefly outlines the main themes in the city's development. For more detail on specific matters – from biographies of famous people to histories of buildings – follow the pointers at the end of each section.

Native peoples

The area that is now the nation's capital was, for most of its history of human habitation, populated by native peoples like the **Piscataway**, who spoke an Algonquin dialect and lived on both banks of the Chesapeake Bay. They were content to live a fairly peaceful existence in tepees, hunting and fishing for game, and their dugout canoes and handwoven baskets are evidence of their long-standing culture in the region.

They did, however, have their enemies – the belligerent **Susquehannocks** were perhaps the most fearsome fellow tribe, scheming and attacking their settlements such as Nacotchtant, around present-day Anacostia. The war-mongering of the Susquehannocks, however, could not alone drive the tribe from the region; predictably, it took the presence of **European settlers** to do that. Although Spanish explorer Pedro Menendez cruised around the southern Chesapeake inlets in the sixteenth century, English colonists would later have more interest in the land and prove to be a more formidable foe for the Piscataway than any other they'd encountered.

> National Museum of the American Indian p.64

European settlement

Sponsored by King James I, **English settlers** under Captain John Smith of the Virginia Company in 1608 established the first successful English colony in America at **Jamestown** on the coast to the south. What is now DC was mostly overlooked – though Smith did explore the Potomac River as far as Great Falls, and perhaps beyond. It wasn't until the 1630s that European settlement in the Chesapeake Basin really took off, with the granting to Lord Baltimore of a royal charter establishing a Catholic colony in the region, **Maryland**, that would welcome members of that persecuted denomination from other parts of the British Empire. This grant was timely, since just eight years later, Parliament under Puritan domination would prove openly hostile to any even remotely Catholic enterprises.

Despite early setbacks, the colonists flourished on the back of a thriving **tobacco trade**. In the later seventeenth century both Virginia and Maryland expanded as English, Irish and Scottish settlers poured into the region, at first allying with the indigenous population of the Piscataway before eventually expelling them from the area. Although Baltimore and other Catholics attempted at first to convert the tribe to Christianity (with little success), much like Protestant colonizers they soon drove the natives further into the wilderness, where they became prey for larger, more dominant tribes. The Europeans also introduced **slaves** from West Africa to work the plantations. The Potomac remained an important commercial thoroughfare, and vibrant new towns sprang up alongside it: notably **Alexandria** in Virginia (1749) and **Georgetown** in Maryland (1751).

| Alexandria | p.177 | Georgetown, history | p.162 |

The Revolutionary War and the creation of the capital

Increasing hostilities with England throughout the 1770s led the colonies – now calling themselves states – to draft the Declaration of Independence in 1776. The **American Revolutionary War** (1775–83), however, had already begun, and George Washington was leading troops of volunteer militia, which later formed into something resembling a continental army. The battle that basically guaranteed American independence – Yorktown, in 1781 – was fought south of DC in Virginia, within 25 miles of the founding colonial site of Jamestown.

After the war, some revolutionary leaders proposed the establishment of a permanent capital city, but conflicting political interests in the new republic made choosing a spot too difficult, so Congress met in several different cities in its early years, including Philadelphia, site of the 1787 **Constitutional Convention**, and New York City, where **George Washington** was inaugurated as the first president of the United States in 1789. The site of present-day DC was chosen for the nation's capital in 1790, largely as a result of **political wrangling**: because the South allowed the federal government to assume the states' Revolutionary War debts (a key Northern demand), the North allowed the new federal capital to be built in the upper South, on the sparsely populated banks of the Potomac River.

With the help of Major **Andrew Ellicott**, a surveyor from Maryland, and the black mathematician and scientist **Benjamin Banneker**, Washington – a mean surveyor himself – suggested a diamond-shaped, hundred-square-mile site at the confluence of the Potomac and Anacostia rivers. Though the land was swampy, it seemed a canny choice: by incorporating the ports of Alexandria in Virginia and Georgetown in Maryland, and building its own port in Anacostia, the city would be ripe for trade, and it was only eighteen miles upriver from Washington's beloved home at Mount Vernon. Maryland ceded roughly seventy square miles of land for its construction, Virginia thirty; and Congress decreed it would be named Washington City, in the Territory (later District) of Columbia, itself a reference to Christopher Columbus. (Thomas Jefferson thought up both monikers.)

| Declaration of Independence | p.120 | Mount Vernon | p.183 |
| Benjamin Banneker | p.93 | George Washington | pp.264–265 |

L'Enfant's plan

For the job of city planner, Washington recommended **Major Pierre Charles L'Enfant**, a former member of his Continental Army staff and a fellow Freemason. Inspired by the city of Paris and the Palace of Versailles, L'Enfant came up with an ambitious blueprint for the capital, one with both a conventional street grid (Thomas Jefferson's suggestion) and diagonal avenues radiating from ceremonial squares and elegant circles. The avenues were named after the fifteen states that existed in 1791, with those named after Northern states placed north of the Capitol, Southern ones to the south; the most populous states – Virginia, New York, Pennsylvania and Massachusetts – were represented by the longest roads. A "Grand Avenue" – later known as the National Mall – formed the centrepiece; government buildings were assigned their own plots; a central canal linked the city's ports; and sculptures, fountains and parks punctuated the design.

Washington was delighted with the scheme, though the existing landowners were less than pleased with the injunction to donate any land needed for public thoroughfares. Moreover, L'Enfant found himself in constant dispute with the District commissioners who had been appointed by Washington to oversee the construction. His obstinacy cost him his job in 1792, and the design of the US Capitol and White House were both later thrown open to public competition.

| The National Mall | p.43 | L'Enfant memorial, Arlington House | p.175 |

Building and rebuilding DC

The first stone of the Executive Mansion – today's **White House** – was laid in 1792, construction of the **US Capitol** followed in 1793, and in 1800 **Congress** and the nation's second president, John Adams, moved from Philadelphia to the nascent city just months before he left office. The following year, **Thomas Jefferson** became the first president to be inaugurated in Washington, DC.

The city was scarcely more than a village, however, with only 3500 free residents, largely based around Capitol Hill and the Executive Mansion. And it was far from complete – 3000 slaves, who lived in the swamp-ridden reaches near the river, laboured on new buildings, wharves and streets. Progress was interrupted by the **War of 1812** with England. Although the war was largely fought in far-flung places like Quebec and upstate New York, the British did score a propaganda coup when in 1814 they sailed up the Potomac to burn the White House, the Capitol and other public buildings to the ground. President James Madison was forced to relocate to a private DC house, known as the **Octagon**, where the peace treaty ending the war was signed in 1814. Congress met in a hastily assembled Brick Capitol until the original was fully restored in 1819.

| The Octagon | p.109 | Presidential inaugurations | p.115 |
| US Capitol, history | p.75 | White House, history | p.98 |

George Washington

The namesake of America's capital city, **George Washington** appropriately shows up around town – in statues, building names, estates, even on the money you carry. And while it took the general a while to establish himself as a war hero, it was his relative lack of egotism, his political dexterity and his natural charm that kept his young republic on a course of independence and, ultimately, self-sufficiency.

The Washington family, originally from the north of **England**, emigrated to America in 1656, a decade after the English Civil War (during which they had been fierce loyalists) and the establishment of Oliver Cromwell's military dictatorship. George Washington was born on February 22, 1732, on his wealthy family's plantation in Westmoreland County, Virginia. Although most of what is known about Washington's early life comes from various nineteenth-century hagiographies, it is clear that he received intermittent schooling and excelled in most outdoor pursuits. Because he wasn't his family's first-born son (primogeniture was a big deal in the Cavalier country of north Virginia), he stood to inherit little property other than a small farm on the Rappahannock River. Washington therefore taught himself how to be a **surveyor**, and in 1748 assisted in the surveying of the new port of Alexandria.

At the age of 21 Washington was selected by Virginia's governor to travel into the Ohio Valley to ascertain the strength of the French forces, which had been steadily encroaching on British turf. Soon after, he was appointed **lieutenant colonel** in the Virginia Regiment and, later, aide-de-camp in the French and Indian War, in which he gained his first battle experience, suffering a bad defeat but gaining respect for his leadership qualities. Finishing his service in the war as regimental commander, Washington had few military successes on which to stake his reputation, but he was elected to the **Virginia House of Burgesses** in Williamsburg nonetheless. Giving up his commission, in January 1759, he married the wealthy **Martha Dandridge Custis** – who had two children from a previous marriage – and settled at **Mount Vernon** after his eldest brother died. For a time Washington led the bucolic life of a gentleman plantation owner, a lifestyle buttressed by a large number of slaves. George and Martha never had any children of their own, but they later became guardians to the youngest two of Martha's grandchildren by her first marriage.

Still serving in the House of Burgesses throughout the 1760s, Washington developed a reputation for honesty and good judgement, and was one of the Virginia delegates at the **Continental Congress** in 1774; the following year, when British soldiers clashed with American volunteers at Lexington and Concord, confrontation turned into revolution. At a second meeting of the Continental Congress in

The antebellum era

Between the War of 1812 and the Civil War, the new capital struggled to make its mark; it was designed to be America's commercial and industrial showpiece, but was consistently overshadowed by Philadelphia and New York, and scarcely had enough residents to make it much of anything except a paper tiger of bureaucracy. **The Mall** – L'Enfant's central thoroughfare – remained a muddy swamp, and construction was slow and piecemeal. Foreign ambassadors collected hardship pay while stationed in this marshy outpost, and criticism was heaped upon the place; early snide detractors included such notable visitors as Charles Dickens (in the 1840s) and Anthony Trollope (1860s).

Despite its critics, however, the capital city was slowly beginning to look the part. **Pennsylvania Avenue** was spruced up as a grand link between the White House and Capitol, monumental buildings like the US Treasury and Patent Office (both by Robert Mills) were added in the 1830s and 1840s, and work started on the

June 1775, the 43-year-old Washington was appointed **commander in chief** of the nascent American forces.

Washington had his limitations as a battlefield tactician; due to early mistakes, his underequipped Continental Army lost more battles than it won. But he did have a knack for imposing order and hierarchy onto the fledgling army and retaining the respect of his forces during trying times. (Throughout the war, Washington shared his soldiers' hardships by spending the winters with them, rather than at Mount Vernon.) He was also a fine judge of talent in his subordinates and promoted such key figures as Friedrich von Steuben and Nathanael Greene, both of whom proved to be excellent tacticians and strategists.

Indeed, Washington proved such an impressive commander that, after the battle at **Yorktown** in 1781 and the establishment of peace two years later, some of his supporters urged him to assume an American "kingship"; instead he resigned his commission and returned to Mount Vernon. Four years later, however, he was back in the political arena. After being unanimously elected as the presiding officer at the 1787 **Constitutional Convention** in Philadelphia – where the Constitution was drawn up and ratified – he was unanimously elected by the electoral college in 1789 as the first **President of the United States**.

Washington defined the uncharted role of president while developing the relationship between the executive and other **branches of government**, as well as the relationship between the federal government and those of the states. During his first term, he even negotiated the political minefield that was choosing the site of the new federal capital. The **capital city** was promptly named after him, and the president laid the cornerstone of the US Capitol in 1793 in a ceremony rich with Masonic symbolism (Washington was a committed member). However, he never lived in Washington or the White House – which wasn't finished until 1800 – shuttling instead between New York, Philadelphia and other Northeastern cities.

Washington was elected to a **second term** in 1793 and would undoubtedly have been granted a third, but in 1797 he was 65 and wanted nothing more than to retire to his farm. Delivering a farewell address to both houses of Congress, he went home to Mount Vernon, where he died two and a half years later on December 14, 1799, from a fever said to have been induced by being caught out in a snowstorm. Congress adjourned for the day, and even the British and French fleets lowered their flags in respect. Martha lived until May 1802, and on her death, Washington's will freed all their slaves. George and Martha are buried together in the grounds of Mount Vernon.

Washington Monument in 1848. British gentleman scientist and philanthropist James Smithson made a huge bequest in 1829, which led to the founding of the Smithsonian Institution; its first home, the **Smithsonian Institution Building** (or the "Castle"), was completed on the Mall in 1855. Despite these advancements, Virginia demanded its share of the capital back in 1846, and the District of Columbia lost two of its major components – Arlington and Alexandria. Only Georgetown remained as an independent city in the District outside of Washington.

Though DC's population increased slowly, throughout the first half of the nineteenth century it never reached 60,000. The balance of the steadily rising black population shifted, however, as the number of runaway slaves from Southern plantations and free blacks jumped dramatically. Separate black schools and churches were established as debate intensified between abolitionists and pro-slavery adherents – the so-called **Snow Riots** (1835) saw intimidation and destruction by white mobs intent on maintaining slavery in the capital. Indeed, as it grew, Washington became a microcosm of the divisions searing the country at large – ideologically polarized residents, each eyeing the other with suspicion;

political combat so fractious as to make dialogue nearly impossible; and the increasing threat of secession in the air. When the domination of the pro-slavery **Democratic Party** – which had ruled the country for all but eight years since 1800 – came to an end in 1860, so too did the bonds of the nation.

The Civil War

Following the Confederate attack on Fort Sumter in South Carolina, which finally propelled the country into civil war, **Abraham Lincoln**'s call to defend the Union in 1861 brought thousands of volunteer soldiers to Washington,

The assassination of Abraham Lincoln

In the days after Robert E. Lee surrendered to Ulysses S. Grant on April 9, 1865, officially ending the Civil War, there was a celebratory mood in Washington, DC. On the evening of Good Friday, April 14, 1865, **President and Mrs Lincoln** went to Ford's Theatre to see top actress Laura Keene perform in the comedy *Our American Cousin*, a play about a yokel who travels to England to claim his inheritance. The president's advisers were never very keen on him appearing in public, but Lincoln, as on previous occasions, overrode their objections. The Lincolns were accompanied by their friends Major Henry Rathbone and his fiancée, Clara Harris; the four took their seats upstairs in the presidential box, just after the play had started.

Conspirators had been plotting to kill the president for weeks. **John Wilkes Booth**, a 26-year-old actor with Confederate sympathies and delusions of grandeur, had first conceived of a plan to kidnap Lincoln during the war and use him as a bargaining chip for the release of Southern prisoners. Booth drew others into the conspiracy, notably **John Surratt**, already acting as a low-level courier for the secessionist cause, whose mother owned a rooming house on H Street, where the plot was hatched. **George Atzerodt** from Maryland was recruited because he knew the surrounding countryside and its hiding places, as was **David Herold**, a pharmacist's clerk in DC; **Lewis Powell** (or Paine, as he was sometimes known) was hired as muscle. With Lee's surrender in April, Booth decided to assassinate rather than kidnap the president; Herold, Atzerodt and Powell were to kill Secretary of State **William Seward** and Vice President **Andrew Johnson**. But these other attacks came to naught: Surratt left the group when the talk turned to murder, Atzerodt chickened out of assassinating Johnson, and while Powell broke into Seward's house and stabbed him in the face and neck, the secretary of state later recovered.

At about 10.15pm, during the third act of the play, when only one actor was on stage and the audience was laughing at a joke, the assassin struck. Lincoln's bodyguard had left the box unattended, and Booth took the opportunity to step inside and shoot Lincoln in the back of the head. Major Rathbone grappled with Booth but was stabbed in the arm with a hunting knife and severely wounded. Booth then jumped the 12ft down onto the stage, catching one of his spurs and fracturing a bone in his left leg as he fell. But he was on his feet immediately – most of the audience thought it was part of the play – and shouted "Sic semper tyrannis!" ("Thus ever to tyrants", the motto of the state of Virginia) before running off backstage and into the alley, where he had a horse waiting.

virtually doubling the city's population. Others left to join the Confederate cause, among them **Robert E. Lee**, who abandoned his estate at Arlington and his Union Army post to take command of the Virginia military. Washington, DC became the epicentre of the Union effort and the North's main supply depot, surrounded by defensive forts (now known as the Fort Circle Parks), its grand Neoclassical buildings turned over to massive makeshift hospitals. Lincoln determined to continue construction in the capital – symbolically, the **Capitol dome** was added in 1863 – despite fear of imminent attack by Southern forces. Though the city was never overrun, several of the bloodiest battles (including Manassas, Antietam and Gettysburg) were fought within ninety miles of it. Because of these factors, an atmosphere of paranoia developed in the capital, and as reports of spies, saboteurs and assassins became legion, Lincoln took such drastic measures as suspending certain civil liberties (such as habeas corpus) for residents of nearby Maryland – thought to be a hotbed of rebel intrigue.

As it dragged on, the Civil War became as much about slavery as about preserving the Union, Lincoln's initial goal. Slavery was outlawed in DC in 1862, and in 1863 the **Emancipation Proclamation** freed all slaves in rebel states – though not those of pro-Union slave states like Maryland and Kentucky. Eventually the South was

First into the presidential box was **Charles Augustus Leale**, a young army doctor. Lincoln was unconscious and labouring badly, and the decision was made to carry him to the nearest house to care for him better. Once inside the **Petersen House**, Lincoln was placed in the small back bedroom, where Leale and the other doctors strived to save him. Soon the house was bulging at the seams, as Mrs Lincoln, her son Robert, Secretary of War Edwin Stanton, various politicians and army officers, and, eventually, Lincoln's pastor, arrived to do what they could. Lincoln never regained consciousness and died at 7.22am the next morning, April 15; Stanton spoke for all when he declaimed, "Now he belongs to the ages" (or, as some historians assert, to the "angels"). Lincoln's body was taken back to the White House, where it lay in state for three days before the funeral.

Booth, meanwhile, had fled on horseback through Maryland with David Herold, stopping at a certain **Doctor Mudd**'s to have his injured leg treated. The pair hid out for several days, but after crossing into Virginia they were eventually surrounded by Union troops at a farm. Herold surrendered, and on the same day, April 26, Booth was shot dead while holed up inside. All the other alleged conspirators were soon captured and sent for trial on May 10 in a military court at **Fort McNair**. They were kept chained and hooded and, after six weeks of evidence, Herold, Powell, Atzerodt and Mary Surratt were sentenced to hang, the punishment being carried out on July 7, 1865. A last-minute reprieve for Mary Surratt – who, although she housed the conspirators, probably knew nothing of the conspiracy – was refused, and she became the first woman to be executed by the US government. Dr Mudd received a life sentence, while the stagehand who held Booth's horse at the theatre got six years, though both were pardoned in 1869 by Andrew Johnson, Lincoln's successor. John Surratt, who fled America, was recaptured in 1867 and also stood trial, but he was freed when the jury couldn't agree on a verdict.

It's hard to say how much of an effect Lincoln's assassination may have had on subsequent, turbulent American history, though it is interesting to note the personal effect that the close-quarters assassination had on the three other occupants of the presidential box that night: ten years later Mary Lincoln – never the most stable of people – was judged insane and committed, and in 1883 Clara Harris (by now Clara Harris Rathbone) was shot by her husband, Henry Rathbone, who died in an asylum in 1911.

defeated by the North's superior strength and economic muscle, not to mention the striking, yet bloody, strategy of attrition by Union commander **Ulysses S. Grant**, who realized that pure, unending carnage was the way to bring the South to its knees. The war ended in April 1865 with Lee's surrender to Grant at Appomattox Court House in Virginia, not far from the initial battle of the war. Five days later, **Lincoln was assassinated** in Washington while attending a play at Ford's Theatre.

Reconstruction and expansion

The period after the Civil War was an era of tremendous growth in DC, as ex-slaves from the South and returned soldiers settled here; within thirty years, the population stood at 300,000 and distinct neighbourhoods had begun to emerge. Black residents now constituted forty percent of the population and enjoyed unprecedented rights and privileges in the aftermath of emancipation. **Suffrage** was extended to all adult men for local DC elections (1866), black public schools were established, the all-black **Howard University** was founded (1867), segregation was prohibited (1870), and ex-slave, orator and abolitionist **Frederick Douglass** was appointed marshal (and, later, recorder of deeds) of DC (1877).

Just as African Americans were beginning to gain some measure of political rights, the District itself was able to take the first small steps toward the enfranchisement of its citizens, an ongoing process ever since (see box, pp.270–271). At the same time, Washington's cultural profile went from strength to strength, boosted after the 1876 Philadelphia Centennial Exhibition when the Smithsonian Institution built America's first **National Museum** (now the Arts and Industries Building) on the Mall to provide a permanent home for the exhibition's artefacts. The **Renwick** and **Corcoran** galleries – two of the earliest public art museums in the country – both opened during this period. The Washington Monument, first of the city's grand presidential memorials, was finally completed in 1884, as DC began to reshape itself as a national showpiece. As its stock rose, place-seekers and lobbyists (a term first coined during Grant's presidency) flooded into the city, seeking attachment to the administration of the day. One such aspirant, Charles Guiteau, was so incensed at being denied a civil-service post that he assassinated **President James Garfield** in 1881, just four months after his inauguration.

Into the twentieth century

By the beginning of the twentieth century, Washington had established itself as a thriving, modern capital with civic and federal buildings to match: in a flurry of construction from the 1870s to the 1890s, fine premises for the **Old Post Office**, **Pension Building** and **Library of Congress** were erected, while Theodore Roosevelt carried out the first full-scale expansion and renovation of the White House (1901). Meanwhile, LeDroit Park, Adams Morgan and Cleveland Park became fashionable suburbs, Georgetown was formally merged with DC, and the Smithsonian branched out again with the establishment of the **National Zoo**.

In 1901, a committee under Senator James McMillan proposed the development and extension of the city's park system. Later, the National Commission of Fine Arts was established to coordinate public improvements and new building design: the country's largest train station, **Union Station**, was completed in the prevailing monumental Beaux-Arts style in 1908, and in 1910, height restrictions were imposed on downtown buildings to preserve the cityscape – ensuring that the Capitol remained the tallest and most prominent government edifice. However, after the high hopes of the Reconstruction years, the city's black population suffered from increasing segregation and loss of civil rights. Housing in black neighbourhoods like Foggy Bottom and Georgetown was in poor shape, federal jobs became harder to come by, and the black population actually decreased.

World War I and the Depression

The US entered World War I in 1917, despite President **Woodrow Wilson**'s avowed efforts to remain neutral; after the war, Washington's population increased again as soldiers returned home. The postwar years were as troubled for DC as they were for the rest of the US. Under Wilson, **Prohibition** was imposed in a futile attempt to improve the morality of the nation, and a number of strikes were violently broken. **Racial tension** increased in this uneasy climate, which saw segregation become entrenched, with the Ku Klux Klan parading at the Washington Monument and race riots, fanned by demobilized white soldiers, breaking out in the city in 1919. Ironically, segregation also worked to boost the fortunes of some of DC's black neighbourhoods: prevented from socializing elsewhere, African Americans made Shaw's **U Street** famous as the "Black Broadway", nurturing stars like Duke Ellington – a small bright spot in an otherwise oppressive system of redlining that would exist for another forty years. Elsewhere, the **Phillips Collection**, America's first modern art museum, opened in 1921, while the building of the **Lincoln Memorial** (1922) and the **Freer Gallery** (1923) represented the last cultural gasps of the McMillan Commission.

Washington, with its government agencies and large federal payroll, was not as hard-hit as rural or industrial areas by the **Great Depression**; unemployed "Bonus Marchers" (see p.76) from the rest of the country descended on the Capitol to register their distress in 1931 and 1932, only to be dispersed by the army under the command of Douglas MacArthur. This episode, along with the economic troubles, was another black mark on the record of President Herbert Hoover and led to Franklin Delano Roosevelt's historic victory in the 1932 election.

Roosevelt's **New Deal**, and, specifically, the **Works Progress Administration** (WPA), put thousands of jobless men to work – in DC, building the Federal

Washington, DC has always had an anomalous place in the Union. It's a **federal district** rather than a state, with no official constitution of its own, and its citizens are denied full representation under the American political system: they have no senator to defend their interests and only a non-voting representative in the House. The capital city shares this position with American Samoa, Guam and the Virgin Islands, but unlike those US territories, citizens of the District are responsible for paying federal taxes. And until 1961, when the 23rd Amendment was passed, DC residents weren't permitted to vote in presidential elections.

Although the city has had a mayor and some sort of elected council since 1802, in the early days so many inhabitants were transients – politicians, lobbyists, lawyers and appointed civil servants – that the local government was denied tax-raising powers; instead, Congress simply appropriated money piecemeal for necessary improvements. In 1871, the District was given **territorial status**. President Grant appointed a governor and city council, and an elected house of delegates and boards of public works and health followed; all adult males (black and white) were eligible to vote. Many of the most significant improvements to the city infrastructure date from this period of limited self-government, with the head of the Board of Public Works, **Alexander "Boss" Shepherd**, instrumental in dredging sewers, paving and lighting streets, and planting thousands of trees. However, Shepherd's improvements and a string of corruption scandals put the city $16 million in debt. Direct control of DC's affairs passed back to Congress in 1874, which later appointed three commissioners to replace the locally elected officials.

And that was how matters stood for a century, until Congress passed the **Home Rule Act** in 1973. Small improvements had already been effected – the first black commissioner (for a city now majority black) was appointed in 1961; later, an elected school board was established. But only in 1974, when the District's first elected mayor in more than a century, **Walter E. Washington**, took office, supported by a fully elected thirteen-member council, did the city wrest back some measure of

Triangle and Supreme Court (1935), among other projects. Despite this kind of progressive economic uplift, racial injustice proved a thornier issue. As just one example, in 1939 the **Daughters of the American Revolution** (DAR) infamously banned black contralto Marian Anderson from singing in their Constitution Hall; Anderson subsequently appeared in front of a huge, desegregated crowd at the Lincoln Memorial, in an early hint of the civil-rights battles to come.

World War II to the 1968 riots

In 1941 the US entered World War II, and a third great wartime influx boosted the population of Washington, DC. Guards were posted at the White House and Capitol, air defences were installed in case of Axis attack, and the **Pentagon** was built in 1943 to accommodate the expanding War Department. The war years also saw the opening of the **National Gallery of Art** (1941), one of the nation's finest museums, and the completion of the **Jefferson Memorial** (1943).

autonomy. However, Congress still retained a legislative veto over any proposed local laws and kept a close watch on spending limits.

Washington was succeeded as mayor in 1978 by Democrat **Marion S. Barry**, who at first was markedly successful in attracting much-needed investment. But long-standing whispers about Barry's turbulent private life – charges of drug addiction in particular – exploded in early 1990, when he was surreptitiously filmed in an FBI sting operation buying and using crack cocaine. By 1995, a Republican Congress finally tired of Barry and of the embarrassment of DC's massive budget deficit and revoked the city's home rule charter. A congressionally appointed financial control board was subsequently given jurisdiction over the city's finances, personnel and various work departments, stripping away what little responsibility the mayor had left.

Washington rebounded under the control board, as deficits became surpluses and city residents could once again afford to be optimistic about their trash being collected. By virtue of its success, the control board put itself out of business in 2001, and full executive power returned to the mayor and the council. But although the District's financial management seems to be improving, a daunting fiscal challenge remains. DC's tax base is too narrow to support the level of services the city requires: two-thirds of the city's workers live (and pay local taxes) in Virginia and Maryland, and roughly forty percent of the land is owned by the government (which excuses itself from taxes). The obvious solution to this problem – a commuter tax – is a nonstarter for political reasons, while past attempts to raise the income tax have only led to more fleeing to the suburbs. Many believe that achieving **statehood** would solve the District's financial conundrum (its licence plates already decry "Taxation Without Representation"). But the crux of granting statehood to DC lies in the realm of national politics: statehood would most likely mean that the District's voters, who are overwhelmingly liberal, would send one Democrat to the House and two to the Senate – DC citizens have never voted for a Republican for president, either, in fifty years. Ultimately, Republicans would almost certainly be able to block such a move with a filibuster.

Following the war, Washington grew as the federal government expanded under presidents Truman and Eisenhower, growing as a result of both the maintenance of New Deal-era programmes and fresh military and economic funds to fight the **Cold War**. By 1960, the city's population reached 800,000, the White House was completely overhauled, neighbouring Foggy Bottom became the seat of various departments and international organizations, and new housing proliferated in suburban Maryland and Virginia.

The war had gone some way toward changing racial perceptions in America, as black soldiers had again enlisted in droves to fight for freedom, and in the postwar years the **civil rights movement** began to gain strength. Segregation of public facilities was finally declared illegal by the Supreme Court ruling on **Brown v. Board of Education**, and schools in DC were desegregated in 1954. A feeling of progressive hope culminated in the close 1960 election victory of **John F. Kennedy** – the youngest president ever elected, and the only Catholic – and was epitomized by **Dr Martin Luther King Jr**'s famous "I Have a Dream" speech during the **March on Washington for Jobs and Freedom** at the Lincoln Memorial in August 1963. Just three months later, however, JFK was assassinated in Dallas and buried in Arlington Cemetery. In 1964, DC citizens voted in a presidential election for the first time, following the 23rd Amendment of 1961, which gave them new electoral rights. The contest was won in a landslide by Lyndon Johnson, who, as vice president, had become president after Kennedy's death.

By the late 1960s, despite the partial enactment of Johnson's **Great Society agenda**, including new civil-rights and Medicare legislation, the growing **Vietnam War** was taking a huge toll on the president's popularity and national cohesion. Demonstrations in Washington were called against poverty and the war itself, and the assassination of Dr Martin Luther King Jr in Memphis in 1968 led to nationwide **race riots**, including the worst in DC's history: parts of Shaw, Logan Circle and Downtown were devastated. The white flight to the suburbs began in earnest, and DC became a predominantly black city.

The Pentagon	p.176	National Gallery of Art	p.63
Jefferson Memorial	p.47	JFK's grave, Arlington	p.172
Lincoln Memorial	p.50	Riots of 1968	p.124

Growth and malaise

The 1970s were a time of momentous political upheaval in Washington, DC. In 1970, DC got its first nonvoting delegate to the House of Representatives; three years later, the Home Rule Act paved the way for the city's first elected mayor – **Walter Washington** – in more than a century; and the **Watergate scandal** of 1974 led to the resignation of President Richard Nixon – still the only such occurrence in US history.

Meanwhile, divisions within the city became increasingly stark. Downtown continued to reshape itself – the **Kennedy Center** opened in 1971, the **Hirshhorn Museum** (1974) and East Wing of the **National Gallery of Art** (1979) were added to the Mall, the K Street business and lobbyist district Downtown thrived, and artsy **Dupont Circle** became one of the city's trendiest neighbourhoods – while Shaw and areas of southeast and northeast Washington slipped further into degradation, with a drug and crime problem that earned DC the enduring tag of "**Murder Capital of America**".

Such contradictions were largely ignored, however, and in 1976, the nation's Bicentennial year, the city celebrated by opening its **Metrorail** system and the **National Air and Space Museum**. Jimmy Carter was sworn in as president in 1977 and, after his inauguration, famously walked the distance from the Capitol to the White House, though his tenure was eventually marked by what he called a "malaise", signified by high petrol prices, inflation and unemployment, plus the taking of American hostages in Iran in 1979 – a crisis that Carter failed to resolve, despite a botched rescue attempt. In November 1980 he lost his job to ex-California governor and *Bedtime for Bonzo* co-star Ronald Reagan.

Home rule in the city	pp.270–271	National Air and Space Museum	p.65
Dupont Circle, history	p.138	Downtown and K Street, development	p.133
Kennedy Center	p.231		

The Reagan era

Under **Ronald Reagan**, the nation's economy boomed and busted as taxes were slashed and the federal budget deficit soared. In DC, the souped-up economy paved the way for drastic Downtown urban-renewal projects; Pennsylvania

Avenue and its buildings – eyesores for three decades – were restored; and yuppies began moving into Adams Morgan and Dupont Circle. Reagan's reputation (and that of his successor, George Bush) was put in question by the Iran-Contra scandal, involving the sale of illegal arms to the official "enemy", Iran, to finance right-wing Nicaraguan guerrillas. At the same time, as American military spending increased dramatically, major new **memorials** were built to Vietnam veterans (1982) and the US Navy (1987).

Culturally, the city flourished. The Smithsonian expanded its collections on the Mall with the addition of the **Sackler Gallery** and **African Art Museum** (both in 1987), the **National Postal Museum** opened (1986), and Union Station was restored (1988). City politics took a colourful turn with the successive mayoral terms of **Marion Barry** (first elected in 1978), whose initial success in attracting investment soon gave way to conflict with Congress, which was to become the hallmark of the following decade. The city began its slide into insolvency just as Bill Clinton was elected president in 1992 on promises to turn the economy around and restructure welfare.

The Clinton years

To the casual eye, it was business as usual in the 1990s in DC – now one of the most touristed cities in America, with almost twenty million visitors a year – as new attractions continued to open, the **FDR Memorial** and Verizon Center foremost among them, both in 1997. Behind the scenes, though, Washington lurched into crisis in the first half of the 1990s, as the federal budget deficit spiralled. During this period, as the city was grappling with its financial woes, the public exposure of President Clinton's affair with intern **Monica Lewinsky** put DC in the national spotlight in a way not seen since the Watergate hearings of the 1970s. As always, the cover-up seemed worse than the crime, but Clinton, who had scored a political victory in the congressional elections of 1998, survived later impeachment hearings.

The situation was different, though, in 2000, when the Supreme Court for the first time decided a presidential election. The Court, in a still-controversial 5–4 decision, awarded the White House to conservative Texas governor **George W. Bush**, whose public fight was successfully shepherded by family crony (and former secretary of state) James Baker, while his opponent, Vice President Al Gore, was content to appear before cameras nonchalantly playing touch football with his family.

The new century

On **September 11, 2001**, terrorists hijacked a United Airlines jet and flew it into the Pentagon, killing nearly two hundred people, including those on the plane.

A second aircraft, probably headed for the US Capitol, crashed in a Pennsylvania field before reaching its target, while two other hijacked planes destroyed New York City's World Trade Center, killing nearly 3000. Soon after, **anthrax** spores were found in a letter mailed to Senate leader Tom Daschle, heightening tensions in an already shaken DC. The House suspended its session for a week and several federal buildings were closed pending investigation and fumigation.

Paradoxically, even while the city was on alert its economic fortunes continued to revive. **Anthony Williams**, a former chief financial officer of the council board (who had won election as mayor in 1998) got credit for lower crime rates, newly paved roads and a revitalized downtown where restaurants, sport and cultural events began to attract visitors to places once overrun by crime. Areas such as Adams Morgan, Dupont Circle and especially the **Penn Quarter** attracted new investment and saw their stately, once-decaying old buildings re-emerge as modern showpieces. Perhaps most tellingly, DC's population stabilized at just above half a million after decades of decline, and the city's property values began to soar in places. Still, many parts of the city remained poverty-stricken, and areas of northeast DC – well away from the capital investment zones – sunk even further into economic blight.

The first decade of the twenty-first century saw more openings of new memorials and museums – among them the **National World War II Memorial** – and visitors returned after some of the terrorist fears ebbed. Washington's **growth** was not without cost, though, as residents priced out of living in the city itself jostled for decent suburban houses near the Metrorail, the thought of doing battle with commuters on the gridlocked Beltway too onerous to imagine. At the same time, places like Shaw and Logan Circle experienced the gentrification that brought new (white) residents even as it drove longer-term (black) residents out.

In November 2006, reform-minded **Adrian Fenty** was elected, becoming at 36 the nation's second-youngest mayor of a major city. Fenty's mayoralty accomplished a good deal, especially the reconfiguration of DC's long-beleaguered school system. Much more conspicuous was the historic 2008 election of **Barack Obama**, the country's first black (or minority) president, who came to the presidency on a wave of emotion and relief after the exhausting tenure of George W. Bush. However, by 2010, voters – still grouchy about the ongoing national economic slump that began in 2007 – decided to hand partial control of Congress back to Republicans and give Obama a congressional adversary for the next two years. Even worse was the fate of Fenty, whose somewhat aloof (some would say arrogant) style chafed many DC voters, who voted him out in favour of the much blander, less engaging Vincent Gray.

| National World War II Memorial | p.47 | 9/11 terrorist attacks | p.273 |
| Penn Quarter | p.124 | | |

Presidents of the USA

Name	Party	Date	State of birth	Notable facts
George Washington	None	1789–97	Virginia	Only president unaffiliated by party
John Adams	Federalist	1797–1801	Massachusetts	First to occupy White House; died on July 4
Thomas Jefferson	Democratic-Republican	1801–09	Virginia	Wrote Declaration of Independence; died on July 4
James Madison	Democratic-Republican	1809–17	Virginia	Co-wrote US Constitution; started War of 1812
James Monroe	Democratic-Republican	1817–25	Virginia	Presided over "Era of Good Feelings"; died on July 4
John Quincy Adams	Democratic-Republican	1825–29	Massachusetts	Elected by Congress, not popular majority; son of John Adams
Andrew Jackson	Democrat	1829–37	South Carolina	"Old Hickory"; last to have served in Revolutionary War, only one to fight 13 duels
Martin Van Buren	Democrat	1837–41	New York	Nickname "Old Kinderhook" may have led to word "OK"
William H. Harrison	Whig	1841	Virginia	"Old Tippecanoe"; died a month after inauguration
John Tyler	Whig	1841–45	Virginia	First unelected president; first to face impeachment attempt
James Polk	Democrat	1845–49	North Carolina	Started Mexican–American War; died 3 months after leaving office
Zachary Taylor	Whig	1849–50	Virginia	"Old Rough and Ready"; died after two years in office
Millard Fillmore	Whig	1850–53	New York	"His Accidency"; not nominated for re-election
Franklin Pierce	Democrat	1853–57	New Hampshire	Distantly related to Barbara Bush; not nominated for re-election
James Buchanan	Democrat	1857–61	Pennsylvania	Only bachelor president; not nominated for re-election
Abraham Lincoln	Republican	1861–65	Kentucky	Preserved Union during the Civil War; first president killed in office
Andrew Johnson	Union	1865–69	North Carolina	Military governor of Tennessee; first president to be impeached
Ulysses S. Grant	Republican	1869–77	Ohio	"Galena Tanner"; Civil War commander of Union forces
Rutherford B. Hayes	Republican	1877–81	Ohio	Elected by Congress, not popular majority; teetotalling wife was called "Lemonade Lucy"
James A. Garfield	Republican	1881	Ohio	Last president born in a log cabin; second killed in office
Chester A. Arthur	Republican	1881–85	Vermont	Diagnosed with fatal kidney disease; not nominated for re-election
Grover Cleveland	Democrat	1885–89	New Jersey	"Uncle Jumbo"; only president married in White House

Benjamin Harrison	Republican	1889–93	Ohio	Elected by Congress, not popular majority; grandson of Pres. William Harrison
Grover Cleveland	Democrat	1893–97	New Jersey	Only president to serve two non-consecutive terms
William McKinley	Republican	1897–1901	Ohio	First to campaign from front porch; third killed in office
Theodore Roosevelt	Republican	1901–09	New York	Fought at San Juan Hill; Teddy Bear named after him
William H. Taft	Republican	1909–13	Ohio	Got stuck in a White House bathtub; became Chief Justice of Supreme Court
Woodrow Wilson	Democrat	1913–21	Virginia	First directly re-elected Democrat in 84 years; retired and died in DC
Warren G. Harding	Republican	1921–23	Ohio	Known for Teapot Dome scandal, affairs with mistresses; died in office
Calvin Coolidge	Republican	1923–29	Vermont	"Silent Cal"; last Republican not to seek re-election
Herbert Hoover	Republican	1929–33	Iowa	First president born west of Mississippi; second longest-lived
Franklin D. Roosevelt	Democrat	1933–45	New York	Only president to serve more than two terms; died in his fourth
Harry S. Truman	Democrat	1945–53	Missouri	"Give 'em hell Harry"; only president to use nuclear weapons
Dwight D. Eisenhower	Republican	1953–61	Texas	Supreme Allied Commander in WWII; last general to be elected
John F. Kennedy	Democrat	1961–63	Massachusetts	Youngest elected president; fourth killed in office
Lyndon B. Johnson	Democrat	1963–69	Texas	"Landslide Lyndon"; last Democrat not to seek re-election
Richard M. Nixon	Republican	1969–74	California	Re-elected with 49 states in 1972; resigned two years later
Gerald Ford	Republican	1974–77	Nebraska	Served as vice president and president; not elected to either position
James (Jimmy) Carter	Democrat	1977–81	Georgia	First Democrat defeated for re-election since Cleveland
Ronald Reagan	Republican	1981–89	Illinois	"The Gipper"; oldest elected president (69 and 73)
George H.W. Bush	Republican	1989–93	Massachusetts	First sitting VP to be elected president since Van Buren
William (Bill) Clinton	Democrat	1993–2001	Arkansas	First Democrat to serve two full terms since FDR; first impeached since Andrew Johnson
George W. Bush	Republican	2001–09	Connecticut	Chosen by US Supreme Court in 2000; (re-)elected in 2004
Barack Obama	Democrat	2009–	Illinois	First black president; first born outside the lower 48 states (Hawaii)

Books

There are plenty of **books** that touch upon the history, politics and personalities of Washington, DC; the problem is in getting an overall picture of
the city. There's no one single, straightforward and up-to-date history of
the District, and visitors through the ages have tended to include their
observations of the capital only as part of wider works about America. However,
every book on American history contains at least a few pages about the founding
of DC; Civil War treatises highlight the city as Lincoln's headquarters (and place
of assassination); and presidential autobiographies and biographies, from those of
George Washington onward, necessarily recount the daily experience of political
and social life in the District.

What follows are some of the better volumes about Washington, DC, including
novels set in the city. Many are available in good bookshops everywhere, and most
in DC itself. Every major museum, gallery and attraction sells related books, too.
The selection in the National Museum of American History is perhaps the finest,
while the Smithsonian Institution publishes a wide range of titles on a variety of
city-related topics. Finally, the White House Historical Association at 740 Jackson
Place, Downtown (gift shop Mon–Fri 9am–4pm; ☎202/737-8292, ⓦwww
.whitehousehistory.org) publishes a series of informative accounts of the White
House, its architecture, contents and occupants.

Note that titles marked "o/p" are not currently in print, though with sufficient
effort on the internet you may be able to locate them.

Guidebooks

Alzina Stone Dale *Mystery Reader's
Walking Guide: DC.* Eight guided walks
around the city in the company of the
words of mystery writers, taken from
some 200 volumes; one of several city-
mystery volumes by this author.

Federal Writers Project *WPA Guide
to Washington DC* (o/p). Classic volume
detailing a history and survey of then-
contemporary DC, from the view
of the 1930s New Deal. Interesting
observations penned when many
of the Neoclassical structures (such
as the Supreme Court and Lincoln
Memorial) were relatively new.

Kathryn Allamong Jacob *Testament
to Union.* Exhaustive record of the
District's Civil War monuments and
memorials, with more than ninety
photographs and accompanying
historical text.

**John J. Protopappas and
Alvin R. McNeal** *Washington on
Foot.* A series of historic treks
around DC, with good maps and
diagrams; along with the major
areas, includes lesser-known spots
like LeDroit Park, Meridian Hill and
Takoma Park, MD.

Art and architecture

Cynthia R. Field, ed. *Paris on the
Potomac: The French Influence on the
Art and Architecture of Washington,*
D.C. Compelling account of how
the District was developed by Pierre
Charles L'Enfant in line with Gallic

concepts of what an imperial city
should look like, realized much
later with the full development of
the city and some of the French-
inspired art movements that flowered
here.

Marjorie Hunt *The Stone Carvers: Master Craftsmen of Washington National Cathedral.* Eye-opening volume about two Italian American artisans who transformed the look of Washington and other cities with their fluid, detailed stonework. Features many fine photos of their work at the Cathedral.

G. Martin Moeller *AIA guide to the Architecture of Washington, D.C.* A handy resource for exploring the city and deciphering the differences between, say, the Federal and Georgian styles, and for the details on all the monuments and memorials.

Luca Molinari *The Italian Legacy in Washington, D.C.: Architecture, Design, Art and Culture.* Although the French usually get credit for being the foremost foreign influence on the city, Washington, DC also had a

considerable Italian presence in its Neoclassical design, Capitol frescoes and park stylings – as evocatively explored in this photo-heavy tome.

David Ovason *The Secret Architecture of Our Nation's Capital: The Masons and the Building of Washington, D.C.* Still controversial in its thesis that Masons like Washington and Jefferson designed the capital according to the tenets of Freemasonry. Formed the blueprint for *The Lost Symbol* (see p.283).

Pamela Scott and Antoinette J. Lee *Buildings of the District of Columbia* (o/p). Though almost two decades old, this is still the best and most comprehensive guide to the structures in the city, with countless stories and facts behind each, explaining the development of the capital.

History and culture

Catherine Allgor *Parlor Politics.* As nineteenth-century DC developed from backwater to capital, the arrival of high society in the shape of the First Ladies and their social circles began to have a growing influence on politics – a thesis encapsulated in the book's subtitle: "In which the ladies of Washington help build a city and a government."

Mark Anderson and Mark Jenkins *Dance of Days: Two Decades of Punk in the Nation's Capital.* Long-overdue story of DC's impact on subversive culture – in this case, the various forms of punk, as practised by seminal acts like Bad Brains, Minor Effect, Henry Rollins and, in more current times, Fugazi.

Tracey Gold Bennett *Washington, D.C. 1861–2006 (Black America Series).* Two-volume saga of the prominent African American presence in the city, beginning in the Civil War era

and continuing up to the present, and powerfully covering emancipation movements, heroic leaders, race riots and gentrification along the way.

Fergus Bordewich *Washington: How Slaves, Idealists and Scoundrels Built the Nation's Capital.* This recent volume shows the early history of the capital, with its backroom deal-making and various political manipulators reminding us that Washington shenanigans weren't invented in the twentieth century.

David Brinkley *Washington Goes to War* (o/p). Acclaimed account of the capital during World War II under FDR, charting its emergence onto the international stage with countless anecdotes and stories of life in the era.

Ron Chernow *Alexander Hamilton.* Standout work that looks at the colourful life, controversial politics and far-sighted economic policies of America's first Treasury secretary – better known as that wig-wearing fellow on the $10 bill, who was on the losing end of a famous duel.

Alistair Cooke *Alistair Cooke's America*. The author's thorough, eloquent overview of American life and customs occasionally touches on DC, as well as US politics. Also worth a look are any of Cooke's other volumes on the American experience.

Kathryn Allamong Jacob *King of the Lobby: The Life and Times of Sam Ward, Man-About-Washington in the Gilded Age*. Engaging tale of a lobbyist's rise during one of the most corrupt eras in national politics, and fascinating for its parallels to today's modern political trickery.

Jeffrey Meyer *Myths in Stone: Religious Dimensions of Washington DC*. Examines the lesser-known spiritual side of the capital, evident in its rituals, culture and architecture, and places the city in a global religious context.

Anthony S. Pitch *The Burning of Washington: The British Invasion of 1814*. Recounting of the dramatic events of the summer of 1814 as the British set fire to the young capital and Francis Scott Key was inspired to write "The Star-Spangled Banner".

Zachary M. Schrag *The Great Society Subway: A History of the Washington Metro*. As the title indicates, not just any old subway history, but one that touches on the social and economic challenges that were addressed with the creation of the District's modern mass transport system, which spared the city from being carved up by freeways like other cities of the time.

James L. Swanson *Manhunt: The 12-Day Chase for Lincoln's Killer*. Excellent re-interpretation of the familiar historical narrative of the Lincoln assassination, presenting a fascinating, moment-by-moment account of the crime and its aftermath in a fast-paced, modern style.

Paul K. Williams *Greater U Street*. Another in an excellent series on DC neighbourhoods in the "Images of America" series, this one focusing on the history and culture of Shaw in the days of "Black Broadway", the Lincoln Theatre and Duke Ellington.

Presidents

See also the *American Presidents* series (Times Books), which covers almost all the presidents, from George Washington to George H.W. Bush, in slim volumes written by noted writers and historians.

Robert Caro *The Years of Lyndon Johnson*. Essential (and ongoing) history of the champion of the Great Society and architect of the Vietnam War. So far the three volumes cover LBJ only to his election as vice president, but these are still rich and revealing volumes about the developing character of this larger-than-life figure – and cumulatively the best biography of any president.

Robert Dallek *An Unfinished Life: John F. Kennedy, 1917–1963*. Detailed and penetrating analysis of JFK's considerable strengths as a leader, as well as his human flaws of philandering and imprudence. The best and most balanced contemporary book on the 35th president.

David Herbert Donald *Lincoln*. Although Lincoln's biography is covered by authors ranging in the hundreds, this is hands-down the definitive volume covering the life and legend of the Railsplitter, who preserved the

Union during the Civil War and helped abolish slavery.

Joseph Ellis *American Sphinx: The Character of Thomas Jefferson*. Thoughtful volume describing the contradictory aspects of the third president, as a proponent of states' rights who expanded the federal government, and as a champion of liberty who owned slaves. Also outstanding is the author's *His Excellency: George Washington*, providing additional insight on a familiar American icon.

Ulysses S. Grant *Personal Memoirs*. Indispensable classic written (with the aid of Mark Twain) while the ex-president was dying, covering his life from childhood to the end of the Civil War. A highly readable and illuminating view of war and sacrifice.

David Maraniss *First in His Class: A Biography of Bill Clinton*. Fine, balanced look at the strengths and weaknesses of the 42nd president, prescient in some ways in foreseeing his successes and pitfalls. Winner of the Pulitzer Prize.

David McCullough *John Adams* and *Truman*. Folksy historian and public-TV personality who's made a career out of resurrecting the reputations of underestimated presidents from the past. The Truman claim to presidential greatness is a lot easier to swallow than that of Adams.

Edmund Morris *The Rise of Theodore Roosevelt* and *Theodore Rex*. Still the essential accounts of the emergence of the New York governor, Spanish-American war hero, corporate trust-buster, namesake of the teddy bear, and "accidental" two-term US president.

Barack Obama *Dreams from My Father: A Story of Race and Inheritance*. The intellectual and literary sensibilities of the current president are in full flower, in this dramatic and compelling memoir of a young man's rise despite his own, and especially his father's, flaws. A rare example of a (future) president writing good literature.

Richard Reeves *President Nixon: Alone in the White House*. A scholar's view of the many momentous decisions made in the heady days of the Nixon White House, and how the paranoia and insularity that were the president's flaws eventually consumed him.

Robert V. Remini *The Life of Andrew Jackson*. Three thick volumes on the life and times of the seventh president, from supporting slavers and Indian removal, to his role as a fervent democratizer/demagogue who threw a chaotic inauguration party for the public that nearly ruined the White House.

Jean Edward Smith *FDR*. While there are scores of books on the titanic figure of the 32nd president, this recent one skilfully synthesizes the voluminous information on his lengthy presidency, from the Depression to the New Deal to World War II.

Bob Woodward and Carl Bernstein *All the President's Men* and *The Final Days*. America's most famous journalistic sleuths tell the gripping story of the unravelling of the Nixon presidency. Although both men have written plenty of investigative books since, none has matched these early classics.

Politics and electioneering

Richard Ben Cramer *What It Takes: The Way to the White House*. The greatest literary interpretation of American electioneering, focusing on the uninspiring 1988 campaign through the use

CONTEXTS | Books

of detailed biographical portraits of six contenders, using interior monologues and a changing authorial voice to get to the core of what animates national leaders.

George Crile *Charlie Wilson's War.* Instructive primer on Washington politics, in which a sex-scandalized congressman and a shadowy CIA agent help to secretly funnel millions of dollars to Afghanistan's Communist-fighting mujahideen – who later became the Taliban. Made into a passable movie.

Doris Kearns Goodwin *Team of Rivals.* Acclaimed volume detailing how Abe Lincoln gathered his party adversaries – men he had beaten for the nomination – and used them to fashion the greatest war cabinet, perhaps the greatest cabinet ever, in US history. Barack Obama claimed this as an influence in creating his own cabinet.

David Halberstam *The Best and the Brightest.* Unforgettable portrait of the proud, swaggering advisers to JFK and LBJ, who, despite their brilliance and advanced college degrees, led the nation into a disastrous war in Vietnam.

John Heilemann and Mark Halperin *Game Change: Obama and the Clintons, McCain and Palin, and the Race of a Lifetime.* Lively, gossipy history of the 2008 presidential race, with plenty of colourful stories to enliven the tale, especially the antics of Sarah Palin.

Richard Hofstadter *The Paranoid Style in American Politics.* Though written in the 1960s, this book continues to be relevant in analyzing extreme political factions based on status anxiety and paranoia, as with some of America's current right-wing movements.

Norman Mailer *The Armies of the Night.* The author's 1967 Pulitzer Prize-winning description of the March on the Pentagon, protesting the Vietnam War, is still essential reading, full of drama and colour – as well as plenty of surly antics by Mailer himself.

Theodore H. White *The Making of the President 1960.* Still one of the quintessential books for understanding American politics, using the Kennedy–Nixon race as a case study for the manufactured stagecraft and imagery of contemporary elections. Subsequent, less groundbreaking but still diverting, volumes cover the next three campaigns to 1972.

Memoirs

Dean Acheson *Present at the Creation: My Years in the State Department.* One of the best volumes about the Cold War as seen from a political insider, in this case Truman's secretary of state, whose careful use of diplomacy steered US policy (and politics). The author's penetrating self-awareness is refreshing, too.

Ben Bradlee *A Good Life.* Autobiography of the executive editor of the *Washington Post*, covering the years between 1968 and 1991, during which Watergate and its fallout made the author America's most famous editor.

Frederick Douglass *The Life and Times of Frederick Douglass.* The third volume (1881) of statesman, orator and ex-slave Frederick Douglass's autobiography sees him living in DC as US marshal and recorder of deeds. But the first volume, *Narrative of the Life of Frederick Douglass: An American Slave* (1845), which covers the author's early life (prior to his arrival in DC), is actually more gripping.

Katharine Graham *Personal History.* Pulitzer Prize-winning autobiography of the *Washington Post* owner and

If Washington has one domestic scandal that still towers above all others, it's **Watergate**, whose various aspects have been exhaustively covered since Woodward and Bernstein first set the ball rolling with *All the President's Men*. For the full story, you could consult Fred Emery's *Watergate: The Corruption of American Politics and the Fall of Richard Nixon* or a host of other eyewitness accounts, most of which are out of print but cheap and easily available on the internet. These include Nixon's own *Memoirs*, Robert Haldeman's *Haldeman Diaries: Inside the Nixon White House*, John Dean's *Blind Ambition* and *Lost Honor*, John Erlichman's *Witness to Power* and G. Gordon Liddy's *Will: The Autobiography of G. Gordon Liddy* – all first-hand (if not completely reliable) testimony from those who were there at the time.

Virtually everyone else involved has written about the affair at some point or other, too, from Watergate burglar James McCord to Judge John Sirica to Mark Felt, whose *G-Man's Life: The FBI, Being "Deep Throat" and the Struggle for Honor in Washington* explains the FBI's role in Watergate, while dancing around his own role as "Deep Throat", the figure who secretly conveyed the key information to reporters. Also interesting, some of the secret tapes recorded by Nixon, betraying his paranoia and prejudices, turn up in Stanley Kutler's *Abuse of Power: The New Nixon Tapes*.

Georgetown society hostess lifts the lid on DC's social and political niceties.

Meg Greenfield *Washington*. Posthumously published memoir by long-time columnist, editorial writer and, eventually, editor of the *Washington Post*. Greenfield writes perceptively about the cocoon-like qualities of DC life and the range of its beguiling personalities.

Marjorie Williams *The Woman at the Washington Zoo: Writings on Politics, Family and Fate*. Intimate and penetrating profiles of Washington insiders from the Bush and Clinton administrations are leavened with the author's own story of her (ultimately losing) battle with liver cancer, in this poignant and evocative memoir-anthology.

Fiction and literature

Henry Adams *Democracy*. A story of electioneering and intrigue set in 1870s Gilded Age-era DC, written (anonymously) by the brilliant historian grandson of John Quincy Adams.

Anonymous *Primary Colors*. Controversial, barely disguised account of a presidential primary campaign by young, charismatic, calculating, philandering, Southern governor Jack Stanton. Its author was eventually unmasked as Washington insider Joe Klein.

William Peter Blatty *The Exorcist*. Seminal horror story about the possession of a teenage girl, written in

1971, set around Georgetown University, and made into one of the scariest films ever.

Charles Dickens *American Notes*. Dickens came here in the early 1840s, when it was still, famously, a "City of Magnificent Intentions". Amusing satirical commentary about the US that's lighter in tone than the author's later, more scabrous, *Martin Chuzzlewit*.

Allen Drury *Advise and Consent* (o/p). Blackmail and slippery Senate politics in Washington's upper echelons in the late 1950s; a cautionary tale that still has an effect half a century after it was written.

James Ellroy *American Tabloid*.
Scandalmongering conspiracy
tale of biblical proportions, tying the
Mafia, JFK, renegade Cubans, and
rogue FBI and CIA officers into an
infernal web of lies and deception,
with all manner of Washington evil at
the epicentre.

Edward P. Jones *Lost in the City*.
Fourteen moving short stories about
residents trying to get by in the
depressed under- and working-class
world of DC in the 1960s and 1970s,
well away from the tourist zones and
halls of political power.

Ward Just *Echo House*. Elegiac, epic
novel of a DC political dynasty and
its intrigues and impact on national
politics, with much to say about the
nature of power in the city.

Sinclair Lewis *It Can't Happen Here*.
Disturbing, oddly humorous tale
of the coming of fascism to the US,
brought by a goofy yet conniving
politician with a folksy, homespun
style – a familiar figure these days.

Robert Littell *The Company* (o/p).
Thick and impressive tale of postwar
subterfuge in which the CIA fights
America's secret battles while fictional
characters cross paths with real-life
Cold Warriors from the time.

Anthony Trollope *North America*.
Two-volume account of Trollope's
visit to the US in the early 1860s.
Picking up where his mother, Fanny,
left off in her contentious *Domestic
Manners of the Americans* (1832),
Trollope offers much carping about
irredeemably vulgar Yanks – though
while his mother actually likes old
Washington, Trollope's not a fan.

Gore Vidal *Burr*; *Lincoln*; *1876*;
Empire; *Hollywood*; *Washington
DC*; *The Golden Age*. DC's – and
America's – most potent and cynical
chronicler sustains a terrific burst
of form in seven hugely enjoyable
novels tracing the history of the US
from the Revolution to modern times
and relying heavily on Washington
set-piece scenes. The moving epic
Lincoln is the best.

Walt Whitman *Leaves of Grass*. The
first edition of this poetic juggernaut
appeared in 1855, and Whitman
added sections to it for the rest of
his life. His war poems, *Drum-Taps*
(1865), were directly influenced by
his work in DC's Civil War hospitals.
Memories of President Lincoln, added
after the assassination, includes the
famous and affecting *"O Captain! My
Captain!"*

Crime and thrillers

Dan Brown *The Lost Symbol*.
Publishing phenomenon that has
inspired all manner of conspiracy
hunters and easily persuadable
readers to go searching for real and
imaginary subterfuge in the capital.
Essential reading for fans of *The Da
Vinci Code*.

Tom Clancy *Debt of Honor*; *Executive
Orders*. Blockbuster thriller writer
who weaves DC scenes into nearly
every tale of spook and terrorist
intrigue. *Debt of Honor* has the
president, his cabinet and most of

Congress perishing in a terrorist attack
on the US Capitol, while *Executive
Orders* sees Jack Ryan taking over as
president of a shattered US.

David Ignatius *A Firing Offense* (o/p).
Washington Post journalist puts his
newspaper experience to good use in
an intelligent espionage thriller that
jumps from DC locations to France
and China.

Charles McCarry *Old Boys* (o/p).
Spy yarn by a long-standing
espionage stylist that has CIA agents
searching for a missing person, with

globe-trotting to China, the Middle East and Europe along the way. His *Shelley's Heart* (o/p) is a page-turning thriller detailing stolen elections, secret societies and other shenanigans, while *Lucky Bastard* (o/p) details the rise of a (familiar) charismatic, liberal, womanizing presidential hopeful.

George P. Pelecanos Hip raconteur who writes pointedly about the city in a series of great thrillers, spanning the years and ethnic divide. *A Firing Offense* (his first), *Nick's Trip* and *Down By the River Where the Dead*

Men Go introduce feisty private eye Nick Stefanos; *King Suckerman* is a tour de force of 1970s drugs and racial tension, while *The Sweet Forever* updates Suckerman's characters to cocaine-riddled 1980s DC. Good later novels include the vivid *Hard Revolution*, *The Night Gardener* and *The Turnaround*.

Margaret Truman *Murder* … Harry's daughter churns out murder-mystery potboilers set in various neighbourhoods and buildings of DC, from Georgetown to the National Cathedral.

Film

I t's possible that more **films** have been set in the District of Columbia than any American city outside of LA or New York. However, despite this celluloid familiarity, few movies (aside from a few penetrating documentaries) have ever really examined life in DC, got to the core of its politics, or looked beyond Capitol Hill or the White House. Therefore, the list of DC films revolves around the decisions, personalities and antics of fictional presidents; the untrustworthy plotting of politicians on the Hill and generals at the Pentagon; and the lovely historic backdrop of Georgetown.

C

CONTEXTS | Film

Comedies and musicals

1776 (Peter H. Hunt, 1972). Amazingly, this musical view of the American Revolution is one of the very few memorable films on the subject – but if you don't enjoy history set to tub-thumping show tunes, it's not for you.

Americathon (Neal Israel, 1979). Memorably bad "comedy" in which a down-on-his-luck presidential sap must rescue the floundering US by holding an oddball telethon; features a cast that somehow includes John Ritter, Meat Loaf, Harvey Korman, Elvis Costello and Jay Leno.

Being There (Hal Ashby, 1979). Unforgettable comedy about a simple-minded gardener (Peter Sellers) who leaves the Washington estate of his deceased employer and unwittingly becomes a political pawn and, possibly, presidential candidate.

Dr Strangelove (Stanley Kubrick, 1964). The archetypical satire of the Cold War Pentagon gone berserk, in which a power-mad general brings the world to the brink of annihilation, fearing a Communist takeover of his "precious bodily fluids".

The President's Analyst (Theodore Flicker, 1967). Political cult film in which James Coburn plays the title character, who gets into all sorts of trouble when various spies and thugs want to find out what he knows. A classic conspiracy-theory satire.

State of the Union (Frank Capra, 1948). Republican bigwig Spencer Tracy asks his estranged wife to return to him to aid his election, putting on a public show for the media and causing all manner of high jinks.

Thank You for Smoking (Jason Reitman, 2006). Goofy and amusing story of master lobbyist Aaron Eckhart's shenanigans shilling for the tobacco industry while navigating a thicket of corporate and personal politics.

Documentaries

American Hardcore (Paul Rachman, 2005). Riveting tale of how the punk style that involved simple, thrashing rhythms, slam-dancing and all manner of aggression found its champions across the US, but especially in DC, where Bad Brains, Minor Threat and Henry Rollins made the capital one of the core cities for the movement.

Fahrenheit 9/11 (Michael Moore, 2004). The ultimate liberal attack on the controversial policies of George W. Bush, which won the Palme d'Or at Cannes and became the most successful documentary in history.

The Fog of War (Errol Morris, 2003). A long dark look at the now-aged

285

former Defense Secretary Robert McNamara, who plunged the US deeper into the Vietnam War despite his own misgivings. Told in the Secretary's own paradoxical, ambivalent words.

Point of Order (Emile de Antonio, 1964). Stark, black-and-white documentary with images taken from the McCarthy hearings of the 1950s, in which the Wisconsin senator's own ranting paranoia and deceptions are made clear before the cameras.

The Trials of Henry Kissinger (Eugene Jarecki, 2003). Angry polemic about the former secretary of state's alleged misdeeds in toppling the government of Chile, illegally bombing Cambodia, and countless other acts of official wickedness. Based on the book and magazine articles by arch-contrarian Christopher Hitchens.

Horror and sci-fi

The Day the Earth Stood Still (Robert Wise, 1951). Classic sci-fi in which an alien makes the mistake of landing his spaceship in Washington, DC, demanding earthlings give up their warlike ways or else. He is, of course, killed, an act which sends his trusty robot companion Gort out for vengeance against the town that wronged him.

The Exorcist (William Friedkin, 1973). The lodestar of religious-horror movies, filmed along 36th Street in Georgetown, giving us unforgettable scenes of evil-possessed Linda Blair speaking and retching with satanic intensity, as well as a famously "head-turning" moment.

Independence Day (Roland Emmerich, 1996). Wildly successful, though crude and ham-fisted, action flick about aliens who greet earth with a barrage of destruction, including blowing up the White House in one of the more famous images of 1990s Hollywood overkill.

Politics

Advise and Consent (Otto Preminger, 1962). Lengthy, close-in view of the tortuous process that Secretary of State nominee Henry Fonda must undergo when subjected to the machinations of Congress – vividly personified in the figure of a drawling Southern pol played with aplomb by Charles Laughton.

All the President's Men (Alan J. Pakula, 1976). Appearing just a few years after the Watergate scandal, one of the few Hollywood films with a premise drawn from real-life politics (crusading journalists exposing a baleful president) that actually made money; shot at many sites across the city.

Backstairs at the White House (various, 1979). Little-remembered but worthy TV mini-series (available on DVD) that depicted the lives and struggles of the servants in the President's Mansion, bearing witness to monumental events and outsize figures from presidents Taft to Eisenhower.

Bob Roberts (Tim Robbins, 1992). Dark satire about a right-wing senatorial candidate who uses charm and folksiness to reach the Capitol. Prescient and still amusing, if a bit ponderous in spots.

Citizen Cohn (Frank Pierson, 1992). Incisive look at the closeted gay arch-McCarthyite Red-hunter and right-wing operative Roy Cohn (James Woods), who reviews his life while dying of AIDS.

Dave (Ivan Reitman, 1993). Another strangely affectionate 1990s portrait of a fictional president, this one being Kevin Kline. An earnest Everyman who's also a look-alike for the president subs after the chief exec has a stroke.

Gabriel Over the White House (Gregory La Cava, 1933). Eerie period piece about a corrupt president who sees the eponymous angel and gets inspired to clean up his act, reform the nation, imprison – and execute – his enemies, and force peace upon other countries at the barrel of a gun.

The Man (Joseph Sargent, 1972). James Earl Jones stars as the president *pro tempore* of the Senate who, after a national tragedy, suddenly becomes US president and has to battle racists and thick-headed politicians determined to dethrone him.

Mr Smith Goes to Washington (Frank Capra, 1939). An exercise in earnest, apple-cheeked faith in the body politic, still loved for its image of populist hero Jimmy Stewart fighting wags and charlatans on Capitol Hill and triumphing with his honesty and courage.

Nixon (Oliver Stone, 1995). A grim look into the brooding mind of the only US president to resign. Anthony Hopkins plays Tricky Dick, doing a gallant job of stifling his Welsh accent and looking appropriately sweaty and paranoid.

Primary Colors (Mike Nichols, 1998). John Travolta plays Jack Stanton, a Southern governor with dangerous libidinal tendencies seeking the presidency. Mildly amusing and strongly familiar.

Thirteen Days (Roger Donaldson, 2001). Riveting insider story detailing how the brothers Kennedy and their crony (Kevin Costner) outflanked the Russians in the potentially world-ending nuclear duel of 1962's Cuban Missile Crisis.

Wag the Dog (Barry Levinson, 1997). Political satire that sounds better than it plays – a president desperate to recover from a sex scandal reacts by declaring war and seeing his popularity jump. All well and good, but the movie loses momentum towards the end.

Thrillers

Arlington Road (Mark Pellington, 1999). Washington terrorism expert Jeff Bridges sees danger in his well-scrubbed neighbour, Tim Robbins, and thinks he may have stumbled onto an authentic homegrown killer. Complications ensue in this gripping though somewhat uneven thriller.

Breach (Billy Ray, 2007). Absorbing depiction of master spy and FBI agent Robert Hanssen, whose antics spying for the Russians were caught in 2001, but only after he'd caused incalculable damage to US national security. This shifty, contradictory figure is memorably played by Chris Cooper.

Fail Safe (Sidney Lumet, 1964). President Henry Fonda plays a slow, excruciating game of nuclear chicken with the Russians as a US bomber crew is sent on a fatal, erroneous errand to destroy cities in the USSR.

The Good Shepherd (Robert DeNiro, 2006). Matt Damon plays a dyed-in-the-wool CIA man whose commitment to the "company" verges on the obsessive, to the point where he endangers his relationships with his family and friends to ferret out Russian moles. Story based on an even stranger historic character, James Jesus Angleton.

In the Line of Fire (Wolfgang Petersen, 1993). Top-notch action-thriller with Secret Service agent Clint Eastwood racing around to protect an undeserving president from the home-made bullets of psycho assassin John Malkovich; filmed around Dupont Circle and Capitol Hill.

National Treasure (Jon Turtletaub, 2004). Fairly ridiculous but enter-taining romp in which Nic Cage needs to snatch a copy of the Declara-tion of Independence in order to root out a historical mystery involving such familiar conspiracists as the Freemasons, Knights Templar, etc.

No Way Out (Roger Donaldson, 1987). A Pentagon-oriented thriller which sees Kevin Costner inves-tigating a crime whose trail leads squarely back to himself, featuring scenes set in Georgetown and a memorable twist ending. Remake of film-noir classic *The Big Clock*.

Seven Days in May (John Frankenheimer, 1964). Striking conspiracy thriller about thuggish general Burt Lancaster plotting a coup to achieve nefarious right-wing ends; Kirk Douglas fights to stop his evil deeds.

Visit us online

www.roughguides.com

Information on over 25,000 destinations around the world

- **Read** Rough Guides' trusted travel info
- **Access** exclusive articles from Rough Guides authors
- **Update** yourself on new books, maps, CDs and other products
- **Enter** our competitions and win travel prizes
- **Share** ideas, journals, photos & travel advice with other users
- **Earn** points every time you contribute to the Rough Guide
  community and get rewards

BROADEN YOUR HORIZONS

Small print and
Index

A Rough Guide to Rough Guides

Published in 1982, the first Rough Guide – to Greece – was a student scheme that became a publishing phenomenon. Mark Ellingham, a recent graduate in English from Bristol University, had been travelling in Greece the previous summer and couldn't find the right guidebook. With a small group of friends he wrote his own guide, combining a highly contemporary, journalistic style with a thoroughly practical approach to travellers' needs.

The immediate success of the book spawned a series that rapidly covered dozens of destinations. And, in addition to impecunious backpackers, Rough Guides soon acquired a much broader and older readership that relished the guides' wit and inquisitiveness as much as their enthusiastic, critical approach and value-for-money ethos.

These days, Rough Guides include recommendations from shoestring to luxury and cover more than 200 destinations around the globe, including almost every country in the Americas and Europe, more than half of Africa and most of Asia and Australasia. Our ever-growing team of authors and photographers is spread all over the world, particularly in Europe, the US and Australia.

In the early 1990s, Rough Guides branched out of travel, with the publication of Rough Guides to World Music, Classical Music and the Internet. All three have become benchmark titles in their fields, spearheading the publication of a wide range of books under the Rough Guide name.

Including the travel series, Rough Guides now number more than 350 titles, covering: phrasebooks, waterproof maps, music guides from Opera to Heavy Metal, reference works as diverse as Conspiracy Theories and Shakespeare, and popular culture books from iPods to Poker. Rough Guides also produce a series of more than 120 World Music CDs in partnership with World Music Network.

Visit www.roughguides.com to see our latest publications.

Rough Guide credits

Text editor: Natasha Foges
Layout: Jessica Subramanian
Cartography: Rajesh Chhibber
Picture editor: Rhiannon Furbear
Production: Louise Minihane
Proofreader: Jan McCann
Cover design: Dan May, Nicole Newman
Photographer: Paul Whitfield
Editorial: London Andy Turner, Keith Drew,
Edward Aves, Alice Park, Lucy White, Jo Kirby,
James Smart, James Rice, Emma Beatson,
Emma Gibbs, Kathryn Lane, Monica Woods,
Mani Ramaswamy, Harry Wilson, Lucy Cowie,
Alison Roberts, Lara Kavanagh, Eleanor Aldridge,
Ian Blenkinsop, Charlotte Melville, Joe Staines,
Matthew Milton, Tracy Hopkins; **Delhi** Madhavi
Singh, Jalpreen Kaur Chhatwal
Design & Pictures: London Scott Stickland,
Dan May, Diana Jarvis, Mark Thomas,

Nicole Newman, Sarah Cummins; **Delhi** Umesh
Aggarwal, Ajay Verma, Ankur Guha, Pradeep
Thapliyal, Sachin Tanwar, Anita Singh, Nikhil
Agarwal, Sachin Gupta
Production: Rebecca Short, Liz Cherry,
Erika Pepe
Cartography: London Ed Wright, Katie Lloyd-
Jones; **Delhi** Ashutosh Bharti, Rajesh Mishra,
Animesh Pathak, Jasbir Sandhu, Swati Handoo,
Deshpal Dabas, Lokamata Sahu
Marketing, Publicity & roughguides.com:
Liz Statham
Digital Travel Publisher: Peter Buckley
Reference Director: Andrew Lockett
Operations Coordinator: Becky Doyle
Operations Assistant: Johanna Wurm
Publishing Director (Travel): Clare Currie
Commercial Manager: Gino Magnotta
Managing Director: John Duhigg

Publishing information

This sixth edition published August 2011 by
Rough Guides Ltd,
80 Strand, London WC2R 0RL
11, Community Centre, Panchsheel Park,
New Delhi 110017, India

Distributed by the Penguin Group

Penguin Books Ltd,
80 Strand, London WC2R 0RL

Penguin Group (USA)
375 Hudson Street, NY 10014, USA

Penguin Group (Australia)
250 Camberwell Road, Camberwell,
Victoria 3124, Australia

Penguin Group (NZ)
67 Apollo Drive, Mairangi Bay, Auckland 1310,
New Zealand

Rough Guides is represented in Canada by
Tourmaline Editions Inc. 662 King Street West,
Suite 304, Toronto, Ontario M5V 1M7

Cover concept by Peter Dyer.

Typeset in Bembo and Helvetica to an original
design by Henry Iles.

Printed in Singapore
© Jules Brown and J.D. Dickey, 2011
Maps © Rough Guides
No part of this book may be reproduced in any
form without permission from the publisher except
for the quotation of brief passages in reviews.
304pp includes index
A catalogue record for this book is available from
the British Library
ISBN: 978-1-40538-226-7
The publishers and authors have done their best
to ensure the accuracy and currency of all the
information in **The Rough Guide to Washington
DC**, however, they can accept no responsibility
for any loss, injury, or inconvenience sustained by
any traveller as a result of information or advice
contained in the guide.

1 3 5 7 9 8 6 4 2

Help us update

We've gone to a lot of effort to ensure that the
sixth edition of **The Rough Guide to Washington
DC** is accurate and up-to-date. However, things
change – places get "discovered", opening hours
are notoriously fickle, restaurants and rooms raise
prices or lower standards. If you feel we've got it
wrong or left something out, we'd like to know,
and if you can remember the address, the price,
the hours, the phone number, so much the better.

Please send your comments with the subject
line "**Rough Guide Washington DC Update**"
to ⑯mail@uk.roughguides.com. We'll credit all
contributions and send a copy of the next edition
(or any other Rough Guide if you prefer) for the
very best emails.
Find more travel information, connect with
fellow travellers and book your trip on ⑯www
.roughguides.com

Acknowledgements

J.D. Dickey Foremost, thanks to editor Natasha Foges, who worked assiduously to improve this guide with her skilful revisions and suggestions. Other thanks are due to those who provided assistance for DC research, insight and accommodation, among them Lisa Scarpelli, Jane Vorwig, Zora O'Neill, Peter Moskos, Emmie Lancaster, Doug Camp, Sara Crocker, Allison Goldstein and Thomas Blaszczyk, along with visitor bureau staff and guides who provided excellent assistance and recommendations. Also valuable to this edition were picture editor Rhiannon Furbear and cartographer Rajesh Chhibber.

Photo credits

All photos © Rough Guides except the following:

Introduction
US Capitol at night © Raimund Koch/Corbis
Man climbing steps to Supreme Court © Paul Quayle/Axiom
American flag by Washington Monument © American Images Inc/Getty
Mural of Barack Obama © Louie Palu/ZUMA Press/Axiom
National Museum of the American Indian © age fotostock/Superstock
Jefferson Memorial aerial view © Guido Alberto Rossi/Tips/Axiom

Things not to miss
01 Washington Monument and Tidal Basin © Lester Lefkowitz/Getty
06 Peacock Room, Whistler Collection © Vespasian/Alamy
07 Arlington National Cemetery © Altrendo/Getty
09 Bond car © Mark Finkenstaedt/International Spy Museum
10 Lincoln Memorial © Aurora Photos/AWL
12 Vietnam Memorial © Walter Bibikow/JAI/Corbis

13 Panda © Mehgan Murphy/Smithsonian's National Zoological Park
14 Wolf Trap © Scott Suchman/Wolf Trap
15 Mount Vernon © Mount Vernon Ladies' Association
16 *Old Ebbitt Grill* © Scott Suchman/DK Images

African American DC colour section
Barack Obama © Chip Somodevilla/Getty
Mount Vernon © Mount Vernon Ladies' Association
Men's bunk house slave quarters © Mount Vernon Ladies' Association
Civil War Reenactors © Jim West/Alamy
Martin Luther King © AFP/Getty
Inauguration Ceremony of Barack Obama © Aurora Photos/AWL Images
Duke Ellington Mural © Hoberman Collection/Superstock
Mural on the back of the *Bohemian Caverns* jazz club © Krista Rossow/Alamy

SMALL PRINT

Index

Map entries are in colour.

O

So now we've told you about the things not to miss, the best places to stay, the top restaurants, the liveliest bars and the most spectacular sights, it only seems fair to tell you about the best travel insurance around

Map symbols

maps are listed in the full index using coloured text

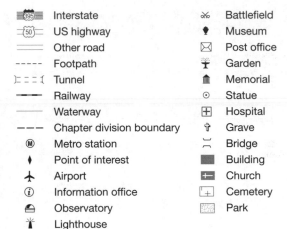

Interstate		Battlefield
US highway		Museum
Other road		Post office
Footpath		Garden
Tunnel		Memorial
Railway		Statue
Waterway		Hospital
Chapter division boundary		Grave
Metro station		Bridge
Point of interest		Building
Airport		Church
Information office		Cemetery
Observatory		Park
Lighthouse		

THE METRORAIL SYSTEM

Shady Grove
Rockville
Twinbrook
White Flint
Grosvenor
Medical Center
Bethesda
Friendship Heights
Tenleytown-AU
Van Ness-UDC
Cleveland Park
Woodley Park-Zoo
Dupont Circle
Farragut North
Foggy Bottom-GWU

Glenmont
Wheaton
Forest Glen
Silver Spring
Takoma
Georgia Ave-Petworth
Columbia Heights
U Street-Cardozo
Shaw-Howard Univ
McPherson Square
Mt Vernon Square
Gallery Pl-Chinatown

Greenbelt
College Park-U of Md
Prince George's Plaza
West Hyattsville
Fort Totten
Brookland-CUA
Rhode Island Ave
New York Ave
Union Station
Judiciary Square

New Carrollton
Landover
Cheverly
Deanwood
Minnesota Ave
Largo Town Center

Potomac River

Rosslyn
Ballston
Clarendon
Virginia Sq-GMU
Court House
East Falls Church
West Falls Church (AIRPORT TRANSFER)
Dunn Loring
Vienna

Farragut West
Metro Center
Federal Triangle
Smithsonian
L'Enfant Plaza
Waterfront

Archives-Navy Meml
Capitol South
Federal Center SW
Eastern Market
Stadium Armory
Potomac Ave
Benning Road
Capitol Heights
Addison Rd
Morgan Blvd

Arlington Cemetery
Pentagon
Pentagon City
Crystal City
National Airport
Braddock Road
Van Dorn Street
King Street
Eisenhower Ave
Huntington
Franconia-Springfield

Navy Yard
Anacostia
Congress Heights
Southern Ave
Naylor Road
Suitland
Branch Ave

Potomac River

Red Line
Glenmont / Shady Grove
Orange Line
New Carrollton / Vienna
Blue Line
Largo Town Center / Franconia-Springfield
Yellow Line
Fort Totten / Huntington
Green Line
Greenbelt / Branch Ave
∞ Interchange transfer station

For Metro information
call ☎ 202/637-7000
or visit ⓦ www.wmata.com

N

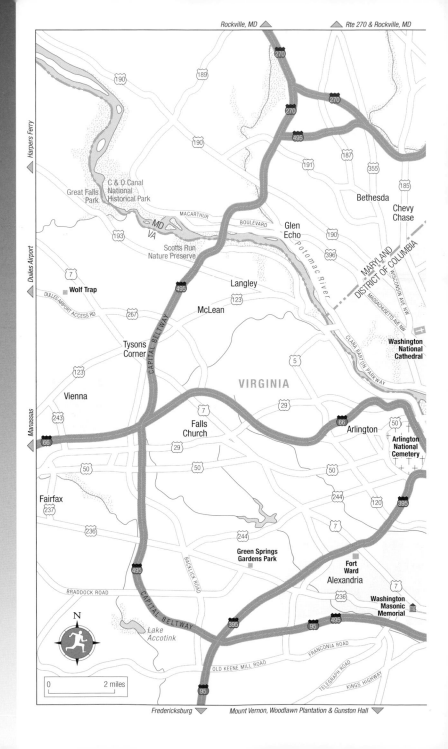

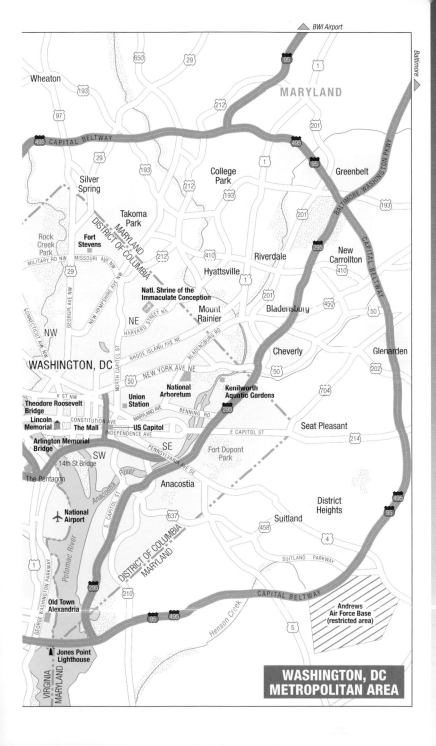

WASHINGTON, DC METROPOLITAN AREA

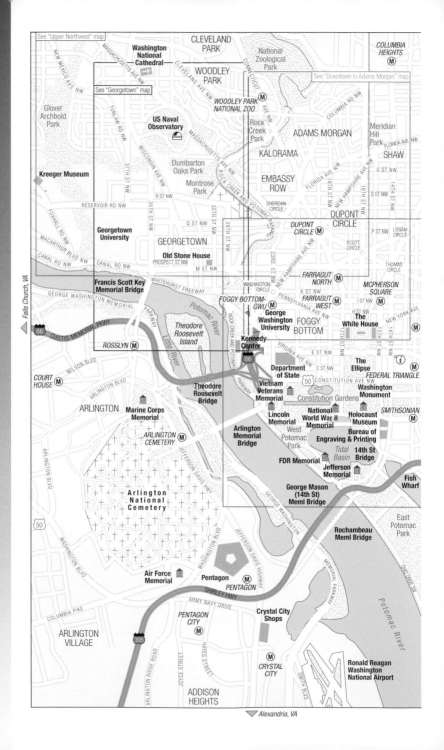

Silver Spring & Takoma Park, MD

President Lincoln's Cottage
National Shrine of the Immaculate Conception
BROOKLAND CUA

WASHINGTON, DC

0   500 yds

GEORGIA AVE NW
29

MICHIGAN AVE
McMillan Reservoir
FRANKLIN ST NE
13TH ST NE
18TH ST NE
N

NORTH CAPITOL ST
Howard University
RHODE ISLAND AVE NE

U STREET CARDOZO
LEDROIT PARK
RHODE ISLAND AVENUE
W ST NE
1

SHAW-HOWARD UNIVERSITY
VERMONT AVE NW
RHODE ISLAND AVE NW

NEW YORK AVE NE
Brentwood Park
WEST VIRGINIA AVE NE
BLADENSBURG RD NE
US National Arboretum

See "Central Washington DC" map
Gallaudet University
M ST NE

Convention Center
9TH ST NW
NORTH CAPITOL ST
NEW YORK AVE
50
FLORIDA AVE NE

N ST NW
M ST NW
MT VERNON SQ-UDC
Greyhound Bus Terminal
NEW JERSEY AVE NW
MASSACHUSETTS AVE NW

MT VERNON SQUARE
K ST NE

GALLERY PLACE
See "Capitol Hill and Southeast DC" map
H ST NE
MARYLAND AVE NE
BENNING RD NE

METRO CENTER
JUDICIARY SQUARE
395
UNION STATION
Union Station
4TH ST NE
F ST NE

E ST NW
PENNSYLVANIA
DOWNTOWN
Senate Offices
STANTON SQUARE
CAPITOL HILL
C ST NE

ARCHIVES-NAVY MEML
AVE NW
CONSTITUTION AVE NE

MADISON DR NW
The Mall
US Capitol
US Supreme Court
Library of Congress
EAST CAPITOL ST
LINCOLN PARK
EAST CAPITOL ST
RFK Stadium

JEFFERSON DR SW
MARYLAND AVE SW
INDEPENDENCE AVE SE
N CAROLINA AVE SE
MASSACHUSETTS AVE SE

FEDERAL CENTER SW
C ST SW
House Offices
SEWARD SQUARE
Eastern Market
11TH ST
STADIUM ARMORY

L'ENFANT PLAZA
NEW JERSEY AVE SE
CAPITOL SOUTH
EASTERN MARKET
4TH ST SE
SOUTH CAROLINA AVE SE
KENTUCKY AVE SE

395
SOUTHWEST WATERFRONT
VIRGINIA AVE SE
PENNSYLVANIA AVE SE
POTOMAC AVE

Thomas Law House
WATERFRONT
SOUTH CAPITOL ST
M ST SE
NAVY YARD
John Philip Sousa Bridge
295

Washington Channel
Wheat Row
Nationals Park
Washington Navy Yard
Navy Museum
ANACOSTIA DRIVE SE
ANACOSTIA FREEWAY

Anacostia River
11th St Bridge
MINNESOTA AVE SE
NAYLOR RD SE

Fort McNair
Frederick Douglass Meml Bridge
ANACOSTIA
ANACOSTIA
GOOD HOPE RD SE
ANACOSTIA
ALABAMA AVE SE

CHELDRIVE SW
ROBBINS ROAD SE
MARTIN LUTHER KING AVE SE
MORRIS ROAD SE
Frederick Douglass National Historic Site
Fort Stanton Park
Anacostia Museum

295
Naval District Washington Anacostia
SUITLAND PARKWAY
GARFIELD HEIGHTS

Phillips
Collection

MASSACHUSETTS AVE NW

CONNECTICUT AVE NW

28TH ST NW

Anderson
House

21ST ST NW

DUPONT
CIRCLE

Washington Club

16TH ST NW

DUPONT
CIRCLE

Ⓜ

CONNECTICUT AVE

N ST NW

SCOTT
CIRCLE

14TH ST NW

Heurich
House

18TH ST NW

St. Matthew's
Cathedral ✚

ROCK CREEK & POTOMAC PARKWAY

M ST NW

Bethune
Council
House

THOMAS
CIRCLE

25TH ST NW

24TH ST NW

23RD ST NW

Mayflower
Hotel

Ⓜ

VERMONT AVE NW

Washington
Post

Georgetown ◄

L ST NW

15TH ST NW

FARRAGUT
NORTH

17TH ST NW

16TH ST NW

WASHINGTON
CIRCLE

K ST NW

FOGGY BOTTOM-
GWU
Ⓜ

PENNSYLVANIA AVE NW

I ST NW

Ⓜ

FARRAGUT
WEST

Ⓜ

MCPHERSON
SQUARE

Watergate
Complex

H ST NW

I ST NW

15TH ST NW

NEW YORK AVE NW

George
Washington
University

FOGGY
BOTTOM

Renwick
Gallery

ROCK CREEK AND POTOMAC

IMF

World
Bank

18TH ST NW

Old
Executive
Office

Treasury

22ND ST NW

21ST ST NW

20TH ST NW

19TH ST NW

G ST NW

F ST NW

Octagon

17TH ST NW

15TH ST NW

Kennedy
Center

66

Corcoran
Gallery of Art

The
White
House

National
Aquarium

Wilson
Building
ⓘ

VIRGINIA AVE NW

E ST NW

Dept of the
Interior

D ST NW

Boy Scout
Memorial

23RD ST NW

Dept
of
State

C ST NW

DAR
Museum

The Ellipse

Original
Patentees
Monument

National
Academy
of Sciences

22ND ST NW

Federal
Reserve

50

CONSTITUTION AVE NW

Dept of
Commerce

PKWY

Lockkeeper's
House

National
Museum of
American
History

Arlington, VA ◄

Vietnam
Veterans
Memorial

Constitution Gardens

Washington
Monument

Lincoln
Memorial

Reflecting Pool

Korean War
Veterans
Memorial

DC War
Memorial

National
World War II
Memorial

US Holocaust
Memorial Museum

Dept of
Agriculture

Arlington
Memorial
Bridge

INDEPENDENCE AVE SW

Bureau of
Engraving
& Printing

West
Potomac
Park

WEST BASIN DRIVE SW

Tidal Basin

14th St
Bridge

Potomac River

OHIO DRIVE SW

FDR
Memorial

Jefferson
Memorial

1

East
Potomac
Park

MEMORIAL PARKWAY

BOUNDARY CHANNEL ROAD

George Mason
(14th St)
Memorial Bridge

CENTRAL WASHINGTON, DC

R ST NW

VERMONT AVE NW

RHODE ISLAND AVE NW

Q ST NW

FLORIDA AVE NE

LOGAN CIRCLE

P ST NW

P ST NW

NEW YORK AVE NE

O ST NW

O ST NW

12TH ST NW
11TH ST NW
10TH ST NW
13TH ST NW
9TH ST NW
8TH ST NW
7TH ST NW
5TH ST NW
4TH ST NW
1ST ST NW
2ND ST NE

N ST NW

N ST NW

NEW JERSEY AVE NW

(50)

M ST NW

M ST NE

NEW YORK AVE

Convention Center

MT VERNON SQ-UDC

Greyhound Bus Terminal

MT. VERNON SQUARE

NORTH CAPITOL ST

K ST NE

National Museum of Women in the Arts

MASSACHUSETTS AVE NW

H ST NE

Smithsonian American Art Museum / National Portrait Gallery

H ST NW

National Building Museum

King Memorial Library

GALLERY PLACE

UNION STATION

METRO CENTER

Tussauds Wax Museum

Verizon Center

Union Station

Ford's Theatre

International Spy Museum

JUDICIARY SQUARE

National Postal Museum

Petersen House

F ST NW

Federal Bureau of Investigation

E ST NW

Old City Hall

PENNSYLVANIA AVE NW

D ST NW

Senate Office Buildings

FEDERAL TRIANGLE

DOWNTOWN

Municipal Center

Dirksen

EPA

IRS

Dept of Justice

National Archives

Newseum

C ST NW

Taft Memorial

Russell

Hart

ARCHIVES-NAVY MEML

National Gallery of Art West Building

US Court House

CONSTITUTION AVE NW

Sculpture Garden & Ice Rink

MADISON DRIVE

National Gallery of Art East Building

CAPITOL HILL

MARYLAND AVE NE

National Museum of Natural History

The Mall

Peace Monument

Supreme Court

Smithsonian Institution

Hirshhorn Museum

National Museum of the American Indian

Grant Meml

US Capitol

EAST CAPITOL ST

Freer Gallery

JEFFERSON DRIVE SW

Library of Congress

SMITHSONIAN

Botanic Garden

Garfield Meml

Jefferson Building

Sackler Gallery

Arts & Industries Building

National Air & Space Museum

INDEPENDENCE AVE SW

Longworth

National Museum of African Art

Bartholdi Fountain

Dept of Education

Dept of Health & Human Services

Rayburn

Cannon

Madison Building

L'ENFANT PLAZA

FEDERAL CENTER SW

House Office Buildings

CAPITOL SOUTH

VIRGINIA AVE SW

E ST SE

Dept of Housing & Urban Development

395

Fish Wharf

Benjamin Banneker Memorial Circle

G ST SW

SOUTHWEST WATERFRONT

N

MAINE AVE SW

WATER ST SW

I ST SW

Washington Channel

0   500 yds

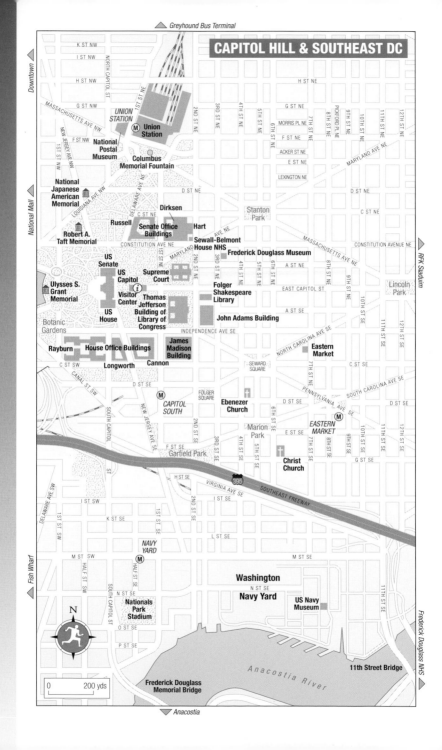

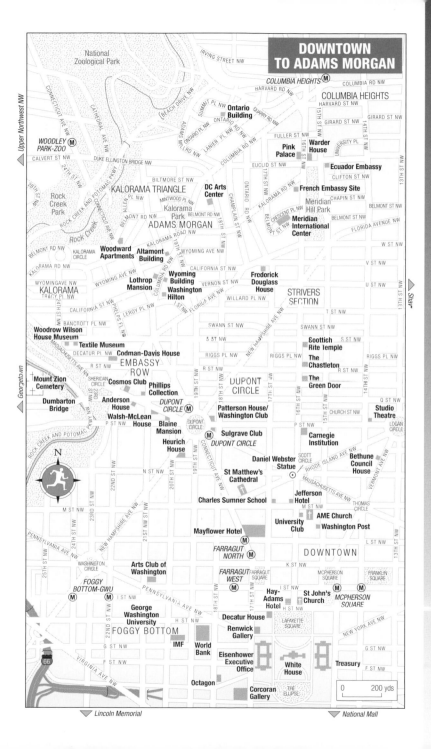

DOWNTOWN TO ADAMS MORGAN

National Zoological Park

IRVING STREET NW

COLUMBIA HEIGHTS Ⓜ

COLUMBIA RD NW

HARVARD RD NW

COLUMBIA HEIGHTS

Upper Northwest NW

HARVARD ST NW

15TH ST NW

GIRARD ST NW

14TH ST NW

Ontario Building

BEACH DRIVE NW

SUMMIT PL NW

QUARRY RD NW

ONTARIO RD NW

GIRARD ST NW

CONNECTICUT AVE NW

CATHEDRAL AVE NW

ADAMS MILL RD NW

LANIER PL NW

FULLER ST NW

16TH ST NW

UNIVERSITY PL

Warder House

Pink Palace

WOODLEY PARK-ZOO Ⓜ

CALVERT ST NW

DUKE ELLINGTON BRIDGE NW

EUCLID ST NW

17TH ST NW

Ecuador Embassy

CLIFTON ST NW

13TH ST NW

24TH ST NW

BILTMORE ST NW

DC Arts Center

CHAMPLAIN ST NW

KALORAMA RD NW

French Embassy Site

CHAPIN ST NW

28TH ST NW

Rock Creek Park

KALORAMA TRIANGLE

MINTWOOD PL NW

Kalorama Park

BELMONT RD NW

Meridian Hill Park

BELMONT ST NW

ONTARIO ST NW

18TH ST NW

Meridian International Center

BELMONT ST NW

Rock Creek

ADAMS MORGAN

BELMONT RD NW

ALLEN PL NW

FLORIDA AVENUE NW

KALORAMA ROAD NW

W ST NW

KALORAMA CIRCLE

Woodward Apartments

Altamont Building

19TH ST NW

WYOMING AVE NW

BELMONT RD NW

V ST NW

Wyoming Building

CALIFORNIA ST NW

Frederick Douglass House

WYOMINGAVE NW

WYOMING AVE NW

Lothrop Mansion

VERNON ST NW

STRIVERS SECTION

U ST NW

13TH ST NW

KALORAMA

TRACY PL NW

Washington Hilton

FLORIDA AVE NW

WILLARD PL NW

CALIFORNIA ST NW

PHELPS PL NW

LEROY PL NW

T ST NW

Shaw

BANCROFT PL NW

SWANN ST NW

SWANN ST NW

Woodrow Wilson House Museum

S ST NW

S ST NW

Scottich Rite Temple

S ST NW

Textile Museum

DECATUR PL NW

RIGGS PL NW

RIGGS PL NW

The Chastleton

RIGGS PL NW

MASSACHUSETTS AVE NW

Codman-Davis House

R ST NW

EMBASSY ROW

R ST NW

DUPONT CIRCLE

The Green Door

R ST NW

14TH ST NW

Georgetown

Mount Zion Cemetery

SHERIDAN CIRCLE

Cosmos Club

Phillips Collection

19TH ST NW

18TH ST NW

16TH ST NW

15TH ST NW

CHURCH ST NW

Q ST NW

Anderson House

DUPONT CIRCLE Ⓜ

Studio Theatre

Dumbarton Bridge

Walsh-McLean House

P ST NW

Blaine Mansion

DUPONT CIRCLE

Patterson House/ Washington Club

P ST NW

Carnegie Institution

LOGAN CIRCLE

ROCK CREEK AND POTOMAC PKWY

Heurich House

19TH ST NW

Sulgrave Club

DUPONT CIRCLE Ⓜ

Bethune Council House

VERMONT AVE NW

N

Daniel Webster Statue

SCOTT CIRCLE

RHODE ISLAND AVE NW

MASSACHUSETTS AVE NW

N ST NW

20TH ST NW

St Matthew's Cathedral ✝

Jefferson Hotel

THOMAS CIRCLE

22ND ST NW

Charles Sumner School

M ST NW

AME Church ✝

University Club

Washington Post

Mayflower Hotel

FARRAGUT NORTH Ⓜ

DOWNTOWN

L ST NW

13TH ST NW

M ST NW

23RD ST NW

24TH ST NW

NEW HAMPSHIRE AVE NW

25TH ST NW

Arts Club of Washington

FARRAGUT WEST Ⓜ

FARRAGUT SQUARE

K ST NW

MCPHERSON SQUARE

FRANKLIN SQUARE

PENNSYLVANIA AVE NW

WASHINGTON CIRCLE

PENNSYLVANIA AVE NW

18TH ST NW

17TH ST NW

I ST NW

Hay-Adams Hotel

I ST NW

St John's Church ✝

Ⓜ

Ⓜ

MCPHERSON SQUARE

13TH ST NW

FOGGY BOTTOM-GWU Ⓜ

Ⓜ

I ST NW

George Washington University

H ST NW

Decatur House

LAFAYETTE SQUARE

NEW YORK AVE NW

FOGGY BOTTOM

IMF

World Bank

Renwick Gallery

G ST NW

G ST NW

66

VIRGINIA AVE NW

Eisenhower Executive Office

White House

Treasury

F ST NW

Octagon

Corcoran Gallery

THE ELLIPSE

0   200 yds

▽ Lincoln Memorial

▽ National Mall

GEORGETOWN

Cleveland Park

Washington National Cathedral

Woodley Mansion

CATHEDRAL AVENUE NW

GARFIELD ST NW

28TH ST NW
27TH ST NW
GARFIELD ST NW

WOODLEY RD NW

Marriott Wardman Park

M

WOODLEY PARK-ZOO

Woodley Park, National Zoo & Adams Morgan

FULTON ST NW

35TH ST NW
34TH PL NW
35TH ST NW
FULTON ST NW
34TH ST NW

31ST PL NW

CLEVELAND AVE NW
NORMANSTONE TERR NW

WOODLAND DR NW
29TH ST NW
31ST ST NW

MASSACHUSETTS AVE NW

EDMUNDS ST NW

DAVIS ST NW

WISCONSIN AVE NW
36TH PL NW

36TH ST NW

OBSERVATORY CIRCLE NW

N

Kreeger Museum

39TH ST NW

CALVERT ST NW

BEECHER ST NW

BENTON ST NW

W ST NW

OBSERVATORY PL NW
HUIDEKOPER PL NW

TUNLAW RD NW
HALL PL NW
W PL NW
37TH ST NW

WISCONSIN AVE NW

US Naval Observatory

OBSERVATORY LANE NW

OBSERVATORY CIRCLE NW

MASSACHUSETTS AVE NW

WHITEHAVEN ST NW

CALVERT ST NW

Omni Shoreham

28TH ST NW
McGILL TERR NW

Rock Creek Park

EDGEVALE TERR NW
BENTON PL NW
ROCK CREEK DR NW

ROCK CREEK & POTOMAC PKWY

BELMONT RD NW
KALORAMA RD NW
WYOMING AVE NW
TRACY PL NW

CALIFORNIA ST NW

MASSACHUSETTS AVE NW

Rock Creek

Dumbarton Bridge/Dupont Circle

Whitehaven Park

WHITEHAVEN PKWY

35TH ST NW
35TH ST NW

39TH ST NW
38TH ST NW
36TH ST NW

T ST NW

S ST NW

R ST NW

Dumbarton Oaks Park

Dumbarton Oaks Garden & Museum

S ST NW

Montrose Park

Oak Hill Cemetery

Duke Ellington School of the Arts

RESERVOIR RD NW

CANTON PL NW
SCOTT PL NW

R ST NW
AVON PL NW
31ST ST NW

DENT PL NW

AVON LA

Mount Zion Cemetery

26TH ST NW

Dumbarton House

Georgetown University Hospital

DENT PL NW

Tudor Place

32ND ST NW
WISCONSIN AVE

Q ST NW

30TH ST NW
29TH ST NW
28TH ST NW
27TH ST NW

Volta Bureau

34TH ST NW

Q ST NW

VOLTA PL NW

33RD ST NW

Georgetown University

Old North

35TH ST NW

P ST NW

P ST NW

O ST NW

O ST NW

DUMBARTON ST NW

Healy Hall

37TH ST NW
36TH ST NW
35TH ST NW

N ST NW

St. John's Episcopal Church

N ST NW

31ST ST NW

OLIVE ST NW

N ST NW

ROCK CREEK & POTOMAC PKWY

Rock Creek

PROSPECT ST NW

Georgetown Park

City Tavern Club

Old Stone House

CANAL RD NW

Historic Car Barn

Francis Scott Key Park

Riggs Bank

Visitor Center

M ST NW

Four Seasons Hotel

Chesapeake & Ohio Canal

Market House

CANAL ST NW

Canal Square

PENNSYLVANIA AVE NW

25TH ST NW

WHITEHURST FREEWAY (K ST NW)

FRANCIS SCOTT KEY BRIDGE

GRACE ST NW

Grace Church

SOUTH ST NW

THOMAS JEFFERSON ST NW

The Foundry

K ST NW

Washington Circle & Foggy Bottom Metro

COPPERWAITHE LA NW

Potomac River

GEORGE WASHINGTON MEMORIAL PKWY

Washington Harbour

Georgetown Waterfront Park

Watergate Complex

I ST NW

VIRGINIA AVE NW

H ST NW

Thompson Boat Center

ROCK CREEK & POTOMAC PKWY

LEE HWY NW

COLONIAL TERR NW
ODE ST NW
KEY BLVD NW

NASH ST NW

FORT MYER DRIVE NW

MOORE ST NW

N 19TH ST NW
19TH ST NW

N LYNN ST NW

WILSON BLVD NW

66

M ROSSLYN

Theodore Roosevelt Island

0   500 yds

Rosslyn & Arlington

Kennedy Center

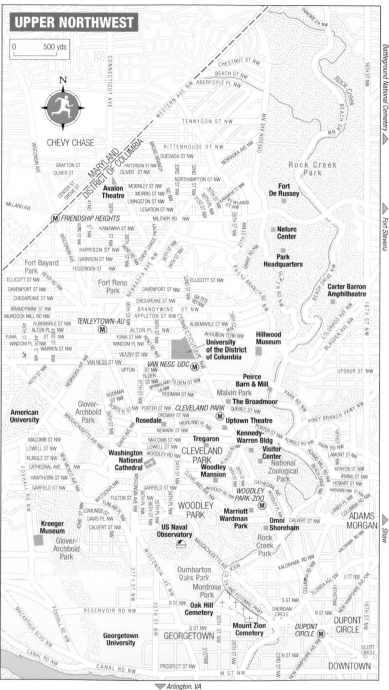

UPPER NORTHWEST

0   500 yds

N

Battleground National Cemetery ▷

Fort Stevens ▷

Shaw ▷

CHESTNUT ST NW
BEACH ST NW
ABERFOYLE PL NW
WESTERN AVE NW
CHEVY CHASE
TENNYSON ST NW
CONNECTICUT AVE
MARYLAND
DISTRICT OF COLUMBIA
RITTENHOUSE ST NW
GRAFTON ST
OUESADA ST NW
OLIVER ST
PATTERSON ST NW
BROAD BRANCH
CENTER ST
33RD
32ND
OLIVER ST
NEBRASKA AVE NW
GROVE ST
NORTHAMPTON ST NW
Rock Creek Park
BROAD BRANCH RD NW
30TH ST NW
OREGON AVE NW
WILLARD AVE
Avalon Theatre
MCKINLEY ST NW
MORRIS ST NW
Fort De Russey
44TH
LIVINGSTON ST NW
LEGATION ST NW
39TH
NEWLANDS
KANAWHA ST NW
27TH ST NW
Ⓜ FRIENDSHIP HEIGHTS
MILITARY RD NW
KANAWHA ST NW
Nature Center
WISCONSIN AVE
GARRISON ST NW
33RD ST NW
34TH ST NW
32ND ST NW
31ST PL NW
Park Headquarters
HARRISON ST NW
30TH ST NW
GRANT RD NW
GARRISON ST NW
RENO RD NW
FESSENDEN ST   NW
Fort Bayard Park
RIVER RD NW
GLEN
Carter Barron Amphitheatre
Fort Reno Park
ELLICOTT ST NW
DAVENPORT ST NW
BEACH DR NW
DAVENPORT ST NW
NEBRASKA AVE NW
CHESAPEAKE ST
COLORADO AVE NW
BRANDYWINE ST NW
GATES
16TH ST NW
MURDOCK MILL RD NW
ALBEMARLE ST NW
BRANDYWINE   ST NW
RD NW
BLAGDEN AVE NW
YUMA
44TH
45TH PL NW
ALTON PL NW
APPLETON ST NW
33RD ST NW
ALBEMARLE ST NW
WINDOM PL NW
33RD ST NW
TENLEYTOWN-AU
Ⓜ
ALTON PL NW
YUMA ST NW
Hillwood Museum
WARREN ST NW
WINDOM PL NW
RENO RD
VEAZEY ST NW
University of the District of Columbia
45TH ST NW
NEBRASKA AVE NW
VAN NESS ST NW
UPTON
AUDUBON TERR NW
CONNECTICUT AVE
VAN NESS UDC Ⓜ
TILDEN
UPSHUR ST NW
American University
RODMAN
ST NW
37TH ST NW
TILDEN ST NW
SPRINGLAND LA NW
Peirce Barn & Mill
Glover-Archbold Park
PORTER ST NW
RODMAN ST NW
Malvin Park
PARK RD NW
MASSACHUSETTS AVE NW
39TH ST NW
PORTER NW
CLEVELAND PARK
The Broadmoor
QUEBEC ST NW
PINEY BRANCH PKWY NW
Rosedale
ORDWAY ST NW
Ⓜ Uptown Theatre
PORTER ST NW
KLINGLE ST NW
18TH ST NW
IDAHO AVE NW
HIGHLAND AVE NW
NEWARK ST NW
Kennedy-Warren Bldg
PARK RD NW
MACOMB ST NW
Tregaron
LAMONT ST NW
LOWELL ST NW
MACOMB ST NW
CLEVELAND
Visitor Center
28TH ST NW
KENYON ST NW
KLINGLE ST NW
WOODLEY RD NW
LOWELL ST NW
PARK
National Zoological Park
IRVING ST NW
CATHEDRAL AVE
Washington National Cathedral
Woodley Mansion
KLINGLE RD NW
ADAMS MILL RD NW
BEACH DRIVE NW
HOBART ST NW
FOXHALL RD NW
HAWTHORN ST NW
WISCONSIN AVE NW
36TH ST NW
34TH ST NW
CLEVELAND AVE NW
HARVARD NW
GARFIELD ST NW
WOODLEY RD NW
WOODLEY PARK-ZOO
LANIER PL NW
CATHEDRAL AVE
GARFIELD ST NW
FULTON ST NW
36TH ST NW
CALVERT ST NW
COLUMBIA RD NW
WATSON PL NW
WOODLEY PARK
CONNECTICUT AVE NW
29TH ST NW
ADAMS MORGAN
EDMUNDS ST
Marriott Wardman Park
DAVIS PL NW
34TH ST NW
Omni Shoreham
CALVERT ST NW
Kreeger Museum
CALVERT ST NW
Rock Creek Park
KALORAMA RD NW
Glover-Archbold Park
US Naval Observatory
MASSACHUSETTS AVE NW
34TH ST NW
KALORAMA RD NW
COLUMBIA RD NW
FLORIDA AVE NW
NEW HAMPSHIRE AVE NW
16TH ST NW
MACARTHUR BLVD NW
FOXHALL RD NW
Dumbarton Oaks Park
ROCK CR EXT AND POTOMAC PKWY
S ST NW
RESERVOIR RD NW
Montrose Park
35TH ST NW
R ST NW
SHERIDAN CIRCLE
S ST NW
DUPONT CIRCLE
R ST NW
Oak Hill Cemetery
30TH ST NW
23RD ST NW
Georgetown University
CANAL RD NW
37TH ST NW
Q ST NW
31ST ST NW
Mount Zion Cemetery
DUPONT CIRCLE Ⓜ
GEORGETOWN
N ST NW
NEW HAMPSHIRE AVE NW
SCOTT CIRCLE
CANAL RD NW
PROSPECT ST NW
M ST NW
DOWNTOWN

▽ Arlington, VA

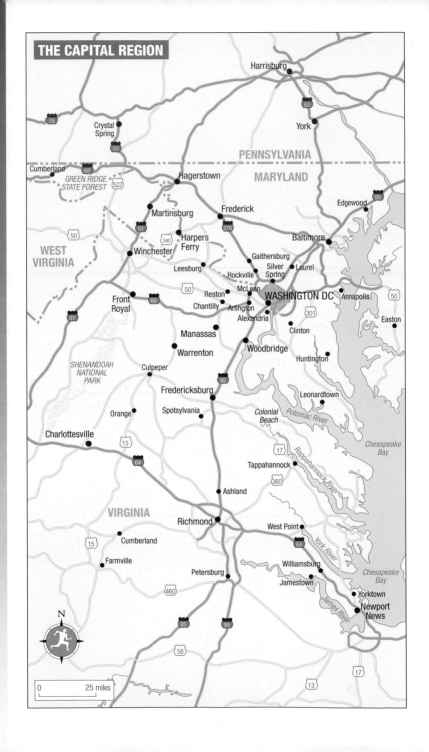

THE CAPITAL REGION